W9-CUO-046

Valuing Employee Stock Options

Founded in 1807, John Wiley & Sons is the oldest independent publishing company in the United States. With offices in North America, Europe, Australia, and Asia, Wiley is globally committed to developing and marketing print and electronic products and services for our customers' professional and personal knowledge and understanding.

The Wiley Finance series contains books written specifically for finance and investment professionals as well as sophisticated individual investors and their financial advisors. Book topics range from portfolio management to e-commerce, risk management, financial engineering, valuation, and financial instrument analysis, as well as much more.

For a list of available titles, visit our Web site at www.WileyFinance.com.

Valuing Employee Stock Options

JOHNATHAN MUN

John Wiley & Sons, Inc.

Published by John Wiley & Sons, Inc., Hoboken, New Jersey.
Published simultaneously in Canada.

For general information on our other products and services, or technical support, please contact our Customer Care Department within the United States at 800-762-2974, outside the United States at 317-572-3993 or fax 317-572-4002.

Wiley also publishes its books in a variety of electronic formats. Some content that appears in print may not be available in electronic books.

For more information about Wiley products, visit our web site at www.wiley.com.

ISBN 0-471-70512-8

Printed in the United States of America.

10 9 8 7 6 5 4 3 2 1

Contents

PART THREE
A Sample Case Study Applying FAS 123

PART FOUR
Options Valuation Results Tables

List of Figures and Tables

FIGURES

TABLES

Preface

This book was written after FASB released its proposed FAS 123 revision in March 2004. As one of the valuation consultants and FASB advisors on the FAS 123 initiative in 2003 and 2004, I would like to illustrate to the finance and accounting world that what FASB has proposed is actually pragmatic and applicable. I am neither for nor against the expensing of employee stock options and would recuse myself from the philosophical and sometimes emotional debate on whether employee stock options should be expensed (that they are a part of an employee's total compensation, paid in part for the exchange of services, and are an economic opportunity cost to the firm just like restricted stocks or other contingent claims issued by the company) or should not be expensed (that they simply dilute the holdings of existing shareholders, are a cashless expense, and if expensed, provide no additional valuable information to the general investor as to the financial health of the company but rather reduce the company's profitability and hence the ability to continue issuing more options to its employees). Rather, as an academic and valuation expert, my concern is with creating a universal standard of understanding on how FAS 123 can be uniformly applied to avoid ambiguity, and not whether employee stock options should be expensed. Therefore, let it not be said that the new ruling is abandoned because it is not pragmatic. This book is also my response to FASB board member Katherine Schipper's direct request to me at the FASB public panel roundtable meeting (Palo Alto, California, June 2004) for assistance in providing more guidance on the overall valuation aspects of FAS 123.

Hopefully the contents of this book will subdue some of the criticisms on how binomial lattices can be used and applied in the real world. The results, tables, graphics, and sample cases illustrated throughout the book were calculated using customized binomial lattice software algorithms I developed to assist FASB in its deliberations, and were based on actual real-life consulting and advisory experience on applying FAS 123. Inexperienced critics will be surprised at some of the findings in the book. For instance, criticisms on the difficulty of finding the highly critical volatility may be unfounded because when real-life scenarios such as vesting, forfeitures, and suboptimal exercise behavior are added to the model, volatility plays a much smaller and less prominent role. In addition, the book illustrates how Monte Carlo simulation with correlations can be added (to simulate volatility, suboptimal exercise behavior multiple, forfeiture rates, as well as other variables for thousands and even hundreds of thousands of simulation scenarios and trials) to provide a precision of up to $0.01 at a 99.9 percent statistical confidence; coupled with a convergence test of the lattice steps, this provides a highly robust modeling methodology. Future editions of this book will include any and all changes to the FAS 123 requirements since the March 2004 proposal.

Parts One and Four are written specifically for the chief financial officer and finance directors, who are interested in understanding what are the impacts and implications of using a binomial lattice versus a Black-Scholes model. Parts Two and Three are targeted more toward the analysts, consultants, and accountants who require the technical knowledge and example cases to execute the analysis.

JOHNATHAN MUN

San Francisco, California
JohnathanMun@cs.com
August 2004

Acknowledgments

The author is greatly indebted to Winny van Veeren of Veritas Software Corporation for her great insights in ESO valuation. In addition, a special word of thanks goes to Bill Falloon, senior editor at John Wiley & Sons, Inc., for his support and encouragement. Finally, many thanks to Mike Tovey, FAS 123 project manager, and members of the board of directors at FASB for graciously allowing me to assist in their deliberations.

J. M.

About the Author

Dr. Johnathan C. Mun is the author of several other well-known books, including *Real Options Analysis: Tools and Techniques* (Wiley, 2002), *Real Options Analysis Course: Business Cases* (Wiley, 2003), *Faith Journey* (Xulon Press, 2003), and *Applied Risk Analysis: Moving Beyond Uncertainty* (Wiley, 2003). He is also the creator of the Real Options Analysis Toolkit software. His books and software have been adopted by major universities in the United States and around the world, and are used widely at a variety of Fortune 500 companies. Dr. Mun has taught seminars and workshops worldwide on the topics of options valuation, risk analysis, simulation, forecasting, financial analysis, and real options analysis. This book is the result of analytical work he did for the Financial Accounting Standards Board in 2003 and 2004, as well as FAS 123 employee stock options valuation advisory and consulting work he has performed at dozens of Fortune 500 firms.

He is currently the Vice President of Analytics at Decisioneering, Inc., the makers of *Real Options Analysis Toolkit* and the *Crystal Ball* suite of products, including applications of Monte Carlo simulation, optimization, options analysis, and forecasting. He heads up the development of real options analysis and financial analytics software products, analytical consulting, training, and technical support. He is also a Visiting and Adjunct Professor and has taught courses in financial management, investments, financial options, real options, economics, and statistics at the undergraduate and graduate MBA levels, as well as chairing several graduate Master's theses committees. He has taught at universities all over the world, from the University of Applied Sciences (Germany and Switzerland) to Golden Gate University (California), St. Mary's College (California), and others. Prior to joining Decisioneering, he was Consulting Manager and Financial Economist in the Valuation Services and Global Financial Services practice of KPMG Consulting and a manager with the Economic Consulting Services practice at KPMG LLP. He has extensive experience in econometric modeling, financial options analysis, real options, economic analysis, and statistics. During his tenure both at Decisioneering and at KPMG Consulting, he consulted with, advised, and trained others in the areas of options analysis, risk analysis, economic forecasting, and financial valuation for many Fortune 500 firms. His experience prior to joining KPMG included being Department Head of Financial Planning and Analysis at Viking, Inc. of FedEx, responsible for performing financial forecasting, economic analysis, and market research. Prior to that, he had also performed some financial planning and freelance financial consulting work.

Dr. Mun received a Ph.D. in Finance and Economics from Lehigh University, where his research and academic interests were in the areas of Investment Finance, Econometric Modeling, Financial Options, Corporate Finance, and Microeconomic Theory. He also has an MBA from Nova Southeastern University and a BS in biology and physics from the University of Miami. He is certified in Financial Risk Management (FRM), a Certified Financial Consultant (CFC), and a Certified Risk Analyst (CRA), and is currently a third-level candidate for the Chartered Financial Analyst (CFA). He is a member of American Mensa, Phi Beta Kappa Honor Society, and Golden Key Honor Society as well as several other professional organizations, including the Eastern and Southern Finance Associations, American Economic Association, and Global Association of Risk Professionals. Finally, he has written many academic articles published in the *Journal of the Advances in Quantitative Accounting and Finance*, *Global Finance Journal*, *International Financial Review*, *Journal of Applied Financial Economics*, *Journal of International Financial Markets, Institutions and Money*, *Financial Engineering News*, *Journal of the Society of Petroleum Engineers*, and *Journal of Financial Analysis*.

He currently resides in California and can be reached via e-mail at JohnathanMun@cs.com.

Valuing Employee Stock Options

PART One

Impacts of the New FAS 123 Methodology

CHAPTER 1

Implications of the New FAS 123 Requirements

A BRIEF INTRODUCTION

In what the *Wall Street Journal* calls "among the most far-reaching steps that the Financial Accounting Standards Board (FASB) has made in its 30 year history,"[1] on March 31, 2004, FASB released a Proposed Statement of Financial Accounting Standards (FAS) on Share-based Payment amending the old FAS Statements 123 and 95 issued in October 1995.[2]

The original 1995 statements required that all share-based payment arrangements with parties other than employees be accounted for in value. The revised 2004 statement retains the principle established in FAS 123 (1995) that a public entity should measure the cost of employee services received in exchange for awards of equity instruments based on the fair value of the instruments at the grant date. In addition, the FASB has reaffirmed the conclusion in the 2004 proposed Statement 123 revision that employee services received in exchange for equity instruments give rise to recognizable compensation cost as the services are used in the issuing entity's operations. Based on that conclusion, this proposed Statement requires that such compensation cost be recognized in the financial statements.

The FASB states in its proposal that it wants to maximize the convergence of U.S. and international accounting standards for *employee stock options* (ESOs), and as such, the proposed 2004 FAS 123 revisions are consistent with the International Accounting Standards Board's *share-based payment* (IFRS 2, issued February 19, 2004). At the date of writing, the proposed Statement will be effective for new awards and portions of existing awards that have not yet vested at the beginning of the first fiscal year starting from December 15, 2004, with a possible delay in effective date to allow corporations to better prepare for the transition. In anticipation of the Standard, many companies such as GE and Coca-Cola have already voluntarily expensed their ESOs at the time of writing. This need for more transparency is in line with the 2002 Sarbanes-Oxley Act, which requires that public companies develop and comply with accepted standards of financial and managerial prudence.

One of the areas of concern is the fair-market valuation of these ESOs. The binomial lattice is the preferred method in the proposed FAS 123 requirements, and critics argue that companies do not necessarily have the resources in-house or the data availability to perform complex valuations that not only are consistent with these new requirements but will pass an audit as well.

The goal of this book is to provide you with a better understanding of the valuation applications of a customized binomial lattice through a systematic and objective assessment of the methodology. This book is concerned only with the valuation of ESOs, and not the management of these options.[3] The analyses performed in this book use my own proprietary customized binomial lattice computer algorithms and my software, the Real Options Analysis Toolkit, and Decisioneering, Inc.'s Crystal Ball Monte Carlo simulation software. This book was written based on my advisory work with FASB in 2003 and 2004, graduate research work in the area of options analysis, actual FAS 123 consulting projects with several Fortune 500 firms, and options software development experience, as well as my prior three books.

This book is divided into four parts. In Part One, the impacts of the 2004 FAS 123 are reviewed. In Chapter 1, the implications of the new FAS 123 requirements with respect to the valuation of ESOs are introduced. Chapter 2 reviews the FAS 123 requirements in more detail, focusing on the methodological requirements. Chapter 3 illustrates the impacts to the valuation results of using a customized binomial lattice versus a traditional *Black-Scholes model* (BSM),[4] as well as where the variation lies. (The traditional BSM described throughout this book is the original model with naïve assumptions without any modifications to include more exotic inputs, which can be very mathematically complex.) The chapter also reviews the selection and justification of the customized binomial lattice, as well as the effects of incorporating vesting, employee suboptimal exercise behavior, forfeiture rates, changing risk-free rates, changing dividends, and changing volatilities over time. Chapter 4 reviews some of the other modifications to value such as nonmarketability, expected life analysis, and dilution. Chapter 5 provides an introduction to using Monte Carlo simulation coupled with binomial lattices to obtain a robust and statistically valid set of option valuation results. Chapter 6 illustrates an example of how the option valuation's fair-market value can be allocated and expensed over the vesting period of the option.

In Part Two, the technical background required to run the BSM and customized binomial lattices are provided. Chapter 7 provides a brief technical background of the BSM and binomial lattice. Chapter 8 provides more detailed technical background on the use of a simple binomial lattice, complete with step-by-step valuation examples. The customized binomial lattice algorithms are briefly explained. Chapter 8's appendix explores in more detail the uses of binomial, trinomial, and multinomial lattices. Chapter 9 deals with how to obtain the model inputs, and their financial, statistical, and analytical justifications.

Chapter 10 in Part Three shows an example ESO fair-market valuation that is based on several real-life cases.[5] Chapter 10's appendix provides a "Getting Started Guide" in using the demo software in the accompanying CD-ROM.

Finally, Part Four provides multiple options valuation results that will prove valuable from the perspective of the analyst all the way to the chief financial officer when it comes to valuing the impact of using the binomial lattice versus BSM. These tables provide a first-pass rough estimate of the fair-market value of the option using a customized binomial lattice, providing management with valuable insights into the possible expenses before having to delve into more detailed, complex, and protracted analyses. In the face of implementing a challenging and potentially complex valuation system, firms need to first obtain a benchmark to understand if these more sophisticated models will provide comparable, lower, or higher values than the BSM.

AN EXECUTIVE SUMMARY OF THE FAS 123 VALUATION IMPLICATIONS

This book broaches the subject of fair-market valuation through an analytical assessment of the three mainstream approaches used in option pricing, and provides guidance on using them, coupled with the mathematical background, sample case study, and demo software to help the reader get started with ESO valuation. The first approach is a set of closed-form models,[6] including the BSM for option pricing and the American option approximation pricing models. The second approach is the use of Monte Carlo path-dependent simulation, including its applications in option pricing as well as its use in simulating the option model's uncertain and probabilistic inputs. The third and final approach is the use of lattices and the customized binomial lattices applied throughout this book. These three sets of methodologies are reviewed based on several criteria, including method applicability, underlying assumptions, robustness of analytical results, and ease of use.[7]

Based on the results illustrated throughout the book, it can be concluded that the BSM, albeit theoretically correct and elegant, is insufficient and inappropriately applied when it comes to quantifying the fair-market value of an ESO. This is because the BSM is applicable only to European options without dividends, where the holder of the option can exercise the option only on its maturity date and the underlying stock does not pay any dividends. However, in reality, most ESOs are American-type options with dividends, where the option holder can execute the option at any time up to (after the vesting period and except blackout dates) and including the maturity date while the underlying stock pays dividends. A stock's price drops by approximately the amount of the dividend on the ex-dividend date, which means that the value of an American stock option (with its ability for early exercise) is greater than that of a European-type option. However, for fairness of comparison, the Generalized Black-Scholes model (GBM) is used—the GBM allows for the inclusion of dividends albeit it is applicable only for valuing European options. The terms BSM and GBM will be used interchangeably throughout this book, which describes the original models developed by Black and Scholes without any modifications (the correct model will be used whenever appropriate).

In addition, under real-world conditions, ESOs have blackout dates and a time to vesting before the employee can execute the option, which is also contingent on the firm and/or the individual employee attaining a specific performance level (e.g., profitability, growth rate, or stock price hitting a minimum barrier before the options become live), and subject to forfeitures when the employee leaves the firm or is terminated prematurely before reaching the vested period. Also, certain options follow a tranching or graduated scale, where a certain percentage of the stock option grants becomes exercisable every year, and if the firm underperforms, it may be required to repurchase the options at a specific termination price. Just as important, the GBM assumes that all employees execute their options optimally—that is, the model assumes that every employee is intelligent enough to execute the option whenever it becomes optimal to do so. In reality, employees tend to execute their stock options prematurely and often suboptimally. The GBM or BSM do not adequately account for this suboptimal early exercise behavior and subsequently overvalue the option (sometimes significantly). The firm may undergo some corporate restructuring (e.g., divestitures, or mergers and acquisitions that may require a stock swap that changes the volatility of the underlying stock) and hence its underlying stock's volatility may change over time. In addition, risk-free rates change over time (both U.S. Treasury spot rates and forward rates fluctuate) and will impact the value of the option. The same applies to dividend policy, where dividend payout ratios can change over the life of an ESO. In addition, ESOs cannot be executed during blackout periods (typically weeks before and afer earnings announcements), and the ESOs in general are nonmarketable and nontransferable (cannot be freely bought or sold in an open market). Finally, options that are granted may sometimes be forfeited by employees when they leave or are terminated during the vesting period (alternatively, employees have a limited time, typically 30 to 90 days, to exercise the portion of the options that have vested, after they leave the firm). All these real-life scenarios make the GBM and BSM insufficient and inappropriate when used to place a fair-market value on the option grant. In summary, firms can implement a variety of provisions that affect the fair value of the options whereas the above list is only a few examples.

Generally speaking, the BSM and GBM typically *overstate* the fair-market value of ESOs where there is suboptimal early exercise behavior coupled with vesting requirements and where employee forfeitures occur, or when the risk-free rates, dividends, and volatilities change over the life of the option. In fact, firms using the BSM and GBM to value and expense ESOs may be significantly overstating their true expense, typically incurring hundreds of thousands to tens of millions of dollars in excess expenses per year.[8]

The analyses in this book illustrate that under very specific conditions (European options with and without dividends) the binomial lattice and Monte Carlo simulation approaches yield identical values to the GBM, indicating that the two former approaches are robust and exact at the limit. When American options with dividends are analyzed, the traditional BSM and GBM undervalue the options, whereas binomial lattices and American options approximation models are more exact. However, when specific real-life business conditions are modeled (i.e., forfeiture rates, probability that the employee leaves or is terminated, time-vesting, blackout dates, tranching, employee suboptimal exercise behavior, changing risk-free rates, and so forth), the American approximation models or Monte Carlo simulation by themselves are also insufficient to capture all of the real-life nuances. Only when the binomial lattice (which is highly flexible in its modeling capabilities) is used will the true fair-market value of the stock option be captured—Monte Carlo simulation can be applied to further simulate the uncertain inputs that go into the binomial lattices. That is, the binomial lattice is used to calculate the American stock option with dividend while the inputs into the binomial lattice can be simulated to capture the uncertainty and probabilistic effects of the real-life conditions mentioned. Basic binomial lattices are extremely easy to use and apply as compared with the other methods. However, in the case of FAS 123, more complex customized binomial lattices are required, but their analytics are based on the simple binomial lattice. In addition, a comparison of other lattices (trinomials and multinomials) indicates that the binomial lattice is still the preferred method (all lattices provide similar results at the limit, while binomial lattices are the easiest and most convenient to compute).

Binomial lattices can be customized to account for exotic events such as stock price barriers (a barrier option exists when the stock option becomes either in-the-money or out-of-the-money only when it hits a stock price barrier), vesting tranches (a specific percent of the options granted becomes vested or exercisable each year), changing volatilities, dividends, and risk-free rates over time (changing business and economic conditions or corporate restructuring), employee suboptimal exercise behaviors (early execution by employees who require liquidity or are risk-averse), forfeitures (employees leaving or terminated during and after the vesting period), and so forth—the same conditions where the BSM and GBM fail miserably. Monte Carlo simulation then can be applied to simulate the probabilities of forfeitures and employee suboptimal behavior, and these simulated values can be used as the inputs into the binomial lattices. *Without the use of binomial lattices, firms may be significantly* overvaluing *ESOs and could potentially end up overexpensing millions of dollars per year.*

In using the highly flexible binomial lattices with Monte Carlo simulation, firms can now create exotic ESOs with different flavors such as performance-based options (i.e., a percentage of ESOs that come into-the-money if the firm hits a particular earnings level, and this percentage may increase based on some graded scale) and value them accordingly.

This book provides a comprehensive review of all the necessary steps and methodologies required to value ESOs. No matter which direction the final requirements lean toward, the methodologies described here can be mixed and matched accordingly.

SUMMARY AND KEY POINTS

- It has been over 30 years since Fischer Black and Myron Scholes derived their option pricing model and significant advancements have been made; therefore, do not restrict stock option pricing to one specific model (the BSM) where a plethora of other models and applications can be explored.
- The three mainstream approaches to valuing stock options are closed-form models (e.g., BSM, GBM, and American option approximation models), Monte Carlo simulation, and binomial lattices.

- The BSM and GBM will typically *overstate* the fair value of ESOs where there is suboptimal early exercise behavior coupled with vesting requirements and option forfeitures. *In fact, firms using the BSM and GBM to value and expense ESOs may be significantly overstating their true expense.*
- The BSM requires many underlying assumptions before it works, and as such, has significant limitations, including being applicable only for European options without dividends. In addition, American option approximation models are very complex and difficult to create in a spreadsheet.[9] The BSM *cannot* account for American options, options based on stocks that pay dividends (the GBM can, however, account for dividends in a European option), forfeitures, underperformance, stock price barriers, vesting periods, blackout dates, changing business environments and volatilities, suboptimal early exercise, and a slew of other conditions.
- Monte Carlo simulation when used alone is another option valuation approach, but is restricted only to European options. Simulation can be used in two different ways: solving the option's fair-market value through path simulations of stock prices, or in conjunction with other approaches (e.g., binomial lattices and closed-form models) to capture multiple sources of uncertainty in the model.[10]
- Binomial lattices are flexible and easy to implement. They are capable of valuing American-type stock options with dividends but require computational power. Software applications should be used to facilitate this computation. Binomial lattices can be used to calculate American options paying dividends and can be easily adapted to solve options with stock price barriers and used in conjunction with Monte Carlo simulation to account for the uncertain input assumptions (e.g., probabilities of forfeiture, suboptimal exercise behavior, vesting, blackout periods, underperformance, and so forth).
- Based on the analyses throughout the book, it is recommended that the use of a model that assumes an ESO is European style, when in fact the option is an exotic American style option with vesting, should not be permitted as this substantially overstates compensation expense. Many factors (e.g., vesting, suboptimal exercise behavior, performance-based options, blackout dates, and forfeitures) influence the fair value of ESOs, and a binomial lattice approach to valuation that considers these factors should be used. Option valuations using BSM, GBM, or other closed-form models should not be permitted when the requirements for those models are not met. Binomial lattice valuation models should be used instead.

CHAPTER 2

The 2004 Proposed FAS 123 Requirements

FAS 123 BACKGROUND

The proposed 2004 FAS 123 revision explains that a better estimate of the fair value of an employee share option may be obtained by using a *binomial lattice model* that incorporates employees' expected exercise and expected post-vesting employment termination behavior than by using a *closed-form model* (such as the Black-Scholes-Merton or *BSM* formula) with a single weighted-average expected option term as an input. Further, this revised statement does not permit the use of the minimum value method as a substitute for the fair-value-based method.[1]

In addition, the 1995 FAS 123 provided alternative methods of measuring and recognizing compensation cost for awards with graded vesting—that is, awards for which different parts vest at different times. The revised 2004 FAS 123 requires a single method under which those different parts are treated as separate awards in estimating fair value and attributing compensation cost.

The 1995 FAS 123 permitted enterprises the option of continuing to use Opinion 25's intrinsic-value method of accounting for share-based payments to employees provided those enterprises supplementally disclosed pro forma net income and related pro forma earnings-per-share information (if earnings per share is presented) as if the fair-value-based method of accounting had been used. For the reasons described in paragraphs C26 through C30 of the proposed 2004 FAS 123 revision, the FASB concluded that such pro forma disclosures are not an appropriate substitute for recognition of compensation cost in the financial statements. The FASB Board of Directors believes fair value is the relevant measurement attribute and grant date is the relevant measurement date.

Further, the FASB has determined that the BSM formula and similar closed-form models do not produce reasonable estimates of fair value because they do not adequately take into account the unique characteristics of employee share options. The FASB recognizes that closed-form models may not necessarily be the best available technique for estimating the fair value of employee share options—they believe that a lattice model (as defined in paragraph E1 of the 2004 FAS 123) is preferable because it offers the greater flexibility needed to reflect the unique characteristics of employee share options and similar instruments. This provides support for the analyses performed throughout the book, which applies the customized binomial lattice.

In addition, the 2004 FAS 123 also suggests that information other than historical volatility should be used in estimating expected volatility, and explicitly notes that defaulting to historical volatility as the estimate of expected volatility without taking into consideration other available information is not appropriate.

The FASB concluded that the 2004 proposed FAS 123 would require a single method of accruing compensation cost for awards with a graded vesting schedule. This statement considers an award with a graded vesting schedule to be in substance separate awards, each with a different fair value measurement and requisite service period, and would require that they be accounted for separately. That treatment results in a recognition pattern that attributes more compensation cost to earlier portions of the combined vesting period of an award and less compensation cost to later portions. This statement would require the modified prospective method of transition for public companies and would not permit retroactive application.

The estimated fair value of an equity instrument on the date it is granted should not reflect the effects of vesting conditions or other restrictions that apply only during the vesting period. Those effects are reflected by recognizing compensation cost only for awards that actually vest because the requisite service is provided.

If observable market prices of identical or similar equity or liability instruments of the entity are not available, the fair value of equity and liability instruments awarded to employees shall be estimated by using a valuation technique that (1) is applied in a manner consistent with the fair value measurement objective and the other requirements of Statement 123, (2) is based on established principles of financial economic theory and generally accepted by experts in that field (paragraph B9 of the 2004 FAS 123), and (3) reflects any and all substantive characteristics of the instrument (except for those characteristics explicitly excluded, such as vesting conditions and reload features).

In estimating the fair value of employee share options at the grant date, the determination of the amount at which the instruments being valued would be exchanged would factor in expectations of the probability that the options would vest (that is, that the service or performance vesting conditions would be satisfied). The estimated fair value of the equity instruments at grant date does not take into account the effect on fair value of vesting conditions and other restrictions prior to vesting.

Several valuation techniques, including a lattice model (an example of which is a binomial model) and a closed-form model (an example of which is the BSM) meet the criteria required by Statement 123 for estimating the fair values of employee share options and similar instruments. Those valuation techniques or models, sometimes referred to as *option-pricing models*, are based on well-established financial economic theory. Those models are used by valuation professionals, dealers in derivative instruments, and other experts to estimate the fair values of options and similar instruments related to equity securities, currencies, interest rates, and commodities. Those models are used to establish trade prices for derivative instruments, to establish fair market values for U.S. tax purposes, and to establish values in adjudications. Both a lattice model and a closed-form model can be adjusted to account for the characteristics of share options and similar instruments granted to employees.

The selection of a valuation model will depend on the substantive characteristics of each arrangement and the availability of data necessary to use the model. A valuation model that is more fully able to capture and better reflects those characteristics is preferable and should be used if it is practicable to do so. For example, the BSM formula, a closed-form model, assumes that option exercises occur at the end of an option's contractual term, and that volatility, dividends, and risk-free interest rates are constant over the option's term. If used to estimate the fair value of employee share options and similar instruments, the BSM formula must be adjusted to take account of certain characteristics of employee share options and similar instruments that are not consistent with the assumptions of the model (e.g., exercise prior to the end of the option's contractual term, and changing volatility and dividends). Because of the nature of the formula, those adjustments take the form of weighted-average assumptions about those characteristics. In contrast, a lattice model can be designed to incorporate certain characteristics of employee share options and similar instruments; it can accommodate changes in dividends and volatility over the option's contractual term, estimates of expected option exercise patterns during the option's contractual term, and blackout periods. A lattice model, therefore, is more fully able to capture and better reflects the characteristics of a particular employee share option or similar instrument in the estimate of fair value.

Entities that do not have reasonable access to the data required by a lattice model may conclude that a closed-form model provides a reasonable estimate of fair value; those entities subsequently may obtain reasonable access to the data and decide to use a lattice model. Further, entities for which compensation cost is not a significant element of the financial statements may conclude that a closed-form model produces estimates of fair value that are not materially different from those produced by a lattice model and that this pattern can be reasonably assumed to persist. Those entities may conclude that a closed-form model provides reasonable estimates of fair value. Public entities for which compensation cost from share option arrangements is a significant element of the financial statements may conclude, when inputs are available, that a lattice model would provide a better estimate of fair value because of its ability to more fully capture and better reflect the characteristics of a particular employee share option or similar instrument in the estimate of fair value.

A U.S. entity issuing an option on its own shares must use as the risk-free interest rates the implied yields from the U.S. Treasury zero-coupon yield curve over the expected term of the option if the entity is using a lattice model incorporating the option's contractual term. If the entity is using a closed-form model, the risk-free interest rate is the implied yield currently available on U.S. Treasury zero-coupon issues with a remaining term equal to the expected term used as the input to the model.

There is likely to be a range of reasonable estimates for expected volatility, dividends, and option term. If no amount within the range is more or less likely than any other amount, an average of the range (its *expected value*) should be used. That entity might base expectations about future volatility on the average volatilities of similar entities for an appropriate period following their going public. Data and assumptions used to estimate the fair value of equity and liability instruments granted to employees should be determined in a consistent manner from period to period.

For employee share options and similar instruments, a lattice model is preferable to a closed-form model and, therefore, is preferable for justifying a change in accounting principle. Once an entity changes its valuation technique for employee share options and similar instruments to a lattice model, it may not change to a less preferable valuation technique.

An entity should not estimate share option fair values based on historical average share option lives, historical share price volatility, or historical dividends (whether stated as a yield or a dollar amount) without considering the extent to which future experience is reasonably expected to differ from historical experience.

Expected term is an input to a closed-form model. However, if an entity uses a lattice model that has been modified to take into account an option's contractual term and employees' expected exercise and post-vesting employment termination behavior, the expected term is estimated based on the resulting output of the lattice. For example, an entity's experience might indicate that option holders tend to exercise those options when the share price reaches 200 percent of the exercise price. If so, that entity might use a lattice model that assumes exercise of the option at each node along each share price path in a lattice at which the early exercise expectation is met, provided that the option is vested and exercisable at that point. Moreover, such a model would assume exercise at the end of the contractual term on price paths along which the exercise expectation is not met but the options are in-the-money at the end of the contractual term. That method recognizes that employees' exercise behavior is correlated with the price of the underlying share. Employees' expected post-vesting employment termination behavior also would be factored in. Expected term then could be estimated based on the output of the resulting lattice.

Other factors that may affect expectations about employees' exercise and postvesting employment termination behavior include the following:

- The vesting period of the award. An option's expected term must at least include the vesting period.
- Employees' past exercise and postvesting employment termination behavior for similar grants.
- Expected volatility of the price of the underlying share.
- Blackout periods and other coexisting arrangements such as agreements that allow for exercise.

Option value is not a linear function of option term; value increases at a decreasing rate as the term lengthens. For example, a two-year option is worth less than twice as much as a one-year option, other things being equal. Accordingly, estimating the fair value of an option based on a single expected term that effectively averages the widely differing exercise and post-vesting employment termination behaviors of identifiable groups of employees will potentially misstate the value of the entire award.

FAS 123 also provides guidance on how volatility can be computed:

- The term structure of the volatility of the share price over the most recent period that is generally commensurate with (1) the contractual term of the option if a lattice model is being used to estimate fair value or (2) the expected term of the option if a closed-form model is being used.

- The implied volatility of the share price determined from the market prices of traded options. Additionally, the term structure of the implied volatility of the share price over the most recent period that is generally commensurate with (1) the contractual term of the option if a lattice model is being used to estimate fair value or (2) the expected term of the option if a closed-form model is being used.
- For public companies, the length of time an entity's shares have been publicly traded. If that period is shorter than the expected term of the option, the term structure of volatility for the longest period for which trading activity is available should be more relevant. A newly public entity also might consider the volatility of similar entities. A nonpublic entity that elects the fair-value-based method might base its expected volatility on the volatilities of entities that are similar except for having publicly traded securities.
- The mean-reverting tendency of volatilities. For example, in computing historical volatility, an entity might disregard an identifiable period of time in which its share price was extraordinarily volatile because of a failed takeover bid or a major restructuring. Statistical models have been developed that take into account the mean-reverting tendency of volatilities.
- Appropriate and regular intervals for price observations. If an entity considers historical volatility or implied volatility in estimating expected volatility, it should use the intervals that are appropriate based on the facts and circumstances and provide the basis for a reasonable fair value estimate. For example, a publicly traded entity might use daily price observations, while a nonpublic entity with shares that occasionally change hands at negotiated prices might use monthly price observations.
- Corporate structure. An entity's corporate structure may affect expected volatility. For instance, an entity with two distinctly different lines of business of approximately equal size may dispose of the one that was significantly less volatile and generated more cash than the other. In that situation, an entity would consider the effect of that disposition in its estimate of expected volatility.

An entity that uses historical share price volatility as its estimate of expected volatility without considering the extent to which future experience is reasonably expected to differ from historical experience (and the other factors cited) would not comply with the requirements of the revised FAS 123. Lattice models can incorporate a term structure of volatilities; that is, a range of expected volatilities can be incorporated into the lattice over an option's contractual term.

Option-pricing models generally call for expected dividend yield as an input. However, the models may be modified to use an expected dividend amount rather than a yield. An entity may use either its expected yield or its expected payments. If the latter is chosen, the entity's historical pattern of increases in dividends should be considered. For example, if an entity's policy generally has been to increase dividends by approximately 3 percent per year, its estimated share option value should not be based on a fixed dividend amount throughout the share option's expected term.

SUMMARY AND KEY POINTS

- FAS 123 shows a preference for the use of binomial lattices for valuing ESOs.
- Modifying the BSM with a single weighted-average expected life is not allowed. Rather, expected life analysis is a result from the binomial lattice, not an input.
- Intrinsic value method is not allowed. Instead, the fair-market value is required.
- At the time of writing, grants with a vesting schedule should be treated as minigrants for the purposes of expense allocation.
- Valuation should be based on grant date.
- Defaulting to historical volatility is not allowed unless all other methods have been exhausted.
- Changing volatilities, risk-free rates, and dividends should be considered instead of using a single-point average input.
- Employee forfeitures and suboptimal exercise behavior should be considered and modeled as well.

CHAPTER 3

Impact on Valuation

A BRIEF DESCRIPTION OF THE DIFFERENT METHODOLOGIES

In options analysis, there are three mainstream methodologies and approaches used to calculate an option's value:

1. Closed-form models like the Black-Scholes model (also known as the Black-Scholes-Merton model, henceforth known as BSM) and its modifications such as the Generalized Black-Scholes model (GBM)
2. Monte Carlo path-dependent simulation methods
3. Lattices (binomial, trinomial, quadranomial, and multinomial lattices)

However, the mainstream methods that are most widely used are the closed-form models (BSM and GSM) and the binomial lattices. No matter which types of stock options problems you are trying to solve, if the binomial lattice approach is used, the solution can be obtained in one of two ways. The first is the use of risk-neutral probabilities, and the second is the use of market-replicating portfolios. Throughout the analysis, the risk-neutral binomial lattice approach is used—and can be simply termed "binomial lattices."[1] The use of a replicating portfolio is more difficult to understand and apply, but the results obtained from replicating portfolios are identical to those obtained through risk-neutral probabilities. So it does not matter which method is used; nevertheless, application and expositional ease should be emphasized, and thus the risk-neutral probability method is preferred.

SELECTION AND JUSTIFICATION OF THE PREFERRED METHOD

Based on the analysis in Chapter 5 and my prior published study that was presented to the FASB's Board of Directors in 2003, it is concluded that the BSM, albeit theoretically correct and elegant, is insufficient and inappropriately applied when it comes to quantifying the fair-market value of ESOs.[2] This is because the BSM is applicable only to European options without dividends, where the holder of the option can exercise the option only on its maturity date and the underlying stock does not pay any dividends.[3]

However, most ESOs are American-type[4] options with dividends, where the option holder can execute the option at any time up to and including the maturity date while the underlying stock pays dividends. In addition, under real-world conditions, ESOs have a time to vesting before the employee can execute the option, which may also be contingent upon the firm and/or the individual employee attaining a specific performance level (e.g., profitability, growth rate, or stock price hitting a minimum barrier before the options become live), and are subject to forfeitures when the employee leaves the firm or is terminated prematurely before reaching the vested period. In addition, certain options follow a tranching or graduated scale, where a certain percentage of the stock option grants become exercisable every year.[5] Next, the option value may be sensitive to the expected economic environment, as characterized by the term structure of interest rates (i.e., the U.S. Treasuries yield curve) where the risk-free rate can change during the life of the option. Finally, the firm may undergo some corporate restructuring (e.g., divestitures, multinational operations, or mergers and acquisitions that may require a stock swap that changes the volatility of the underlying stock). All these real-life scenarios make the BSM insufficient and inappropriate when used to place a fair-market value on the option grant. In summary, firms can implement a variety of provisions that affect the fair value of the options; the above list is only a few examples. The closed-form models such as the BSM or the GBM—the latter accounts for the inclusion of dividend yields—are inflexible and cannot be modified to accommodate these real-life conditions. Hence, the binomial lattice approach is chosen.

It is shown in Chapter 5 that under very specific conditions (European options without dividends), the binomial lattice and Monte Carlo simulation approaches yield identical values to the BSM, indicating that the two former approaches are robust and exact at the limit. However, when specific real-life business conditions are modeled (i.e., probability of forfeiture, probability that the firm or stock underperforms, time-vesting, suboptimal exercise behavior, and so forth), only the binomial lattice with its highly flexible nature will provide the true fair-market value of the ESO. Binomial lattices can account for real-life conditions such as stock price barriers (a barrier option exists when the stock option becomes either in-the-money or out-of-the-money only when it hits a stock price barrier), vesting tranches (a specific percent of the options granted becomes vested or exercisable each year), changing volatilities (business conditions changing or corporate restructuring), and so forth—the same conditions where a BSM fails miserably.

The BSM takes into account only the following inputs: stock price, strike price, time to maturity, a single risk-free rate, and a single volatility. The GBM accounts for the same inputs as well as a single dividend rate. Hence, in accordance with the proposed FAS 123 requirements, the BSM and GBM fail to account for real-life conditions. On the contrary, the binomial lattice can be customized to include the stock price, strike price, time to maturity, a single risk-free rate and/or multiple risk-free rates changing over time, a single volatility and/or multiple volatilities changing over time, a single dividend rate and/or multiple dividend rates changing over time, plus all the other real-life factors including but not limited to vesting periods, changing suboptimal early exercise behaviors, multiple blackout periods, and changing forfeiture rates over time. It is important to note that the customized binomial lattice results revert to the GBM if these real-life conditions are negligible.

Therefore, based on the justifications above, and in accordance with the requirements and recommendations set forth by the proposed FAS 123, which prefers the binomial lattice, it is hereby concluded that the customized binomial lattice is the best and preferred methodology to calculate the fair-market value of ESOs.

APPLICATION OF THE PREFERRED METHOD

It must be noted here that a standard binomial lattice takes only the six GBM inputs plus a step size input, and is insufficient and inadequate to model ESOs under FAS 123. A special customized binomial lattice was developed to incorporate these additional exotic and changing inputs over time. This customized binomial lattice is used throughout the book. Please contact the author for further information about the software and algorithms used.

In applying the customized binomial lattice methodology, several inputs have to be determined, including:

- Stock price at grant date
- Strike price of the option grant
- Time to maturity of the option

- Risk-free rate over the life of the option
- Dividend yield of the option's underlying stock over the life of the option
- Volatility over the life of the option
- Vesting period of the option grant
- Suboptimal exercise behavior multiple of employees over the life of the option
- Forfeiture and employee turnover rates over the life of the option
- Blackout dates when the options cannot be exercised, from the postvesting period until maturity

The analysis assumes that the employee cannot exercise the option when it is still in the vesting period. Further, if the employee is terminated or decides to leave voluntarily during this vesting period, the option grant will be forfeited and presumed worthless. In contrast, after the options have been vested, employees tend to exhibit erratic exercise behavior where an option will be exercised only if it breaches some multiple of the contractual strike price, and not before. This is termed the suboptimal exercise behavior multiple.[6] However, the options that have vested must be exercised within a short period if the employee leaves voluntarily or is terminated, regardless of the suboptimal behavior threshold—that is, if forfeiture occurs (measured by the historical option forfeiture rates as well as employee turnover rates). Finally, if the option expiration date has been reached, the option will be exercised if it is in-the-money, and expire worthless if it is at-the-money or out-of-the-money. The next section details the results obtained from such an analysis. Further, Chapters 9 and 10 provide more details on the selection and justification of the input parameters used, while the following section provides a theoretical and empirical justification of the results.

TECHNICAL JUSTIFICATION OF METHODOLOGY EMPLOYED

This section illustrates some of the technical justifications that make up the price differential between the GBM and the customized binomial lattice models. Figure 3.1 shows a tornado chart and how each input variable in a customized binomial lattice drives the value of the option.[7] Based on the chart, it is clear that volatility is not the single key variable that drives option value.[8] In fact, when vesting, forfeiture, and suboptimal early exercise behavior elements are added to the model, their effects dominate that of volatility. Of course the tornado chart will not always look like Figure 3.1,

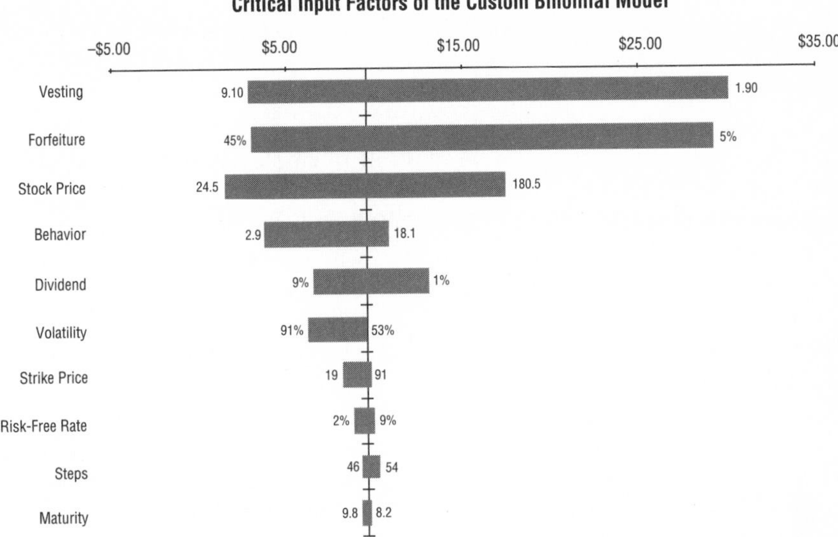

FIGURE 3.1 Tornado chart listing the critical input factors of a customized binomial model.

as it will change depending on the inputs. The chart only illustrates a specific case and should not be generalized across all cases.

In contrast, volatility is a significant variable in a simple BSM as can be seen in Figure 3.2. This is because there is less interaction among input variables, due to the fewer input variables, and for most ESOs that are issued at-the-money, volatility plays an important part when there are no other dominant inputs.

In addition, the interactions between these new input variables are nonlinear. Figure 3.3 shows a spider chart[9] and it can be seen that vesting, forfeiture rates, and suboptimal behavior multiples have nonlinear effects on option value. That is, the lines in the spider chart are not straight but curve at certain areas, indicating that there are nonlinear effects in the model. This means that we cannot generalize these three variables' effects on option value (for instance, we cannot generalize that if a 1 percent increase in forfeiture rate will decrease option value by 2.35 percent, it means that a 2 percent increase in forfeiture rate drives option value down 4.70 percent, and so forth). This is because the variables interact differently at different input levels. The conclusion is that we really cannot say a priori what the direct effects are of changing one variable on the magni-

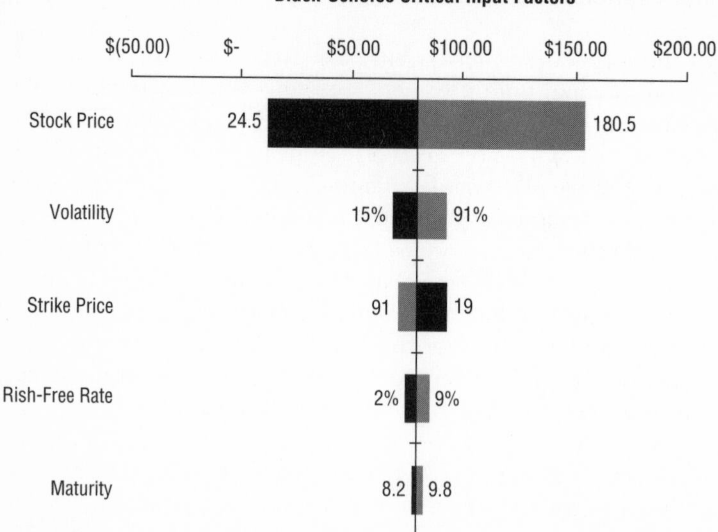

FIGURE 3.2 Tornado chart listing the critical input factors of the BSM.

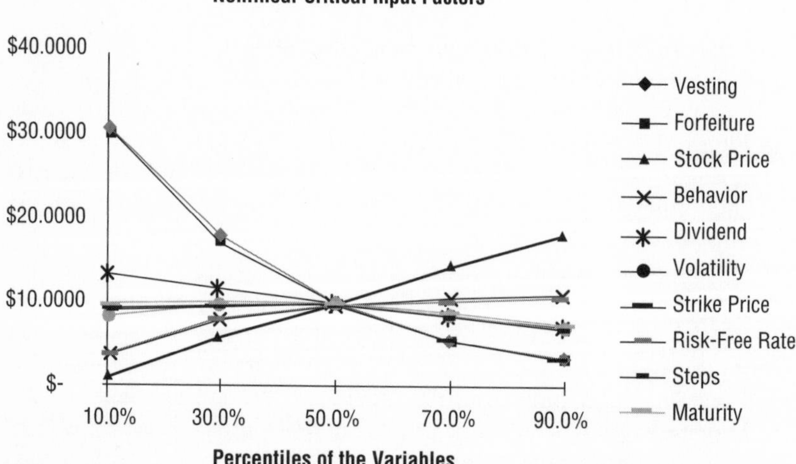

FIGURE 3.3 Spider chart showing the nonlinear effects of input factors in the binomial model.

tude of the final option value. More detailed analysis will have to be performed in each case.

Although the tornado and spider charts illustrate the impact of each input variable on the final option value, its effects are static. That is, one variable is tweaked at a time to determine its ramifications on the option value. However, as shown, the effects are sometimes nonlinear, which means we need to change all variables simultaneously to account for their interactions. Figure 3.4 shows a Monte Carlo simulated dynamic sensitivity chart where forfeiture, vesting, and suboptimal exercise behavior multiples are determined to be important variables, while volatility is again relegated to a less important role. The dynamic sensitivity chart perturbs all input variables simultaneously for thousands of trials, and captures the effects on the option value. This approach is valuable in capturing the net interaction effects among variables at different input levels.

From this preliminary sensitivity analysis, we conclude that incorporating forfeiture rates, vesting, and suboptimal early exercise behavior is vital to obtaining a fair-market valuation of ESOs due to their significant contributions to option value. In addition, we cannot generalize each input's potential nonlinear effects on the final option value. Detailed analysis has to be performed to obtain the option's value every time.

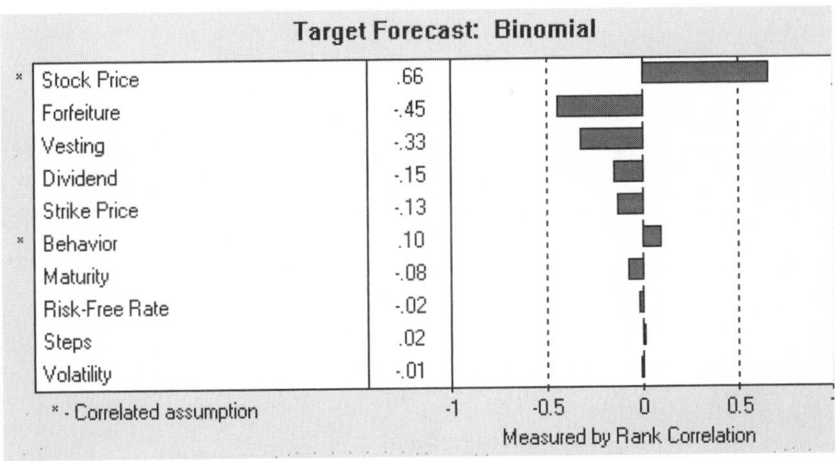

FIGURE 3.4 Dynamic sensitivity with simultaneously changing input factors in the binomial model.

OPTIONS WITH VESTING AND SUBOPTIMAL BEHAVIOR

Employee stock option holders tend to execute their options suboptimally because of liquidity needs (pay off debt, down payment on a home, vacations), personal preferences (risk-averse perception that the stock price will go down in the future), or lack of knowledge (firms do not provide guidance to their employees on optimal timing or optimal thresholds to exercise their options). Therefore, further investigation into the elements of suboptimal exercise behavior and vesting is needed, and the analysis yields the chart shown in Figure 3.5.[10] Here we see that at lower suboptimal behavior multiples (within the range of 1 to 6), the stock option value can be significantly lower than that predicted by the BSM. With a 10-year vesting stock option, the results are identical regardless of the suboptimal behavior multiple—its flat line bears the same value as the BSM result. This is because for a 10-year vesting of a 10-year maturity option, the option reverts to a perfect European option, where it can be exercised only at expiration. The BSM provides the correct result in this case.

However, when suboptimal exercise behavior multiple is low, the option value decreases. This is because employees holding the option will tend to exercise the option suboptimally—that is, the option will be exercised earlier and at a lower stock price than optimal. Hence, the option's

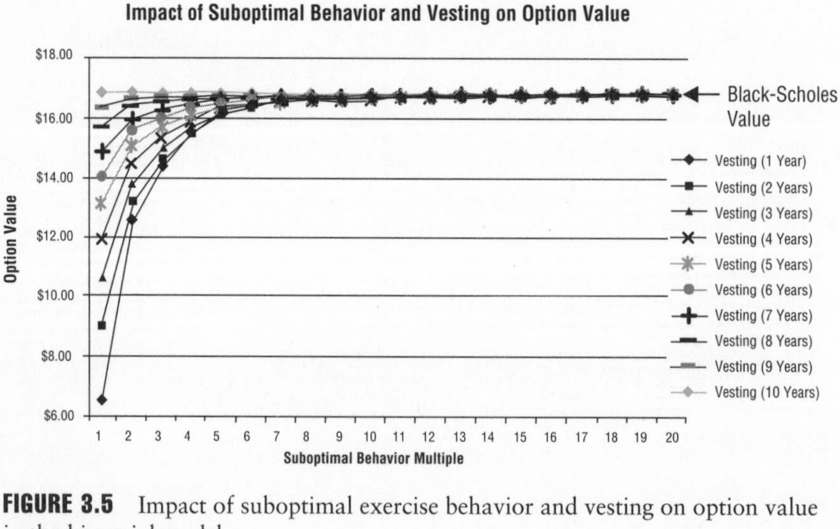

FIGURE 3.5 Impact of suboptimal exercise behavior and vesting on option value in the binomial model.

upside value is not maximized. As an example, suppose an option's strike price is $10 while the underlying stock is highly volatile. If an employee exercises the option at $11 (this means a 1.10 suboptimal exercise multiple), he or she may not be capturing the entire upside potential of the option as the stock price can go up significantly higher than $11 depending on the underlying volatility. Compare this to another employee who exercises the option when the stock price is $20 (suboptimal exercise multiple of 2.0) versus one who does so at a much higher stock price. Thus, lower suboptimal exercise behavior means a lower fair-market value of the stock option.

This suboptimal exercise behavior has a higher impact when stock prices at grant date are forecast to be high. Figure 3.6 shows that (at the lower end of the suboptimal exercise behavior multiples) a steeper slope occurs the higher the initial stock price at grant date.[11]

Figure 3.7 shows that for higher volatility stocks, the suboptimal region is larger and the impact to option value is greater, but the effect is gradual.[12] For instance, for the 100 percent volatility stock (Figure 3.7), the suboptimal region extends from a suboptimal exercise behavior multiple of 1.0 to approximately 9.0 versus from 1.0 to 2.0 for the 10 percent volatility stock. In addition, the vertical distance of the 100 percent volatility stock extends from $12 to $22 with a $10 range, as compared to $2 to $10 with an $8 range. Therefore, the higher the stock price at grant date and

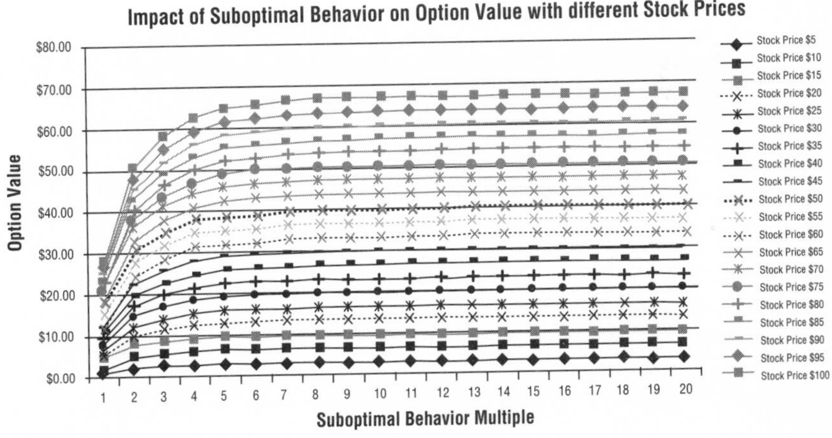

FIGURE 3.6 Impact of suboptimal exercise behavior and stock price on option value in the binomial model.

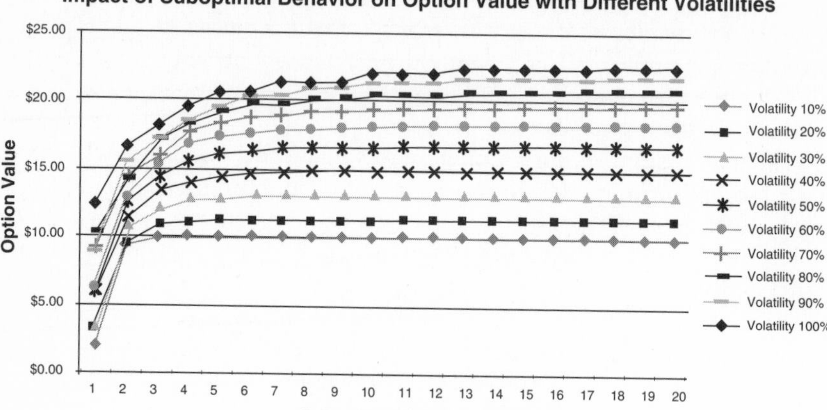

FIGURE 3.7 Impact of suboptimal exercise behavior and volatility on option value in the binomial model.

the higher the volatility, the greater the impact of suboptimal behavior will be on the option value. *In all cases, the BSM results are the horizontal lines in the charts (Figures 3.6 and 3.7). That is, the BSM will always generate the maximum option value assuming optimal exercise behavior, and overexpense the option significantly.*

OPTIONS WITH FORFEITURE RATES

Figure 3.8 illustrates the reduction in option value when the forfeiture rate increases.[13] The rate of reduction changes depending on the vesting period. The longer the vesting period, the more significant the impact of forfeitures will be. This illustrates once again the nonlinear interacting relationship between vesting and forfeitures (that is, the lines in Figure 3.8 are curved and nonlinear). This is intuitive because the longer the vesting period, the lower the compounded probability that an employee will still be employed in the firm and the higher the chances of forfeiture, reducing the expected value of the option. Again, we see that the BSM result is the highest possible value assuming a 10-year vesting in a 10-year maturity option with zero forfeiture. *The BSM will always generate the maximum option value assuming all options will fully vest, and overexpense the option significantly.*

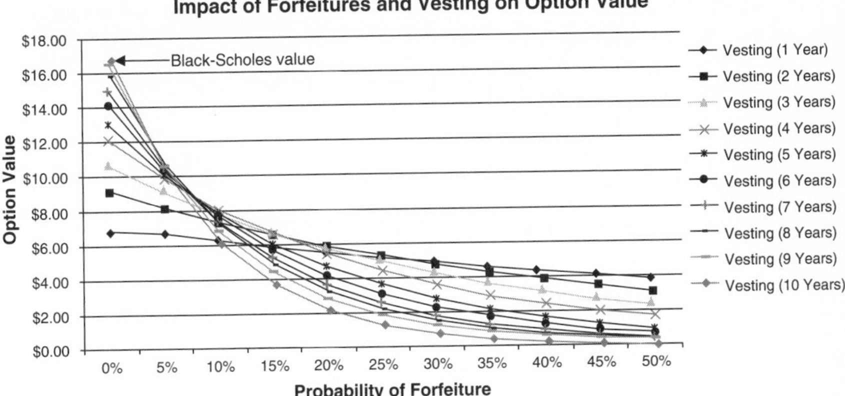

FIGURE 3.8 Impact of forfeiture rates and vesting on option value in the binomial model.

OPTIONS WHERE RISK-FREE RATE CHANGES OVER TIME

Another input assumption is the risk-free rate. Tables 3.1 and 3.2 illustrate the effects of changing risk-free rates over time on option valuation. Due to the time-value-of-money, discounting more heavily in the future will reduce the option's value. Tables 3.1 and 3.2 compare several risk-free yield curve characteristics: flat, upward sloping, downward sloping, smile, and frown. Table 3.1 indicates that a changing risk-free rate over time has a negligible effect on option value for a simple option (i.e., setting suboptimal exercise behavior multiple to 100, vesting to zero, forfeiture to zero, and dividends to zero recreates a basic call option where the BSM is sufficient). The changing risk-free rate in the binomial lattice yields $64.89 with 1,000 lattice steps, identical to the BSM results. Notice that the valuations are identical regardless of how the risk-free rates change over time.

However, when exotic variables are included as in Table 3.2, where suboptimal exercise behavior multiple is 1.8, vesting is 4 years, and forfeiture rate is 10 percent, these tend to interact with the changing risk-free rates. In all cases, the binomial lattice taking into account the changing risk-free rate will yield lower values than the naïve BSM and forfeiture-rate-modified BSM results. In addition, comparing the base case scenario of a flat yield curve or constant 5.50 percent risk-free rate (option value $25.92) with the other scenarios, the results are now different due to this new interaction. For instance, when the term structure of interest rates increases over time, the

TABLE 3.1 Effects of Changing Risk-Free Rates on Option Value

Basic Input Parameters		Year	Static Base Case	Increasing Risk-Free Rates	Decreasing Risk-Free Rates	Risk-Free Rate Smile	Risk-Free Rate Frown
Stock Price	$100.00	1	5.50%	1.00%	10.00%	8.00%	3.50%
Strike Price	$100.00	2	5.50%	2.00%	9.00%	7.00%	4.00%
Maturity	10.00	3	5.50%	3.00%	8.00%	5.00%	5.00%
Volatility	45.00%	4	5.50%	4.00%	7.00%	4.00%	7.00%
Dividend Rate	0.00%	5	5.50%	5.00%	6.00%	3.50%	8.00%
Lattice Steps	1,000	6	5.50%	6.00%	5.00%	3.50%	8.00%
Suboptimal Behavior	100.00	7	5.50%	7.00%	4.00%	4.00%	7.00%
Vesting Period	0.00	8	5.50%	8.00%	3.00%	5.00%	5.00%
Forfeiture Rate	0.00%	9	5.50%	9.00%	2.00%	7.00%	4.00%
		10	5.50%	10.00%	1.00%	8.00%	3.50%
		Average	5.50%	5.50%	5.50%	5.50%	5.50%
		BSM using 5.50% Average Rate	$64.89	$64.89	$64.89	$64.89	$64.89
		Forfeiture Modified BSM using 5.50% Average Rate	$64.89	$64.89	$64.89	$64.89	$64.89
		Changing Risk-Free Binomial Lattice	$64.89	$64.89	$64.89	$64.89	$64.89

TABLE 3.2 Effects of Changing Risk-Free Rates with Exotic Inputs on Option Value

Basic Input Parameters		Year	Static Base Case	Increasing Risk-Free Rates	Decreasing Risk-Free Rates	Risk-Free Rate Smile	Risk-Free Rate Frown
Stock Price	$100.00	1	5.50%	1.00%	10.00%	8.00%	3.50%
Strike Price	$100.00	2	5.50%	2.00%	9.00%	7.00%	4.00%
Maturity	10.00	3	5.50%	3.00%	8.00%	5.00%	5.00%
Volatility	45.00%	4	5.50%	4.00%	7.00%	4.00%	7.00%
Dividend Rate	4.00%	5	5.50%	5.00%	6.00%	3.50%	8.00%
Lattice Steps	1,000	6	5.50%	6.00%	5.00%	3.50%	8.00%
Suboptimal Behavior	1.80	7	5.50%	7.00%	4.00%	4.00%	7.00%
Vesting Period	4.00	8	5.50%	8.00%	3.00%	5.00%	5.00%
Forfeiture Rate	10.00%	9	5.50%	9.00%	2.00%	7.00%	4.00%
		10	5.50%	10.00%	1.00%	8.00%	3.50%
		Average	5.50%	5.50%	5.50%	5.50%	5.50%
		BSM using 5.50% Average Rate	$37.45	$37.45	$37.45	$37.45	$37.45
		Forfeiture Modified BSM using 5.50% Average Rate	$33.71	$33.71	$33.71	$33.71	$33.71
		Changing Risk-Free Binomial Lattice	$25.92	$24.31	$27.59	$26.04	$25.76

option value calculated using a customized changing risk-free rate binomial lattice is lower ($24.31) than that calculated using a constant or average rate. The reverse is true for a downward-sloping yield curve. In addition, Table 3.2 shows a risk-free yield curve frown (low rates followed by high rates followed by low rates) and a risk-free yield curve smile (high rates followed by low rates followed by high rates). In summary, the results indicate that using a single average risk-free rate will overestimate an upward-sloping yield curve, underestimate a downward-sloping yield curve, overestimate a yield curve frown, and underestimate a yield curve smile. The illustration here is for a typical case and may not be generalized to include all cases.

OPTIONS WHERE VOLATILITY CHANGES OVER TIME

Similar to the changing risk-free rate analysis, Table 3.3 illustrates the effects of changing volatilities on an ESO. If volatility changes over time, the option model using a single average volatility over time will overestimate the true option value of a volatility stream that gradually increases over time starting from a low level. In all other cases, the average volatility model will underestimate the true value of the option. The illustration here is for a typical case and may not be generalized to include all cases.

OPTIONS WHERE DIVIDEND YIELD CHANGES OVER TIME

Dividend yield is an interesting variable that has very little interaction with other exotic input variables. Dividend yield has a close-to-linear effect on option value, whereas the other exotic input variables do not. For instance, Table 3.4 illustrates the effects of different maturities (in years) on the same option.[14] The higher the maturity, the higher the option value but the option value increases at a decreasing rate. In contrast, Table 3.5 illustrates the linear effects of dividends even when some of the exotic inputs have been changed. Whatever the change in variable is, the effects of dividends are always very close to linear. While Table 3.5 illustrates many options with unique dividend rates, Table 3.6 illustrates the effects of changing dividends over time on a single option. That is, Table 3.5's

TABLE 3.3 Effects of Changing Volatilities on Option Value

Basic Input Parameters		Year	Static Base Case	Increasing Volatilities	Decreasing Volatilities	Volatility Smile	Volatility Frown
Stock Price	$100.00	1	55.00%	10.00%	100.00%	80.00%	35.00%
Strike Price	$100.00	2	55.00%	20.00%	90.00%	70.00%	40.00%
Maturity	10.00	3	55.00%	30.00%	80.00	50.00%	50.00%
Risk-Free Rate	5.50%	4	55.00%	40.00%	70.00%	40.00%	70.00%
Dividend Rate	0.00%	5	55.00%	50.00%	60.00^	35.00%	80.00%
Lattice Steps	10	6	55.00%	60.00%	50.00%	35.00%	80.00%
Suboptimal Behavior	1.80	7	55.00%	70.00%	40.00%	40.00%	70.00%
Vesting Period	4.00	8	55.00%	80.00%	30.00%	50.00%	50.00%
Forfeiture Rate	10.00%	9	55.00%	90.00%	20.00%	70.00%	40.00%
		10	55.00%	100.00%	10.00%	80.00%	35.00%
		Average	55.00%	55.00%	55.00%	55.00%	55.00%
		BSM using 55% Average Rate	$71.48	$71.48	$71.48	$71.48	$71.48
		Forfeiture Modified BSM using 55% Average Rate	$64.34	$64.34	$64.34	$64.34	$64.34
		Changing Volatilities Binomial Lattice	$38.93	$32.35	$45.96	$39.56	$39.71

TABLE 3.4 Nonlinear Effects of Maturity

	1.8 Behavior Multiple 1-Year Vesting 10% Forfeiture Rate	
Maturity	Option Value	Change
1	$25.16	
2	$32.41	28.84%
3	$35.35	9.08%
4	$36.80	4.08%
5	$37.87	2.91%
6	$38.41	1.44%
7	$38.58	0.43%

TABLE 3.5 Linear Effects of Dividends

	1.8 Behavior Multiple 4-Year Vesting 10% Forfeiture Rate		1.8 Behavior Multiple 1-Year Vesting 10% Forfeiture Rate		3.0 Behavior Multiple 1-Year Vesting 10% Forfeiture Rate	
Dividend Rate	Option Value	Change	Option Value	Change	Option Value	Change
0%	$42.15		$42.41		$49.07	
1%	$39.94	–5.24%	$41.47	–2.20%	$47.67	–2.86%
2%	$37.84	–5.27%	$40.55	–2.22%	$46.29	–2.89%
3%	$35.83	–5.30%	$39.65	–2.24%	$44.94	–2.92%
4%	$33.92	–5.33%	$38.75	–2.26%	$43.61	–2.95%
5%	$32.10	–5.37%	$37.87	–2.28%	$42.31	–2.98%

	$50 Stock Price 1.8 Behavior Multiple 1-Year Vesting 10% Forfeiture Rate		1.8 Behavior Multiple 1-Year Vesting 5% Forfeiture Rate	
Dividend Rate	Option Value	Change	Option Value	Change
0%	$21.20		$45.46	
1%	$20.74	–2.20%	$44.46	–2.20%
2%	$20.28	–2.22%	$43.47	–2.23%
3%	$19.82	–2.24%	$42.49	–2.25%
4%	$19.37	–2.26%	$41.53	–2.27%
5%	$18.93	–2.28%	$40.58	–2.29%

TABLE 3.6 Effects of Changing Dividends over Time

Scenario	Option Value	Change	Notes
Static 3% Dividend	$39.65	0.00%	Dividends are kept steady at 3%
Increasing Gradually	$40.94	3.26%	1% to 5% with 1% increments (average of 3%)
Decreasing Gradually	$38.39	–3.17%	5% to 1% with –1% increments (average of 3%)
Increasing Jumps	$41.70	5.19%	0%, 0%, 5%, 5%, 5% (average of 3%)
Decreasing Jumps	$38.16	–3.74%	5%, 5%, 5%, 0%, 0% (average of 3%)

results are based on comparing different options with different dividend rates, whereas Table 3.6's results are based on a single option whose underlying stock's dividend yields are changing over the life of the option.[15]

Clearly, a changing-dividend option has some value to add in terms of the overall option valuation results. Therefore, if the firm's stock pays a dividend, then the analysis should also consider the possibility of dividend yields changing over the life of the option.

OPTIONS WHERE BLACKOUT PERIODS EXIST

The last item of interest is blackout periods, which can be modeled in the binomial lattice. These are the dates on which ESOs cannot be executed. These dates are usually several weeks before and several weeks after an earnings announcement (usually on a quarterly basis). In addition, only senior executives with fiduciary responsibilities have these blackout dates, and hence, their proportion is relatively small compared to the rest of the firm. Table 3.7 illustrates the calculations of a typical ESO with different blackout dates.[16] In the case where there are only a few blackout days a month, there is little difference between options with blackout dates and those without blackout dates. In fact, if the suboptimal behavior multiple is small (a 1.8 ratio is assumed in this case), blackout dates at strategic times will actually prevent the option holder

TABLE 3.7 Effects of Blackout Periods on Option Value

Blackout Dates	Option Value
No blackouts	$43.16
Every 2 years evenly spaced	$43.16
First 5 years annual blackouts only	$43.26
Last 5 years annual blackouts only	$43.16
Every 3 months for 10 years	$43.26

from exercising suboptimally and sometimes even increase the value of the option ever so slightly.

Table 3.7's analysis assumes only a small percentage of blackout dates in a year (for example, during several days in a year, the ESO cannot be executed). This may be the case for certain so-called brick-and-mortar companies, and as such, blackout dates can be ignored. However, in other firms such as those in the biotechnology and high-tech industries, blackout periods play a more significant role. For instance, in a biotech firm, blackout periods may extend 4 to 6 weeks every quarter, straddling the release of its quarterly earnings. In addition, blackout periods prior to the release of a new product may exist. Therefore, the proportion of blackout dates with respect to the life of the option may reach upward of 35 to 65 percent per year. In such cases, blackout periods will significantly affect the value of the option. For instance, Table 3.8 illustrates the differences between a customized binomial lattice with and without blackout periods.[17] By adding in the real-life elements of blackout periods, the ESO value is further reduced by anywhere between 10 and 35 percent depending on the rate of forfeiture and volatility. As expected, the reduction in value is nonlinear, as the effects of blackout periods will vary depending on the other input variables involved in the analysis.

Table 3.9 shows the effects of blackouts under different dividend yields and vesting periods, while Table 3.10 illustrates the results stemming from different dividend yields and suboptimal exercise behavior multiples. Clearly, it is almost impossible to predict the exact impact unless a detailed analysis is performed, but the range can be generalized to be typically between 10 and 20 percent.

TABLE 3.8 Effects of Significant Blackouts (Different Forfeiture Rates and Volatilities)

% Difference between No Blackout Periods versus Significant Blackouts	Volatility (25%)	Volatility (30%)	Volatility (35%)	Volatility (40%)	Volatility (45%)	Volatility (50%)
Forfeiture Rate (5%)	–17.33%	–13.18%	–10.26%	–9.21%	–7.11%	–5.95%
Forfeiture Rate (6%)	–19.85%	–15.17%	–11.80%	–10.53%	–8.20%	–6.84%
Forfeiture Rate (7%)	–22.20%	–17.06%	–13.29%	–11.80%	–9.25%	–7.70%
Forfeiture Rate (8%)	–24.40%	–18.84%	–14.71%	–13.03%	–10.27%	–8.55%
Forfeiture Rate (9%)	–26.44%	–20.54%	–16.07%	–14.21%	–11.26%	–9.37%
Forfeiture Rate (10%)	–28.34%	–22.15%	–17.38%	–15.35%	–12.22%	–10.17%
Forfeiture Rate (11%)	–30.12%	–23.67%	–18.64%	–16.45%	–13.15%	–10.94%
Forfeiture Rate (12%)	–31.78%	–25.11%	–19.84%	–17.51%	–14.05%	–11.70%
Forfeiture Rate (13%)	–33.32%	–26.48%	–21.00%	–18.53%	–14.93%	–12.44%
Forfeiture Rate (14%)	–34.77%	–27.78%	–22.11%	–19.51%	–15.78%	–13.15%

TABLE 3.9 Effects of Significant Blackouts (Different Dividend Yields and Vesting Periods)

% Difference between No Blackout Periods versus Significant Blackouts	Vesting (1)	Vesting (2)	Vesting (3)	Vesting (4)
Dividends (0%)	–8.62%	–6.93%	–5.59%	–4.55%
Dividends (1%)	–9.04%	–7.29%	–5.91%	–4.84%
Dividends (2%)	–9.46%	–7.66%	–6.24%	–5.13%
Dividends (3%)	–9.90%	–8.03%	–6.56%	–5.43%
Dividends (4%)	–10.34%	–8.41%	–6.90%	–5.73%
Dividends (5%)	–10.80%	–8.79%	–7.24%	–6.04%
Dividends (6%)	–11.26%	–9.18%	–7.58%	–6.35%
Dividends (7%)	–11.74%	–9.58%	–7.93%	–6.67%
Dividends (8%)	–12.22%	–9.99%	–8.29%	–6.99%
Dividends (9%)	–12.71%	–10.40%	–8.65%	–7.31%
Dividends (10%)	–13.22%	–10.81%	–9.01%	–7.64%

TABLE 3.10 Effects of Significant Blackouts (Different Dividend Yields and Suboptimal Exercise Behaviors)

% Difference between No Blackout Periods versus Significant Blackouts	Dividends (0%)	Dividends (1%)	Dividends (2%)	Dividends (3%)	Dividends (4%)	Dividends (5%)	Dividends (6%)	Dividends (7%)	Dividends (8%)	Dividends (9%)	Dividends (10%)
Suboptimal Behavior Multiple (1.8)	–1.01%	–1.29%	–1.58%	–1.87%	–2.16%	–2.45%	–2.75%	–3.06%	–3.36%	–3.67%	–3.98%
Suboptimal Behavior Multiple (1.9)	–1.01%	–1.29%	–1.58%	–1.87%	–2.16%	–2.45%	–2.75%	–3.06%	–3.36%	–3.67%	–3.98%
Suboptimal Behavior Multiple (2.0)	–1.87%	–2.29%	–2.72%	–3.15%	–3.59%	–4.04%	–4.50%	–4.96%	–5.42%	–5.90%	–6.38%
Suboptimal Behavior Multiple (2.1)	–1.87%	–2.29%	–2.72%	–3.15%	–3.59%	–4.04%	–4.50%	–4.96%	–5.42%	–5.90%	–6.38%
Suboptimal Behavior Multiple (2.2)	–4.71%	–5.05%	–5.39%	–5.74%	–6.10%	–6.46%	–6.82%	–7.19%	–7.57%	–7.95%	–8.34%
Suboptimal Behavior Multiple (2.3)	–4.71%	–5.05%	–5.39%	–5.74%	–6.10%	–6.46%	–6.82%	–7.19%	–7.57%	–7.95%	–8.34%
Suboptimal Behavior Multiple (2.4)	–4.71%	–5.05%	–5.39%	–5.74%	–6.10%	–6.46%	–6.82%	–7.19%	–7.57%	–7.95%	–8.34%
Suboptimal Behavior Multiple (2.5)	–6.34%	–6.80%	–7.28%	–7.77%	–8.26%	–8.76%	–9.27%	–9.79%	–10.32%	–10.86%	–11.41%
Suboptimal Behavior Multiple (2.6)	–6.34%	–6.80%	–7.28%	–7.77%	–8.26%	–8.76%	–9.27%	–9.79%	–10.32%	–10.86%	–11.41%
Suboptimal Behavior Multiple (2.7)	–6.34%	–6.80%	–7.28%	–7.77%	–8.26%	–8.76%	–9.27%	–9.79%	–10.32%	–10.86%	–11.41%
Suboptimal Behavior Multiple (2.8)	–6.34%	–6.80%	–7.28%	–7.77%	–8.26%	–8.76%	–9.27%	–9.79%	–10.32%	–10.86%	–11.41%
Suboptimal Behavior Multiple (2.9)	–8.62%	–9.04%	–9.46%	–9.90%	–10.34%	–10.80%	–11.26%	–11.74%	–12.22%	–12.71%	–13.22%
Suboptimal Behavior Multiple (3.0)	–8.62%	–9.04%	–9.46%	–9.90%	–10.34%	–10.80%	–11.26%	–11.74%	–12.22%	–12.71%	–13.22%

SUMMARY AND KEY POINTS

- Option valuation can be performed by applying Monte Carlo path-dependent simulation, closed-form models (BSM, GBM, and the like), and lattices (binomial, trinomial, multinomial, and the like).
- Only binomial lattices can account for real-world exotic inputs such as vesting, forfeitures, blackouts, and suboptimal exercise behavior, as well as risk-free rates, dividends, and volatilities changing during the life of the option. The other inputs into the binomial lattice are the same as the GBM or simulation models (stock price, strike price, maturity, a single risk-free rate, a single dividend yield, and a single volatility).
- Stock price, maturity, risk-free rate, and volatility are all positively correlated to ESO value, whereas strike price and dividend yield are negatively correlated to the ESO value.
- Some of these exotic inputs may have a greater impact on the option value than volatility, and if accounted for correctly may potentially reduce the fair-market value of the ESO.
- These exotic inputs have nonlinear and interacting effects on option value.
- Vesting, suboptimal exercise behavior, and forfeitures will all reduce the option value.
- An increasing (decreasing) risk-free rate over time will reduce (increase) an option's value.
- Increasing volatilities over time starting from a low level will tend to decrease the option value slightly as compared to using an average volatility.
- Blackout periods tend to have significant effects on option value if they occur frequently throughout the year.

CHAPTER 4

Haircuts on Nonmarketability, Modified Black-Scholes with Expected Life, and Dilution

NONMARKETABILITY ISSUES

ESOs are neither directly transferable to someone else nor freely tradable in the open market. Under such circumstances, it can be argued based on sound financial and economic theory that a nonmarketability and non-transferability discount can be appropriately applied to the ESO. However, this is not a simple task as will be discussed.

A simple and direct application of a discount should not be based on an arbitrarily chosen percentage *haircut* on the resulting binomial lattice result. Instead, a more rigorous analysis can be performed using a *put option*. A call option is the contractual right, but not the obligation, to *purchase* the underlying stock at some predetermined contractual strike price within a specified time, while a put option is a contractual right but not the obligation, to *sell* the underlying stock at some predetermined contractual price within a specified time. Therefore, if the holder of the ESO cannot sell or transfer the rights of the option to someone else, then the holder of the option has given up his or her rights to a put option (i.e., the employee has written or sold the firm a put option). Calculating the put option and discounting this value from the call option provides a theoretically correct and justifiable nonmarketability and nontransferability discount to the existing option.

However, care should be taken in analyzing this haircut or discounting feature. The same inputs that go into the customized binomial lattice to calculate a call option should also be used to calculate a customized binomial lattice for a put option. That is, the put option must also be under the same risks (volatility that can change over time), economic environment (risk-free rate structure that can change over time), corporate financial policy (a static or changing dividend yield over the life of the option), contractual obligations (vesting, maturity, strike price, and blackout dates), investor irrationality and nonmarketability (suboptimal early exercise behavior), firm performance (stock price at grant date), and so forth.

Albeit nonmarketability discounts or haircuts are not explicitly discussed in detail in FAS 123, the valuation analysis is performed in Table 4.1 anyway, for the sake of completeness. It is up to each firm's management to decide if haircuts should and can be applied. Table 4.1 shows the customized binomial lattice valuation results of a typical ESO.[1] Table 4.2 shows the results from a nonmarketability analysis performed using a down-and-in upper barrier modified put option with the same exotic inputs (vesting, blackouts, forfeitures, suboptimal early exercise behavior, and so forth) calculated using the customized binomial lattice model. The discounts range from 22 to 53 percent. These calculated discounts look somewhat significant but are actually in line with market expectations.[2] As these discounts are not explicitly sanctioned by FASB, be careful using them in determining the fair-market value of the ESOs.

The marketability discount can be captured and calculated in several ways. The first is using the corresponding put option as described previously. The second approach is to calculate the relevant carrying cost of the option and adjusting an artificially inflated dividend yield to convert the ESO into a *soft option*, thereby discounting the value of the ESO appropriately. This soft option method is more difficult to apply and is susceptible to more subjectivity than using a put option. The put option approach is more advantageous in that all of its inputs have already been predetermined in the ESO valuation. Simply deducting the corresponding put option value from the calculated ESO value would give you the nonmarketability- and nontransferability-adjusted ESO valuation. The third approach is to take market comparables and calculate the corresponding percentage marketability discount that is appropriate for similar types of assets (contingent claims issued by firms with similar functions, markets, risks, and doing business in similar geographical locations). This third method is usually difficult to perform due to lack of pertinent information and data. Therefore, the best alternative is still the use of the corresponding put option to offset the calculated ESO value.

Still others would claim that the use of the suboptimal exercise behavior multiple in the customized binomial lattice is sufficient to account for the nonmarketability and nontransferability aspects of the ESO. In reality, employees tend to exercise their options early and suboptimally anyway, regardless of the suboptimal exercise behavior multiple. This occurs be-

TABLE 4.1 Customized Binomial Lattice Valuation Results

Customized Binomial Lattice (Option Valuation)	Behavior (1.20)	Behavior (1.40)	Behavior (1.60)	Behavior (1.80)	Behavior (2.00)	Behavior (2.20)	Behavior (2.40)	Behavior (2.60)	Behavior (2.80)	Behavior (3.00)
Forfeiture (0.00%)	$24.57	$30.53	$36.16	$39.90	$43.15	$45.87	$48.09	$49.33	$50.40	$51.31
Forfeiture (5.00%)	$22.69	$27.65	$32.19	$35.15	$37.67	$39.74	$41.42	$42.34	$43.13	$43.80
Forfeiture (10.00%)	$21.04	$25.22	$28.93	$31.29	$33.27	$34.88	$36.16	$36.86	$37.45	$37.94
Forfeiture (15.00%)	$19.58	$23.13	$26.20	$28.11	$29.69	$30.94	$31.93	$32.46	$32.91	$33.29
Forfeiture (20.00%)	$18.28	$21.32	$23.88	$25.44	$26.71	$27.70	$28.48	$28.89	$29.23	$29.52
Forfeiture (25.00%)	$17.10	$19.73	$21.89	$23.17	$24.20	$25.00	$25.61	$25.93	$26.19	$26.41
Forfeiture (30.00%)	$16.02	$18.31	$20.14	$21.21	$22.06	$22.70	$23.19	$23.44	$23.65	$23.82
Forfeiture (35.00%)	$15.04	$17.04	$18.61	$19.51	$20.20	$20.73	$21.12	$21.32	$21.49	$21.62
Forfeiture (40.00%)	$14.13	$15.89	$17.24	$18.00	$18.58	$19.01	$19.33	$19.49	$19.63	$19.73

TABLE 4.2 Nonmarketability and Nontransferability Discount

Haircut (Customized Binomial Lattice Modified Put)	Behavior (1.20)	Behavior (1.40)	Behavior (1.60)	Behavior (1.80)	Behavior (2.00)	Behavior (2.20)	Behavior (2.40)	Behavior (2.60)	Behavior (2.80)	Behavior (3.00)
Forfeiture (0.00%)	$11.33	$11.33	$11.33	$11.33	$11.33	$11.33	$11.33	$11.33	$11.33	$11.33
Forfeiture (5.00%)	$10.76	$10.76	$10.76	$10.76	$10.76	$10.76	$10.76	$10.76	$10.76	$10.76
Forfeiture (10.00%)	$10.23	$10.23	$10.23	$10.23	$10.23	$10.23	$10.23	$10.23	$10.23	$10.23
Forfeiture (15.00%)	$ 9.72	$ 9.72	$ 9.72	$ 9.72	$ 9.72	$ 9.72	$ 9.72	$ 9.72	$ 9.72	$ 9.72
Forfeiture (20.00%)	$ 9.23	$ 9.23	$ 9.23	$ 9.23	$ 9.23	$ 9.23	$ 9.23	$ 9.23	$ 9.23	$ 9.23
Forfeiture (25.00%)	$ 8.77	$ 8.77	$ 8.77	$ 8.77	$ 8.77	$ 8.77	$ 8.77	$ 8.77	$ 8.77	$ 8.77
Forfeiture (30.00%)	$ 8.34	$ 8.34	$ 8.34	$ 8.34	$ 8.34	$ 8.34	$ 8.34	$ 8.34	$ 8.34	$ 8.34
Forfeiture (35.00%)	$ 7.92	$ 7.92	$ 7.92	$ 7.92	$ 7.92	$ 7.92	$ 7.92	$ 7.92	$ 7.92	$ 7.92
Forfeiture (40.00%)	$ 7.52	$ 7.52	$ 7.52	$ 7.52	$ 7.52	$ 7.52	$ 7.52	$ 7.52	$ 7.52	$ 7.52
Nonmarketability and Nontransfer-ability Discount (%)	**Behavior (1.20)**	**Behavior (1.40)**	**Behavior (1.60)**	**Behavior (1.80)**	**Behavior (2.00)**	**Behavior (2.20)**	**Behavior (2.40)**	**Behavior (2.60)**	**Behavior (2.80)**	**Behavior (3.00)**
Forfeiture (0.00%)	46.09%	37.09%	31.32%	28.39%	26.25%	24.69%	23.55%	22.96%	22.47%	22.07%
Forfeiture (5.00%)	47.43%	38.92%	33.43%	30.62%	28.57%	27.08%	25.98%	25.42%	24.95%	24.57%
Forfeiture (10.00%)	48.60%	40.55%	35.35%	32.68%	30.73%	29.32%	28.28%	27.75%	27.31%	26.95%
Forfeiture (15.00%)	49.62%	42.01%	37.08%	34.57%	32.73%	31.40%	30.43%	29.93%	29.53%	29.19%
Forfeiture (20.00%)	50.52%	43.31%	38.66%	36.29%	34.57%	33.33%	32.42%	31.96%	31.59%	31.28%
Forfeiture (25.00%)	51.32%	44.48%	40.09%	37.86%	36.25%	35.10%	34.26%	33.84%	33.49%	33.22%
Forfeiture (30.00%)	52.03%	45.53%	41.38%	39.29%	37.79%	36.72%	35.95%	35.56%	35.25%	35.00%
Forfeiture (35.00%)	52.67%	46.48%	42.56%	40.60%	39.20%	38.21%	37.50%	37.15%	36.86%	36.63%
Forfeiture (40.00%)	53.24%	47.34%	43.64%	41.80%	40.49%	39.57%	38.92%	38.60%	38.34%	38.14%

cause of a variety of personal reasons (need for liquidity, need to pay off a debt, down payment to buy a home, a child's college tuition fees being due, and so forth), as well as the employee's lack of knowledge on how to capitalize on and maximize the value of an option (i.e., when is it optimal to execute or what is the optimal trigger price for execution). Also, suppose an employee has decided to leave the firm (or is being terminated). He or she has a set period (usually 15 to 45 days) to execute the ESOs if they are in-the-money. Further suppose that the ESO is currently exactly at-the-money (stock price is yielding $50 and the contractual strike price is also $50). This means that the ESO has a value of zero. In contrast, if this were a tradable and marketable security, due to time value and volatility, the same option can be sold in the market for some value greater than zero. Thus, the employee loses out on this marketability value, regardless of his or her suboptimal exercise behavior multiple threshold. So, a marketability discount should be allowed on top of the ESO valuation that has already been adjusted for the suboptimal exercise behavior multiple.

EXPECTED LIFE ANALYSIS

The 2004 proposed FAS 123 revision expressly prohibits the use of a modified BSM with a single expected life. The requirements are rather explicit:

> *A better estimate of the fair value of an employee share option may be obtained by using a binomial lattice model that incorporates employees' expected exercise and expected post-vesting employment termination behavior than by using a closed-form model (such as the Black-Scholes-Merton formula) with a single weighted-average expected option term as an input.*

In addition, the Standard provides an alternative to estimating expected life of an option:

> *Expected term is an input to a closed-form model. However, if an entity uses a lattice model that has been modified to take into account an option's contractual term and employees' expected exercise and post-vesting employment termination behavior, the expected term is estimated based on the resulting output of the lattice.*
>
> *For example, an entity's experience might indicate that option holders tend to exercise those options when the share price reaches 200 percent of the exercise price. If so, that entity might use a lattice model that assumes exercise of the option at each node along each*

> *share price path in a lattice at which the early exercise expectation is met, provided that the option is vested and exercisable at that point. Moreover, such a model would assume exercise at the end of the contractual term on price paths along which the exercise expectation is not met but the options are in-the-money at the end of the contractual term. That method recognizes that employees' exercise behavior is correlated with the price of the underlying share. Employees' expected post-vesting employment termination behavior also would be factored in. Expected term then could be estimated based on the output of the resulting lattice.*

This means that instead of using an expected life as the *input* into the BSM to obtain the similar results as in a customized binomial lattice, the analysis should be done the other way around. That is, using vesting requirements, suboptimal exercise behavior multiples, forfeiture or employee turnover rates, and the other standard option inputs, calculate the valuation results using the customized binomial lattice. This result can then be compared with a modified BSM and the expected life can then be *imputed*. Excel's goal-seek function can be used to obtain the imputed expected life of the option by setting the BSM result equal to the customized binomial lattice. The resulting expected life can then be compared with historical data as a secondary verification of the results, that is, if the expected life falls within reasonable bounds based on historical performance. This is the correct approach because measuring the expected life of an option is very difficult and inaccurate. FAS 123 provides further guidance on this issue:

> *Option value is not a linear function of option term; value increases at a decreasing rate as the term lengthens. For example, a two-year option is worth less than twice as much as a one-year option, other things being equal. Accordingly, estimating the fair value of an option based on a single expected term that effectively averages the widely differing exercise and post-vesting employment termination behaviors of identifiable groups of employees will potentially misstate the value of the entire award.*

Table 4.3 illustrates the use of Excel's goal-seek function to impute the expected life into the BSM by setting the BSM results to the customized binomial lattice results.

Table 4.4 illustrates another case where the expected life can be imputed, but this time the forfeiture rates are not set at zero. In this case, the BSM results will need to be modified. For example, the customized binomial lattice result of $5.41 is obtained with a 15 percent forfeiture

TABLE 4.3 Imputing the Expected Life for the BSM Using the Binomial Lattice Results

	Customized Binomial Lattice Results to Impute the Expected Life for BSM *Applying Different Suboptimal Behavior Multiples*						
Stock Price	$20.00	$20.00	$20.00	$20.00	$20.00	$20.00	$20.00
Strike Price	$20.00	$20.00	$20.00	$20.00	$20.00	$20.00	$20.00
Maturity	10.00	10.00	10.00	10.00	10.00	10.00	10.00
Risk-Free Rate	3.50%	3.50%	3.50%	3.50%	3.50%	3.50%	3.50%
Dividend	0.00%	0.00%	0.00%	0.00%	0.00%	0.00%	0.00%
Volatility	50.00%	50.00%	50.00%	50.00%	50.00%	50.00%	50.00%
Vesting	4.00	4.00	4.00	4.00	4.00	4.00	4.00
Suboptimal Behavior	**1.10**	**1.50**	**2.00**	**2.50**	**3.00**	**3.50**	**4.00**
Forfeiture Rate	0.00%	0.00%	0.00%	0.00%	0.00%	0.00%	0.00%
Lattice Steps	1,000	1,000	1,000	1,000	1,000	1,000	1,000
Binomial	$ 8.94	$10.28	$11.03	$11.62	$11.89	$12.18	$12.29
BSM	$12.87	$12.87	$12.87	$12.87	$12.87	$12.87	$12.87
Expected Life	*4.42*	*5.94*	*6.95*	*7.83*	*8.26*	*8.74*	*8.93*
Modified BSM	$ 8.94	$10.28	$11.03	$11.62	$11.89	$12.18	$12.29

TABLE 4.4 Imputing the Expected Life for the BSM Using the Binomial Lattice Results under Nonzero Forfeiture Rates

	Customized Binomial Lattice Results to Impute the Expected Life for BSM *Applying Different Forfeiture Rates*						
Stock Price	$20.00	$20.00	$20.00	$20.00	$20.00	$20.00	$20.00
Strike Price	$20.00	$20.00	$20.00	$20.00	$20.00	$20.00	$20.00
Maturity	10.00	10.00	10.00	10.00	10.00	10.00	10.00
Risk-Free Rate	3.50%	3.50%	3.50%	3.50%	3.50%	3.50%	3.50%
Dividend	0.00%	0.00%	0.00%	0.00%	0.00%	0.00%	0.00%
Volatility	50.00%	50.00%	50.00%	50.00%	50.00%	50.00%	50.00%
Vesting	4.00	4.00	4.00	4.00	4.00	4.00	4.00
Suboptimal Behavior	1.50	1.50	1.50	1.50	1.50	1.50	1.50
Forfeiture Rate	**0.00%**	**2.50%**	**5.00%**	**7.50%**	**10.00%**	**12.50%**	**15.00%**
Lattice Steps	1,000	1,000	1,000	1,000	1,000	1,000	1,000
Binomial	$10.28	$9.23	$8.29	$7.44	$6.69	$6.02	$5.41
BSM	$12.87	$12.87	$12.87	$12.87	$12.87	$12.87	$12.87
Expected Life	***5.94***	***4.71***	***3.77***	***3.03***	***2.45***	***1.99***	***1.61***
Modified BSM*	$10.28	$9.23	$8.29	$7.44	$6.69	$6.02	$5.41
Expected Life	***5.94***	***4.97***	***4.19***	***3.55***	***3.02***	***2.59***	***2.22***
Modified BSM†	$10.28	$9.23	$8.29	$7.44	$6.69	$6.02	$5.41

*Note: Uses the binomial lattice result to impute the expected life for a modified BSM.
†Note: Uses the binomial lattice but also accounts for the forfeiture rate to modify to BSM.

rate. This means that the BSM result needs to be BSM(1 – 15%) = $5.41 using the modified expected life method. The expected life that yields the BSM value of $6.36 [$5.41/85% is $6.36, and $6.36(1 – 15%) is $5.41] is 2.22 years.

DILUTION

In most cases, the effects of dilution can be safely ignored as the proportion of ESO grants is relatively small compared to the total equity issued by the company. In investment finance theory, the market has already anticipated the exercise of these ESOs and the effects have already been accounted for in the stock price. Once a new grant is announced, the stock price will immediately and fully incorporate this news and account for any dilution that may occur. This means that as long as the valuation is performed after the announcement is made, then the effects of dilution are nonexistent. The proposed 2004 FAS 123 revisions do not explicitly provide guidance in this area. Given that the FASB has decided to ignore the issue of dilution, and the fact that forecasting stock prices (as part of estimating the effects of dilution) is fairly difficult and inaccurate at best, plus the fact that the dilution effects are small in proportion compared to all the equity issued by the firm, the effects of dilution are assumed to be minimal, and can be safely ignored.

SUMMARY AND KEY POINTS

- ESOs are nontransferable and hence nonmarketable.
- Typically, a marketability discount is deducted from the fair-market value of assets that cannot be sold openly in the market but the proposed FAS 123 does not explicitly allow a marketability discount.
- Analysis shows that marketability discounts on ESOs range from 22 to 53 percent, which is in line with market expectations.
- The 2004 proposed FAS 123 prohibits the use of a single expected life as an input into the GBM or BSM. Instead, the expected life can be imputed from the results of a customized binomial lattice and can be used as a secondary verification of the results to be benchmarked against historical average lives of ESOs.
- The effects of dilution are negligible as stock prices have already adjusted once the ESO grants are announced. In addition, the proportion of ESOs to the total equity in the company is relatively small to have any significant impact.

CHAPTER 5

Applicability of Monte Carlo Simulation

INTRODUCTION TO THE ANALYSIS

Analyses in previous chapters clearly indicate that using the BSM alone is insufficient to measure the true fair-market value of ESOs. Option pricing has made vast strides since 1973 when Fischer Black and Myron Scholes published their path-breaking paper providing a model for valuing European options. While Black and Scholes' derivations are mathematically complex, other approaches broached in this book, namely those using Monte Carlo simulation and binomial lattices, provide much simpler applications but at the same time enable a similar wellspring of information.[1] In fact, applying binomial lattices with Monte Carlo simulation has been made much easier with the use of software and spreadsheets.

This chapter focuses on the applicability of Monte Carlo simulation as it pertains to valuing stock options and as a means of simulating the inputs that go into a customized binomial lattice—that is, used in conjunction with binomial lattices. This chapter begins with a brief review of the three types of option pricing methodologies and continues with a quantitative assessment of their analytical robustness under different conditions. The simulation approach to valuing options will be shown to be precise when it comes to valuing simple European options without dividends. In contrast, when it comes to American or mixed options with exotic features (vesting, forfeiture, suboptimal behavior, and blackout dates), the simulation approach to valuing options breaks down and cannot be used. The binomial lattice is a much better candidate when these exotic elements exist. However, Monte Carlo simulation still proves to be a powerful and useful tool for simulating the uncertain input variables with correlations, and allows tens of thousands of scenarios to enter into a customized binomial lattice. It is shown later in this chapter that a precision-controlled simulation can increase the confidence of the results and narrow the errors to less than a $0.01 precision with a 99.9 percent statistical confidence level, increasing the confidence of the valuation results.

In the rest of the chapter a brief review of the three mainstream approaches is made and the valuation results are then compared. The simulation approach to valuation will be shown not to be applicable by itself; but when coupled with the customized binomial lattices, it provides a powerful analytical tool that yields robust results.

The Black-Scholes Model

In order to fully understand and use the BSM, one needs to understand the assumptions under which the model was constructed. These are essentially the caveats that go into using the BSM option pricing model. These assumptions are violated quite often, but the model still holds up to scrutiny when applied appropriately to European options. A European option is the type of option that can be exercised only on its expiration date and not before. In contrast, most executive stock options awarded are American options, where the holder of the option is allowed to exercise at any time (except on blackout dates) once the award has been fully vested.

The main assumption that goes into the BSM is that the underlying asset's price structure follows a Brownian Motion with static drift and volatility parameters, and that this motion follows a Markov-Weiner stochastic process. In other words, it assumes that the returns on the stock prices follow a lognormal distribution. The other assumptions are fairly standard, including a fair and timely efficient market with no riskless arbitrage opportunities, no transaction costs, and no taxes. Price changes are also assumed to be continuous and instantaneous. Finally, the risk-free rate and volatility are assumed to be constant throughout the life of the option, and the stock pays no dividends.[2] However, for fairness of comparison, a modification of the BSM is used—the GBM. This modification allows the incorporation of dividends in a standard European option.

Monte Carlo Path Simulation

Monte Carlo simulation can be easily adapted for use in an options valuation paradigm. There are multiple uses of Monte Carlo simulation including its use in risk analysis and forecasting. Here, the discussion focuses on two distinct applications of Monte Carlo simulation: solving a stock option valuation problem versus obtaining a range of solved option values. Although these two approaches are discussed separately, they can be used together in an analysis.

Applying Monte Carlo Simulation to Obtain a Stock Options Value

Monte Carlo simulation can be applied to solve an options valuation problem, that is, to obtain a fair-market value of the stock option. Recall that the mainstream approaches in solving options problems are the binomial approach, closed-form equations, and simulation. In the simulation approach, a series of forecast stock prices are created using the Brownian Motion stochastic process, and the option maximization calculation is applied to the series' end nodes, and discounted back to time zero, at the risk-free rate.

Note that simulation can be easily used to solve European-type options, but it is fairly difficult to apply simulation to solve American-type options.[3] In fact, certain academic texts list Monte Carlo simulation's major limitation as that it can be used to solve only European-type options.[4] If the number of simulation trials are adequately increased, coupled with an increase in the simulation time-steps, the results stemming from Monte Carlo simulation also approach the BSM value for a European option.

Binomial Lattices

Binomial lattices, in contrast, are easy to implement and easy to explain. They are also highly flexible, but require significant computing power and lattice steps to obtain good approximations, as will be seen in the next chapter. The results from closed-form solutions can be used in conjunction with the binomial lattice approach when presenting a complete stock options valuation solution. Binomial lattices are particularly useful in capturing the effect of early exercise as in an American option with dividends, vesting and blackout periods, suboptimal early exercise behaviors, forfeitures, performance-based vesting, changing volatilities and business environments, changing dividend yield, changing risk-free rates, and so forth—the same real-life conditions that cannot be accounted for in the BSM, GBM, or simulation. Binomial lattices can even account for exotic events such as stock price barriers (a barrier option exists when the stock option becomes either in-the-money or out-of-the-money only when it hits a stock price barrier), vesting tranches (a specific percent of the options granted becomes vested or exercisable each year, or that senior management has different option grants than regular employees), and so forth. Monte Carlo simulation can then be applied to simulate the probabilities of forfeitures and underperformance of the firm, and use these as the inputs into the binomial lattices.[5]

Analytical Comparison

The following presents a results comparison of the three methods discussed. The main goal of the analysis is to show that under certain restrictive conditions, all three methodologies provide identical results, indicating that all three methods are robust and correct. However, when conditions are changed to mirror real-life scenarios, binomial lattices provide a much more accurate fair-value assessment than the GBM and BSM approaches, where the latter approaches may sometimes overvalue and at other times undervalue the ESO.

Figure 5.1 illustrates a comparative analysis of the three different options valuation methodologies for a simple set of inputs. The usual inputs in the options valuation model are: expiration in years, stock price, volatility, risk-free rate, dividend rate, and strike price. Notice that with a simple set of inputs where the stock is assumed not to pay any dividends, the binomial approach with 5,000 steps yields \$39.43, identical to the BSM of \$39.43. The path simulation approach also yields a value of \$39.43.[6] Notice in addition, that the American closed-form model results indicate identical values when no dividend payments exist, and that all methods yield the same values in a European option. In American options when a dividend exists, the values obtained from the three methodologies are vastly different, as seen in Table 5.1 (a–d).

When a dividend yield exists, that is, when the underlying firm's stocks pay dividends, the results from a BSM or GBM are no longer robust or correct, because early execution is optimal, making the stock option, an American-type option, more valuable than is estimated using the BSM. Table 5.1 (a–d) illustrates this point. For instance, panel (a) of Table 5.1 shows the results from a BSM, and panel (b) is the binomial lattice for a European option, while the panel (c) shows the results from an American closed-form approximation model, and panel (d) shows the binomial approach for an American option. Notice that for all four panels, the first column results are identical when no dividends exist. This indicates that all four methodologies are robust and consistent and provide identical values at the limit, under the condition of no dividends and are all valid for European-type options. However, when dividends exist, the BSM breaks down and is no longer valid, especially when the option is of the American type.

Applying Monte Carlo Simulation for Statistical Confidence and Precision Control

Alternatively, Monte Carlo simulation can be applied to obtain a range of calculated stock option fair values. That is, any of the inputs into the stock

Comparing Approaches

Input Parameters	
Expiration in Years	5.00
Volatility	35.00%
Initial Stock Price	$100.00
Risk-Free Rate	5.00%
Dividend Rate	0.00%
Strike Cost	$100.00

European Option Results	
Binomial Approach	$39.43
Black-Scholes Model	$39.43
Path-Dependent Simulation	$39.43
Generalized Black-Scholes	$39.43

American Option Results	
Binomial Approach	$39.43
Black-Scholes Model	N/A
Path Dependent Simulation	N/A
Closed-Form Approximation Model	$39.43

Simulation Calculation	
Simulate Value	0.00
Payoff Function	19.47

Binomial Steps 5,000 Steps ▼

Binomial Steps 5,000 Steps ▼

Time	Simulate	Steps	Value	Value (2)	Time	Simulate	Steps	Value	Value (2)	Time	Simulate	Steps	Value
0	0.00	0.00	100.00	100.00	21	–0.05	–0.09	82.87	86.17	42	–1.30	–3.87	35.01
1	–0.59	–4.40	95.60	95.60	22	0.24	1.78	84.65	88.32	43	–1.27	–3.40	31.61
2	–0.85	–6.14	89.46	89.18	23	–2.00	–13.05	71.61	72.91	44	1.13	2.88	34.48
3	1.23	8.81	98.28	99.03	24	–0.66	–3.49	68.11	68.03	45	–0.29	–0.70	33.79
4	–0.62	–4.56	93.72	94.39	25	1.20	6.57	74.68	77.68	46	1.34	3.64	37.42
5	0.94	7.14	100.85	102.01	26	–1.59	–9.13	65.55	65.45	47	0.43	1.34	38.77
6	0.84	6.92	107.77	108.87	27	–0.54	–2.59	62.96	61.49	48	0.17	0.61	39.38
7	–1.17	–9.60	98.17	99.96	28	–1.38	–6.65	56.30	50.92	49	–0.69	–2.03	37.35
8	–1.02	–7.62	90.55	92.20	29	–1.50	–6.48	49.83	39.42	50	–0.78	–2.19	35.16
9	–0.09	–0.40	90.15	91.76	30	0.20	0.89	50.71	41.20	51	0.62	1.79	36.95
10	–0.66	–4.40	85.76	86.88	31	0.24	1.06	51.78	43.30	52	–1.64	–4.66	32.29
11	–0.99	–6.45	79.30	79.36	32	–1.65	–6.55	45.23	30.64	53	–0.68	–1.64	30.65
12	0.35	2.36	81.66	82.33	33	–0.88	–2.99	42.23	24.03	54	–1.90	–4.48	26.17
13	2.12	13.76	95.42	99.18	34	–1.29	–4.17	38.07	14.16	55	–0.52	–0.99	25.17
14	–0.27	–1.75	93.67	97.35	35	–0.50	–1.40	36.67	10.50	56	1.04	2.12	27.29
15	–1.49	–10.72	82.95	85.91	36	–0.26	–0.64	36.03	8.75	57	0.21	0.51	27.80
16	–0.57	–3.48	79.48	81.72	37	0.65	1.92	37.95	14.06	58	0.52	1.19	28.99
17	0.06	0.58	80.06	82.45	38	0.54	1.69	39.63	18.51	59	–0.78	–1.70	27.29
18	0.87	5.67	85.73	89.53	39	–0.57	–1.67	37.96	14.29	60	0.00	0.06	27.35
19	–0.34	–2.08	83.65	87.10	40	–0.42	–1.15	36.81	11.27	61	1.17	2.57	29.92
20	–0.14	–0.69	82.96	86.27	41	0.68	2.06	38.88	16.87	62	1.64	3.92	33.84

FIGURE 5.1 Comparing the three approaches.

TABLE 5.1 (a–d) The Three Approaches' Comparison Results

	Black-Scholes Model	Dividend (0.00%)	Dividend (1.00%)	Dividend (2.00%)	Dividend (3.00%	Dividend (4.00%)	Dividend (5.00%)	Dividend (6.00%)	Dividend (7.00%)	Dividend (8.00%)	Dividend (9.00%)	Dividend (10.00%)	
	Years (1.00)	$16.13	$16.13	$16.13	$16.13	$16.13	$16.13	$16.13	$16.13	$16.13	$16.13	$16.13	1
	Years (2.00)	$23.75	$23.75	$23.75	$23.75	$23.75	$23.75	$23.75	$23.75	$23.75	$23.75	$23.75	2
	Years (3.00)	$29.78	$29.78	$29.78	$29.78	$29.78	$29.78	$29.78	$29.78	$29.78	$29.78	$29.78	3
	Years (4.00)	$34.91	$34.91	$34.91	$34.91	$34.91	$34.91	$34.91	$34.91	$34.91	$34.91	$34.91	4
(a)	Years (5.00)	$39.43	$39.43	$39.43	$39.43	$39.43	$39.43	$39.43	$39.43	$39.43	$39.43	$39.43	5
	Years (6.00)	$43.47	$43.47	$43.47	$43.47	$43.47	$43.47	$43.47	$43.47	$43.47	$43.47	$43.47	6
	Years (7.00)	$47.14	$47.14	$47.14	$47.14	$47.14	$47.14	$47.14	$47.14	$47.14	$47.14	$47.14	7
	Years (8.00)	$50.48	$50.48	$50.48	$50.48	$50.48	$50.48	$50.48	$50.48	$50.48	$50.48	$50.48	8
	Years (9.00)	$53.55	$53.55	$53.55	$53.55	$53.55	$53.55	$53.55	$53.55	$53.55	$53.55	$53.55	9
	Years (10.00)	$56.39	$56.39	$56.39	$56.39	$56.39	$56.39	$56.39	$56.39	$56.39	$56.39	$56.39	10
		1	2	3	4	5	6	7	8	9	10	11	

	Binomial Approach (European)	Dividend (0.00%)	Dividend (1.00%)	Dividend (2.00%)	Dividend (3.00%)	Dividend (4.00%)	Dividend (5.00%)	Dividend (6.00%)	Dividend (7.00%)	Dividend (8.00%)	Dividend (9.00%)	Dividend (10.00%)	
	Years (1.00)	$16.13	$15.51	$14.91	$14.33	$13.76	$13.21	$12.68	$12.16	$11.66	$11.17	$10.70	1
	Years (2.00)	$23.74	$22.42	$21.16	$19.95	$18.79	$17.69	$16.63	$15.62	$14.66	$13.74	$12.87	2
	Years (3.00)	$29.78	$27.71	$25.75	$23.90	$22.15	$20.50	$18.95	$17.49	$16.12	$14.84	$13.64	3
	Years (4.00)	$34.91	$32.06	$29.39	$26.89	$24.57	$22.40	$20.39	$18.53	$16.80	$15.21	$13.74	4
(b)	Years (5.00)	$39.43	$35.76	$32.37	$29.24	$26.36	$23.71	$21.27	$19.05	$17.01	$15.16	$13.48	5
	Years (6.00)	$43.47	$38.98	$34.87	$31.11	$27.69	$24.58	$21.76	$19.22	$16.92	$14.85	$13.00	6
	Years (7.00)	$47.13	$41.80	$36.97	$32.60	$28.66	$25.13	$21.96	$19.13	$16.62	$14.38	$12.40	7
	Years (8.00)	$50.48	$44.29	$38.74	$33.78	$29.36	$25.43	$21.95	$18.88	$16.17	$13.80	$11.74	8
	Years (9.00)	$53.55	$46.50	$40.25	$34.71	$29.82	$25.53	$21.77	$18.49	$15.63	$13.17	$11.04	9
	Years (10.00)	$56.38	$48.47	$41.52	$35.42	$30.10	$25.47	$21.46	$18.01	$15.04	$12.50	$10.33	10
		1	2	3	4	5	6	7	8	9	10	11	

TABLE 5.1 (a–d) *(Continued)*

(c)

Closed-Form Approximation (American)	Dividend (0.00%)	Dividend (1.00%)	Dividend (2.00%)	Dividend (3.00%)	Dividend (4.00%)	Dividend (5.00%)	Dividend (6.00%)	Dividend (7.00%)	Dividend (8.00%)	Dividend (9.00%)	Dividend (10.00%)	
Years (1.00)	$16.13	$15.51	$14.91	$14.33	$13.79	$13.33	$12.88	$12.45	$12.05	$11.67	$11.31	1
Years (2.00)	$23.75	$22.43	$21.16	$19.99	$18.96	$18.10	$17.26	$16.49	$15.77	$15.11	$14.49	2
Years (3.00)	$29.78	$27.71	$25.77	$24.03	$22.58	$21.33	$20.16	$19.10	$18.12	$17.22	$16.40	3
Years (4.00)	$34.91	$32.06	$29.45	$27.20	$25.37	$23.76	$22.30	$20.98	$19.78	$18.68	$17.69	4
Years (5.00)	$39.43	$35.77	$32.51	$29.80	$27.61	$25.67	$23.95	$22.40	$21.01	$19.75	$18.61	5
Years (6.00)	$43.47	$39.00	$35.12	$31.99	$29.47	$27.23	$25.26	$23.52	$21.96	$20.56	$19.30	6
Years (7.00)	$47.14	$41.84	$37.39	$33.86	$31.03	$28.51	$26.33	$24.42	$22.71	$21.19	$19.83	7
Years (8.00)	$50.48	$44.37	$39.38	$35.48	$32.35	$29.58	$27.22	$25.15	$23.32	$21.69	$20.24	8
Years (9.00)	$53.55	$46.64	$41.14	$36.90	$33.49	$30.49	$27.96	$25.75	$23.81	$22.09	$20.56	9
Years (10.00)	$56.39	$48.69	$42.71	$38.15	$34.48	$31.27	$28.58	$26.25	$24.21	$22.41	$20.82	10
	1	2	3	4	5	6	7	8	9	10	11	

(d)

Binomial Approach (American)	Dividend (0.00%)	Dividend (0.00%)	Dividend (0.00%)	Dividend (0.00%)	Dividend (0.00%)	Dividend (0.00%)	Dividend (0.00%)	Dividend (0.00%)	Dividend (0.00%)	Dividend (0.00%)	Dividend (0.00%)	
Years (1.00)	$16.13	$15.51	$14.91	$14.34	$13.83	$13.36	$12.93	$12.52	$12.14	$11.77	$11.42	1
Years (2.00)	$23.74	$22.42	$21.17	$20.03	$19.05	$18.16	$17.35	$16.59	$15.89	$15.23	$14.61	2
Years (3.00)	$29.78	$27.71	$25.79	$24.13	$22.70	$21.43	$20.27	$19.21	$18.24	$17.34	$16.51	3
Years (4.00)	$34.91	$32.06	$29.50	$27.35	$25.50	$23.88	$22.42	$21.10	$19.89	$18.79	$17.79	4
Years (5.00)	$39.43	$35.78	$32.61	$29.98	$27.76	$25.81	$24.08	$22.52	$21.12	$19.86	$18.70	5
Years (6.00)	$43.47	$39.02	$35.26	$32.19	$29.61	$27.37	$25.40	$23.64	$22.07	$20.66	$19.8	6
Years (7.00)	$47.13	$41.88	$37.56	$34.08	$31.17	$28.66	$26.47	$24.54	$22.82	$21.28	$19.90	7
Years (8.00)	$50.48	$44.42	$39.57	$35.71	$32.49	$29.74	$27.36	$25.26	$23.41	$21.77	$20.30	8
Years (9.00)	$53.55	$46.70	$41.35	$37.12	$33.63	$30.66	$28.10	$25.86	$23.90	$22.16	$20.62	9
Years (10.00)	$56.38	$48.76	$42.93	$38.36	$34.61	$31.44	$28.72	$26.36	$24.29	$22.48	$20.87	10
	1	2	3	4	5	6	7	8	9	10	11	

options valuation model can be chosen for Monte Carlo simulation if they are uncertain and stochastic. Distributional assumptions are assigned to these variables, and the resulting options values using the BSM, GBM, path simulation, or binomial lattices are selected as forecast cells. These modeled uncertainties include the probability of forfeiture and the employees' suboptimal exercise behavior. The simulation examples throughout this book use Decisioneering, Inc.'s Crystal Ball software.

The results of the simulation are essentially a distribution of the stock option values. Keep in mind that the simulation application here is used to vary the inputs to an options valuation model to obtain a range of results, not to model and calculate the options themselves. However, simulation can be applied both to simulate the inputs to obtain the range of options results and also to solve the options model through path-dependent simulation.

Monte Carlo simulation, named after the famous gambling capital of Monaco, is a very potent methodology. Monte Carlo simulation creates artificial futures by generating thousands and even millions of sample paths of outcomes and looks at their prevalent characteristics, and its simplest form is a random number generator that is useful for forecasting, estimation, and risk analysis. A simulation calculates numerous scenarios of a model by repeatedly picking values from a user-predefined *probability distribution* for the uncertain variables and using those values for the model. As all those scenarios produce associated results in a model, each scenario can have a *forecast*. Forecasts are events (usually with formulas or functions) that you define as important outputs of the model.

Simplistically, think of the Monte Carlo simulation approach as picking golf balls out of a large basket repeatedly with replacement. The size and shape of the basket depend on the distributional *assumptions* (e.g., a normal distribution with a mean of 100 and a standard deviation of 10, versus a uniform distribution or a triangular distribution) where some baskets are deeper or more symmetrical than others, allowing certain balls to be pulled out more frequently than others. These balls are colored differently to represent their respective frequency or probabilities of occurrence. The number of balls pulled repeatedly depends on the number of *trials* simulated. For a large model with multiple related assumptions, imagine the large model as a very large basket, where many baby baskets reside. Each baby basket has its own set of different-colored golf balls that are bouncing around. Sometimes these baby baskets are linked to each other (if there is a *correlation* between the variables) and the golf balls are bouncing in tandem while others are bouncing independently of one another. The balls that are picked each time from these interactions within the model are tabulated and recorded, providing a *forecast* result of the simulation.

These concepts can be applied to ESO valuation. For instance, the simulated input assumptions are those inputs that are highly uncertain and can vary in the future, such as stock price at grant date, volatility, forfeiture rates, and suboptimal early exercise behavior multiples. Clearly, variables that are objectively obtained, such as risk-free rates (U.S. Treasury yields for the next 1 month to 20 years are published), dividend yield (determined from corporate strategy), vesting period, strike price, and blackout periods (determined contractually in the option grant) should not be simulated. In addition, the simulated input assumptions can be correlated. For instance, forfeiture rates can be negatively correlated to stock price—if the firm is doing well, its stock price usually increases, making the option more valuable, thus making the employees less likely to leave and the firm less likely to lay off its employees. Finally, the output forecasts are the option valuation results.

The analysis results will be distributions of thousands of options valuation results, where all the uncertain inputs are allowed to vary according to their distributional assumptions and correlations, and the customized binomial lattice model will take care of their interactions. The resulting average (if the distribution is not skewed) or median (if the distribution is highly skewed) options value is used. Hence, instead of using single-point estimates of the inputs to provide a single-point estimate of options valuation, all possible contingencies and scenarios in the input variables will be accounted for in the analysis through Monte Carlo simulation.

Table 5.2 shows the results obtained using the customized binomial lattices based on single-point inputs of all the variables. The model takes exotic inputs such as vesting, forfeiture rates, suboptimal exercise behavior multiples, blackout periods, and changing inputs (dividends, risk-free rates, and volatilities) over time. The resulting option value is $31.42. This analysis can then be extended to include simulation. Table 5.2 and Figures 5.2 to 5.6 illustrate the use of simulation coupled with customized binomial lattices.[7]

For instance, Figure 5.2 illustrates how the input assumptions are obtained through a distributional-fitting routine. Using historical data, comparable data, forecast projections, or management assumptions, the correct distributions are obtained through a rigorous statistical hypothesis test. Figure 5.3 shows all the input assumptions used in the model. Notice that only volatility, forfeiture rate, and suboptimal exercise behavior multiple are simulated. The rest of the input variables are either contractually fixed or objectively obtained (e.g., risk-free rates from the U.S. Treasury) and their fluctuations are negligible. Figure 5.4 shows how some assumptions can be correlated in the simulation. For instance, the change in volatility in year 4 of the analysis is assumed to be correlated to the

TABLE 5.2 Single-Point Result Using a Customized Binomial Lattice

Risk-Free Rate		Volatility		Dividend Yield		Suboptimal Behavior	
Year	Rate	Year	Rate	Year	Rate	Year	Multiple
1	3.50%	1	35.00%	1	1.00%	1	1.80
2	3.75%	2	35.00%	2	1.00%	2	1.80
3	4.00%	3	35.00%	3	1.00%	3	1.80
4	4.15%	4	45.00%	4	1.50%	4	1.80
5	4.20%	5	45.00%	5	1.50%	5	1.80

		Forfeiture Rate		Blackout Dates	
Stock Price	$100				
Strike Price	$100	Year	Rate	Month	Step
Time to Maturity	5	1	5.00%	12	12
Vesting Period	1	2	5.00%	24	24
Lattice Steps	60	3	5.00%	36	36
		4	5.00%	48	48
Option Value	**$31.42**	5	5.00%	60	60

volatility in the past three years. Here we assume that the risk in the firm's stock is autocorrelated.[8] Other examples may include a negative correlation between stock prices and forfeiture rates, and so forth.

Rather than randomly deciding on the correct number of trials to run in the simulation, statistical significance and precision control are set up to run the required number of trials automatically. Figure 5.5 shows that a 99.9 percent statistical confidence on a $0.01 error precision control is se-

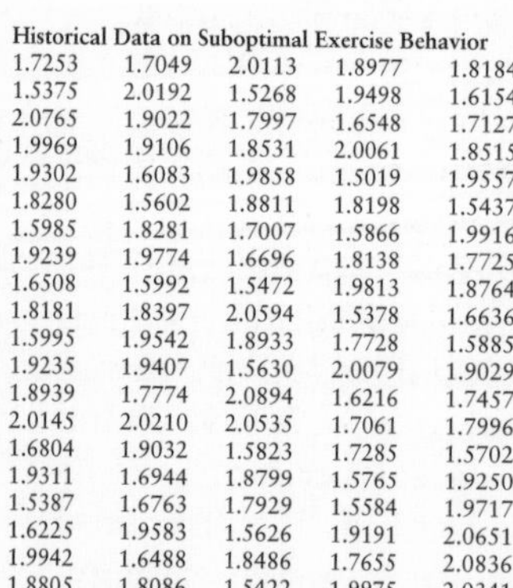

Historical Data on Suboptimal Exercise Behavior

1.7253	1.7049	2.0113	1.8977	1.8184
1.5375	2.0192	1.5268	1.9498	1.6154
2.0765	1.9022	1.7997	1.6548	1.7127
1.9969	1.9106	1.8531	2.0061	1.8515
1.9302	1.6083	1.9858	1.5019	1.9557
1.8280	1.5602	1.8811	1.8198	1.5437
1.5985	1.8281	1.7007	1.5866	1.9916
1.9239	1.9774	1.6696	1.8138	1.7725
1.6508	1.5992	1.5472	1.9813	1.8764
1.8181	1.8397	2.0594	1.5378	1.6636
1.5995	1.9542	1.8933	1.7728	1.5885
1.9235	1.9407	1.5630	2.0079	1.9029
1.8939	1.7774	2.0894	1.6216	1.7457
2.0145	2.0210	2.0535	1.7061	1.7996
1.6804	1.9032	1.5823	1.7285	1.5702
1.9311	1.6944	1.8799	1.5765	1.9250
1.5387	1.6763	1.7929	1.5584	1.9717
1.6225	1.9583	1.5626	1.9191	2.0651
1.9942	1.6488	1.8486	1.7655	2.0836
1.8805	1.8086	1.5422	1.9975	2.0341

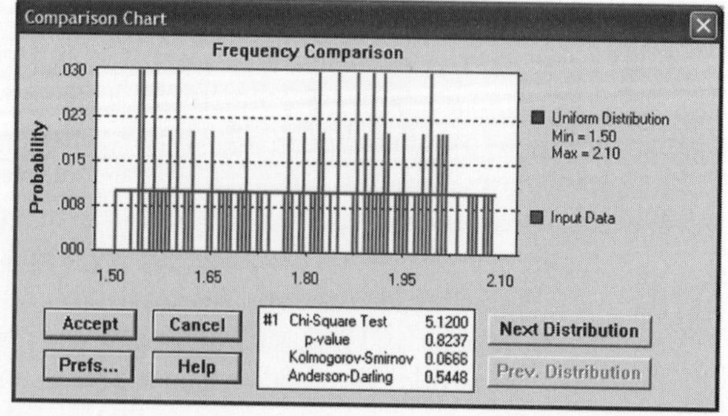

FIGURE 5.2 Distributional-fitting using historical, comparable, or forecast data.

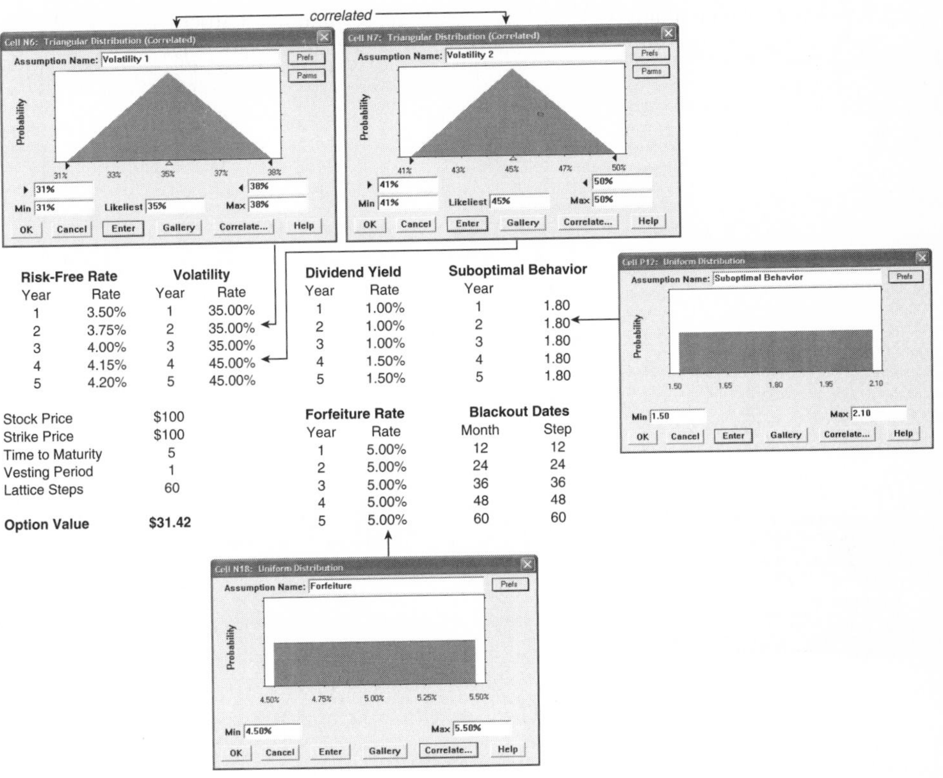

FIGURE 5.3 Monte Carlo input assumptions.

lected.[9] This highly stringent set of parameters means that an adequate number of trials will be run to ensure that the results will fall within a $0.01 error variability 99.9 percent of the time. Of course the precision assumes that the input parameters are correct and accurate. For instance, the simulated average result was $31.32 (Figure 5.7). This means that 999 out of 1,000 times, the true option value will be accurate to within $0.01 of $31.32. These measures are statistically valid and objective.

Figure 5.6 shows the complete options valuation distribution and that the 5 percent probability in the main body is between $31.32 and $31.54. Figure 5.7 shows the results after performing 145,510 simulation trials where the resulting average binomial lattice value of $31.32 is precise to within $0.01 at a 99.9 percent statistical confidence. Armed with this result, firms should be confident with the analysis that it is statistically valid and robust after running these many thousands of trials or scenarios.

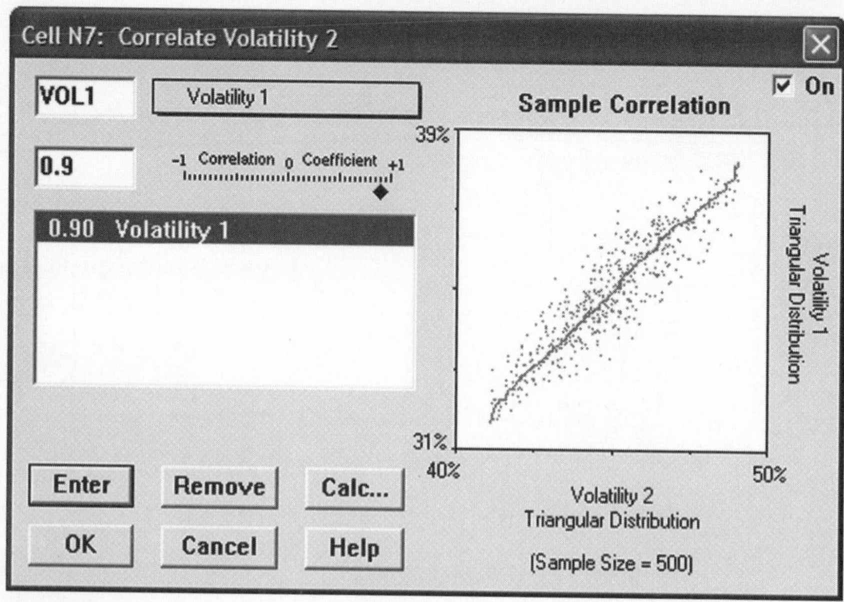

FIGURE 5.4 Correlating input assumptions.

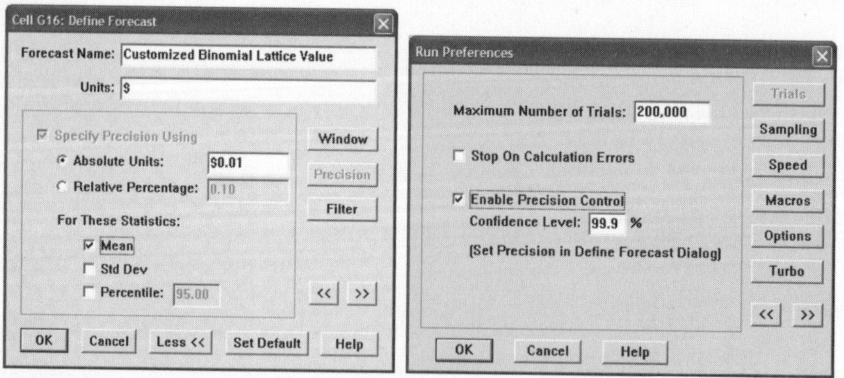

FIGURE 5.5 Statistical confidence restrictions and precision control.

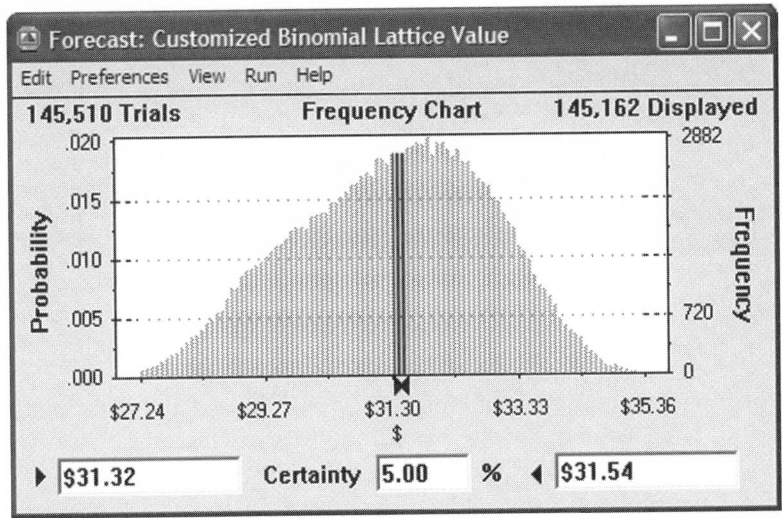

FIGURE 5.6 Probability distribution of options valuation results.

Forecast: Customized Binomial Lattice Value

Edit Preferences View Run Help

Cell G16 **Statistics**

Statistic	Value	Precision
Trials	145,510	
Mean	$31.32	$0.01
Median	$31.43	$0.02
Mode	---	
Standard Deviation	$1.57	$0.01
Variance	$2.46	
Skewness	-0.21	
Kurtosis	2.43	
Coeff. of Variability	0.05	
Range Minimum	$26.59	
Range Maximum	$35.62	
Range Width	$9.03	
Mean Std. Error	$0.00	

*Statistics highlighted are tested for $0.01 precision at 99.90% confidence

FIGURE 5.7 Options valuation result at $0.01 precision with 99.9 percent confidence.

Without the use of simulation, these precision levels cannot be ascertained directly from the binomial lattices.

Note that although a binomial lattice is by itself a discrete simulation (volatility captures the uncertainty of the stock price evolution over time, as seen in Chapter 8), simulating the inputs that go into the lattice is theoretically sound and does not constitute double counting. For example, volatility accounts for the stock's risk whereas simulation accounts for the uncertainties of the levels of the input variables. That is, Monte Carlo simulation captures the uncertainty of certain input variables in a lattice and does not affect in any way how the lattice calculation works. In essence, it is similar to creating multiple lattices under different input scenarios and capturing their results statistically. Therefore, instead of trying to ascertain the exact input values, ranges of input values can be used and the simulation methodology will statistically account for all combinations of scenarios to calculate the best possible estimate of the fair-market value of the ESOs.

SUMMARY AND KEY POINTS

- Monte Carlo simulation can be applied to value an option as well as to simulate the uncertain inputs in an options model.
- Monte Carlo simulation can be used only to value European options, and hence has limited use in options valuation.
- However, when coupled with the customized binomial lattices, Monte Carlo can simulate and correlate uncertain variables (e.g., forfeitures, suboptimal exercise behavior multiples, and volatility) that enter the binomial model.
- Monte Carlo simulation can also be conditioned to produce results within a specified error under certain statistical confidence levels, such as a precision control of $0.01 error around the results with a 99.9 percent statistical confidence.

CHAPTER 6

Expense Attribution Schedule

ESO EXPENSE ATTRIBUTION SCHEDULE AS MINIGRANTS

The ESOs valued will have to be attributed over the life of the option. This expense attribution can employ a straight-line method that is simple and takes the value of the ESO and evenly allocates its value starting from the vested period and extending to the option's maturity. The alternative approach is to treat each grant as a separate award, effectively creating multiple minigrants over time. It is still unclear at the time of writing which method will be chosen, but the exposure draft seems to prefer the minigrant approach. This chapter focuses on the more complex minigrant approach.

The 2004 proposed FAS 123 revisions require that each ESO grant be treated as separate awards for the purposes of expensing the ESO over its vesting life.

> *The 1995 FAS 123 provided alternative methods of measuring and recognizing compensation cost for awards with graded vesting—that is, awards for which different parts vest at different times. The revised 2004 FAS 123 requires a single method under which those different parts are treated as separate awards in estimating fair value and attributing compensation cost.*

To illustrate the separate awards or minigrant expense allocation, Table 6.1 shows the total ESO valuation results.[1] The total valuation for the firm's ESO using the customized binomial lattice is \$813.99 million, compared to \$914.34 million using the naïve BSM or \$863.96 million using the modified BSM. Clearly there is over a \$49.96 million reduction in expenses when using the customized binomial lattice approach.

Using the customized binomial lattice result of \$813.99 million, the option grants have to be first allocated per FAS 123 before the actual expenses

TABLE 6.1 Example Valuation Summary

	Per Share Closing Stock Price				48 Months Vest		6 Month Cliff and then 42 Month Vest	
Date	Conservative	Aggressive	Average		New Hire Grant	Acquisition	Focal	Total
End Dec 04/Start Jan 05	$45.17	$50.70	$47.93	**Jan-05**	550,000			550,000
End Jan 05/Start Feb 05	$45.89	$51.52	$48.70	February	550,000			550,000
End Feb/Start Mar	$46.61	$52.34	$49.48	March	550,000			550,000
End Mar/Start Apr	$47.34	$53.16	$50.25	April	550,000			550,000
End Apr/Start May	$48.06	$53.98	$51.02	May	550,000			550,000
End May/Start Jun	$48.78	$54.81	$51.79	June	605,000			605,000
End Jun/Start July	$49.51	$55.63	$52.57	July	605,000			605,000
End July/Start Aug	$50.23	$56.45	$53.34	August	605,000			605,000
End Aug/Start Sep	$50.95	$57.27	$54.11	September	605,000	2,500,000		3,105,000
End Sep/Start Oct	$51.68	$58.09	$54.89	October	605,000			605,000
End Oct/Start Nov	$52.40	$58.92	$55.66	November	605,000		7,492,100	8,097,100
End Nov/Start Dec	$53.13	$59.74	$56.43	December	605,000			605,000
End Dec/Start Jan 06	$53.85	$60.56	$57.20	**Jan-06**	605,000			605,000
End Jan 06/Start Feb 06	$54.55	$61.36	$57.95	February	605,000			605,000
End February/Start March	$55.25	$62.15	$58.70	March	605,000			605,000
End March/Start Apr	$55.95	$62.95	$59.45	April	605,000			605,000
End Apr/Start May	$56.66	$63.75	$60.20	May	605,000			605,000
End May/Start Jun	$57.36	$64.55	$60.95	June	665,500			665,500
End Jun/Start July	$58.06	$65.34	$61.70	July	665,500			665,500
End July/Start Aug	$58.76	$66.14	$62.45	August	665,500			665,500
End Aug/Start Sep	$59.46	$66.94	$63.20	September	665,500	3,000,000		3,665,500
End Sep/Start Oct	$60.16	$67.74	$63.95	October	665,500			665,500
End Oct/Start Nov	$60.87	$68.53	$64.70	November	665,500		8,241,310	8,906,810
End Nov/Start Dec	$61.57	$69.33	$65.45	December	665,500			665,500

TABLE 6.1 *(Continued)*

	Options Valuation (Monthly)				Options Valuation (Cliff Vesting)		
Date	Conservative	Aggressive	Average	Date	Conservative	Aggressive	Average
Jan-05	$17.39	$19.52	$18.46	**Jan-05**	$17.42	$19.55	$18.49
February	$17.67	$19.84	$18.76	February	$17.70	$19.87	$18.78
March	$17.95	$20.16	$19.05	March	$17.98	$20.19	$19.08
April	$18.23	$20.47	$19.35	April	$18.26	$20.50	$19.38
May	$18.51	$20.79	$19.65	May	$18.54	$20.82	$19.68
June	$18.79	$21.11	$19.95	June	$18.81	$21.14	$19.88
July	$19.06	$21.42	$20.24	July	$19.09	$21.45	$20.27
August	$19.34	$21.74	$20.54	August	$19.37	$21.77	$20.57
September	$19.62	$22.05	$20.84	September	$19.65	$22.09	$22.87
October	$19.90	$22.37	$21.14	October	$19.93	$22.41	$21.17
November	$20.18	$22.69	$21.43	November	$20.21	$22.72	$21.47
December	$20.46	$23.00	$21.73	December	$20.49	$23.04	$21.46
Jan-06	$20.74	$23.32	$22.03	**Jan-06**	$20.77	$23.36	$22.06
February	$21.01	$23.63	$22.32	February	$21.04	$23.66	$22.35
March	$21.28	$23.94	$22.61	March	$21.31	$23.97	$22.64
April	$21.55	$24.24	$22.89	April	$21.58	$24.28	$22.93
May	$21.82	$24.55	$23.18	May	$21.85	$24.59	$23.22
June	$22.09	$24.86	$23.47	June	$22.12	$24.89	$23.51
July	$22.36	$25.16	$23.76	July	$22.39	$25.20	$23.80
August	$22.63	$25.47	$24.05	August	$22.66	$25.51	$24.09
September	$22.90	$25.78	$24.34	September	$22.93	$25.82	$24.38
October	$23.17	$26.09	$24.63	October	$23.20	$26.12	$24.66
November	$23.44	$26.39	$24.92	November	$23.47	$26.43	$24.95
December	$23.71	$26.70	$25.20	December	$23.75	$26.74	$25.24

TABLE 6.1 *(Continued)*

	Total Options Expense (Binomial): $813,997,675.53				Options Valuation (Black-Scholes)		
Date	Conservative	Aggressive	Average	Date	Conservative	Aggressive	Average
Jan-05	$ 9,566,052.74	$ 10,737,306.72	$ 10,151,679.73	**Jan-05**	$19.55	$21.94	$20.75
February	$ 9,719,311.21	$ 10,911,406.31	$ 10,315,358.76	February	$19.86	$22.30	$21.08
March	$ 9,872,590.87	$ 11,085,484.73	$ 10,479,037.80	March	$20.18	$22.66	$21.42
April	$ 10,025,849.35	$ 11,259,584.33	$ 10.642,716.84	April	$20.49	$23.01	$21.75
May	$ 10,179,107.83	$ 11,433,662.74	$ 10,806,395.88	May	$20.80	$23.37	$22.09
June	$ 11,365,602.93	$ 12,768,538.58	$ 12,067,082.40	June	$21.12	$23.72	$22.42
July	$ 11,534,210.56	$ 12,960,024.83	$ 12,247,106.05	July	$21.43	$24.08	$22.75
August	$ 11,702,794.88	$ 13,151,534.39	$ 12,427,152.99	August	$21.74	$24.43	$23.09
September	$ 60,926,665.19	$ 68,479,589.19	$ 64,703,067.40	September	$22.06	$24.79	$23.42
October	$ 12,039,963.53	$ 13,534,530.21	$ 12,787,246.87	October	$22.37	$25.15	$23.76
November	$163,625,443.32	$183,963,675.91	$173,794,559.61	November	$22.68	$25.50	$24.09
December	$ 12,377,155.48	$ 13,917,526.02	$ 13,147,340.75	December	$23.00	$25.86	$24.43
Jan-06	$ 12,545,739.81	$ 14,109,035.88	$ 13,327,387.69	**Jan-06**	$23.31	$26.21	$24.76
February	$ 12,709,221.87	$ 14,294,860.42	$ 13,502,052.80	February	$23.61	$26.56	$25.09
March	$ 12,872,727.23	$ 14,480,685.27	$ 13,676,694.60	March	$23.92	$26.90	$25.41
April	$ 13,036,232.59	$ 14,666,510.11	$ 13,851,359.70	April	$24.22	$27.25	$25.73
May	$ 13,199,714.65	$ 14,852,311.66	$ 14,026,024.81	May	$24.52	$27.59	$26.06
June	$ 14,699,542.02	$ 16,541,950.16	$ 15,620,733.27	June	$24.83	$27.94	$26.38
July	$ 14,879,372.29	$ 16,746,357.48	$ 15,812,865.89	July	$25.13	$28.28	$26.71
August	$ 15,059,202.56	$ 16,950,764.81	$ 16,004,996.50	August	$25.44	$28.63	$27.03
September	$ 83,935,039.46	$ 94,488,780.60	$ 89,211,839.45	September	$25.74	$28.98	$27.36
October	$ 15,418,914.35	$ 17,359,579.47	$ 16,389,234.10	October	$26.04	$29.32	$27.68
November	$209,062,661.14	$235,401,537.28	$222,232,270.95	November	$26.35	$29.67	$28.01
December	$ 15,778,600.52	$ 17,768,368.50	$ 16,773,471.70	December	$26.65	$30.01	$28.33
			$813,997,675.53				

TABLE 6.1 *(Continued)*

	Total Options Expense (Black-Scholes): $914,341,297.69			Main Input Assumptions & Results		
Date	**Conservative**	**Aggressive**	**Average**	**Year**	**Risk-Free Rate**	
Jan-05	$ 10,752,660.26	$ 12,069,200.79	$ 11,410,930.53	1	1.21%	
February	$ 10,924,929.47	$ 12,264,896.33	$ 11,594,912.90	2	2.19%	
March	$ 11,097,222.49	$ 12,460,568.06	$ 11,778,895.27	3	3.21%	
April	$ 11,269,491.70	$ 12,656,263.59	$ 11,962,877.65	4	3.85%	
May	$ 11,441,760.91	$ 12,851,935.32	$ 12,146,860.02	5	4.68%	
June	$ 12,775,433.13	$ 14,352,393.94	$ 13,563,926.63	6	4.59%	
July	$ 12,964,955.45	$ 14,567,632.85	$ 13,766,281.05	7	5.11%	
August	$ 13,154,451.58	$ 14,782,897.94	$ 13,968,661.66	8	4.91%	
September	$ 68,484,227.49	$ 76,974,043.30	$ 72,729,068.19	9	5.25%	
October	$ 13,533,443.84	$ 15,213,401.93	$ 14,373,422.88	10	5.59%	
November	$183,662,838.36	$206,491,668.93	$195,077,253.65			
December	$ 13,912,462.28	$ 15,643,905.92	$ 14,778,184.10	Time to Maturity		10
Jan-06	$ 14,101,958.41	$ 15,859,171.01	$ 14,980,564.71	Dividend		0.00%
February	$ 14,285,719.38	$ 16,068,046.23	$ 15,176,895.90	Volatility		49.91%
March	$ 14,469,506.53	$ 16,276,921.46	$ 15,373,200.90	Suboptimal Behavior		1.8531
April	$ 14,653,293.69	$ 16,485,796.69	$ 15,569,532.09	Forfeiture Rate		5.51%
May	$ 14,837,054.65	$ 16,694,645.72	$ 15,765.863.28	Vesting		1 month and 6 months
June	$ 16,522,925.99	$ 18,593,873.04	$ 17,558,385.11	Steps		4,200
July	$ 16,725,063.05	$ 18,823,635.79	$ 17,774,349.43	Total Black-Scholes		$914,341,298
August	$ 16,927,200.11	$ 19,053,398.54	$ 17,990,313.73	Total Binomial		$813,997,676
September	$ 94,346,643.11	$106,209,508.20	$100,277,996.32	Adjusted Black-Scholes		$863,961,092
October	$ 17,331,531.85	$ 19,512,924.04	$ 18,422,213.54	Difference		($49,963,417)
November	$234,664,248.79	$264,228,555.25	$249,446,594.79			
December	$ 17,735,834.78	$ 19,972,420.73	$ 18,854,113.35			
			$914,341,297.69			

TABLE 6.2 Grant Allocation (Monthly Graded Vesting Expense Allocations. Month of Grant: January; Size of Grant: 550,000 Options)

Jan	Feb	Mar	Apr	May	Jun	Jul	Aug	Sept	Oct	Nov	Dec	Jan	Feb	Mar	Apr	May	Jun	Jul	Aug	Sept	Oct	Nov	Dec
11,458																							
5,729	5,729																						
3,819	3,819	3,819																					
2,865	2,865	2,865	2,865																				
2,292	2,292	2,292	2,292	2,292																			
1,910	1,910	1,910	1,910	1,910	1,910																		
1,637	1,637	1,637	1,637	1,637	1,637	1,637																	
1,432	1,432	1,432	1,432	1,432	1,432	1,432	1,432																
1,273	1,273	1,273	1,273	1,273	1,273	1,273	1,273	1,273															
1,146	1,146	1,146	1,146	1,146	1,146	1,146	1,146	1,146	1,146														
1,042	1,042	1,042	1,042	1,042	1,042	1,042	1,042	1,042	1,042	1,042													
955	955	955	955	955	955	955	955	955	955	955	955												
881	881	881	881	881	881	881	881	881	881	881	881	881											
818	818	818	818	818	818	818	818	818	818	818	818	818	818										
764	764	764	764	764	764	764	764	764	764	764	764	764	764	764									
716	716	716	716	716	716	716	716	716	716	716	716	716	716	716	716								
674	674	674	674	674	674	674	674	674	674	674	674	674	674	674	674	674							
637	637	637	637	637	637	637	637	637	637	637	637	637	637	637	637	637	637						
603	603	603	603	603	603	603	603	603	603	603	603	603	603	603	603	603	603	603					
573	573	573	573	573	573	573	573	573	573	573	573	573	573	573	573	573	573	573	573				
546	546	546	546	546	546	546	546	546	546	546	546	546	546	546	546	546	546	546	546	546			
521	521	521	521	521	521	521	521	521	521	521	521	521	521	521	521	521	521	521	521	521	521		
498	498	498	498	498	498	498	498	498	498	498	498	498	498	498	498	498	498	498	498	498	498	498	
477	477	477	477	477	477	477	477	477	477	477	477	477	477	477	477	477	477	477	477	477	477	477	477
458	458	458	458	458	458	458	458	458	458	458	458	458	458	458	458	458	458	458	458	458	458	458	458
441	441	441	441	441	441	441	441	441	441	441	441	441	441	441	441	441	441	441	441	441	441	441	441
424	424	424	424	424	424	424	424	424	424	424	424	424	424	424	424	424	424	424	424	424	424	424	424
409	409	409	409	409	409	409	409	409	409	409	409	409	409	409	409	409	409	409	409	409	409	409	409
395	395	395	395	395	395	395	395	395	395	395	395	395	395	395	395	395	395	395	395	395	395	395	395
382	382	382	382	382	382	382	382	382	382	382	382	382	382	382	382	382	382	382	382	382	382	382	382
370	370	370	370	370	370	370	370	370	370	370	370	370	370	370	370	370	370	370	370	370	370	370	370
358	358	358	358	358	358	358	358	358	358	358	358	358	358	358	358	358	358	358	358	358	358	358	358
347	347	347	347	347	347	347	347	347	347	347	347	347	347	347	347	347	347	347	347	347	347	347	347
337	337	337	337	337	337	337	337	337	337	337	337	337	337	337	337	337	337	337	337	337	337	337	337
327	327	327	327	327	327	327	327	327	327	327	327	327	327	327	327	327	327	327	327	327	327	327	327
318	318	318	318	318	318	318	318	318	318	318	318	318	318	318	318	318	318	318	318	318	318	318	318
310	310	310	310	310	310	310	310	310	310	310	310	310	310	310	310	310	310	310	310	310	310	310	310
302	302	302	302	302	302	302	302	302	302	302	302	302	302	302	302	302	302	302	302	302	302	302	302
294	294	294	294	294	294	294	294	294	294	294	294	294	294	294	294	294	294	294	294	294	294	294	294
286	286	286	286	286	286	286	286	286	286	286	286	286	286	286	286	286	286	286	286	286	286	286	286
279	279	279	279	279	279	279	279	279	279	279	279	279	279	279	279	279	279	279	279	279	279	279	279
273	273	273	273	273	273	273	273	273	273	273	273	273	273	273	273	273	273	273	273	273	273	273	273
266	266	266	266	266	266	266	266	266	266	266	266	266	266	266	266	266	266	266	266	266	266	266	266
260	260	260	260	260	260	260	260	260	260	260	260	260	260	260	260	260	260	260	260	260	260	260	260
255	255	255	255	255	255	255	255	255	255	255	255	255	255	255	255	255	255	255	255	255	255	255	255
249	249	249	249	249	249	249	249	249	249	249	249	249	249	249	249	249	249	249	249	249	249	249	249
244	244	244	244	244	244	244	244	244	244	244	244	244	244	244	244	244	244	244	244	244	244	244	244
239	239	239	239	239	239	239	239	239	239	239	239	239	239	239	239	239	239	239	239	239	239	239	239
51,090	39,632	33,903	30,083	27,219	24,927	23,017	21,381	19,948	18,675	17,529	16,488	15,533	14,551	13,833	13,069	12,353	11,679	11,042	10,439	9,866	9,321	8,800	8,302

TABLE 6.2 *(Continued)*

Monthly Graded Vesting Expense Allocations																								
Month of Grant: January												Size of Grant: 550,000 options												
Jan	Feb	Mar	Apr	May	Jun	Jul	Aug	Sept	Oct	Nov	Dec	Jan	Feb	Mar	Apr	May	Jun	Jul	Aug	Sept	Oct	Nov	Dec	Total
458																								
441	441																							
424	424	424																						
409	409	409	409																					
395	395	395	395	395																				
382	382	382	382	382	382																			
370	370	370	370	370	370	370																		
358	358	358	358	358	358	358	358																	
347	347	347	347	347	347	347	347	347																
337	337	337	337	337	337	337	337	337	337															
327	327	327	327	327	327	327	327	327	327	327														
318	318	318	318	318	318	318	318	318	318	318	318													
310	310	310	310	310	310	310	310	310	310	310	310	310												
302	302	302	302	302	302	302	302	302	302	302	302	302	302											
294	294	294	294	294	294	294	294	294	294	294	294	294	294	294										
286	286	286	286	286	286	286	286	286	286	286	286	286	286	286	286									
279	279	279	279	279	279	279	279	279	279	279	279	279	279	279	279	279								
273	273	273	273	273	273	273	273	273	273	273	273	273	273	273	273	273	273							
266	266	266	266	266	266	266	266	266	266	266	266	266	266	266	266	266	266	266						
260	260	260	260	260	260	260	260	260	260	260	260	260	260	260	260	260	260	260	260					
255	255	255	255	255	255	255	255	255	255	255	255	255	255	255	255	255	255	255	255	255				
249	249	249	249	249	249	249	249	249	249	249	249	249	249	249	249	249	249	249	249	249	249			
244	244	244	244	244	244	244	244	244	244	244	244	244	244	244	244	244	244	244	244	244	244			
239	239	239	239	239	239	239	239	239	239	239	239	239	239	239	239	239	239	239	239	239	239	239		
7,824	7,366	6,925	6,501	6,092	5,696	5,314	4,945	4,587	4,240	3,903	3,575	3,257	2,947	2,648	2,352	2,065	1,786	1,513	1,247	986	732	483	239	550,000

TABLE 6.3 Monthly Graded-Vesting Grants Allocation

Month	Grants	January 2005	February	March	April	May	June	July	August
January 2005	550,000	51,090.38	39,632.05	33,902.88	30,083.44	27,218.86	24,927.19	23,017.47	21,380.56
February	550,000		51,090.38	39,632.05	33,902.88	30,083.44	27,218.86	24,927.19	23,017.47
March	550,000			51,090.38	39,632.05	33,902.88	30,083.44	27,218.86	24,927.19
April	550,000				51,090.38	39,632.05	33,902.88	30,083.44	27218.86
May	550,000					51,090.38	39,632.05	33,902.88	30,083.44
June	605,000						56,199.42	43,595.26	37,293.17
July	605,000							56,199.42	43,595.26
August	605,000								56,199.42

TABLE 6.4 Final Expense Allocation

Expense Allocation Summary							
Total Valuation (Customized Binomial Lattice)					$813,997,675.53		
Expense Allocation	**2005**	**2006**	**2007**	**2008**	**2009**	**2010**	**Total**
Custom Binomial	$92,197,733	$271,222,335	$267,662,000	$125,765,601	$48,567,875	$8,582,132	$813,997.676

can be quantified. This is done through dividing the actual 48-month graded vesting grant into 48 minigrants per month. This is done in Table 6.2, where the single grant in January of 550,000 issues is divided into a 48 × 48 matrix. The total allocation to January is 51,090 issues, and so forth. The total grants for the 48 months equal the original 550,000 issues. This is simply a single grant in January.

Table 6.3 shows multiple grants on a monthly basis starting from January.[2] Using these allocations, the option valuation result is multiplied by the number of grants on a per-month vesting basis to yield the results shown in Table 6.4. Notice that over the next 6 years, the allocation is complete and the total expense is $813.99 million, identical to the total valuation result shown in Table 6.1.

SUMMARY AND KEY POINTS

- The 2004 proposed FAS 123 revisions require that each ESO grant be treated as separate awards for the purposes of expensing the ESO over its vesting life.
- The total expenses allocated over the vesting period should always be identical to the total valuation results.

PART Two

Technical Background of the Binomial Lattice and Black-Scholes Models

CHAPTER 7

Brief Technical Background

BLACK-SCHOLES MODEL

The basic BSM is summarized as follows:

$$Call = S\Phi\left[\frac{\ln(S/X)+(rf+\sigma^2/2)T}{\sigma\sqrt{T}}\right] - Xe^{-rf(T)}\Phi\left[\frac{\ln(S/X)+(rf-\sigma^2/2)T}{\sigma\sqrt{T}}\right]$$

$$Put = Xe^{-rf(T)}\Phi\left[-\frac{\ln(S/X)+(rf-\sigma^2/2)T}{\sigma\sqrt{T}}\right] - S\Phi\left[-\frac{\ln(S/X)+(rf+\sigma^2/2)T}{\sigma\sqrt{T}}\right]$$

where Φ is the cumulative standard-normal distribution function
S is the value of the forecast stock price at grant date
X is the option's contractual strike price
rf is the nominal risk-free rate
σ is the annualized volatility
T is the time to expiration of the option

To illustrate its use, let us assume that an option exists such that both the stock price (S) and the strike price (X) are \$100, the time to expiration (T) is one year with a 5 percent annualized risk-free rate (rf) for the same duration, while the annualized volatility (σ) of the underlying asset is 25 percent. The BSM calculation yields \$12.3360:

$$Call = S\Phi\left[\frac{\ln(S/X)+(rf+\sigma^2/2)T}{\sigma\sqrt{T}}\right] - Xe^{-rf(T)}\Phi\left[\frac{\ln(S/X)+(rf-\sigma^2/2)T}{\sigma\sqrt{T}}\right]$$

$$Call = \$100\Phi\left[\frac{\ln\left(\frac{\$100}{\$100}\right)+\left(0.05+\frac{1}{2}0.25^2\right)(1)}{0.25\sqrt{1}}\right] - \$100e^{-0.05(1)}\Phi\left[\frac{\ln\left(\frac{\$100}{\$100}\right)+\left(0.05-\frac{1}{2}0.25^2\right)(1)}{0.25\sqrt{1}}\right]$$

$$Call = \$100\Phi(0.3250) - \$100(0.9512)\Phi(0.0750) = \$100(0.6274) - \$95.12(0.5299) = \$12.3360$$

The cumulative standard-normal distribution function can be solved in Excel by using its "NORMSDIST( )" function.

In addition, you can create calculation codes within Excel's Visual Basic for Applications (VBA) environment. Following are the VBA codes for the BSM for estimating call and put options. The equations for the BSM are simplified to functions in Excel named "BlackScholesCall" and "BlackScholesPut."

```
Public Function BlackScholesCall(Stock As Double, Strike As Double,
    Time As Double, Riskfree _
As Double, Volatility As Double) As Double
Dim D1 As Double, D2 As Double
D1 = (Log(Stock / Strike) + (Riskfree + 0.5 * Volatility ^ 2 ) * Time) /
    (Volatility * Sqr(Time))
D2 = D1 – Volatility * Sqr(Time)
BlackScholesCall = Stock * Application.NormSDist(D1) – Strike *
    Exp(–Time * Riskfree) * _
  Application.NormSDist(D2)
End Function
Public Function BlackScholesPut(Stock As Double, Strike As Double,
    Time As Double, Riskfree _
As Double, Volatility As Double) As Double
Dim D1 As Double, D2 As Double
D1 = (Log(Stock / Strike) + (Riskfree + 0.5 * Volatility ^ 2 ) * Time) /
    (Volatility * Sqr(Time))
D2 = D1 – Volatility * Sqr(Time)
BlackScholesPut = Strike * Exp(–Time * Riskfree) *
    Application.NormSDist(–D2) – Stock * _
  Application.NormSDist(–D1)
End Function
```

As an example, entering the function in Excel:

"=BlackScholesCall(100,100,1,5%,25%)"

results in 12.3360 and entering the function in Excel:

"=BlackScholesPut(100,100,1,5%,25%)"

results in 7.4589.

Note that *Log* is a natural logarithm function in VBA and *Sqr* is square root, and make sure there is a space before the underscore in the code.

MONTE CARLO SIMULATION MODEL

In the simulation approach for estimating European options, a series of forecast stock prices are created using the Geometric Brownian Motion stochastic process, and the options maximization calculation is applied to the end point of the series, and discounted back to time zero, at the risk-free rate. That is, starting with an initial seed value of the underlying stock price, simulate out multiple future pathways using a Geometric Brownian Motion, where $\delta S_t = S_{t-1}\left(rf(\delta t) + \sigma\varepsilon\sqrt{\delta t}\right)$. That is, the change in asset value δS_t at time t is the value of the asset in the previous period S_{t-1} multiplied by the Brownian Motion $\left(rf(\delta t) + \sigma\varepsilon\sqrt{\delta t}\right)$. The term rf is the risk-free rate, δt is the time-steps, σ is the volatility, and ε is the simulated value from a standard-normal distribution with mean of zero and a variance of one. Other variations of Brownian Motions exist but for illustration purposes, this simple version will be used.

The first step in Monte Carlo simulation is to decide on the number of time-steps to simulate. In the example, 10 steps were chosen for simplicity. Starting with the initial stock price of \$100 (S_0), the change in value from this initial value to the first period is seen as $\delta S_1 = S_0\left(rf(\delta t) + \sigma\varepsilon\sqrt{\delta t}\right)$. Hence, the stock price at the first time-step is equivalent to $S_1 = S_0 + \delta S_1 = S_0 + S_0\left(rf(\delta t) + \sigma\varepsilon\sqrt{\delta t}\right)$. The stock price at the second time-step is hence $S_2 = S_1 + \delta S_2 = S_1 + S_1\left(rf(\delta t) + \sigma\varepsilon\sqrt{\delta t}\right)$, and so forth, all the way until the terminal tenth time-step. Notice that because ε changes on each simulation trial, each simulation trial will produce an entirely different asset-evolution pathway. At the end of the tenth time-step, the maximization process is then applied. That is, for a simple European option with a \$100 implementation cost, the function is simply $C_{10,i} = Max[S_{10,i} - X, 0]$. This is the call value $C_{10,i}$ at time 10 for the ith simulation trial. This value is then discounted at the risk-free rate to obtain the call value at time zero, that is, $C_{0,i} = C_{10,i}e^{-rf(T)}$. This is a single-point estimate for a single simulated pathway. A forecast distribution of the thousands of simulated pathways is collected and the mean of the distribution is the expected value of the option. On the one hand, it must be stressed that Monte Carlo simulation can be applied only to calculate European options, and not American options, making it less suitable for use in valuing ESOs. On the other hand, Monte Carlo can be used to simulate the uncertain input variables that go into the customized binomial lattice model as seen in Chapter 5.

BINOMIAL LATTICES

Binomial lattices, in contrast to the other methods, are easy to implement and easy to explain. They are also highly flexible but require significant computing power and time-steps to obtain good approximations, as will be seen later. It is important to note, however, that at the limit, results obtained through the use of binomial lattices tend to approach those derived from closed-form solutions, and hence, it is always recommended that both approaches be used to benchmark the results. The results from closed-form solutions may be used in conjunction with the binomial lattice approach when presenting a complete financial options valuation solution in the most basic European options analysis. However, when real-life cases are added into the analysis (forfeitures, vesting, suboptimal exercise behavior multiples, and blackout dates), the results diverge because the closed-form models such as the BSM or GBM cannot account for these added variables.

Following is an example to illustrate the point of binomial lattices approaching the results of a closed-form model. Let us look again at the European call option presented previously, but this time, calculated using the GBM:

$$Call = Se^{-qT}\Phi\left[\frac{\ln(S/X)+(rf-q+\sigma^2/2)T}{\sigma\sqrt{T}}\right] - Xe^{-rT}\Phi\left[\frac{\ln(S/X)+(rf-q-\sigma^2/2)T}{\sigma\sqrt{T}}\right]$$

Using the previous example where both the stock price (S) and the strike price (X) are \$100, the time to expiration (T) is one year with a 5 percent risk-free rate (*rf*) for the same duration, while the volatility (σ) of the underlying asset is 25 percent with no dividends (*q*). The GBM calculation yields $12.3360, similar to the BSM calculations, while using a binomial lattice we obtain the following results:

N = 10 steps	$12.0923
N = 20 steps	$12.2132
N = 50 steps	$12.2867
N = 100 steps	$12.3113
N = 1,000 steps	$12.3335
N = 10,000 steps	$12.3358
N = 50,000 steps	$12.3360

Notice that even in this simplified example, as the number of time-steps (*N*) gets larger, the value calculated using the binomial lattice approaches the GBM closed-form solution. Suffice it to say, many steps are required for a good estimate using binomial lattices. It has been shown in past research that 1,000 time-steps are usually sufficient for a good approximation for up to 2 decimals. Chapter 10 provides a case example of how to find the optimal number of lattice steps and to test for results convergence in a binomial lattice.

SUMMARY AND KEY POINTS

- The three mainstream approaches used to solve simple options are the GBM and BSM closed-form models, path-dependent simulation, and binomial lattices.
- BSM is highly inflexible and can be applied to solve only European options.
- Path-dependent simulations are also applicable for solving only European options.
- Binomial lattices are more flexible and can be used to solve both American and European options and are capable of handling other exotic input variables that exist in real-life ESOs.

CHAPTER 8

Binomial Lattices in Technical Detail

This chapter introduces the reader to some basics of options valuation and a step-by-step approach to analyzing them. The methods introduced include closed-form models, partial-differential equations, and binomial lattices through the use of risk-neutral probabilities. The advantages and disadvantages of each method are discussed. But the focus is on the use of binomial lattices. In addition, the theoretical underpinnings and black-box analytics surrounding the binomial equations are demystified here, leading the reader through a set of simplified discussions on how certain binomial models are solved, without the use of fancy mathematics.

OPTIONS VALUATION: BEHIND THE SCENES

In options analysis, there are multiple methodologies and approaches used to calculate an option's value. These range from using closed-form equations like the Black-Scholes model (BSM) or Generalized Black-Scholes model (GBM) and its modifications, Monte Carlo path-dependent simulation methods, lattices (e.g., binomial, trinomial, quadranomial, and multinomial trees), and variance reduction and other numerical techniques, to using partial-differential equations, and so forth. However, the mainstream methods that are most widely used are the closed-form solutions, partial-differential equations, and the binomial lattices.

Closed-form solutions are models like the BSM or GBM, where there exist equations that can be solved given a set of input assumptions. For instance, $A + B = C$ is a closed-form equation, where given any two of the three variables, you obtain a unique answer to the third variable. Closed-form solutions are exact, quick, and easy to implement with the assistance of some basic programming knowledge but are difficult to explain because they tend to apply highly technical stochastic calculus mathematics when it comes to options valuation. They are also very specific in nature, with very limited modeling flexibility.

Binomial lattices, in contrast, are easy to implement and easy to explain. They are also highly flexible but require significant computing power and time-steps to obtain good approximations, as we will see later in this chapter. It is important to note, however, that in the limit, and under certain assumptions, results obtained through the use of binomial lattices tend to approach those derived from closed-form solutions, and hence, it is always recommended that the BSM or GBM be used to benchmark the binomial lattice results, as we will also see later in this chapter. The results from closed-form solutions may be used in conjunction with the binomial lattice approach when presenting a complete ESO valuation solution. In this chapter we will explore these mainstream approaches and compare their results, as well as when each approach may be best used, when analyzing the more common types of options—starting with common plain-vanilla calls and puts.

Here is the same example seen in Chapter 7 used to illustrate the point of binomial lattices approaching the results of a closed-form solution. Let us look at a *European call option* as calculated using the GBM specified here:

$$Call = Se^{-qT}\Phi\left[\frac{\ln(S/X)+(rf-q+\sigma^2/2)T}{\sigma\sqrt{T}}\right] - Xe^{-rT}\Phi\left[\frac{\ln(S/X)+(rf-q-\sigma^2/2)T}{\sigma\sqrt{T}}\right]$$

Let us once again assume that both the stock price (S) and the strike price (X) are \$100, the time to expiration (T) is one year with a 5 percent risk-free rate (rf) for the same duration, while the volatility (σ) of the underlying asset is 25 percent with no dividends (q). The GBM calculation yields \$12.3360, while using a binomial lattice we obtain the following results:

$N = 10$ steps	\$12.0923
$N = 20$ steps	\$12.2132
$N = 50$ steps	\$12.2867
$N = 100$ steps	\$12.3113
$N = 1{,}000$ steps	\$12.3335
$N = 10{,}000$ steps	\$12.3358
$N = 50{,}000$ steps	\$12.3360

Notice that even in this simplified example, as the number of time-steps (N) gets larger, the value calculated using the binomial lattice approaches the closed-form GBM solution. Do not worry about the computation at this point as we will detail the stepwise calculations of the binomial lattice in a moment. Suffice it to say, many steps are required for a good estimate using binomial lattices. It has been shown in past research that 1,000 time-steps are usually sufficient for a good approximation.

We can define time-steps as the number of branching events in a lattice. For instance, the binomial lattice in Figure 8.1 has three time-steps, starting from time 0. The first time-step has two nodes (S_0u and S_0d), while the second time-step has three nodes (S_0u^2, S_0ud, and S_0d^2), and so on. Therefore, to obtain a 1,000-step lattice, we need to calculate 1, 2, 3 . . . 1,001 nodes, which is equivalent to calculating 501,501 nodes. If we intend to perform 10,000 simulation trials on the options calculation, we will need approximately 5×10^9 nodal calculations, equivalent to 299 Excel spreadsheets or 4.6 GB of memory space. This is definitely a daunting task, to say the least, and we clearly see here the need for using software to facilitate such calculations.[1] One noteworthy item is that the lattice in Figure 8.1 is called a *recombining lattice*, where at time-step 2, the middle node (S_0ud) is the same as time-step 1's lower bifurcation of S_0u and upper bifurcation of S_0d.

Figure 8.2 shows an example of a two time-step binomial lattice that is nonrecombining. That is, the center nodes in time-step 2 are different (S_0ud' is not the same as S_0du'). In this case, the computational time and resources are even higher due to the exponential growth of the number of

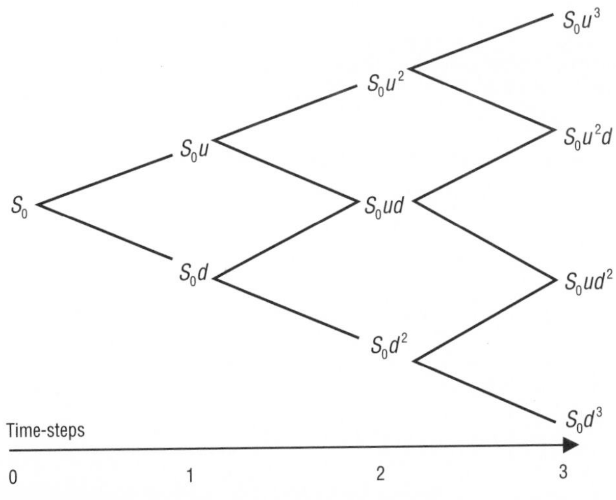

FIGURE 8.1 A three-step recombining lattice.

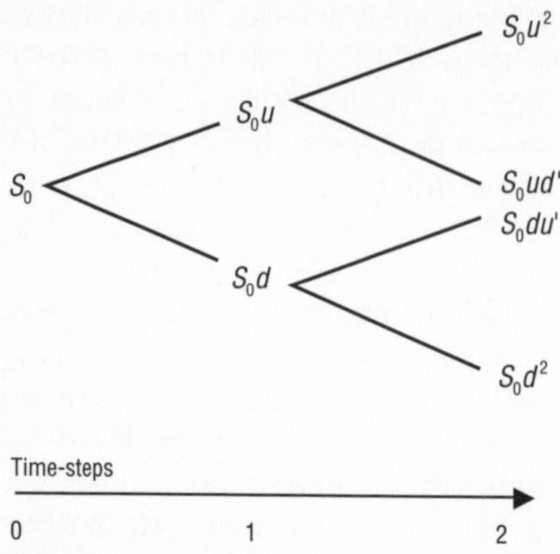

FIGURE 8.2 A two-step nonrecombining lattice.

nodes—specifically, 2^0 nodes at time-step 0, 2^1 nodes at time-step 1, 2^2 nodes at time-step 2, and so forth, until $2^{1,000}$ nodes at time-step 1,000 or approximately 2×10^{301} nodes, taking your computer potentially years to calculate the entire binomial lattice manually! Recombining and nonrecombining binomial lattices yield the same results at the limit, so it is definitely easier to use recombining lattices for most of our analysis. However, there are exceptions where nonrecombining lattices are required, especially when there are two or more stochastic underlying variables or when volatility of the single underlying variable changes over time.

As you can see, closed-form solutions certainly have computational ease compared to binomial lattices. However, it is more difficult to tweak, explain, audit, and trust the exact nature of a fancy black-box stochastic calculus equation than it would be to explain a binomial lattice that branches up and down. Because both methods tend to provide the same results in the limit anyway, for ease of exposition, the binomial lattice should be used. There are also other issues to contend with in terms of advantages and disadvantages of each technique. For instance, closed-form solutions are mathematically elegant but very difficult to derive and are highly specific in nature. Tweaking a closed-form equation requires facility with sophisticated stochastic mathematics. Binomial lattices, however, although sometimes computationally stressful, are easy to build and require no more than simple algebra, as we will see later. Binomial lattices are also very flexible in that they can be tweaked easily to accommodate most types of real-life ESO problems. The recommended approach when dealing with the valuation of ESOs is to show a small lattice, say five steps, of the algorithm used. Then, using software applications[2] calculate the more accurate lattice with at least 1,000 steps and use that as the result.[3] Of course care must be taken in choosing the actual number of steps as the lattice must satisfy a convergence criterion and the lattice must be conditioned such that the nodes fall on the right time scale to account for blackout and vesting periods. (Contact the author for more information on the software applications and proprietary algorithms used.)

We continue the rest of the chapter with introductions to various types of common real-life ESO problems and their associated solutions, using closed-form models, partial-differential equations, and binomial lattices, wherever appropriate. We further assume, for simplicity, the use of recombining lattices, with only five time-steps shown in most cases. The reader can very easily extend these five time-step examples into thousands of time-steps using the same methodology.

BINOMIAL LATTICES

In the binomial world, several basic similarities are worth mentioning. No matter the types of real-life ESO problems you are trying to solve, if the binomial lattice approach is used, the solution can be obtained in one of two ways. The first is the use of risk-neutral probabilities, and the second is the use of market-replicating portfolios. Throughout this book, the former approach is used.[4] The use of a replicating portfolio is more difficult to understand and apply, but for basic option types, the results obtained from replicating portfolios are identical to those obtained through risk-neutral probabilities. So it does not matter which method is used; nevertheless, application and expositional ease should be emphasized. However, the replicating portfolios method is fairly restrictive as compared to the more flexible risk-neutral probability approach, where only the latter can accommodate solving customized binomial lattices with real-life requirements such as suboptimal exercise behavior, vesting, forfeiture rates, and changing inputs over time (e.g., dividend, risk-free rate, and volatility).

Market-replicating portfolios' predominant assumptions are that there are no arbitrage opportunities and that there exist a number of traded assets in the market that can be obtained to replicate the existing asset's payout profile. This is more difficult to justify as ESOs are nontradable and nonmarketable. A simple illustration is in order here. Suppose you own a portfolio of publicly traded stocks that pay a set percentage *dividend* per period. You can, in theory, assuming no trading restrictions, taxes, or transaction costs, purchase a second portfolio of several *non-dividend-paying* stocks and/or bonds and replicate the payout of the first portfolio of *dividend-paying* stocks. You can, for instance, sell a particular number of shares (and/or obtain bond coupon payments) per period to replicate the first portfolio's dividend payout amount at every time period. Hence, if both payouts are identical although their stock/bond compositions are different, the value of both portfolios should then be identical. Otherwise, there will be arbitrage opportunities, and market forces will tend to make them equilibrate in value. This makes perfect sense in a financial securities world where stocks are freely traded and highly liquid.

Compare that to using something called risk-neutral probability. Simply stated, instead of using an evolution of risky future stock prices, calculate the options values at these future dates, weight them using the risk-neutral probabilities, and discount them at a risk-free rate to the present time. Thus, using these risk-adjusted probabilities on the options values allows the analyst to discount these future option values (whose risks have now been accounted for) at the risk-free rate. This is the essence of binomial lattices as applied in valuing options. The results that obtain are identical to the market-replicating approach.

Let us now see how easy it is to apply risk-neutral valuation. In any options model, there is a minimum requirement of at least two lattices. The first lattice is always the lattice of the underlying stock price, while the second lattice is the option valuation lattice. No matter what real-life variations of the ESO model are of interest, the basic structure almost always exists, taking the form:

$$\text{Inputs}: S, X, \sigma, T, rf, b$$

$$u = e^{\sigma\sqrt{\delta t}} \text{ and } d = e^{-\sigma\sqrt{\delta t}} = \frac{1}{u}$$

$$p = \frac{e^{(rf-b)(\delta t)} - d}{u - d}$$

The basic inputs are the stock price at grant date (S), contractual strike price of the option (X), annualized volatility of the natural logarithm of the underlying stock returns in percent (σ), time to maturity in years (T), risk-free rate or the annualized rate of return on a riskless asset (rf), and annualized dividend yield in percent (b). In addition, the binomial lattice approach requires two other sets of calculations, the up and down factors (u and d) as well as a risk-neutral probability measure (p). We see from the equations above that the up factor is simply the exponential function of the stock's volatility multiplied by the square root of time-steps or stepping time (δt). Time-steps or stepping time is simply the time scale between steps. That is, if an option has a one-year maturity and the binomial lattice that is constructed has 10 steps, each step has a stepping time of 0.1 years. The volatility measure is an annualized value; multiplying it by the square root of time-steps breaks it down into the time-step's equivalent volatility. The down factor is simply the reciprocal of the up factor. In addition, the higher the volatility measure, the higher the up and down factors. This reciprocal magnitude ensures that the lattices are recombining because the up and down steps have the same magnitude but different signs; at places along the future path these binomial bifurcations must meet.

Note that the additional real-life variables mentioned earlier come into play later in the second option valuation lattice. For this current example, we will consider only a simple plain-vanilla call option to illustrate the inner-workings of the lattice model. We will then delve into the specifics of the customized lattice later in the chapter. Nonetheless, it is important to note that no matter how specialized and customized the lattices become, the same underlying two-lattice structure almost always exists when it comes to valuing ESOs.

The second required calculation is that of the risk-neutral probability, defined simply as the ratio of the exponential function of the difference between risk-free rate and dividend, multiplied by the stepping time less the down factor, to the difference between the up and down factors. This risk-neutral probability value is a mathematical intermediate and by itself has no particular meaning. One major error users commit is to extrapolate these probabilities as some kind of subjective or objective probabilities that a certain event will occur. Nothing is further from the truth. There is no economic or financial meaning attached to these risk-neutralized probabilities save that it is an intermediate step in a series of calculations. Armed with these values, you are now on your way to creating a binomial lattice of the underlying asset value, shown in Figure 8.3.

Starting with the present value of the underlying asset at time zero (S_0), multiply it with the up (u) and down (d) factors as shown in Figure 8.3, to create a binomial lattice. Remember that there is one bifurcation at each node, creating an up and a down branch. The intermediate branches are all recombining. This evolution of the underlying asset shows that if the volatility is zero, in a deterministic world where there are no uncertainties, the lattice would be a straight line, and the stock price will always be the same tomorrow as it is today, making the option value simply its intrinsic value or stock price less strike price. As the strike price is almost always set as the stock price at grant date for most ESOs, the valuation of the option is hence zero. This is the essence of the intrinsic value method. In other words, if volatility (σ) is zero, then the up $\left(u = e^{\sigma\sqrt{\delta t}}\right)$ and down $\left(d = e^{-\sigma\sqrt{\delta t}}\right)$ jump sizes are equal to one and

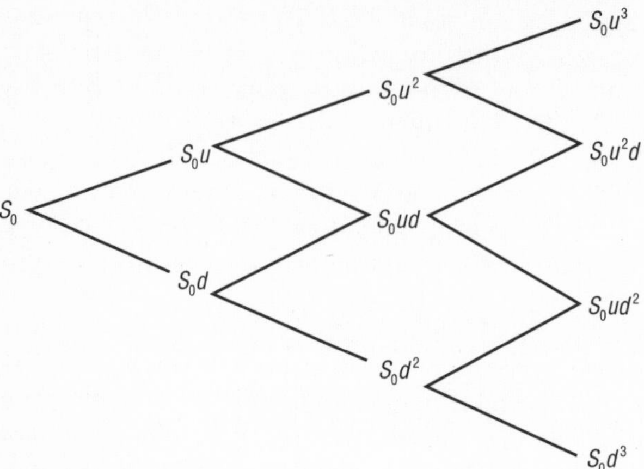

FIGURE 8.3 The underlying stock price lattice.

the lattice becomes a straight line. It is because there are uncertainties and risks in the stock market, as captured by the volatility measure, that the lattice is not a straight horizontal line but comprises up and down movements. It is this up and down uncertainty of the stock price that generates the value in an option. The higher the volatility measure, the higher the up and down factors as previously defined, the higher the potential value of an option as higher uncertainties exist and the potential upside for the option increases.

THE LOOK AND FEEL OF UNCERTAINTY

In options valuation, the first step is to create a series of future stock prices. These stock prices are forecasts of the unknown future. In a simple example, say the stock prices are assumed to follow a straight-line, the future stock prices are all known with certainty—that is, no uncertainty exists—and hence, there exists zero volatility around the forecast values as shown in Figure 8.4. However, in reality, business conditions are hard to forecast. Uncertainty exists, and the actual future stock prices may look more like those in Figure 8.5. That is, at certain time periods, actual stock prices may be above, below, or at the forecast levels. For instance, at any time period, the stock price may fall within a range of values with a certain percent probability. As an example, the first year's stock price may fall anywhere between \$48 and \$52. The actual values are shown to fluctuate around the forecast values at an average volatility of 20 percent.[5] Certainly this exam-

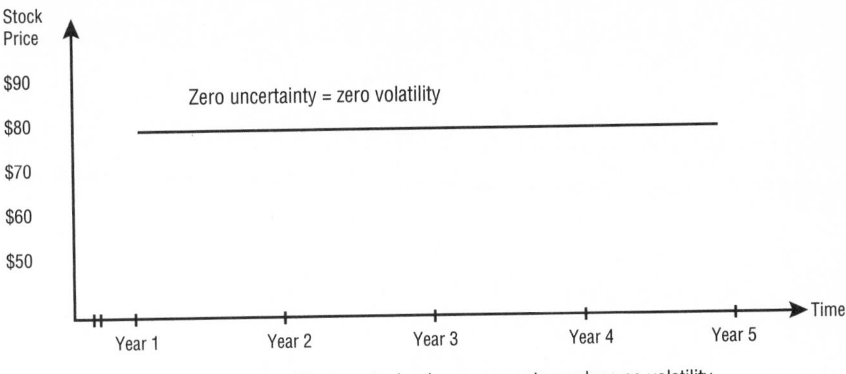

FIGURE 8.4 Zero volatility stock.

ple provides a much more accurate view of the true nature of the stock market, which is fairly difficult to predict with any amount of certainty.

Figure 8.6 shows two sample forecast stock prices around the straight-line forecast value. The higher the uncertainty or risk around the forecast stock prices, the higher the volatility. The darker line with 20 percent volatility fluctuates more wildly around the forecast values. These values can be quantified using Monte Carlo simulation. For instance, Figure 8.7 also shows the Monte Carlo simulated probability distribution

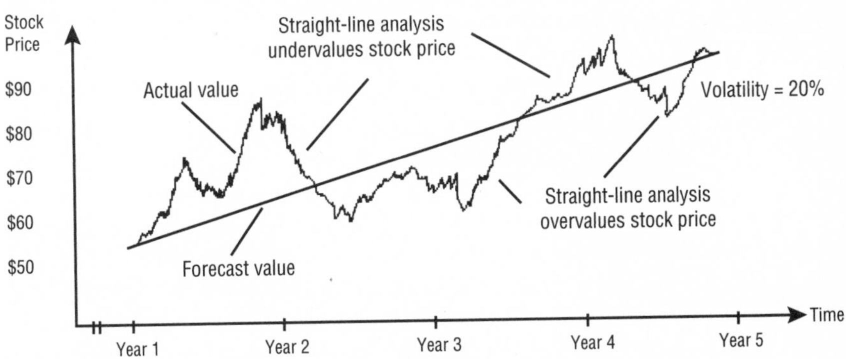

FIGURE 8.5 Twenty percent volatility stock.

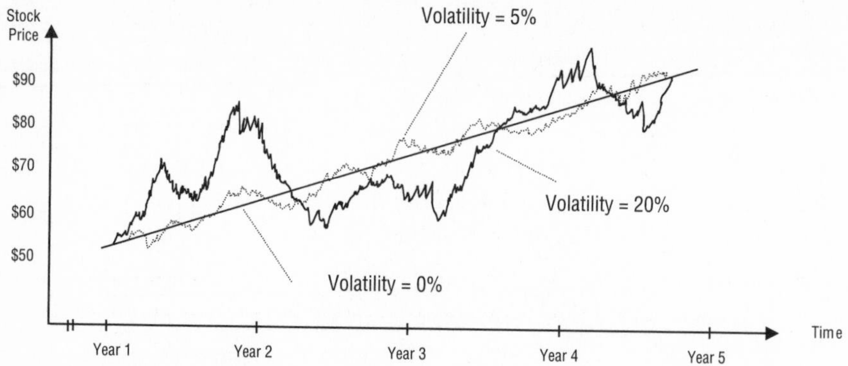

The higher the uncertainty, the higher the volatility and the higher the fluctuation of actual stock price around the simple straight-line forecast. When volatility is zero, the values collapse to the forecast straight-line value.

FIGURE 8.6 A graphical view of volatility.

output for the 5 percent volatility line, where 95 percent of the time the actual values will fall between $51.0 and $69.8. Contrast this to a 95 percent confidence range of between $40.5 and $92.3 for the 20 percent volatility case. This implies that the actual future stock prices can fluctuate anywhere in these ranges, where the higher the volatility, the wider the range of uncertainty on the probability distribution. Therefore, the width of the distribution (measured by volatility, standard deviation, variance, range, and so forth) is indicative of the stock's risk profile. The wider the distribution implies the higher the fluctuations around the forecast value, and the higher the volatility.

A STOCK OPTION PROVIDES VALUE IN THE FACE OF UNCERTAINTY

As seen in Figures 8.6 and 8.7, Monte Carlo simulation was used to generate a Brownian Motion stochastic process to quantify the levels of uncertainty in future stock prices. For instance, simulation accounts for the range and probability that actual stock prices can be above or below the strike price but does not provide the option value per se. Only when probabilistic simulation is used in conjunction with other techniques will the option value be obtained.[6]

Path-dependent simulation using Brownian Motion processes is a *continuous* simulation approach, where all possible stock price paths are

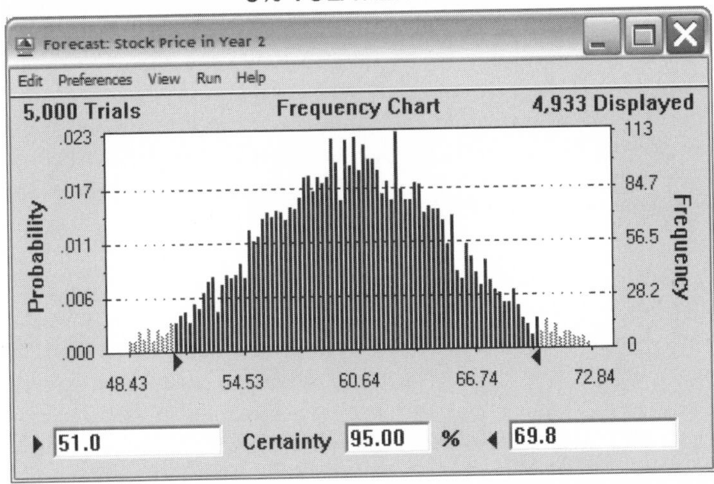

20% VOLATILITY

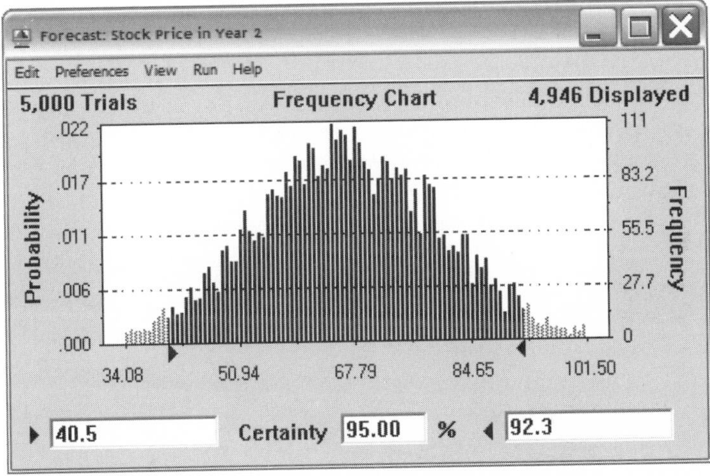

FIGURE 8.7 Monte Carlo probability distribution of stock prices.

simulated probabilistically, either using historical volatilities and drift rates (or growth rate) or forecasted volatilities and drift rates. The BSM is also dependent on the Brownian Motion stochastic process where by applying some stochastic calculus to this process, the options pricing model can be solved *mathematically*. In fact, the binomial lattice has its origins in the Brownian Motion as we will see later in this chapter. The binomial lattice is simply a *discrete* simulation of the Brownian Motion, which means that the higher the number of steps in a lattice, the closer the results will get to the continuous case. For the basic plain-vanilla European call and put options, the results from these three methods approach the same value because they start from the same Brownian Motion assumptions. The difference is, with more exotic and real-life events added into the model (for example, vesting, forfeiture, blackouts, and suboptimal behavior), only the binomial lattice can handle the valuation due to its modeling flexibility.

Consider Figure 8.8. The area above the strike price means that executing a call option will yield considerable value. Conversely, put options are valuable when the stock price is below the strike price. The Brownian Motion simulation will yield the relevant probabilities the stock price will be below or above the strike price, and it is then up to the options valuation calculations to determine the expected value of these options at every point in time, and discount them to the present (grant date).

BINOMIAL LATTICES AS A DISCRETE SIMULATION OF UNCERTAINTY

As uncertainty (measured by volatility) drives the option value, we need to further the discussion on the nature of uncertainty. Figure 8.9 shows a "cone of uncertainty," where we can depict uncertainty as increasing over time. This is the case even when volatility remains constant over the life of the option. Notice that risk may or may not increase over time, but uncer-

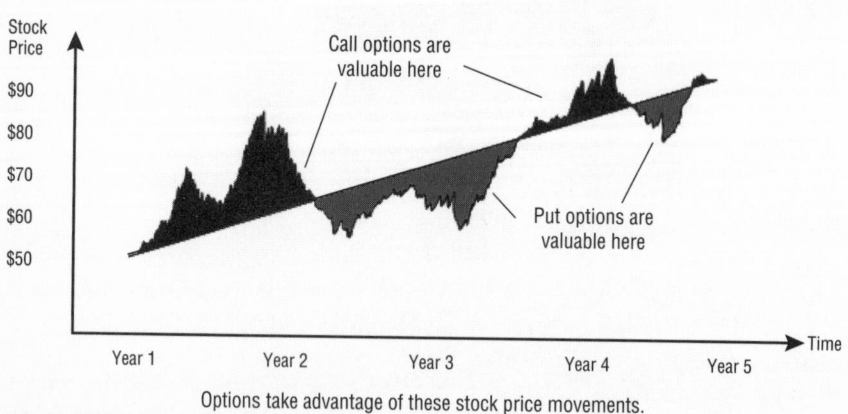

FIGURE 8.8 Call and put options.

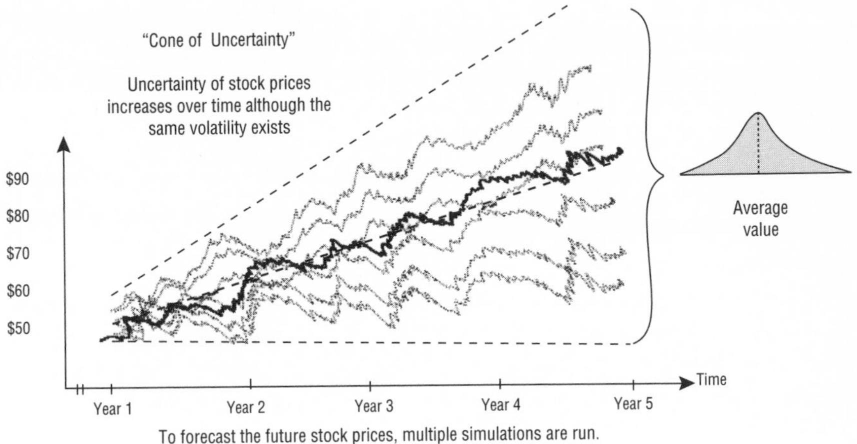

FIGURE 8.9 Cone of uncertainty.

tainty does increase over time. For instance, it is usually much easier to predict business conditions a few months in advance, but it becomes more and more difficult the further one goes into the future, even when business risks remain unchanged. This is the nature of the cone of uncertainty. If we were to attempt to forecast future stock prices while attempting to quantify uncertainty using simulation, a well-prescribed method is to simulate thousands of stock price paths over time, as shown in Figure 8.9. Based on all the simulated paths, a probability distribution can be constructed at each time period. The simulated pathways were generated using a Brownian Motion with a fixed volatility. A Brownian Motion can be depicted as

$$\frac{\delta S}{S} = \mu(\delta t) + \sigma\varepsilon\sqrt{\delta t}$$

where a percent change in the variable S or stock price denoted

$$\frac{\delta S}{S}$$

is simply a combination of a deterministic part ($\mu\delta t$) and a stochastic part $(\sigma\varepsilon\sqrt{\delta t})$. Here, μ is a drift term or growth rate parameter that increases at a factor of time-steps δt, while σ is the volatility parameter, growing at the rate of the square root of time, and ε is a simulated variable, usually following a normal distribution with a mean of zero and a variance of one. Note that the different types of Brownian Motions are widely regarded and accepted as standard assumptions necessary for pricing options. Brownian Motions are also widely used in predicting stock prices.

Notice that the volatility (σ) remains constant throughout several thousand simulations. Only the simulated variable (ε) changes every time. One of the required assumptions in options modeling is the reliance on Brownian Motion. Although the risk or volatility measure (σ) in this example remains constant over time, the level of uncertainty increases over time at a factor of $(\sigma\sqrt{\delta t})$. That is, the level of uncertainty grows at the square root of time and the more time passes, the harder it is to predict the future. This is seen in the cone of uncertainty, where the width of the cone increases over time.

Based on the cone of uncertainty, which depicts uncertainty as increasing over time, we can clearly see the similarities in triangular shape between a cone of uncertainty and a binomial lattice as shown in Figure 8.10. In essence, a binomial lattice is simply a discrete simulation of the cone of

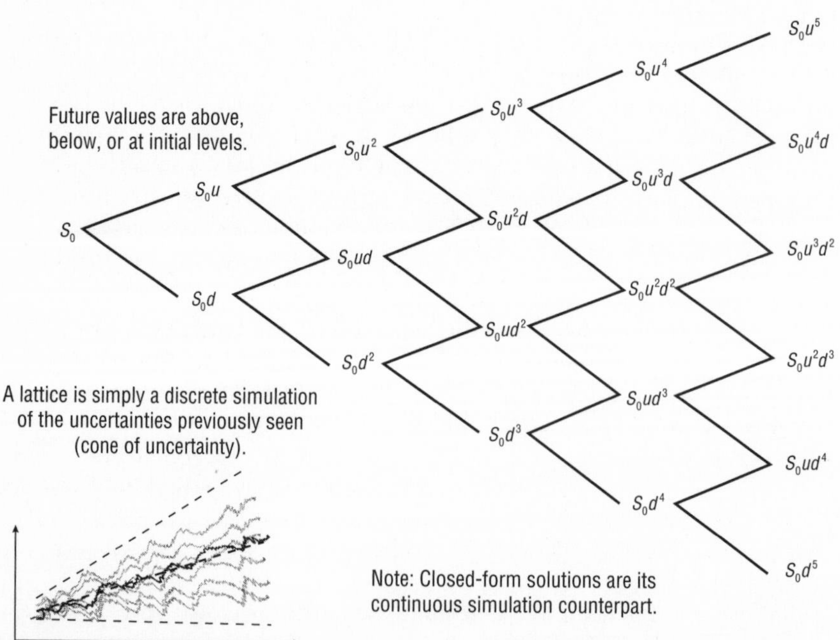

FIGURE 8.10 The binomial lattice as a discrete simulation.

uncertainty. Whereas a Brownian Motion is a continuous stochastic simulation process, a binomial lattice is a discrete simulation process. At the limit, where the time-steps approach zero and the number of steps approach infinity, the results stemming from a binomial lattice approach those obtained from a Brownian Motion process in a basic European call or put option. Solving a Brownian Motion in a discrete sense yields the binomial equations, while solving it in a continuous sense yields closed-form equations like the BSM or GBM and other models.

As a side note, multinomial models that involve more than two bifurcations at each node, such as the trinomial (three-branch) models or quadranomial (four-branch) models, require a similar Brownian Motion assumption but are mathematically more difficult to solve. See Appendix 8A for more details on comparing binomial and trinomial lattices. No matter how many branches stem from each node, these models provide exactly the same results in the limit for plain-vanilla European options, the difference being that the more branches at each node, the faster the results are reached. For instance, a binomial model may require a hundred steps to solve a particular ESO problem, while a trinomial model probably only requires half the number of steps to achieve convergence but the computation time takes longer due to more branching events at each node.

To continue the exploration into the nature of binomial lattices, Figure 8.11 shows the different binomial lattices with different volatilities. This means that the higher the volatility, the wider the range and spread of values between the upper and lower branches of each node in the lattice. Because binomial lattices are discrete simulations, the higher the volatility, the wider the spread of the distribution. This can be seen on the terminal nodes, where the range between the highest and lowest values at the terminal nodes is higher for higher volatilities than the range of a lattice with a lower volatility. This is exactly what was seen in Figure 8.7.

At the extreme, where volatility equals zero, the lattice collapses into a straight line. This straight line is akin to the straight line shown in Figure 8.4. This is important because if there is zero uncertainty and risk, meaning that all future stock prices are known with absolute certainty, then there is no options value. The intrinsic value method is sufficient. It is because business, economic, and market conditions are fraught with uncertainty, and hence volatility exists and can be captured using a binomial lattice. Therefore, the intrinsic value method can be seen as a special case of an options model, when uncertainty is negligible and volatility approaches zero, and the options value is simply the stock price at grant date less the contractual strike price. As most ESOs are granted at-the-money, which means the strike price is set at the grant date's stock price, the intrinsic value method will provide an ESO value of zero.

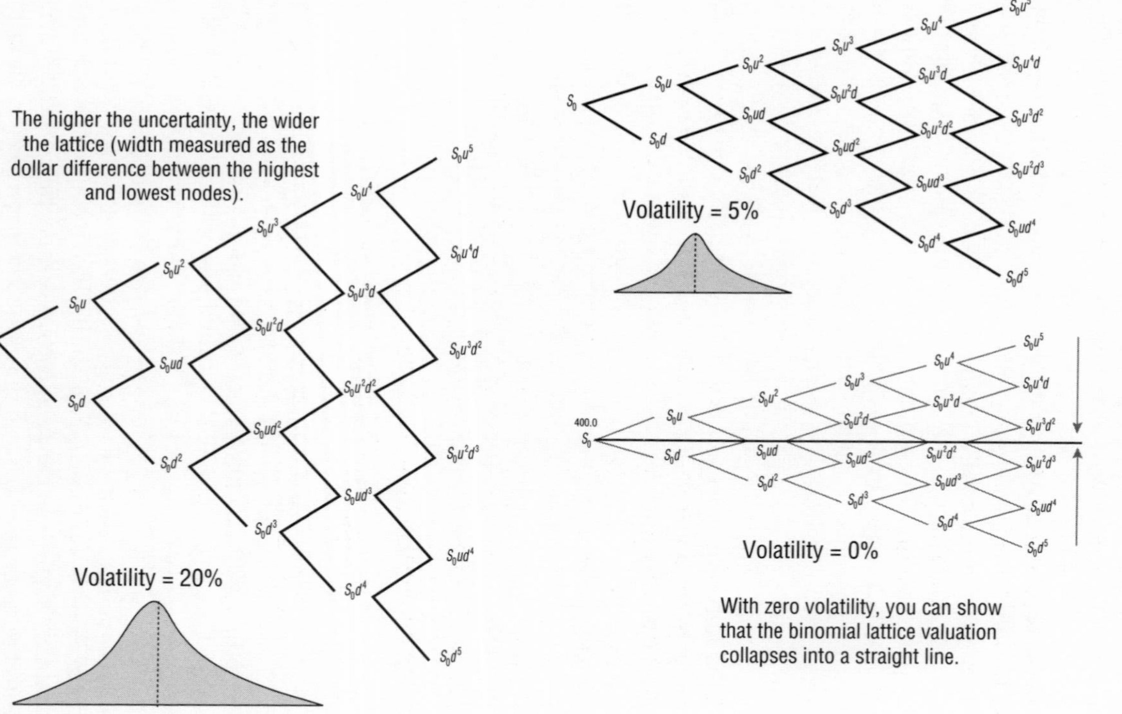

The higher the uncertainty, the wider the lattice (width measured as the dollar difference between the highest and lowest nodes).
Volatility = 20%
Volatility = 5%
Volatility = 0%
400.0
With zero volatility, you can show that the binomial lattice valuation collapses into a straight line.

FIGURE 8.11 Lattice views with different volatilities.

SOLVING A SIMPLE EUROPEAN CALL OPTION USING BINOMIAL LATTICES

Another key concept in the use of binomial lattices is the idea of steps and precision. For instance, if a five-year option is valued using five steps, each time-step size (δt) is equivalent to one year. Conversely, if 50 steps are used, then δt is equivalent to 0.1 years per step. Recall that the up and down step sizes were $e^{\sigma\sqrt{\delta t}}$ and $e^{-\sigma\sqrt{\delta t}}$, respectively. The smaller δt is, the smaller the up and down steps, and the more granular the lattice values will be.

An example is in order. Figure 8.12 shows the example of a simple European call option. Suppose the call option has an underlying stock price of \$100 and a strike price of \$100 expiring in one year. Further, suppose that the corresponding risk-free rate is 5 percent and the calculated volatility of historical logarithmic returns is 25 percent. Because the option pays no dividends and is exercisable only at termination, a BSM equation will

Example of a European *financial* call option with a stock price (S) of \$100, a strike price (X) of \$100, a 1-year expiration (T), 5% risk-free rate (r), and 25% volatility (σ) with no dividend payments.

Using the Black-Scholes equation, we obtain \$12.3360.

$$Call = S\Phi\left[\frac{\ln(S/X)+(r+\sigma^2/2)T}{\sigma\sqrt{T}}\right] - Xe^{-rT}\Phi\left[\frac{\ln(S/X)+(r-\sigma^2/2)T}{\sigma\sqrt{T}}\right]$$

Using a 5-step binomial approach, we obtain \$12.79.

Step 1 in the binomial approach:

$$\text{Given } S=100, X=100, \sigma=0.25, T=1, rf=0.05$$

$$u=e^{\sigma\sqrt{\delta t}}=1.1183 \text{ and } d=e^{-\sigma\sqrt{\delta t}}=0.8942$$

$$p=\frac{e^{rf(\delta t)}-d}{u-d}=0.5169$$

FIGURE 8.12 European call option solved using the BSM and binomial lattices.

suffice. As seen previously, the call option value calculated using the BSM is \$12.3360, which is obtained by (calculations shown are rounded):

$$Call = S\Phi\left[\frac{\ln(S/X) + (r + \sigma^2/2)T}{\sigma\sqrt{T}}\right] - Xe^{-rf(T)}\Phi\left[\frac{\ln(S/X) + (r - \sigma^2/2)T}{\sigma\sqrt{T}}\right]$$

$$Call = 100\Phi\left[\frac{\ln(100/100) + (0.05 + 0.25^2/2)1}{0.25\sqrt{1}}\right] - 100e^{-0.05(1)}\Phi\left[\frac{\ln(100/100) + (0.05 - 0.25^2/2)1}{0.25\sqrt{1}}\right]$$

$$Call = 100\Phi[0.325] - 95.13\Phi[0.075] = 100(0.6274) - 95.13(0.5298) = 12.3360$$

A binomial lattice can also be applied to solve this problem (Figures 8.13 and 8.14). The first step is to solve the binomial lattice equations, that is, to calculate the up step size (u), down step size (d), and risk-neutral probability (p). This assumes that the stepping-time (δt) is 0.2 years (one-year expiration divided by five steps). The calculations proceed as follows:

$$u = e^{\sigma\sqrt{\delta t}} = e^{0.25\sqrt{0.2}} = 1.1183$$

$$d = e^{-\sigma\sqrt{\delta t}} = e^{-0.25\sqrt{0.2}} = 0.8942$$

$$p = \frac{e^{rf(\delta t)} - d}{u - d} = \frac{e^{0.05(0.2)} - 0.8942}{1.1183 - 0.8942} = 0.5169$$

Figure 8.13 illustrates the first lattice in the binomial approach. In an options world, this lattice is created based on the evolution of the underlying stock price at grant date to forecast the future until maturity. The starting point is the \$100 initial stock price at grant date. This \$100 value evolves over time due to the volatility that exists. For instance, the \$100 value becomes \$111.8 (\$100 × 1.118) on the upper bifurcation at the first time period and \$89.4 (\$100 × 0.894) on the lower bifurcation by multiplying the stock prices by their respective up and down step sizes. This up and down compounding effect continues until the end terminal, where given a 25 percent annualized volatility, stock prices can, after a period of five years, be anywhere between \$57.2 and \$174.9.[7] Recall that if volatility is zero, then the lattice collapses into a straight line where at every time-step interval, the value of the stock will be \$100 (this is because up and down step sizes are equal to 1.0). It is when volatility exists that stock prices can vary within this \$57.2 to \$174.9 interval.

Notice on the lattice in Figure 8.13 that the values are path-independent. That is, the value on node H can be attained through the multiplica-

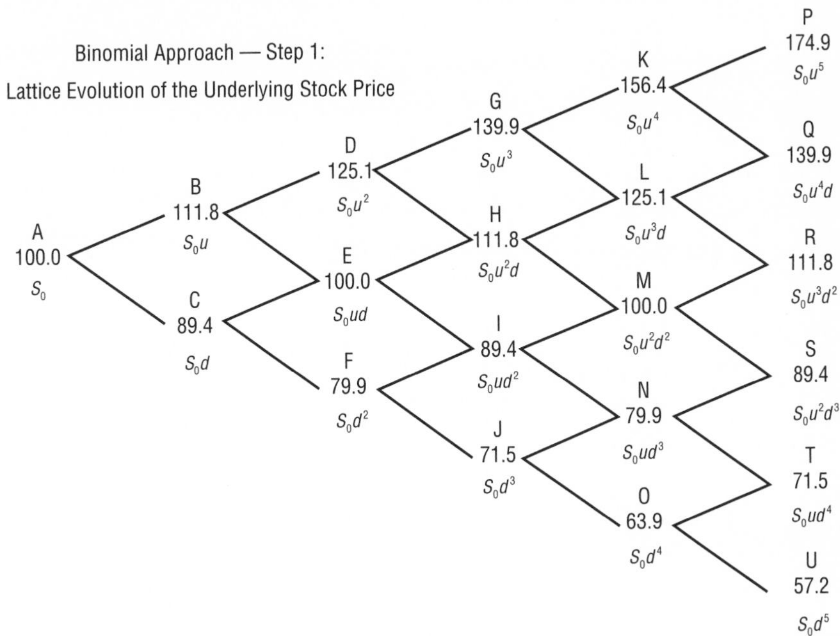

FIGURE 8.13 First lattice evolution of the underlying stock price.

tion of S_0u^2d, which can be arrived at by going through paths ABEH, ABDH, or ACEH. The value of path ABEH is $S \times u \times d \times u$, the value of path ABDH is $S \times u \times u \times d$, and the value of path ACEH is $S \times d \times u \times u$, all of which yields S_0u^2d.

Figure 8.14 shows the calculation of the European option's valuation lattice. The valuation lattice is calculated in two steps, starting with the *terminal* node and then the *intermediate* nodes, through a process called backward induction. For instance, the circled terminal node shows a value of \$74.9, which is calculated through the maximization between executing the option and letting the option expire worthless if the cost exceeds the benefits of execution. The value of executing the option is calculated as \$174.9 – \$100, which yields \$74.9. The value \$174.9 comes from Figure 8.13's (node P) lattice of the underlying asset, and \$100 is the cost of executing the option, leaving a value of \$74.9.

The second step is the calculation of intermediate nodes. The circled intermediate node illustrated in Figure 8.14 is calculated using a risk-neutral probability analysis. Using the previously calculated risk-neutral

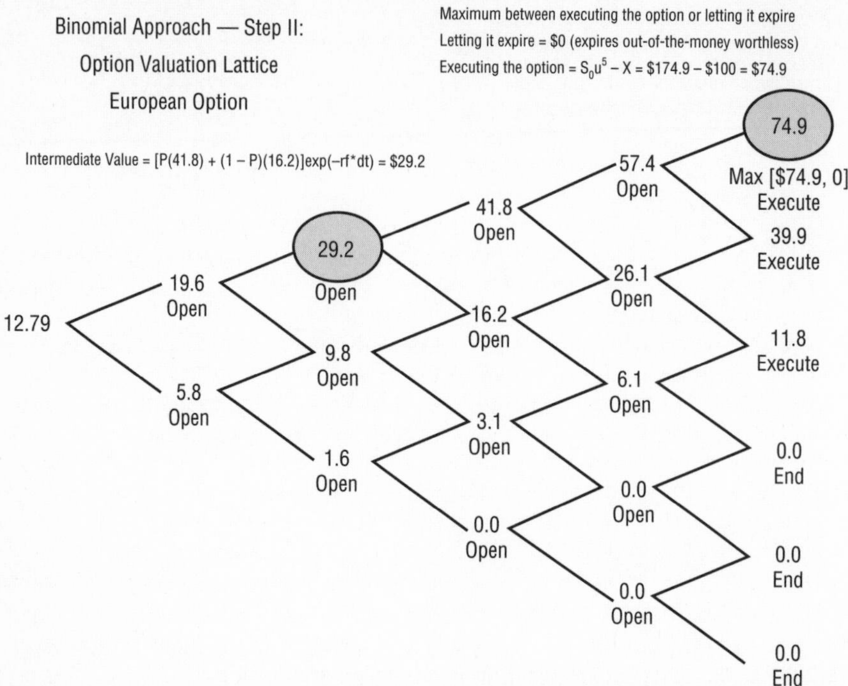

FIGURE 8.14 Second option valuation lattice (European call without dividends).

probability of 0.5169, a backward induction analysis is obtained through:

$$[(p)up + (1 - p)down]\exp[(-riskfree)(\delta t)]$$
$$[(0.5169)41.8 + (1 - 0.5169)16.2]\exp[(-0.05)(0.2)] = 29.2$$

Using this backward induction calculation all the way back to the starting period, the option's value at time zero is calculated as $12.79.

GRANULARITY LEADS TO PRECISION

Table 8.1 shows a series of calculations using a BSM closed-form solution, binomial lattices with different steps, and Monte Carlo simulation.

TABLE 8.1 Comparison of Results

More Steps Equal Higher Accuracy		
– Black-Scholes: $12.3360		
– Binomial:		
• N = 5 steps	$12.7946	→ OVERESTIMATES
• N = 10 steps	$12.0932	UNDERESTIMATES
• N = 20 steps	$12.2132	UNDERESTIMATES
• N = 50 steps	$12.2867	UNDERESTIMATES
• N = 100 steps	$12.3113	UNDERESTIMATES
• N = 1,000 steps	$12.3335	UNDERESTIMATES
• N = 10,000 steps	$12.3358	
• N = 50,000 steps	$12.3360	→ EXACT VALUE
– Simulation: (10,000 simulations: $12.3360)		

Notice that for the binomial lattice, the higher the number of steps, the more accurate the results become. At the limit, when the number of steps approaches infinity—that is, the time between steps (δt) approaches zero—the discrete simulation in a binomial lattice approaches that of a continuous model, which is the closed-form solution. The BSM is applicable here because there are no dividend payments and the option is executable only at termination. When the number of steps approaches 50,000, the results converge. However, in most cases, the level of accuracy becomes sufficient when the number of steps reaches 1,000. Notice that the third method, using Monte Carlo simulation, also converges at 10,000 simulations on 100 steps.

Table 8.2 shows another concept of binomial lattices. When there are more time-steps in a lattice, the underlying lattice shows more granularities, and hence provides a higher precision. The first lattice shows five steps and the second 20 steps (truncated at 10 steps due to space limitations). Notice the similar values that occur over time. For instance, the value 111.83 in the first lattice occurs at step 1 versus step 2 in the second lattice. All the values in the first lattice recur in the second lattice, but the second lattice is more granular in the sense that more intermediate values exist. As seen in Table 8.1, the higher number of steps means a higher precision due to the higher granularity.

TABLE 8.2 Higher Lattice Steps Equals Higher Granularity and Precision

5 Time-Steps

100.00	(111.83)	[125.06]	139.85	158.39	174.90
	(89.42)	[100.00]	111.83	126.06	138.85
		[79.96]	89.42	100.00	111.83
			71.50	79.96	89.42
				63.94	71.50
					67.18

20 Time-Steps

100.00	105.75	(111.83)	118.26	[125.06]	132.25	139.85	147.89	158.39	165.39	174.90
	94.56	100.00	105.75	111.83	118.26	125.06	132.25	139.85	147.89	158.39
		(89.42)	94.56	[100.00]	105.75	111.83	118.26	125.06	132.25	139.85
			84.56	89.42	94.56	100.00	105.75	111.83	118.26	125.06
				[79.96]	84.56	89.42	84.56	100.00	105.75	111.83
					76.82	79.96	84.56	89.42	94.56	100.00
						71.50	75.62	79.96	84.56	89.42
							67.62	71.50	75.62	79.96
								63.94	67.62	71.60
									60.46	63.94
										57.18

SOLVING AMERICAN AND EUROPEAN OPTIONS WITH DIVIDENDS

The example calculations in Figure 8.14 illustrate the valuation of a European call option without dividends. To continue with the example, Figure 8.15 shows an American call option without dividends. Notice that the \$12.79 options valuation result is identical to the European option without dividends (Figure 8.14). This is because it is never optimal to exercise a call option before maturity when there are no dividends, and when there are no other real-life impacts such as vesting, suboptimal exercise behavior, and possibilities of forfeiture; therefore the American call option's value equals the European call option's value for the simple option.

Figure 8.16 shows a European option with its underlying stock paying an annualized 4 percent dividend yield. The resulting valuation is \$10.47.

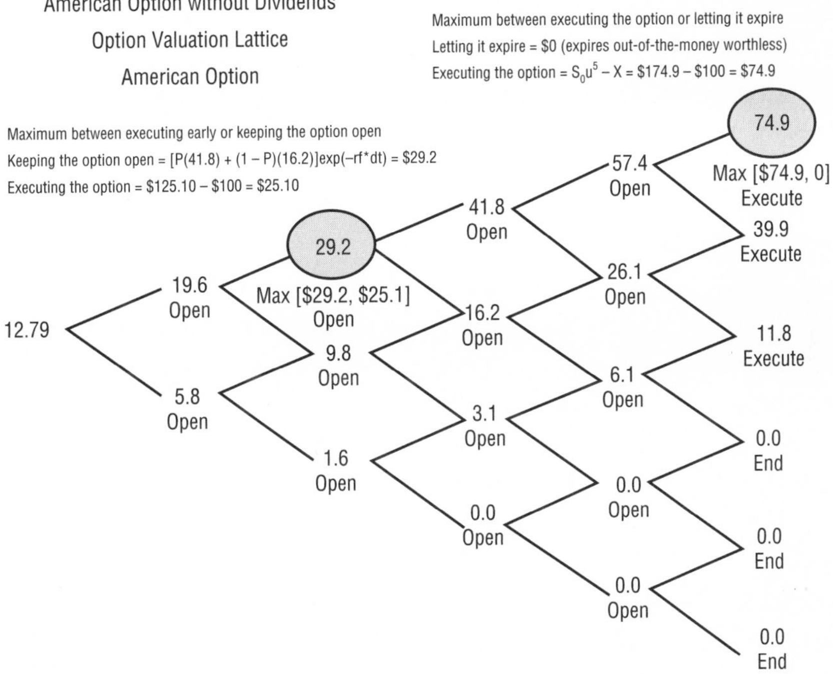

FIGURE 8.15 Second option valuation lattice (American option without dividends).

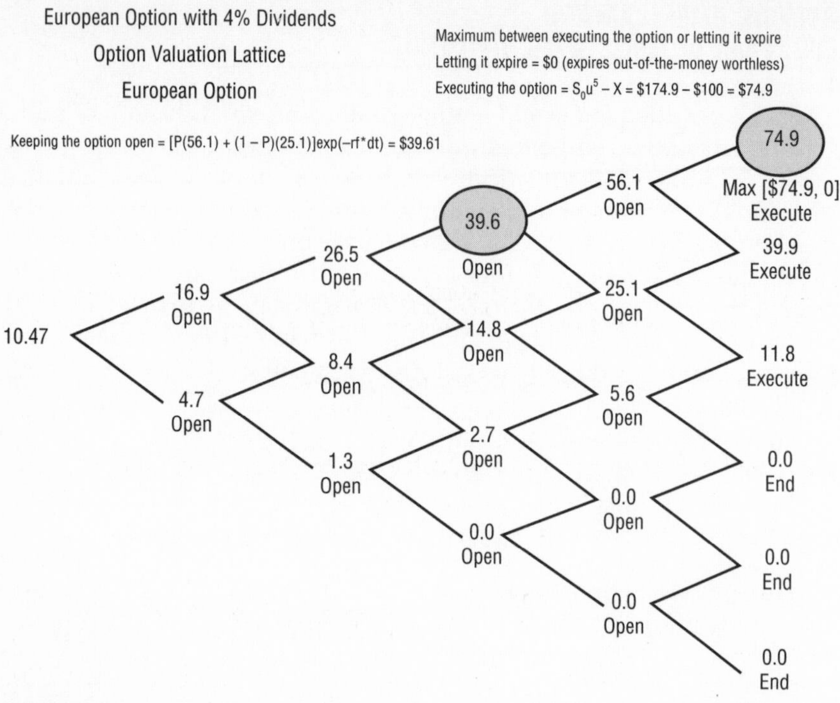

FIGURE 8.16 Second option valuation lattice (European option with dividends).

Notice that the risk-neutral probability is no longer 0.5169 but 0.4810 by incorporating the dividend yield (q):

$$p = \frac{e^{(rf-q)\delta t} - d}{u-d} = \frac{e^{(0.05-0.04)0.2} - 0.8942}{1.1183 - 0.8942} = 0.4810$$

In contrast, Figure 8.17 shows the computations for an American call option where the underlying stock pays dividends. The difference between the calculations in Figures 8.16 and 8.17 is that the American option has the ability to be exercised before expiration. Therefore, the intermediate value of $39.9 in Figure 8.17 is obtained by calculating the profit maximization decision between exercising now and thereby receiving $39.85 or keeping the option open for future execution and obtaining an expected value of $39.73 after adjusting for future option values through the risk-neutral probability. The final options valuation result is $10.50 (American with

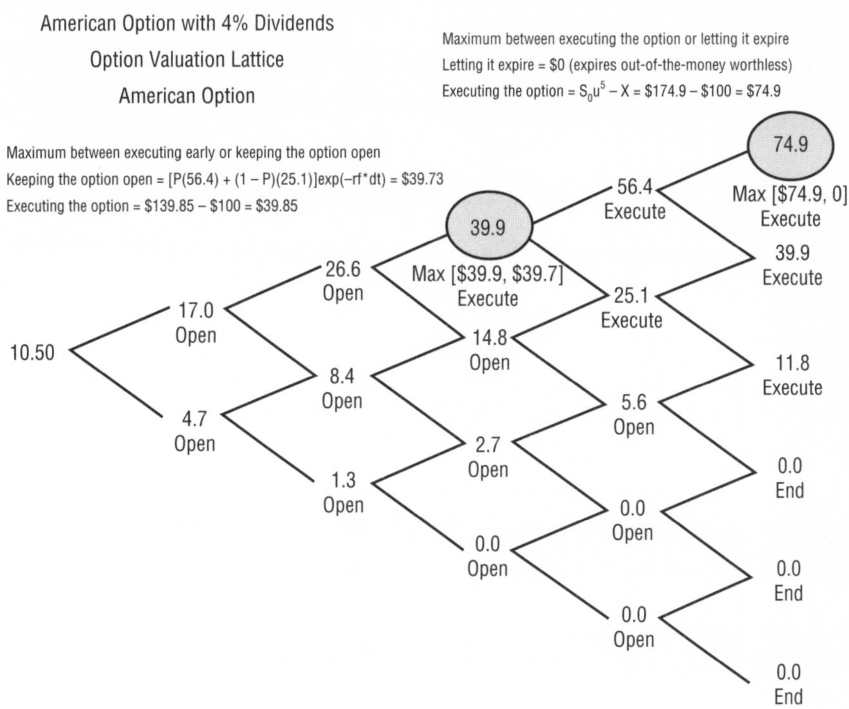

FIGURE 8.17 Second option valuation lattice (American option with dividends).

dividends), which is less than $12.79 (American without dividends), and slightly greater than $10.47 (European with dividends).

In other words, an American call option is worth the same as a European call option if the underlying stock pays no dividends and as long as there are no exotic variables interacting in the option execution decisions. Both American and European call options are worth less if their underlying stock pays a dividend. In addition, an American call option is worth slightly more than a European call option if the underlying stock pays a dividend, and the difference depends on how high the dividend yield is—the higher the yield, the higher the difference in value. This is because the stock price drops by the amount of the dividend paid on the ex-dividend date (in most cases, the stock prices have already instantaneously adjusted for this way in advance of a dividend payment) and therefore, the call option is worth less whether it is American or European, if the underlying stock pays a dividend. The American call option, with its ability for early execution, will be worth slightly more than the European call option by being able to execute the option earlier. The higher the dividend yield, the lower the stock price drops, and the higher the value of being able to execute earlier before the stock price drops.

CUSTOMIZING THE BINOMIAL LATTICE

Notice that the options valuation methodology using risk-neutral probabilities is simple and consistently applied to European and American options. We then added a simple complexity called dividends. Yet the basic methodology remains the same, the only difference being that the dividend is imputed into the risk-neutral probability calculation, and that the American call option can be exercised prior to and including the expiration date. The same methodology underlies the proprietary algorithms used in the customized binomial lattice model—the specifics of the algorithms themselves are not discussed here due to their complexity, but their generalities and a simple version of the model are discussed next.

The customized binomial lattice analysis assumes that the holder of the option cannot exercise the option when it is still in the vesting period; that is, the employee is holding a European call option during the vesting period. Further, if the employee is terminated or decides to leave voluntarily during this vesting period, the option grant will be forfeited and presumed worthless. In other words, the forfeiture rate calculated by the annualized employee turnover rate and calibrated with the proportion of options forfeitures in the past few years is used to condition the lattice tree to zero if the employee is terminated or leaves during this vesting period. In contrast, after the options have been vested, the option converts to an American option such that the holder of the option can execute at any time up to expiration. In certain options, blackout dates exist, implying that the options cannot be executed during these weeks or months. These dates usually coincide with several weeks before and several weeks after a major earnings release. The option then becomes a Bermudan option, where it is a mixture of American and European options—Bermudan options have certain time periods where they can be exercised. When calculating such options, the number of steps in a lattice model needs to be calibrated to align these dates on specific nodes.

Next, employees tend to exhibit erratic exercise behavior where an option will be exercised only if it breaches some multiple of the contractual strike price, and not before. This is termed the suboptimal exercise behavior multiple.[8] This is important as based on the example valuations previously discussed, the option is exercised when it is *optimal* to do so. The problem is that one never really truly knows when it is indeed optimal to hold or execute the option. It is preposterous to say that all employees granted stock options in a large corporation have facility with lattice modeling, stock price forecasting, and optimal trigger value estimations. Therefore, employees tend to exercise their options more from their intuition, expectations, gut feel, emotion, financial need, and other subjective criteria. Hence, if an execution is not optimal but is done anyway this means that the exercise behavior is suboptimal by definition. In addition, as discussed in Chapter 4, using suboptimal exercise behavior multiples can account for some elements of nonmarketability and nontransferability of the options. That is, the only way to liquidate or sell the option is to exercise it earlier than when it is optimal to do so.

In addition, the options that have vested must be exercised within a short period if the employee leaves voluntarily or is terminated, regardless of the suboptimal behavior threshold—that is, if forfeiture occurs (measured by the historical forfeiture rates). Also, if the option expiration date has been reached, the option will be exercised if it is in-the-money, and expire worthless if it is at-the-money or out-of-the-money.

Finally, all other aspects of the models are allowed to change over the life of the option, including risk-free rates, volatilities, suboptimal early exercise behavior multiples, forfeiture rates, and dividend yields. Changing any one of these items will also change the risk-neutral probabilities over time. Changing the volatilities over time will also change the up and down step sizes as well as require a nonrecombining lattice. All of these changing variables together with the exotic inputs will yield significant interaction effects that are nonlinear, and their results cannot be guessed at or determined without actually running the models. Therefore, due to the complex nature of variable interactions, changing inputs, and exotic inputs, the complete algorithm is not included in this book but a portion of the recombining lattice algorithm is presented next.[9] In addition, solved valuation results are provided in Parts Three and Four of this book.

THE CUSTOMIZED BINOMIAL LATTICE MODEL

The customized binomial lattice using a recombining lattice is defined as:

For $n = N$ at the terminal nodes, the option values at those nodes are:

$$\Omega_{N,m} = Max\left[S_0 e^{(2m-N)\sigma_{i,n}\sqrt{\delta t}} - X, 0\right] \text{ for all } m = 0 \text{ to } N, \text{ and for all } i$$

values of σ at the appropriate steps,

where $\Omega_{n,m}$ is the option value at step n on the lattice and node location m, where m goes from 0 to n, the step number in the *lattice. In addition, S_0 is the stock price at grant date, $\sigma_{i,n}$ is the ith volatility appropriate to the particular step n at time $n(\delta t)$. In addition, δt is the stepping-time calculated as the total time to maturity divided by the number of steps, while X is the contractual strike price.*

For all intermediate steps when $0 \le n \le N-1$, backward induction is applied such that:

For all $n = N-1$ to 0, $m = 0$ to n, and for all i values of σ, β, B, rf, q, and Φ at the appropriate steps in the lattice where:

$$\text{If } n(\delta t) \ge v \text{ and } S_0 e^{(2m-n)\sigma_{i,n}\sqrt{\delta t}} \ge XB_{i,n} \text{ and } n(\delta t) \ne \beta_{i,n} \text{ then}$$

$$\Omega_{n,m} = Max\left[S_0 e^{(2m-n)\sigma_{i,n}\sqrt{\delta t}} - X, 0\right]$$

or

$$\text{If } n(\delta t) \ge v \text{ and } S_0 e^{(2m-n)\sigma_{i,n}\sqrt{\delta t}} < XB_{i,n} \text{ and } n(\delta t) \ne \beta_{i,n} \text{ then}$$

$$\Omega_{n,m} = \Phi_{i,n}(\delta t) Max\left[S_0 e^{(2m-n)\sigma_{i,n}\sqrt{\delta t}} - X, 0\right] +$$

$$[1-\Phi_{i,n}(\delta t)]\left[\left(\left(e^{(rf_{i,n}-q_{i,n})\delta t} - e^{-\sigma_{i,n}\sqrt{\delta t}}\right)\Big/\left(e^{\sigma_{i,n}\sqrt{\delta t}} - e^{-\sigma_{i,n}\sqrt{\delta t}}\right)\right)\Omega_{n+1,m+1} + \left(\left(e^{\sigma_{i,n}\sqrt{\delta t}} - e^{(rf_{i,n}-q_{i,n})\delta t}\right)\Big/\left(e^{\sigma_{i,n}\sqrt{\delta t}} - e^{-\sigma_{i,n}\sqrt{\delta t}}\right)\right)\Omega_{n+1,m}\right] e^{-rf_{i,n}(\delta t)}$$

or

$$\text{If } n(\delta t) < v \text{ or } n(\delta t) = \beta_{i,n} \text{ then}$$

$$\Omega_{n,m} = [1-\Phi_{i,n}(\delta t)]\left[\left(\left(e^{(rf_{i,n}-q_{i,n})\delta t} - e^{-\sigma_{i,n}\sqrt{\delta t}}\right)\Big/\left(e^{\sigma_{i,n}\sqrt{\delta t}} - e^{-\sigma_{i,n}\sqrt{\delta t}}\right)\right)\Omega_{n+1,m+1} + \left(\left(e^{\sigma_{i,n}\sqrt{\delta t}} - e^{(rf_{i,n}-q_{i,n})\delta t}\right)\Big/\left(e^{\sigma_{i,n}\sqrt{\delta t}} - e^{-\sigma_{i,n}\sqrt{\delta t}}\right)\right)\Omega_{n+1,m}\right] e^{-rf_{i,n}(\delta t)}$$

Where v is the vesting period in years, $\beta_{i,n}$ are all the blackout dates, $B_{i,n}$ is the ith suboptimal behavior multiple, $\Phi_{i,n}$ is the ith forfeiture rate corresponding to the relevant time-step appropriate to the particular step n at time $n(\delta t)$, $q_{i,n}$ is the ith dividend yield corresponding to the relevant time-step appropriate to the particular step n at time $n(\delta t)$, and $rf_{i,n}$ is the ith risk-free rate corresponding to the relevant time-step appropriate to the particular step n at time $n(\delta t)$.

The model is then extended to a nonrecombining lattice to account for changing volatilities over time. To facilitate the computation of a recombining lattice and to make it mathematically tractable, at each constant volatility period the previously given recombining lattice is used, where at the point of inflection, each recombined terminal node has its own recombining lattice. I created this software algorithm and associated models and presented the results to FASB in 2003. This model and its associated algorithms are an advancement over other published models in that this model accounts for changing values over time and the application of combining lattices to recreate a nonrecombining lattice, the inclusion of forfeitures, suboptimal exercise behavior multiple, vesting, and blackout dates such that Monte Carlo simulation can be applied to simulate the inputs as well as for error precision and statistical confidence control.

Finally, it must be stressed that the customized binomial lattice model can be adapted to any alternative accounting methods that have been proposed. As an example, the alternative Bulow-Shoven option accounting system[10] shortens the time frame involved in modeling a grant's value to 90 days and uses actual liquid market prices as an input (a type of mark-to-market approach, reducing the need for forecasting). Because most programs require employees who leave the company to exercise their options within 90 days, the Bulow-Shoven approach would assume that a new grant is made every quarter, requiring a company to subtract the value of extending its existing options another three months as an expense, along with the three-month cost of any newly-granted options. The option valuation model used in the proposed Bulow-Shoven system is the modified BSM. Instead of using the modified BSM, the customized binomial lattice is actually more appropriate here, in that the lattice can account for all the exotic variables that do have an effect on the shortened option, which cannot be captured by the BSM. For instance, if a significant portion of the 90 days are blackout dates (e.g., 90%) the BSM will significantly and incorrectly overvalue the option. However, be aware of the pitfalls of using this method, namely, marking-to-market always provides the best data for the analysis, the actual market prices, but firms will now be unable to perform any strategic financial planning and decision making in advance (estimating the total ESO expenses months or years before the actual grant date). They will be susceptible to additional higher earnings and stock price volatility (if the ESO grants are a significant expense to the firm, their values will fluctuate with the market prices every 90 days and earnings will be very volatile quarter to quarter, unnecessarily incorporating part of the additional market volatility into the income statements), and they may also have insufficient information to perform the analysis (thinly traded stocks, private equity placements, private entities, and firms with no publicly traded short-term options). This author believes that the Bulow-Shoven approach is theoretically correct and elegant but it has some pragmatic issues that firms have to seriously consider before adopting it. Finally, be aware that the Bulow-Shoven method is an alternative accounting system, not an alternative options valuation model, which means that the customized binomial lattice presented previously can still be used in such a system if FASB offers it as an approved alternative and if firms decide to adopt it.

TREATMENT OF FORFEITURE RATES

One note of caution in the aforementioned model is the application of forfeiture rates. The treatment of forfeiture rates will also yield a difference in the options valuation results. Specifically, forfeiture rates can be applied inside a customized binomial lattice model (calculations are performed inside the previously given lattice algorithm) versus outside (adjusting the results after obtaining them from the binomial lattice). The valuation obtained will in most cases and under most conditions be different. At the time of writing, it is still unknown toward which direction the final FAS 123 requirements will lean. Table 8.3 illustrates some of the nontrivial differences in valuation between using forfeitures inside versus outside of the binomial lattice for a typical ESO. Applying forfeiture rates internal to the lattice consistently provides a lower value than when applied outside the lattice.

If the forfeiture rate is applied inside the lattice, which in my opinion is the correct method, then when using the customized binomial lattice algorithm, simply input the forfeiture rate as is. In addition, the forfeiture rates can also be allowed to change over time in the customized binomial lattice algorithm. If the forfeiture rate is applied outside the lattice, simply set all forfeiture rates to zero in the binomial lattice and multiply the valuation results by (1 – *Forfeiture*).[11] To understand the theoretical implications of inside versus outside treatments of forfeiture rates, we first need to understand how forfeiture rates are used in the model.

When applied inside the lattice, the forfeiture rate is used to condition the customized binomial lattice to zero if the employee is terminated or leaves during the vesting period. Post-vesting, the forfeiture rate is used to condition the lattice to execute the option if it is in-the-money or it is allowed to expire worthless otherwise, regardless of the suboptimal exercise behavior multiple when the employee leaves. This is important because due to the nonlinear interactions among variables, by putting the forfeiture rates inside the lattice, these interactions will be played out in the model—for instance, forfeiture dominates when an

TABLE 8.3 Comparing the Application of Forfeiture Rates

Comparing ESO Valuation on Applying Forfeitures Inside versus Outside Lattices								
Stock Price	$ 50	$ 50	$ 50	$ 50	$ 50	$ 50	$ 50	$ 50
Strike Price	$ 50	$ 50	$ 50	$ 50	$ 50	$ 50	$ 50	$ 50
Maturity	10	10	10	10	10	10	10	10
Risk-Free Rate	3.5%	3.5%	3.5%	3.5%	3.5%	3.5%	3.5%	3.5%
Dividend	0%	0%	0%	0%	0%	0%	0%	0%
Volatility	55%	55%	55%	55%	55%	55%	55%	55%
Lattice Steps	1,000	1,000	1,000	1,000	1,000	1,000	1,000	1,000
Vesting Period	1.0	1.0	1.0	1.0	1.0	1.0	1.0	1.0
Suboptimal Behavior	1.80	1.80	1.80	1.80	1.80	1.80	1.80	1.80
Forfeiture Rate	**0.00%**	**2.50%**	**5.00%**	**7.50%**	**10.00%**	**12.50%**	**15.00%**	**20.00%**
Naïve BSM	$34.02	$34.02	$34.02	$34.02	$34.02	$34.02	$34.02	$34.02
Customized Binomial (Inside Forfeiture)	$22.60	$21.45	$20.40	$19.44	$18.56	$17.75	$16.99	$15.63
Customized Binomial (Outside Forfeiture)	$22.60	$22.04	$21.47	$20.91	$20.34	$19.78	$19.21	$18.08
Difference	$ 0.00	($0.58)	($1.07)	($1.46)	($1.78)	($2.03)	($2.22)	($2.45)

employee leaves, but suboptimal exercise behavior and vesting dominate the value when there are no forfeitures, and the employee's actions will depend on the rate of forfeiture and suboptimal exercise behavior multiple. This rate is applied inside the customized binomial lattice. That is, at certain nodes, the lattice value becomes worthless going forward as the option is terminated due to forfeiture. This is more applicable in real life where if an employee who holds a large ESO grant leaves, his or her ESOs become worthless going forward (in the vesting period or post-vesting if the ESO is at-the-money or out-of-the-money). In other words, each option grant has a different expected life (the point where forfeiture occurs is the point where the option's value reverts to zero or is executed if in-the-money), and the backward induction calculation used will result in different values compared to applying forfeiture rates outside the lattice.

In contrast, when used outside the lattice, this means that all grants will never be forfeited in the valuation analysis. Forfeiture adjustments will occur only afterward. In other words, all ESOs will mature and their values will be based on the total length of maturity. Then, these values are adjusted for forfeitures. This is less likely to happen in real life because this implies that all employees who are terminated or leave voluntarily will leave only at the end of the maturity period. If this were the case, then at maturity, the vesting period would have been over anyway, and by definition, employees will be able to exercise their ESOs if they are in-the-money. Thus, adjusting the forfeitures this way makes little sense. In addition, by setting the forfeiture rates outside of the lattice, any and all interactions among forfeiture, vesting, and suboptimal exercise behavior (see the examples on nonlinearity and interactions among variables provided earlier in Chapter 3) will be lost. Finally, setting the forfeiture rates outside the lattice means that the employee's employment status plays no role in determining whether an ESO will be executed. This also makes no sense. If an employee forfeits his or her ESO after being vested, he or she has a limited time to execute the options or lose them. Also, leaving the forfeiture rate outside assumes that employees will execute an ESO when the stock price exceeds the suboptimal exercise threshold regardless of their employment status, which again violates the contractual requirements in the ESO, especially when the employee has already forfeited the option.

With that said, no matter how forfeitures are applied, the higher the forfeiture rate, the lower the option value becomes. However, as seen in Table 8.3, valuing the option using forfeiture rates based on applying them internally in a lattice reduces the option value more than applying them external to the lattice, and sometimes the magnitude of this reduction is nontrivial.

SUMMARY AND KEY POINTS

- The GBM and BSM, path-dependent simulations, and binomial lattices yield the same results in plain-vanilla European call and put options, but their results differ when real-life ESO conditions are applied.
- Binomial lattices are simply discrete simulations of future stock prices.
- The higher the number of binomial lattice steps, the more precise the answer. However, the optimal number of lattice steps has to be found by conditioning for timing and convergence.
- Most ESO options can be solved in a two-lattice model.
- The principal calculations required in the binomial lattice are the stepping time, up step size, down step size, and risk-neutral probability.
- The first lattice is the evolution of the underlying stock price and proceeds from the left (present) to the right (future).
- The second lattice is the option valuation lattice and proceeds from the right (future) to the left (present) using a process called backward induction.
- Other exotic inputs enter into the analysis in the second valuation lattice.
- American call options are identical in value to European call options when there are no dividends and no exotic variables to interact with the option execution decisions. However, when dividends exist, American call options are worth a little more than their European counterparts due to their ability to execute early and before the stock price drops on the ex-dividend date.

APPENDIX 8A—BINOMIAL, TRINOMIAL, AND MULTINOMIAL LATTICES

When the term *lattices* is used, it applies not only to binomial lattices (two branches protruding from each node) but also to trinomials (three branches protruding from each node), quadranomials (four branches protruding from each node), and so forth. Lattices with greater than two nodes are usually collectively known as *multinomial lattices*. This appendix shows that the results stemming from these multinomial lattices yield identical values to those from the binomial lattices, but convergence is achieved faster in multinomial lattices. However, this benefit of faster convergence is offset by the significantly higher computational time and mathematical complexity such that the best approach is still the use of binomial lattices.

Figure 8A.1 shows a three-step recombining binomial lattice, while Figure 8A.2 shows a three-step recombining trinomial lattice.

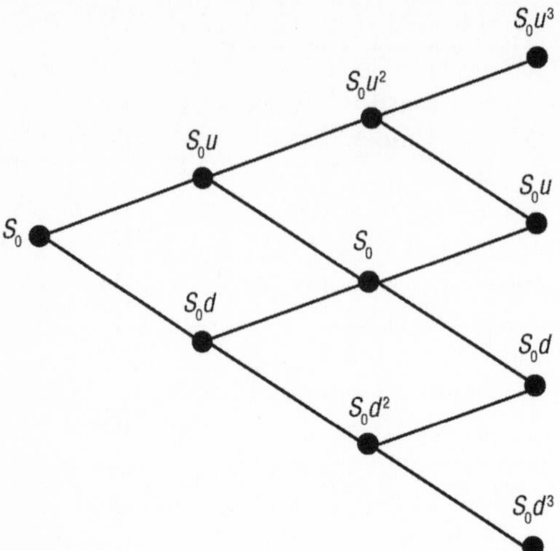

FIGURE 8A.1 Three-step recombining binomial lattice.

Clearly a binomial lattice is much easier to build than the trinomial. In terms of visualization and auditing the computations, trinomial and other multinomial lattices can become intractable very quickly. In addition, notice that all the values represented in a binomial lattice are repeated in a trinomial lattice. That is, the nodal values of both lattices—and for that matter, all multinomial lattices—are repeated from one lattice to another, regardless of how many branches stem from each node. The difference is that in order to obtain the same frequency of nodal values as in the trinomial lattices, we must add more steps to the binomial lattice.

To illustrate the comparability of results, Table 8A.1 shows the results of a simple American call option with basic inputs. Notice that convergence at \$33.66 is achieved after 1,000 steps in the trinomial lattice but 2,000 steps are required for the binomial lattice. This reduction of steps is repeated in Table 8A.2 when exotic inputs are included (suboptimal exercise behavior multiple, forfeiture rate, and vesting period). For instance, convergence at \$20.64 is achieved in the binomial lattice in 5,000 steps but only 4,000 steps are needed in the trinomial lattice.

This reduction in step size seems on the surface a modeling improvement. However, the computation time required for the trinomial lattice

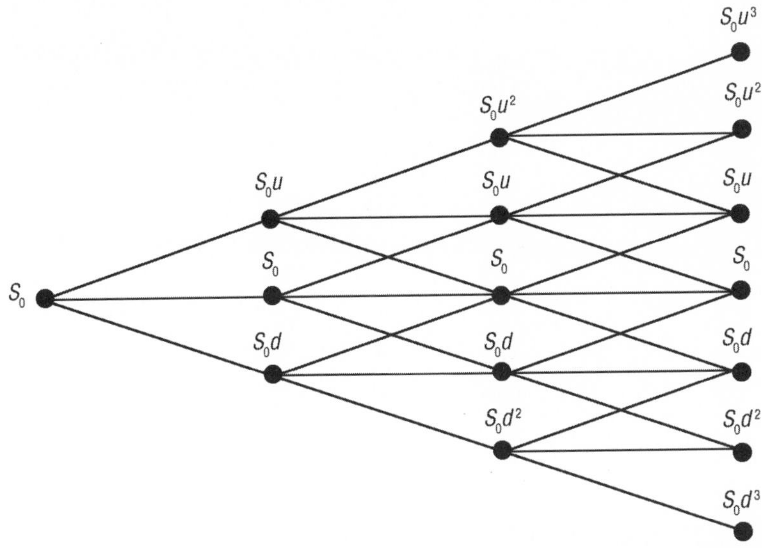

FIGURE 8A.2 Three-step recombining trinomial lattice.

is sometimes 50 to 200 times longer for the same number of steps. That is, one can compute a 5,000-step binomial lattice in about 2 to 6 seconds depending on the complexity of the model and one's computer speed, whereas it can take up to 20 minutes to compute a trinomial lattice with 4,000 steps. Seeing that the results are identical in the limit, and trinomials and other multinomial lattices take a much longer time to compute plus the math becomes much more cumbersome, it only makes sense to keep using the binomial lattice as the preferred method. Using multinomial lattices therefore provides no additional benefit. The additional granularity required (e.g., specific stock price levels falling on specific nodes) that the trinomial lattice provides can be obtained by increasing the number of binomial lattice steps. Finally, if volatility is allowed to change over time, nonrecombining lattices are required. A nonrecombining multinomial lattice becomes mathematically intractable very quickly, and even the world's fastest supercomputers cannot solve a multiple changing volatility option using nonrecombining multinomial lattices for several thousand steps within our lifetimes!

TABLE 8A.1 Binomial and Trinomial Results (Basic Inputs)

Lattice Steps	10	50	100	250	500	1,000	2,000	3,000	4,000	5,000
Binomial Lattice Value*	$33.11	$33.55	$33.60	$33.64	$33.65	$33.65	$33.66	$33.66	$33.66	$33.66
Trinomial Lattice Value*	$33.38	$33.60	$33.63	$33.65	$33.65	$33.66	$33.66	$33.66	$33.66	$33.66

*$50 stock price, $50 strike price, 10-year maturity, 5% risk-free rate, 0% dividend, and 50% volatility.

TABLE 8A.2 Binomial and Trinomial Results (Exotic Inputs)

Lattice Steps	10	50	100	250	500	1,000	2,000	3,000	4,000	5,000
Binomial Lattice Value*	$20.18	$21.00	$20.65	$20.82	$20.64	$20.72	$20.64	$20.65	$20.66	$20.64
Trinomial Lattice Value*	$20.92	$20.62	$21.03	$20.80	$20.83	$20.64	$20.72	$20.69	$20.64	$20.64

*$50 stock price, $50 strike price, 10-year maturity, 5% risk-free rate, 2% dividend, 50% volatility, 4-year vesting, 2.5 suboptimal exercise behavior multiple, and 5% forfeiture rate.

CHAPTER 9

The Model Inputs

STOCK AND STRIKE PRICE

The stock price required for the ESO valuation analysis is based on some future grant date's stock price forecast. Typically, the strike price is set to the stock price at grant date, or issued at-the-money. In an options world, the binomial lattice is created based on the evolution of the underlying stock price starting at grant date to forecast the future until the maturity date based on the underlying stock's volatility.

The forecast stock price at grant date can be obtained from various sources. The first is from the firm's own finance department and investor relations department, where stock price forecasts are usually available. These forecasts tend to be obtained using a straight-line growth approximation and can be used as a baseline. A stock price consensus of Wall Street analysts can be used as well. Sometimes, actual prices will be forecasted, and in certain other cases we can use the earnings per share (EPS), price to earnings (PE) ratio, and price to earnings growth (PEG) ratio to forecast stock prices. For instance, if the PE is expected (based on historical data) to remain flat for the term of the option, the EPS projections at the grant date can be multiplied by this PE ratio to obtain the forecast stock price. If the PE ratio is expected to grow (i.e., PEG is not zero), then the PE at grant date can be computed through the PEG. The same multiplication with the EPS can then be applied and the stock price forecast obtained.

Another approach is the use of econometric modeling. A well-prescribed method is to simulate thousands of stock price paths over time using a Brownian Motion process. Based on all the simulated paths, a probability distribution can be constructed at each time period of interest. A simple Brownian Motion can be depicted as

$$\frac{\delta S}{S} = \mu(\delta t) + \sigma\varepsilon\sqrt{\delta t}$$

where a percent change in the variable S or stock price denoted

$$\frac{\delta S}{S}$$

is simply a combination of a deterministic part ($\mu(\delta t)$) and a stochastic part $\left(\sigma\varepsilon\sqrt{\delta t}\right)$. Here, μ is a drift term or growth rate parameter that increases at a factor of time-steps δt, while σ is the volatility parameter, growing at a rate of the square root of time, and ε is a simulated variable, usually following a normal distribution with a mean of zero and a variance of one. Note that the different types of Brownian Motion are widely regarded and accepted as standard assumptions necessary for pricing options. Brownian Motions are also widely used in predicting stock prices. See Chapter 10 for example applications and results of applying the Brownian Motion process to forecast stock prices at grant date.

TIME TO MATURITY

The time to maturity for the option is probably the simplest of all to obtain. It is whatever the life of the option is based on the grant. This is the contractual life of the option, and is usually between 5 and 10 years.

RISK-FREE RATE

The risk-free rate can be obtained from the U.S. Treasury web site at www.ustreas.gov. The available rates are typically spot rates. In the analysis, if we assume a single risk-free rate over the life of the option, then a spot rate with an equivalent maturity date as the option can be used. However, if we assume that the risk-free rate will change over the life of the option, then implied forward rates need to be determined.

Spot rates are the risk-free interest rates from time zero to some time in the future. For instance, a two-year spot rate applies from year 0 to year 2, while a five-year spot rate applies from year 0 to year 5, and so forth, whereas implied forward rates can be obtained by *bootstrapping* the spot rates. Forward rates are interest rates that apply between two future periods. For instance, a one-year forward rate three years from now applies to the period from year 3 to year 4. Hence, in creating a forward yield curve or forward rates term structure, the binomial lattice valuation model can apply the relevant forward rates to discount the option value with respect to the appropriate time. For instance, using backward induction on the lattice, the lattice steps between years 9 and 10 will be discounted using the one-year forward rate nine years from now, while the lattice steps between years 8 and 9 will be discounted using the one-year forward rate eight years from now. The valuation lattice will then account for the relevant step sizes and use the pro-rated forward rate to apply the discounting.

DIVIDEND YIELD

Dividend yield is a simple input that can be obtained from corporate dividend policies. Dividend yield is the total dividend payments computed as a percentage of stock price that is paid out over the course of a year. The typical dividend yield is between 0 and 7 percent. In fact, about 45 percent of all publicly traded firms in the United States pay dividends. Of those who pay a dividend, 85 percent of them have a yield of 7 percent or below, and 95 percent of them have a yield of 10 percent or below.[1] The customized binomial lattice takes either single-point estimates of future dividends or a series of changing dividend yields. These estimates of changing yields will have to come from corporate finance departments or senior management strategies. The one major pitfall of using multiple dividend yields is that once the ESO valuation is announced (and their inputs provided) to the public, a change in dividend policy is a major signal to the stock market and stock prices will react and adjust instantly to account for this new information.[2] Hence, the stock price at grant date will no longer be valid. In addition, prematurely announcing dividend policy changes may yield undesired effects on the stock price, or would detract from the desired effects if the change in dividend policy is announced at other more strategic times. Therefore, great care should be taken when considering a series of changing dividend yields.

VOLATILITY

One of the most difficult input parameters to estimate in an ESO valuation analysis is the volatility of stock prices. Following is a review of several methods used to calculate volatility, together with a discussion of their potential advantages and shortcomings.

Logarithmic Stock Price Returns Approach

The logarithmic stock price returns approach calculates the volatility using historical closing stock prices and their corresponding logarithmic returns, as illustrated here. Starting with a series of historical stock prices, convert them into relative returns. Then take the natural logarithms of these relative returns. The standard deviation of these natural logarithm returns is the volatility of the underlying stock used in an options analysis. Notice that the number of returns is one less than the total number of periods. That is, in this example, for time periods 0 to 5, we have six stock prices but only five returns.

Time Period	Historical Stock Prices	Stock Price Relative Returns	Natural Logarithm of Stock Price Returns (*X*)
0	\$100	—	—
1	\$125	\$125/\$100 = 1.25	LN (\$125/\$100) = 0.2231
2	\$ 95	\$ 95/\$125 = 0.76	LN (\$ 95/\$125) = –0.2744
3	\$105	\$105/\$ 95 = 1.11	LN (\$105/\$ 95) = 0.1001
4	\$155	\$155/\$105 = 1.48	LN (\$155/\$105) = 0.3895
5	\$146	\$146/\$155 = 0.94	LN (\$146/\$155) = –0.0598

The volatility estimate is then calculated as

$$volatility = \sqrt{\frac{1}{n-1}\sum_{i=1}^{n}\left(x_i - \overline{x}\right)^2} = 25.58\%$$

where X is the natural logarithm of stock returns, n is the number of Xs, and $\overline{x}$ is the average X value. Clearly there are advantages and shortcomings to this simple approach. This method is very easy to implement and this approach is mathematically valid and is widely used in estimating volatility of financial assets. Remember to annualize the volatility (see the next section on *Annualizing Volatilities*).

There are several caveats in estimating volatility this way. The periodicity used (daily, weekly, and monthly closing stock prices can be used) will determine the volatility. In addition, the time period used will also skew the volatility measurements. Fortunately, the proposed FAS 123 revision provides some guidance:

> *For public companies, the length of time an entity's shares have been publicly traded [should be used to estimate the stock's volatility]. If that period is shorter than the expected term of the option, the term structure of volatility for the longest period for which trading activity is available should be more relevant.*

In addition, the requirements state that:

> *Appropriate and regular intervals for price observations should be used. If an entity considers historical volatility or implied volatility in estimating expected volatility, it should use the intervals that are appropriate based on the facts and circumstances and provide the basis for a reasonable fair value estimate. For example, a publicly traded entity might use daily price observations, while a nonpublic entity with shares that occasionally change hands at negotiated prices might use monthly price observations.*

Annualizing Volatility

No matter the approach, the volatility estimate used in an ESO analysis has to be an annualized volatility. Depending on the periodicity of the stock price data used, the volatility calculated should be converted into annualized values using $\sigma\sqrt{T}$, where T is the number of periods in a year. For instance, if the calculated volatility using monthly stock price data is 10 percent, the annualized volatility is

$$10\%\sqrt{12} = 35\%$$

This 35 percent figure should be used in the options analysis. Similarly, T is 365 for daily data (typically 250 to 256 if correcting for number of trading days), 4 for quarterly data, 2 for semiannual data, and 1 for annual data.

GARCH Model

The proposed FAS 123 requirement is fairly explicit in stating that:

> *In addition, the 2004 FAS 123 also suggests that information other than historical volatility should be used in estimating expected volatility, and explicitly notes that defaulting to historical volatility as the estimate of expected volatility without taking into consideration other available information is not appropriate.*

As such, other avenues of volatility estimates must also be considered in our due diligence. One method for estimating future volatilities is through the use of econometric models. GARCH (Generalized Autoregressive Conditional Heteroskedasticity) models are a family of econometric models that can be utilized to estimate the stock's volatility. GARCH models are used mainly in analyzing financial time-series data, in order to ascertain their conditional variances and volatilities. These volatilities are used to value options, but the amount of historical data necessary for a good volatility estimate remains significant. Usually, hundreds of data points are required to obtain good GARCH estimates. This means that firms that just went public or stocks that are infrequently and thinly traded may have insufficient data to run a GARCH model.

For instance, a GARCH (1,1) model takes the form of

$$y_t = x_t \gamma + \varepsilon_t$$
$$\sigma_t^2 = \omega + \alpha \varepsilon_{t-1}^2 + \beta \sigma_{t-1}^2$$

where the first equation's dependent variable (y_t) is a function of exogenous variables (x_t) with an error term (ε_t). The second equation estimates the variance (squared volatility σ_t^2) at time t, which depends on a historical mean (ω), news about volatility from the previous period, measured as a lag of the squared residual from the mean equation (ε_{t-1}^2), and volatility from the previous period (σ_{t-1}^2). The exact modeling specification of a GARCH model is beyond the scope of this book and will not be discussed. Suffice it to say that detailed knowledge of econometric modeling (model specification tests, structural breaks, and error estimation) is required to run a GARCH model, making it less accessible to the general analyst.

Market Proxy Approach

An often used (not to mention abused and misused) method in estimating volatility applies to publicly available market data. That is, for estimating the volatility of a particular firm's stock options, a set of market comparable firms' publicly traded stock prices are used. These firms should have functions, markets, and risks similar to those of the project under review. Then, using closing stock prices, the standard deviation of natural logarithms of relative returns is calculated. The methodology is identical to that used in the logarithm of relative stock returns approach previously alluded to. The problem with this method is the assumption that the risks inherent in comparable firms are identical to the risks inherent in the specific firm's stocks under analysis. The issue is that a firm's equity prices are subject to investor overreaction and psychology in the stock market, as well as countless other exogenous variables that are seemingly irrelevant when estimating the volatility of the target firm. In addition, the market valuation of a large public firm depends on multiple interacting and diversified projects. Therefore, using comparable firms with different internal projects may yield erroneous volatility benchmarks.

However, if no other means of measuring volatility are available (especially for firms that have just gone public where no historical data are available), or if a benchmark against estimated volatilities is required, this comparable method can be applied. Industry- or sector-specific indexes can also be used as a volatility benchmark. In fact, using an industry or market index (e.g., S&P 500, Wilshire 5000) helps firms obtain a good-enough volatility estimate, eliminating the need for fancy econometric modeling, guesswork, or subjective manipulation. Using market indices will also create a solid comparability basis among firms, while facilitating the audit process by providing more transparency to the investing public. In the author's view, this is the best and simplest approach for large-scale implementation of FAS 123.

Implied Volatilities Approach

> *The implied volatility of the share price determined from the market prices of traded options [can also be used].*

This requirement indicates that we can use market data on available stock options openly traded in the market. Long-term Equity Anticipation Securities (LEAPS) is a vehicle that can be used to estimate the underlying stock's volatility; LEAPS are long-term stock options, and when time passes such that there are six months or so remaining, LEAPS revert to regular stock options. However, due to lack of trading, the bid-ask spread on LEAPS tends to be larger than for regularly traded equities. Finding the two LEAPS closest to the stock price forecast at grant date and obtaining their implied volatilities on both bid and ask is a simple task. The implied volatilities calculated based on call options written on the firm's underlying stock can also be used. The problem is that not all stocks have LEAPS or options written on them, and if there are, the time to maturity on these vehicles may be shorter than the ESOs'.

VESTING

Almost all ESOs contain a vesting period provision whereby during the vesting period, the employee cannot exercise the option. Upon completion of the vesting period, the option then can be exercised up to and including the maturity date. If an employee is terminated or voluntarily leaves the firm during the vesting period, the ESOs automatically become worthless. The two basic types of vesting are the graded-vesting schedule and the cliff-vesting schedule. In graded vesting, a proportion of each grant is vested each month, quarter, or year. For instance, for a 48-month graded-vesting option, 1/48 of the options granted will vest every month. In a cliff-vesting option, all ESOs granted on a specific date will vest at the same time. For instance, a 6-month cliff-vesting option means that if the employee leaves the firm or is terminated during this 6-month vesting period, all of the options will expire worthless. In other situations, cliff-vesting can be coupled with graded-vesting schedules—a 48-month vesting option may have a 6-month cliff-vesting with a subsequent 42-month graded-vesting schedule. However, for the purposes of expensing the grants, each grant is divided into many *minigrants* that are issued over the course of the vesting period. The typical vesting schedules for a 10-year maturity are 48 months vesting monthly (graded vesting), and 6 months or 1 year (cliff vesting). See Chapter 6 for details on creating and allocating expense schedules based on these minigrants.

SUBOPTIMAL EXERCISE BEHAVIOR MULTIPLE

The suboptimal exercise behavior multiple is probably one of the more confusing input variables in the valuation of ESOs. This multiple is simply the ratio of the stock price when the option is exercised to the contractual strike price, and is tabulated based on historical exercise patterns. However, the historical data collected should first be refined. That is, behavior multiples right before and right after termination should be discarded. This is because employees who are terminated or leave the firm voluntarily will have a very different post-vesting behavior prior to termination, and will have a certain amount of time (typically 2 to 8 weeks) after termination to execute the vested portion of their ESO. This forced behavior is not typical of the regular employee and should not be considered in the analysis. Further, if data exist, the behaviors of senior executives should be treated separately from the rest of the employee pool. Senior executives tend to not require too much liquidity and their tenure in a company is usually more stable. For newly public firms without sufficient historical data on past employee exercise behaviors, an offsetting put option can be used instead, to account for the early exercise behavior due to the ESO's nonmarketability and nontransferability characteristics. (See Chapter 4 for details.)

The ESO valuation using the customized binomial lattice assumes that after the options have been vested, employees tend to exhibit erratic exercise behavior where an option will be exercised only if it breaches some multiple of the contractual strike price, and not before. This multiple is the suboptimal exercise behavior multiple. However, the options that have vested must be exercised within a short period if the employee leaves voluntarily or is terminated, regardless of the suboptimal behavior threshold—that is, if forfeiture occurs (measured by the historical forfeiture rates).

Research has shown that the typical suboptimal behavior multiple ranges from 1.5 to 3.0. For instance, Carpenter provided some empirical evidence that for a 10-year maturity option, the exercise multiple is 2.8 for senior executives.[3] Huddart and Lang showed that the average multiple was 2.2 for all employees, not just senior executives.[4] In addition, my own research and consulting activities show that the typical multiple lies between 1.2 and 3.0.

Because in using historical data, a large set of exercise behavior multiple data points can be obtained, rather than using a single-point estimate such as the mean or median, Monte Carlo simulation can be performed on the exercise multiple and used in conjunction with the customized binomial lattices. See Chapter 5 for details on running Monte Carlo simulations.

FORFEITURES

Forfeiture rates calculate the proportion of option grants that are forfeited per year through employee terminations or when employees leave voluntarily. Therefore, the forfeiture rate is calculated by the annualized employee turnover rate and calibrated with the proportion of option forfeitures in the past years. Forfeiture is used to condition the customized binomial lattice to zero if the employee is terminated or leaves during the vesting period. Post-vesting, the forfeiture rate is used to condition the lattice to execute the option if it is in-the-money or it is allowed to expire worthless otherwise, regardless of the suboptimal exercise behavior multiple when the employee leaves.

The higher the forfeiture rate, the higher the rate of reduction in option value, but the rate of reduction moves in a nonlinear fashion. The rate of reduction also changes depending on the vesting period. The higher the vesting period, the more significant the impact of forfeitures. This illustrates once again the nonlinear relationship between vesting and forfeitures. This is intuitive because the longer the vesting period, the lower the compounded probability that an employee will still be employed in the firm and the higher the chances of forfeiture, reducing the expected value of the option. The BSM result is the highest possible value assuming a 10-year vesting in a 10-year maturity option with zero forfeiture. Hence, if the analysis considers forfeiture rates, the option valuation will in most cases be less than the BSM result.[5]

Finally, forfeiture rates can be negatively correlated to stock price—if the firm is doing well, its stock price usually increases, making the option more valuable and making the employees less likely to leave and the firm less likely to lay off its employees. Because the rate of forfeitures is uncertain (forfeiture rate fluctuations typically occur in the past due to business and economic environments, and will most certainly fluctuate again in the future) and is negatively correlated to the stock price, it is best to apply a correlated Monte Carlo simulation on forfeiture rates in conjunction with the customized binomial lattices.

BLACKOUT PERIODS

Blackout periods are the specific dates that officers, directors, and principal stakeholders of a publicly traded corporation are restricted from executing their ESOs or participating in any equity trades. Sometimes other senior-level employees who have fiduciary duties (such as the senior accountants preparing the quarterly earnings statements, or the investor relations specialist responsible for preparing the news conference to release said statements) are also bound by the same restrictions, as prescribed in Section 16 of the 1934 Securities Act. These blackout dates typically fall anywhere from one to four weeks prior to an earnings release, to one to four weeks after an earnings release.

There are several issues to consider when it comes to blackout dates. First, for a long-term maturity option (5 to 10 years), the effects of blackouts can be negligible if they are few and far between, but can be significant if they are frequent and long (see Chapter 3 for details). In the customized binomial model, the blackout periods are converted into specific lattice step numbers, where during these periods the option cannot be executed. In the case of the high-tech and biotech industries where additional blackout restrictions are imposed, typically straddling the release of a new product, Monte Carlo simulation can be applied to simulate these discrete events and blackout periods.

LATTICE STEPS

The choice of the optimal number of lattice steps is *crucial* in obtaining a valid and robust options valuation result. To illustrate, the customized binomial lattice can be very easily conditioned to account for blackouts or non-trading days, where the holder of the option cannot execute the option even if it is in-the-money, optimal, vested, forfeited, or if the stock price exceeds the suboptimal behavior threshold. In order to condition the lattice to account for these blackouts, the lattice converts from a European option prior to vesting to an American option after the vesting period, but periodically converts back to a European option during the blackout dates. These oscillations in option types need to fall on specific lattice nodes, so the first step in lattice conditioning includes calibrating the lattice steps to include a timing aspect as well as a convergence aspect. Chapter 10 illustrates an example of calibrating the number of lattice steps to achieve convergence, while Chapter 5 shows the second part of the lattice conditioning through the use of Monte Carlo simulation to achieve a prespecified level of statistically valid result (for instance, a result that is at the 99.9 percent confidence level with a precision of $0.01).

Typically, the minimum number of lattice steps for a recombining lattice is 1,000 for obtaining valid results. For nonrecombining lattices, the number of lattice steps has to undergo more calibration to determine the optimal number. This is due to the exponential computational load required to compute a nonrecombining lattice. One simple approach to test for convergence is to progressively increase the number of steps and chart the option valuation results. Then, applying bootstrap simulation on these values, obtain the statistical distribution of the option values and determine using a hypothesis test at what step the option results have converged. Simply testing several lattice steps and choosing the one that provides the lowest option value, in my opinion, violates the essence of FAS 123. Therefore, due diligence has to be performed here.

SUMMARY AND KEY POINTS

- Stock price is determined through investor relations or corporate finance department estimates, Wall Street analyst expectations, or running path-dependent simulations.
- Strike price is usually set at the stock price level at grant date such that the ESO is issued at-the-money.
- Maturity is set contractually in the option, and is typically 5 to 10 years.
- Risk-free rate is obtained from the U.S. Treasuries web site. Spot rates are used for single-input models, whereas bootstrapped implied forward rates are used in the changing risk-free rate customized binomial lattice models.
- Dividend yield is obtained from corporate finance departments or based on corporate dividend policies, and may be allowed to change over time. Typical dividend yields are between 0 and 10 percent.
- Volatility can be estimated several ways: historical prices, GARCH modeling, market proxies, and implied volatilities from exchange-traded options and LEAPS.
- Vesting is contractually set in the option, and is typically between 1 month and 4 years in length.

- Suboptimal exercise behavior multiple is calculated using historical option executions by nonterminated employees, and is typically between 1.2 and 3.0.
- Forfeiture rates are computed via employee turnover rates and the proportion of options grants that are forfeited each year.
- Blackout periods are contractually set by the firm and are typically set several weeks before to several weeks after a major earnings announcement.
- Lattice steps should be at least 1,000 for recombining lattices, and should be calibrated with respect to their convergence levels and timing of executions.

PART Three

A Sample Case Study Applying FAS 123

CHAPTER 10

A Sample Case Study

This chapter provides an example case study with detailed empirical justifications for the input assumptions used in the ESO valuation. These inputs were obtained based on the 2004 proposed FAS 123 revision requirements and recommendations, and are used in the customized binomial lattice model. The customized binomial lattice used is a proprietary algorithm that incorporates the traditional BSM inputs (stock price, strike price, time to maturity, risk-free rate, dividend, and volatility) plus additional inputs including time to vesting, changing forfeiture rates, changing suboptimal exercise behavior multiples, blackout dates, changing risk-free rates, changing dividends, and changing volatilities over time.[1] This proprietary algorithm can be run to accommodate hundreds to thousands of lattice steps as well as incorporate Monte Carlo simulation of uncertain inputs whenever necessary. The following sections describe how each of the inputs was derived in the valuation analysis. The analysis is an excerpt from several real-life FAS 123 consulting projects. The numbers and assumptions have been changed to maintain client confidentiality but the results and conclusions are still equally valid. The case study here goes through in selecting and justifying each input parameter in the customized binomial lattice model, and showcases some of the results generated in the analysis. Some of the more analytically intensive but equally important aspects have been omitted for the sake of brevity.

STOCK PRICE AND STRIKE PRICE

The first two inputs into the customized binomial lattice are the stock price and strike price. For the ESOs issued, the strike price is always set at the stock price at grant date. This means obtaining the stock price will also yield the strike price. Table 10.1 lists the stock prices estimated by the firm's investor relations department. Conservative and aggressive closing

TABLE 10.1 Stock Price Forecast from Investor Relations

Estimate of Stock Price per Investor Relations			
	Per Share Stock Price		
Grant Date	**Conservative**	**Aggressive**	**Comment**
4-Mar-04	$37.51	$37.51	Actual
2-Apr-04	$33.40	$33.40	Actual
May-04	$34.87	$35.56	Computed
Jun-04	$36.34	$37.72	Computed
Jul-04	$37.81	$39.88	Computed
Aug-04	$39.28	$42.05	Computed
Sep-04	$40.75	$44.21	Computed
Oct-04	$42.22	$46.37	Computed
Nov-04	$43.69	$48.53	Computed
Dec-04	$45.17	$50.70	Per Investor Relations
Jan-05	$45.89	$51.52	Computed
Feb-05	$46.61	$52.34	Computed
Mar-05	$47.34	$53.16	Computed
Apr-05	$48.06	$53.98	Computed
May-05	$48.78	$54.81	Computed
Jun-05	$49.51	$55.63	Computed
Jul-05	$50.23	$56.45	Computed
Aug-05	$50.95	$57.27	Computed
Sep-05	$51.68	$58.09	Computed
Oct-05	$52.40	$58.92	Computed
Nov-05	$53.13	$59.74	Computed
Dec-05	$53.85	$60.56	Per Investor Relations

stock prices were provided for a period of 24 months, generated using growth curve estimations. For instance, the closing stock price for December 2004 is estimated to be between $45.17 and $50.70. In order to perform due diligence on the stock price forecast at grant date, several other approaches were used. Twelve analyst expectations were obtained and their results were averaged. In addition, econometric modeling with Monte Carlo simulation was used to forecast the stock price. Using a path-dependent stochastic simulation model (Figure 10.1),[2] the average stock price was forecast to be $47.22 (Figure 10.2), consistent with the investor relations stock price. The valuation analysis will use all three stock prices, and the final result used will be the average of these three stock price forecasts.

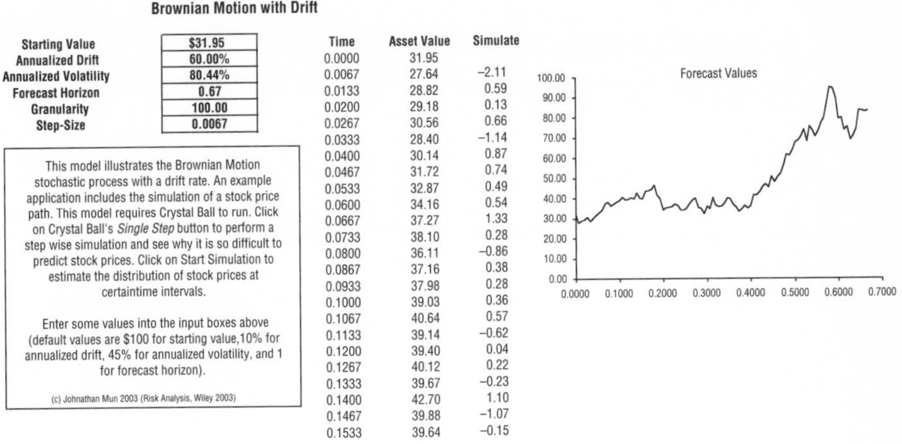

FIGURE 10.1 Stock price forecast using stochastic path-dependent simulation techniques.

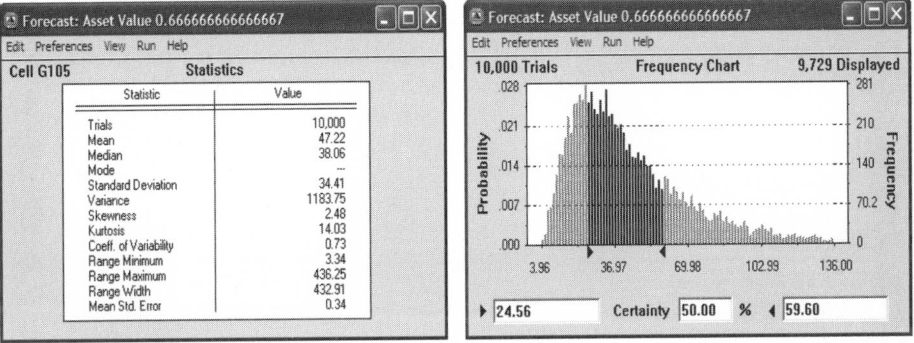

FIGURE 10.2 Results of stock price forecast using Monte Carlo simulation.

MATURITY

The next input is the option's maturity date. The contractual maturity date is 10 years on each option issue. This is consistent throughout the entire ESO plan. Therefore, 10 years is used as the input in the binomial lattice model.

RISK-FREE RATES

The next input parameter is the risk-free rate. A detailed listing of the U.S. Treasury spot yields were downloaded from www.ustreas.gov as seen in Table 10.2. Using the spot yield curve, the spot rates were bootstrapped to obtain the forward yield curve as seen in Table 10.3. Spot rates are the interest rates from time zero to some time in the future. For instance, a two-year spot rate applies from year 0 to year 2 while a five-year spot rate applies from year 0 to year 5, and so forth. However, we require the forward rates for the options valuation, which we can obtain from bootstrapping the spot rates. Forward rates are interest rates that apply between two future periods. For instance, a one-year forward rate three years from now applies to the period from year 3 to year 4. Based on the date of valuation, the highlighted risk-free rates in Table 10.3 are the rates used in the changing risk-free rate binomial lattice model (i.e., 1.21%, 2.19%, 3.21%, 3.85%, and so forth).[3]

DIVIDENDS

The firm's stocks pay no dividends, and this parameter will always be set to zero. In other cases, if dividend yields exist, these yields are entered into the model, including any expected changes to dividend policy over the life of the option.

VOLATILITY

Volatility is the next input assumption in the customized binomial lattice model. There are several ways volatility can be measured, and in the interest of full disclosure and due diligence, all methods are used in this study. Table 10.4 shows the first method used to estimate the changing volatility of the firm's stock prices using the Generalized Autoregressive Conditional Heteroskedasticity (GARCH) model. The inputs to the model are all available historical stock prices since going public. The results indicate that the standard GARCH (1,1) model is inadequate to forecast the stock's volatility due to the low R-squared,[4] low F-statistics,[5] and bad Akaike and Schwarz criterion statistics. As such, GARCH analysis is found to be unsuitable for forecasting the volatility for valuing the firm's ESOs and its results are abandoned. Only GARCH (1,1) is shown in this example. In reality, multiple other model specifications were run and analyzed.

TABLE 10.2 U.S. Treasuries Risk-Free Spot Rates

Date	1mo	3mo	6mo	1yr	2yr	3yr	5yr	7yr	10yr	20yr
2/2/2004	0.87	0.94	1.03	1.29	1.83	2.36	3.18	3.70	4.18	5.02
2/3/2004	0.93	0.94	1.02	1.27	1.78	2.30	3.12	3.65	4.13	4.98
2/4/2004	0.91	0.94	1.01	1.27	1.80	2.32	3.15	3.67	4.15	5.00
2/5/2004	0.89	0.94	1.02	1.29	1.85	2.40	3.21	3.72	4.20	5.02
2/6/2004	0.89	0.93	1.01	1.26	1.77	2.29	3.12	3.63	4.12	4.95
2/9/2004	0.89	0.94	1.02	1.25	1.76	2.26	3.08	3.60	4.09	4.93
2/10/2004	0.91	0.95	1.02	1.27	1.82	2.33	3.13	3.64	4.13	4.97
2/11/2004	0.89	0.93	1.00	1.23	1.73	2.23	3.03	3.56	4.05	4.90
2/12/2004	0.90	0.93	1.00	1.24	1.75	2.26	3.07	3.58	4.10	4.94
2/13/2004	0.90	0.92	0.98	1.21	1.70	2.19	3.01	3.54	4.05	4.92
2/17/2004	0.90	0.95	1.00	1.21	1.70	2.20	3.02	3.54	4.05	4.91
2/18/2004	0.93	0.94	1.00	1.23	1.72	2.22	3.03	3.55	4.05	4.91
2/19/2004	0.93	0.94	1.00	1.23	1.70	2.20	3.02	3.54	4.05	4.91
2/20/2004	0.93	0.94	1.01	1.26	1.75	2.25	3.08	3.59	4.10	4.96
2/23/2004	0.95	0.97	1.02	1.22	1.69	2.21	3.03	3.55	4.05	4.92
2/24/2004	0.97	0.97	1.02	1.23	1.69	2.20	3.01	3.53	4.04	4.90
2/25/2004	0.96	0.96	1.02	1.23	1.67	2.16	2.98	3.51	4.02	4.89
2/26/2004	0.97	0.96	1.02	1.23	1.69	2.18	3.01	3.54	4.05	4.92
2/27/2004	0.95	0.96	1.01	1.21	1.66	2.13	3.01	3.48	3.99	4.85

Source: http://www.ustreas.gov/offices/domestic-finance/debt-management/interest-rate/yield20040201.html.

TABLE 10.3 Forward Risk-Free Rates Resulting from Bootstrap Analysis

	Annual Forward Curve									
Years	1	2	3	4	5	6	7	8	9	10
2/2/2004	1.29%	2.37%	3.43%	4.01%	4.84%	4.75%	5.27%	4.99%	5.31%	5.63%
2/3/2004	1.27%	2.29%	3.35%	3.95%	4.78%	4.72%	5.25%	4.94%	5.26%	5.58%
2/4/2004	1.27%	2.33%	3.37%	3.99%	4.83%	4.72%	5.24%	4.96%	5.28%	5.60%
2/5/2004	1.29%	2.41%	3.51%	4.03%	4.85%	4.75%	5.26%	5.01%	5.33%	5.65%
2/6/2004	1.26%	2.28%	3.34%	3.96%	4.80%	4.66%	5.17%	4.94%	5.27%	5.60%
2/9/2004	1.25%	2.27%	3.27%	3.91%	4.74%	4.65%	5.17%	4.91%	5.24%	5.57%
2/10/2004	1.27%	2.37%	3.36%	3.94%	4.75%	4.67%	5.18%	4.95%	5.28%	5.61%
2/11/2004	1.23%	2.23%	3.24%	3.84%	4.65%	4.63%	5.16%	4.87%	5.20%	5.53%
2/12/2004	1.24%	2.26%	3.29%	3.89%	4.71%	4.61%	5.12%	4.97%	5.32%	5.67%
2/13/2004	1.21%	2.19%	3.18%	3.84%	4.67%	4.61%	5.14%	4.91%	5.25%	5.59%
2/17/2004	1.21%	2.19%	3.21%	3.85%	4.68%	4.59%	5.11%	4.91%	5.25%	5.59%
2/18/2004	1.23%	2.21%	3.23%	3.85%	4.67%	4.60%	5.12%	4.89%	5.23%	5.56%
2/19/2004	1.23%	2.17%	3.21%	3.85%	4.68%	4.59%	5.11%	4.91%	5.25%	5.59%
2/20/2004	1.26%	2.24%	3.26%	3.92%	4.76%	4.62%	5.13%	4.96%	5.30%	5.64%
2/23/2004	1.22%	2.16%	3.26%	3.86%	4.69%	4.60%	5.12%	4.89%	5.23%	5.56%
2/24/2004	1.23%	2.15%	3.23%	3.83%	4.65%	4.58%	5.10%	4.90%	5.24%	5.58%
2/25/2004	1.23%	2.11%	3.15%	3.81%	4.64%	4.58%	5.11%	4.88%	5.22%	5.56%
2/26/2004	1.23%	2.15%	3.17%	3.85%	4.69%	4.61%	5.14%	4.91%	5.25%	5.59%
2/27/2004	1.21%	2.11%	3.08%	3.90%	4.79%	4.43%	4.90%	4.85%	5.19%	5.53%

TABLE 10.4 Generalized Autoregressive Conditional Heteroskedasticity for Forecasting Volatility

Dependent Variable: LOGRETURNS
Method: ML–ARCH
Date: 04/10/04 Time: 10:48
Sample: 1901 2603
Included observations: 703
Convergence achieved after 30 iterations

	Coefficient	Std. Error	z-Statistic	Prob.
GARCH	–4.36065	1.794356	–2.430222	0.0151
C	0.004958	0.002188	2.266192	0.0234
	Variance Equation			
C	3.10E-07	2.12E-06	0.145964	0.8839
ARCH(1)	0.031233	0.005472	5.707787	0.0000
GARCH(1)	0.971900	0.004750	204.5979	0.0000

R-squared	0.010575	Mean dependent var	–0.001054
Adjusted R-squared	0.004905	S.D. dependent var	0.038647
S.E. of regression	0.038552	Akaike info criterion	–3.841624
Sum squared resid	1.037432	Schwarz criterion	–3.809224
Log likelihood	1355.311	F-statistic	1.865084
Durbin-Watson stat	2.125897	Prob(F-statistic)	0.114774

Two additional approaches are used to estimate volatility. The first is to use historical stock prices for the last quarter, last one year, last two years, and last four years (equivalent to the vesting period). These closing prices are then converted to natural logarithmic returns and their sample standard deviations are then annualized to obtain the annualized volatilities seen in Table 10.5.[6]

In addition, Long-term Equity Anticipation Securities (LEAPS) can be used to estimate the underlying stock's volatility. LEAPS are long-term stock options, and when time passes such that there are six months or so remaining, LEAPS revert to regular stock options. However, due to lack of trading, the bid-ask spread on LEAPS tends to be larger than for regularly traded equities. Table 10.5 lists the two LEAPS closest to the stock price forecast at grant date. Implied volatilities on both bid and ask are listed in Table 10.5.

After performing due diligence on the estimation of volatilities, it is found that a GARCH econometric model was insufficiently specified to be of statistical validity. Hence, we reverted back to using the implied volatilities of long-

TABLE 10.5 Volatility Estimates

	Volatility
4 Years	72.50%
2 Years	58.00%
1 Year	46.25%
Quarter	43.55%
LEAP: $45 Bid	45.50%
LEAP: $45 Ask	47.50%
LEAP: $50 Bid	41.50%
LEAP: $50 Ask	44.50%
Volatility Inputs: Triangular distribution with the following parameters into Monte Carlo simulation	
Min	41.50%
Average	49.91%
Max	72.50%

term options or LEAPS, and compared them with historical volatilities. The best single-point estimate of the volatility going forward would be an average of all estimates or 49.91 percent as shown in Table 10.5. However, due to this large spread, Monte Carlo simulation was applied by running a simulation on these volatility rates; thus, every volatility calculated here will be used in the analysis. For the purposes of benchmarking, the Wilshire 5000 and Standard & Poors 500 indices for the same period were found to be 20.7% and 20.5% respectively. The firm's stock price has a stable beta of 2.3, making the beta-adjusted volatility 47%, which falls within the calculated volatility range.

VESTING

All ESOs granted by the firm vest in two different tranches: one month and six months. The former are options granted over a period of 48 months, where each month 1/48 of the options vest, until the fourth year when all options are fully vested. The latter is a cliff-vesting grant, where if the employee leaves within the first six months, the entire option grant is forfeited. After the six months, each additional month vests 1/42 additional portions of the options. Consequently, one-month (1/12 years) and six-month (1/2 year) vesting are used as inputs in the analysis. The results of the analysis are simply the valuation of the options. To obtain the actual expenses, each 48-

month vesting option is divided into 48 *minigrants* and expensed over the vesting period. See Chapter 6 for details on allocating expense schedules.

SUBOPTIMAL EXERCISE BEHAVIOR MULTIPLE

The next input is the suboptimal exercise behavior multiple. In order to obtain this input, data on all options exercised within the past year were collected. We used the past year, as trading from 2000 to 2002 was highly volatile and we believe the high-tech bubble caused extreme events in the stock market to occur that were not representative of our expectations of the future. In addition, only the past year's data are available. Figure 10.3 illustrates the calculations performed. (The table is truncated to save space.) The suboptimal exercise behavior multiple is simply the ratio of the stock price when it was exercised to the contractual strike price of the option. Terminated employees or employees who left voluntarily were excluded from the analysis. This is because employees who leave the firm have a limited time to execute the portion of their options that have vested. In addition, all unvested options will expire worthless. Finally, employees who decide to leave the firm would have potentially known this in advance and hence have a different exercise behavior than a regular employee. Suboptimal exercise behavior does not play a role under these circumstances. The event of an employee leaving is instead captured in the rate of forfeiture. The median behavior multiple is found to be 1.85, and is the input used in the analysis.

The median is used as opposed to the mean value because the distribution is highly skewed (the coefficient of skewness is 39.9), and as means are highly susceptible to outliers, the median is preferred. Figure 10.3's histogram shows that the median is much more representative of the central tendency of the distribution than the average or mean. In order to verify that this is the case, two additional approaches are applied to validate the use of the median: trimmed ranges and statistical hypothesis tests. Table 10.6 illustrates a trimmed range where the range of the suboptimal exercise behavior multiple such that the option holder will exercise at a stock price exceeding $500 is ignored. This is justified because given the current stock price it is highly improbable that it will exceed this $500 threshold.[7] The median calculated using this subjective trimming is 1.84, close to the initial global median of 1.85.

In addition, a more objective analysis, the statistical hypothesis test, was performed using the single-variable one-tailed t-test, and the 99.99th statistical percentile (alpha of 0.0001) from the t-distribution (the t-distribution was used to account for the distribution's skew and kurtosis—its extreme values and fat tails) was found to be 3.92 (Table 10.7). The median calculated from the suboptimal exercise behavior range between 1.0 and 3.92 yielded 1.76.

Employee ID	Option Number	Exercise Date	Shares	Value Basis	Option Price	Grant Date	Termination Date	Behavior Multiplier
38509	10518	08/28/2003	469	$34.2900	$11.3333	08/05/98		3.0256
59850	89961	08/28/2003	2,269	$34.2900	$15.1389	02/16/99		2.2650
88519	95867	09/03/2003	2,194	$36.9200	$28.7200	08/31/01		1.2855
1942	41038	12/31/2003	352	$37.2000	$16.2600	11/19/02		2.2878
86393	14289	12/31/2003	488	$37.2000	$28.7200	08/31/01		1.2953
24881	5025	09/29/2003	2,108	$32.4600	$21.8055	08/10/99		1.4886
3722	16831	10/28/2003	880	$37.2600	$16.2600	11/19/02		2.2915
22351	2200	08/28/2003	127	$33.5000	$16.2600	11/19/02	03/16/04	
28862	34637	07/28/2003	99	$30.6000	$16.2600	11/19/02		1.8819
55587	36058	10/30/2003	29	$37.5400	$16.2600	11/19/02		2.3087
37498	35882	10/30/2003	155	$37.5400	$19.0600	04/04/03		1.9696
91075	46869	07/28/2003	309	$30.6000	$19.0600	04/04/03		1.6055
42903	30738	12/01/2003	300	$38.2784	$17.7100	11/04/02	04/09/04	
97583	80763	09/02/2003	20	$34.5000	$16.2600	11/19/02		2.1218
99128	25998	09/03/2003	224	$36.0000	$16.2600	11/19/02		2.2140
95193	5817	09/02/2003	23	$34.5000	$28.7200	08/31/01		1.2013
70651	81744	11/14/2003	2,000	$36.5700	$11.1389	07/15/98		3.2831
97264	46899	11/24/2003	1,000	$36.7800	$11.1389	07/15/98		3.3019
30371	75145	12/15/2003	511	$37.1700	$11.1389	07/15/98		3.3370
35472	77678	12/30/2003	1,500	$37.2850	$11.1389	07/15/98		3.3473
7897	20244	12/15/2003	1,000	$37.1550	$11.1389	07/15/98		3.3356
687	36156	10/30/2003	1,100	$37.5400	$28.7200	08/31/01		1.3071

Max	160.5263
Min	1.0000
Average	3.3576
Median	1.8530

Note: Do not include terminated behavior

FIGURE 10.3 Estimating suboptimal exercise behavior multiples (table truncated).

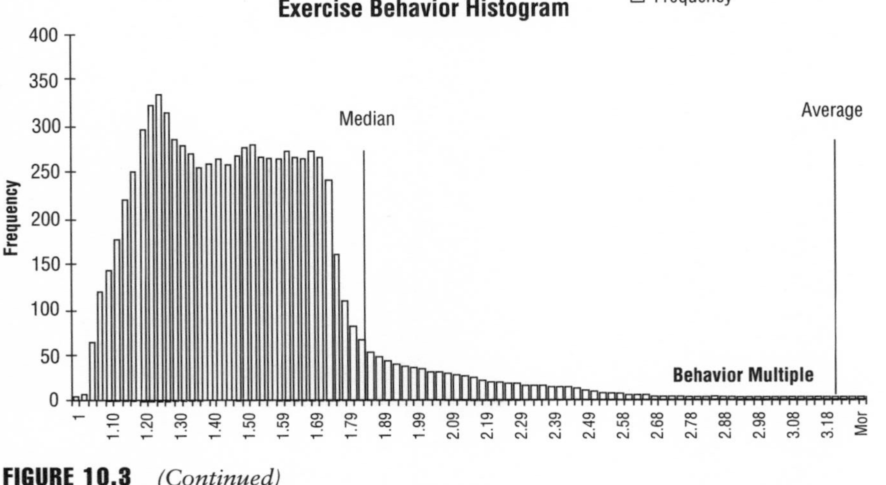

FIGURE 10.3 *(Continued)*

TABLE 10.6 Estimating Suboptimal Exercise Behavior Multiple with Trimmed Ranges (Table Truncated)

Behavior Multiplier		Untrimmed	> = $500 Trimmed	
	Average	3.3576	2.3462	
160.5263	**Median**	1.8530	1.8450	
151.9787	Note: Do not include terminated behavior.			
135.4962				
127.7468	At a stock price of $33.18, the multiple is too high!			
119.1431	We trim outliers above a stock price of $500 as unreasonable.			
66.5517	Exercise if exceeding $2,208.19			<<--data not used
66.5517	Exercise if exceeding $2,208.19			
66.5517	Exercise if exceeding $2,208.19			
66.5517	Exercise if exceeding $2,208.19			
66.5517	Exercise if exceeding $2,208.19			
66.1379	Exercise if exceeding $2,194.46			
66.1379	Exercise if exceeding $2,194.46			
65.9437	Exercise if exceeding $2,188.01			
65.3793	Exercise if exceeding $2,169.29			
64.7759	Exercise if exceeding $2,149.26			
64.5837	Exercise if exceeding $2,142.89			<<--rows hidden to
64.5837	Exercise if exceeding $2,142.89			conserve space
15.1412	Exercise if exceeding $502.39			
15.1185	Exercise if exceeding $501.63			
15.0910	Exercise if exceeding $500.72			
15.0737	Exercise if exceeding $500.15			<<--data not used
14.9927	Exercise if exceeding $497.46			<<--data used
14.9287	Exercise if exceeding $495.33			
14.9145	Exercise if exceeding $494.86			
14.8723	Exercise if exceeding $493.46			
14.8499	Exercise if exceeding $492.72			
14.8433	Exercise if exceeding $492.50			
14.8156	Exercise if exceeding $491.58			
14.7880	Exercise if exceeding $490.67			
14.7847	Exercise if exceeding $490.55			
14.7780	Exercise if exceeding $490.34			<<--data used

TABLE 10.7 Estimating Suboptimal Exercise Behavior Multiples with Statistical Hypothesis Tests

One-Sample Hypothesis t-Test:
Suboptimal Exercise Behavior
Test of null hypothesis: mean = 3.754
Test of alternate hypothesis: mean < 3.754
Alpha one-tail of 1%

Variable	N	Mean	StDev	SE Mean
Behavior	8,530	3.469	11.312	0.122

Variable	99.99%	Upper Bound	T	P
Behavior		3.925	–2.33	0.01

Therefore, the 99.99th statistical percentile cut-off is 3.925.

The average for the range between 1.000 and 3.925 is

Average	1.7954
Median	1.7689

Therefore, with the three values indicating a suboptimal behavior multiple at around 1.7689, 1.8450 and 1.8531, using the median of all data points provides the best indication as all data are used . . .
The resulting suboptimal behavior multiple used is
Global Median 1.8531

We therefore conclude that using the global median of 1.85 is the most conservative and best represents the employees' suboptimal exercise behavior.[8]

FORFEITURE RATE

The rate of forfeiture is calculated by comparing the number of grants that were canceled to the total number of grants. This value is calculated on a monthly basis and the results are shown in Table 10.8. The average forfeiture rate is calculated to be 5.51 percent. In addition, the average employee turnover rate for the past four years was 5.5 percent annually. Therefore, 5.51 percent is used in the analysis.

NUMBER OF STEPS

The higher the number of lattice steps, the higher the precision of the results. Figure 10.4 illustrates the convergence of results obtained using a BSM closed-form model on a European call option without dividends, and

TABLE 10.8 Estimating Forfeiture Rates (Table Truncated)

Cancellations							Sum 241,374	Count 133		Years 0.34
Name	ID	Number	Grant Date	Plan	Cancel Date	Cancel Reason	Shares	Price	Total Price	Days to Cancellation
	18292	NI273832	8/4/2003	2003	12/31/2003	Termination-Voluntary	4,300	$30.8800	$132,784.00	149
	18159	00273892	8/4/2003	2003	12/31/2003	Termination-Involuntary	330	$30.8800	$ 10,190.40	149
	16794	00273401	7/25/2003	2003	12/31/2003	Termination-Voluntary	2,000	$30.7600	$ 61,520.00	159
	16807	NI273719	7/25/2003	2003	12/31/2003	Termination-Voluntary	2,000	$30.7600	$ 61,520.00	159
	16666	00273415	7/25/2003	2003	12/31/2003	Termination-Involuntary	2,000	$30.7600	$ 61,520.00	159
	16666	00273771	7/25/2003	2003	12/31/2003	Termination-Involuntary	3,134	$30.7600	$ 96,401.84	159
	18023	00273288	7/3/2003	2003	12/31/2003	Termination-Voluntary	4,900	$29.4200	$144,158.00	181
	5257	00273015	5/2/2003	1993	12/31/2003	Termination-Voluntary	333	$23.6900	$ 7,888.77	243
	17598	NI272903	5/2/2003	1993	12/31/2003	Termination-Voluntary	2,916	$23.6900	$ 69,080.04	243
	16897	00273721	7/25/2003	2003	12/26/2003	Termination-Voluntary	2,750	$30.7600	$ 84,590.00	154
	17063	P0002027	6/26/2003	PR98	12/26/2003	Termination-Voluntary	404	$28.4600	$ 11,497.84	183
	16897	P0001979	4/1/2003	PR98	12/26/2003	Termination-Voluntary	2,022	$24.6300	$ 49,801.86	269
	8092	NI273111	6/4/2003	2003	12/23/2003	Termination-Voluntary	1,281	$28.4590	$ 36,455.98	202
	19094	00274451	12/4/2003	2003	12/22/2003	Termination-Voluntary	5,600	$37.3200	$208,992.00	18
	5428	00272981	5/2/2003	1993	12/19/2003	Termination-Voluntary	462	$23.6900	$ 10,944.78	231
	5428	00272795	4/4/2003	1993	12/19/2003	Termination-Voluntary	462	$19.0600	$ 8,805.72	259
	18103	00273913	8/4/2003	2003	12/15/2003	Termination-Voluntary	8	$30.8800	$ 247.04	133
	8102	NI272622	3/4/2003	1993	12/9/2003	Termination-Voluntary	396	$16.0600	$ 6,359.76	280
	5361	00273024	5/2/2003	1993	12/5/2003	Termination-Voluntary	875	$23.6900	$ 20,728.75	217
	18911	00274455	12/4/2003	2003	12/4/2003	Termination-Voluntary	750	$37.3200	$ 27,990.00	0
	17840	00273283	7/3/2003	2003	12/4/2003	Termination-Voluntary	3,500	$29.4200	$102,970.00	154
	18721	00274339	11/4/2003	2003	12/3/2003	Termination-Involuntary	900	$37.0500	$ 33,345.00	29

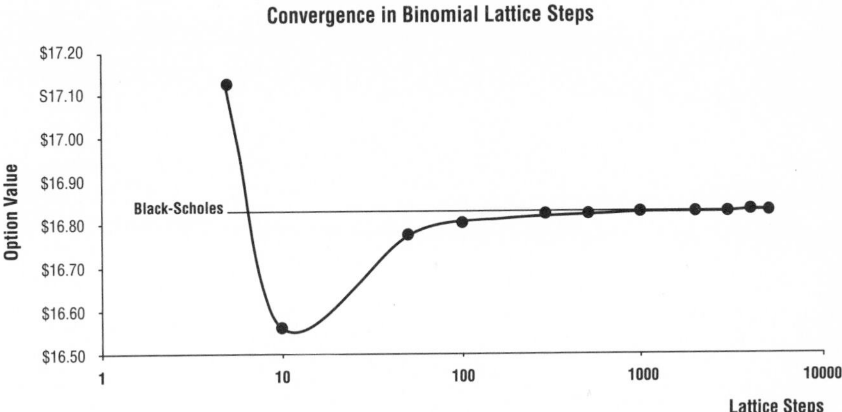

FIGURE 10.4 Convergence of the binomial lattice to closed-form solutions.

comparing its results to the basic binomial lattice. Convergence is generally achieved at 1,000 steps. As such, the analysis results will use 1,000 steps whenever possible.[9] Due to the high number of steps required to generate the results, software-based mathematical algorithms are used.[10] For instance, a nonrecombining binomial lattice with 1,000 steps has a total of 2×10^{301} nodal calculations to perform, making manual computation impossible without the use of specialized algorithms.[11]

Table 10.9 illustrates the calculation of convergence by using progressively higher lattice steps. The progression is based on sets of 120 steps (12 months per year multiplied by 10 years). The results are tabulated and the median of the average results is calculated. It shows that 4,200 steps is the best estimate in this customized binomial lattice, and this input is used throughout the analysis.[12]

RESULTS AND CONCLUSIONS

Using the customized binomial lattice methodology coupled with Monte Carlo simulation, the fair-market values of the options at different grant dates and different forecast stock prices are listed in Table 10.10. For instance, the grant date of January 2005 has a conservative stock price forecast of $45.17 and its resulting binomial lattice result is $17.39 for the one-month-vesting option, and $17.42 for the six-month-vesting option. In contrast, if we modified the BSM to use the expected life of the option (which was set to the lowest possible value of four years, equivalent to the vesting period of four years),[13] the option's value is still significantly

TABLE 10.9 Convergence of the Customized Binomial Lattice (Table Truncated)

Stock Price	$45.17	$45.17	$45.17	$45.17	$45.17	$45.17	$45.17	$45.17	$45.17	$45.17	$45.17	$45.17	$45.17	$45.17
Strike Price	$45.17	$45.17	$45.17	$45.17	$45.17	$45.17	$45.17	$45.17	$45.17	$45.17	$45.17	$45.17	$45.17	$45.17
Maturity	10	10	10	10	10	10	10	10	10	10	10	10	10	10
Risk-Free Rate	1.21%	1.21%	1.21%	1.21%	1.21%	1.21%	1.21%	1.21%	1.21%	1.21%	1.21%	1.21%	1.21%	1.21%
Volatility	49.91%	49.91%	49.91%	49.91%	49.91%	49.91%	49.91%	49.91%	49.91%	49.91%	49.91%	49.91%	49.91%	49.91%
Dividend	0%	0%	0%	0%	0%	0%	0%	0%	0%	0%	0%	0%	0%	0%
Lattice Steps	10	50	100	120	600	1,200	1,800	2,400	3,000	3,600	4,200	4,800	5,400	6,000
Suboptimal Behavior	1.8531	1.8531	1.8531	1.8531	1.8531	1.8531	1.8531	1.8531	1.8531	1.8531	1.8531	1.8531	1.8531	1.8531
Vesting	0.08	0.08	0.08	0.08	0.08	0.08	0.08	0.08	0.08	0.08	0.08	0.08	0.08	0.08
Binomial Option Value	$20.55	$17.82	$17.32	$18.55	$17.55	$13.08	$13.11	$12.93	$12.88	$12.91	$13.00	$13.08	$12.93	$13.06

Segments	Steps	Results	Average
1	120	$18.55	$13.91
5	600	$17.55	$13.45
10	1,200	$13.08	$13.00
15	1,800	$13.11	$12.99
20	2,400	$12.93	$12.97
25	3,000	$12.88	$12.97
30	3,600	$12.91	$12.99
35	4,200	$13.00	$13.00
40	4,800	$13.08	$13.02
45	5,400	$12.93	$12.99
50	6,000	$13.06	$13.06
		Median	$13.00

TABLE 10.10 Analytical Customized Binomial Lattice Results (Table Truncated)

	Per Share Closing Stock Price				48 Months Vest		6 Month Cliff and then 42 Month Vest	
Date	Conservative	Aggressive	Average		New Hire Grant	Acquisition	Focal	Total
End Dec 04/Start Jan 05	$45.17	$50.70	$47.93	**Jan-05**	550,000			550,000
End Jan 05/Start Feb 05	$45.89	$51.52	$48.70	February	550,000			550,000
End Feb/Start Mar	$46.61	$52.34	$49.48	March	550,000			550,000
End Mar/Start Apr	$47.34	$53.16	$50.25	April	550,000			550,000
End Apr/Start May	$48.06	$53.98	$51.02	May	550,000			550,000
End May/Start Jun	$48.78	$54.81	$51.79	June	605,000			605,000
End Jun/Start July	$49.51	$55.63	$52.57	July	605,000			605,000
End July/Start Aug	$50.23	$56.45	$53.34	August	605,000			605,000
End Aug/Start Sep	$50.95	$57.27	$54.11	September	605,000	2,500,000		3,105,000
End Sep/Start Oct	$51.58	$58.09	$54.89	October	605,000			605,000
End Oct/Start Nov	$52.40	$58.92	$55.66	November	605,000		7,492,100	8,097,100
End Nov/Start Dec	$53.13	$59.74	$56.43	December	605,000			605,000
End Dec/Start Jan 06	$53.85	$60.56	$57.20	**Jan-06**	605,000			605,000
End Jan 06/Start Feb 06	$54.55	$61.36	$57.95	February	605,000			605,000
End February/Start March	$55.25	$62.15	$58.70	March	605,000			605,000
End March/Start Apr	$55.95	$62.95	$59.45	April	605,000			605,000
End Apr/Start May	$56.66	$63.75	$60.20	May	605,000			605,000
End May/Start Jun	$57.36	$64.55	$60.95	June	665,500			665,500
End Jun/Start July	$58.06	$65.34	$61.70	July	665,500			665,500
End July/Start Aug	$58.76	$66.14	$62.45	August	665,500			665,500
End Aug/Start Sep	$59.46	$66.94	$63.20	September	665,500	3,000,000		3,665,500
End Sep/Start Oct	$60.16	$67.74	$63.95	October	665,500			665,500
End Oct/Start Nov	$60.87	$68.53	$64.70	November	665,500		8,241,310	8,906,810
End Nov/Start Dec	$61.57	$69.33	$65.45	December	665,500			665,500

TABLE 10.10 *(Continued)*

	Options Valuation (Monthly)				Options Valuation (Cliff Vesting)		
Date	Conservative	Aggressive	Average	Date	Conservative	Aggressive	Average
Jan-05	$17.39	$19.52	$18.46	**Jan-05**	$17.42	$19.55	$18.49
February	$17.67	$19.84	$18.76	February	$17.70	$19.87	$18.78
March	$17.95	$20.16	$19.05	March	$17.98	$20.19	$19.08
April	$18.23	$20.47	$19.35	April	$18.26	$20.50	$19.38
May	$18.51	$20.79	$19.65	May	$18.54	$20.82	$19.68
June	$18.79	$21.11	$19.95	June	$18.81	$21.14	$19.98
July	$19.06	$21.42	$20.24	July	$19.09	$21.45	$20.27
August	$19.34	$21.74	$20.54	August	$19.37	$21.77	$20.57
September	$19.62	$22.05	$20.84	September	$19.65	$22.09	$20.87
October	$19.90	$22.37	$21.14	October	$19.93	$22.41	$21.17
November	$20.18	$22.69	$21.43	November	$20.21	$22.72	$21.47
December	$20.46	$23.00	$21.73	December	$20.49	$23.04	$21.76
Jan-06	$20.74	$23.32	$22.03	**Jan-06**	$20.77	$23.36	$22.06
February	$21.01	$23.63	$22.32	February	$21.04	$23.66	$22.35
March	$21.28	$23.94	$22.61	March	$21.31	$23.97	$22.64
April	$21.55	$24.24	$22.89	April	$21.58	$24.28	$22.93
May	$21.82	$24.55	$23.18	May	$21.85	$24.59	$23.22
June	$22.09	$24.86	$23.47	June	$22.12	$24.89	$23.51
July	$22.36	$25.16	$23.76	July	$22.39	$25.20	$23.80
August	$22.63	$25.47	$24.05	August	$22.66	$25.51	$24.09
September	$22.90	$25.78	$24.34	September	$22.93	$25.82	$24.38
October	$23.17	$26.09	$24.63	October	$23.20	$26.12	$24.66
November	$23.44	$26.39	$24.92	November	$23.47	$26.43	$24.95
December	$23.71	$26.70	$25.20	December	$23.75	$26.74	$25.24

TABLE 10.10 *(Continued)*

	Total Options Expense (Binomial): $813,997,675.53				Options Valuation (Black-Scholes)		
Date	Conservative	Aggressive	Average	Date	Conservative	Aggressive	Average
Jan-05	$ 9,566,052.74	$ 10,737,306.72	$ 10,151,679.73	**Jan-05**	$19.55	$21.94	$20.75
February	$ 9,719,311.21	$ 10,911,406.31	$ 10,315,358.76	February	$19.86	$22.30	$21.08
March	$ 9,872,590.87	$ 11,085,484.73	$ 10,479,07.80	March	$20.18	$22.66	$21.42
April	$ 10,025,849.35	$ 11,259,584.33	$ 10,642,716.84	April	$20.49	$23.01	$21.75
May	$ 10,179,107.83	$ 11,433,662.74	$ 10,806,395.88	May	$20.80	$23.37	$22.09
June	$ 11,365,602.93	$ 12,768,538.58	$ 12,067,082.40	June	$21.12	$23.72	$22.42
July	$ 11,534,210.56	$ 12,960,024.83	$ 12,247,106.05	July	$21.43	$24.08	$22.75
August	$ 11,702,794.88	$ 13,151,534.39	$ 12,427,152.99	August	$21.74	$24.43	$23.09
September	$ 60,926,665.19	$ 68,479,589.19	$ 64,703,067.40	September	$22.06	$24.79	$23.42
October	$ 12,039,963.53	$ 13,534,530.21	$ 12,787,246.87	October	$22.37	$25.15	$23.76
November	$163,625,443.32	$183,963,675.91	$173,794,559.61	November	$22.68	$25.50	$24.09
December	$ 12,377,155.48	$ 13,917,526.02	$ 13,147,340.75	December	$23.00	$25.86	$24.43
Jan-06	$ 12,545,739.81	$ 14,109,035.58	$ 13,327,387.69	**Jan-06**	$23.31	$26.21	$24.76
February	$ 12,709,221.87	$ 25,395,860.42	$ 13,502,052.80	February	$23.61	$26.56	$25.09
March	$ 12,872,727.23	$ 14,480,685.27	$ 13,676,694.60	March	$23.92	$26.90	$25.41
April	$ 13,036,232.59	$ 14,666,510.11	$ 13,851,359.70	April	$24.22	$27.25	$25.73
May	$ 13,199,714.65	$ 14,852,311.66	$ 14,026,024.81	May	$24.52	$27.59	$26.06
June	$ 14,699,542.02	$ 16,541,950.16	$ 15,620,733.27	June	$24.83	$27.94	$26.38
July	$ 14,879,372.29	$ 16,746,357.48	$ 15,812,864.89	July	$25.13	$28.28	$26.71
August	$ 15,059,202.56	$ 16,950,764.81	$ 16,004,996.50	August	$25.44	$28.63	$27.03
September	$ 83,935,039.46	$ 94,488,780.60	$ 89,211,839.45	September	$25.74	$28.98	$27.36
October	$ 15,418,914.35	$ 17,359,579.47	$ 16,389,234.10	October	$26.04	$29.32	$27.68
November	$209,062,661.14	$235,401,537.28	$222,232,270.95	November	$26.35	$29.67	$28.01
December	$ 15,778,600.52	$ 17,768,368.50	$ 16,773,471.70	December	$26.65	$30.01	$28.33

TABLE 10.10 *(Continued)*

	Total Options Expense (Black-Scholes): $914,341,297.69			Main Input Assumptions & Results		
Date	**Conservative**	**Aggressive**	**Average**	**Year**	**Risk-free Rate**	
Jan-05	$ 10,752,660.26	$ 12,069,200.79	$ 11,410,930.53	1	1.21%	
February	$ 10,924,929.47	$ 12,264,896.33	$ 11,594,912.90	2	2.19%	
March	$ 11,097,222.49	$ 12,460,568.06	$ 11,778,895.27	3	3.21%	
April	$ 11,269,491.70	$ 12,656,263.59	$ 11,962,877.65	4	3.85%	
May	$ 11,441,760.91	$ 12,851,935.32	$ 12,146,860.02	5	4.68%	
June	$ 12,775,433.13	$ 14,352,393.94	$ 13,563,926.63	6	4.59%	
July	$ 12,964,955.45	$ 14,567,632.85	$ 13,766,281.05	7	5.11%	
August	$ 13,154,451.58	$ 14,782,897.94	$ 13,968,661.66	8	4.91%	
September	$ 68,484,227.49	$ 76,974,043.30	$ 72,729,068.19	9	5.25%	
October	$ 13,533,443.84	$ 15,213,401.93	$ 14,373,422.88	10	5.59%	
November	$183,662,838.36	$206,491,668.93	$195,077,253.65			
December	$ 13,912,462.28	$ 15,643,905.92	$ 14,778,184.10	Time to Maturity		10
Jan-06	$ 14,101,958.41	$ 15,859,171.01	$ 14,980,564.71	Dividend		0.00%
February	$ 14,285,719.38	$ 16,068,046.23	$ 15,178,895.90	Volatility		49.91%
March	$ 14,469,506.53	$ 16,276,921.46	$ 15,373,200.90	Suboptimal Behavior		1.8531
April	$ 14,653,293.69	$ 16,485,796.69	$ 15,569,532.90	Forfeiture Rate		5.51%
May	$ 14,837,054.65	$ 16,694,645.72	$ 15,765,863.28	Vesting		1 month and 6 months
June	$ 16,522,925.99	$ 18,593,873.04	$ 17,558,386.11	Steps		4,200
July	$ 16,725,063.05	$ 18,823,635.79	$ 17,774,349.42	Total Black-Scholes		$914,341,298
August	$ 16,927,200.11	$ 19,053,398.54	$ 17,990,313.73	Total Binomial		$813,997,676
September	$ 94,346,643.11	$106,209,508.20	$100,277,996.32	Adjusted Black-Scholes		$863,961,092
October	$ 17,331,531.85	$ 19,512,924.04	$ 18,422,213.54	Difference		($ 49,963,417)
November	$234,664,248.79	$264,228,555.25	$249,446,594.79			
December	$ 17,735,834.78	$ 19,972,420.73	$ 18,854,113.35			

higher at $19.55. This is a $2.16 cost reduction compared to using the BSM, or a 12.42 percent reduction in cost for this simple option alone. When all the options are calculated and multiplied by their respective grants, the total *valuation* under the traditional BSM is $863,961,092 after accounting for the 5.51 percent forfeiture rate. In contrast, the total *valuation* for the customized binomial lattice is $813,997,676, a reduction of $49,963,417 over the period of two years. Figure 10.5 and Table 10.11 show one sample calculation in detail.

Figure 10.5 illustrates a sample result from a 124,900-trial Monte Carlo simulation run on the customized binomial lattice where the error is within $0.01 with a 99.9 percent statistical confidence that the fair-market value of the option granted at January 2005 is $17.39. Each grant illustrated in Table 10.10 will have its own simulation result like the one in Figure 10.5.

The example illustrated in Table 10.11 shows a naïve BSM result of $26.91 versus a binomial lattice result of $17.39 (the BSM using an adjusted four-year life is $19.55). This $9.52 differential can be explained by contribution in parts. In order to understand this lower option value as compared to the naïve BSM results, Table 10.12 illustrates the contribution to options valuation reduction.

The difference between the naïve BSM valuation of $26.91 versus a

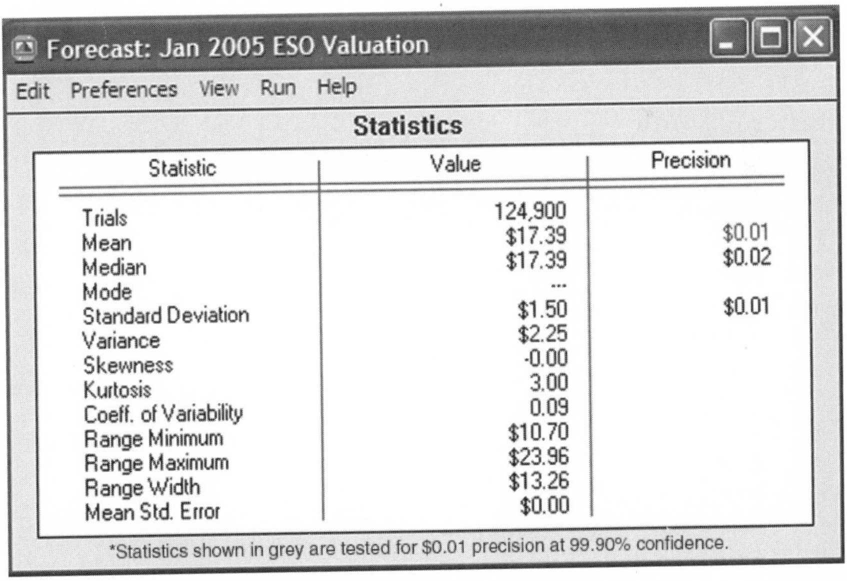

Forecast: Jan 2005 ESO Valuation

Edit Preferences View Run Help

Statistics

Statistic	Value	Precision
Trials	124,900	
Mean	$17.39	$0.01
Median	$17.39	$0.02
Mode	---	
Standard Deviation	$1.50	$0.01
Variance	$2.25	
Skewness	-0.00	
Kurtosis	3.00	
Coeff. of Variability	0.09	
Range Minimum	$10.70	
Range Maximum	$23.96	
Range Width	$13.26	
Mean Std. Error	$0.00	

*Statistics shown in grey are tested for $0.01 precision at 99.90% confidence.

FIGURE 10.5 Monte Carlo simulation of ESO valuation result.

TABLE 10.11 Options Valuation Results

	Conservative Stock Price	Aggressive Stock Price	Average of Two Stock Prices	Forfeiture Year	5.51% Risk Free
Stock Price	$45.17	$50.70	$47.93	1	1.21%
Strike Price	$45.17	$50.70	$47.93	2	2.19%
Maturity	10	10	10	3	3.21%
Risk-Free Rate	1.21%	1.21%	1.21%	4	3.85%
Volatility	49.91%	49.91%	49.91%	5	4.68%
Dividend	0%	0%	0%	6	4.59%
Lattice Steps	4,200	4,200	4,200	7	5.11%
Suboptimal Exercise Behavior	1.8531	1.8531	1.8531	8	4.91%
Vesting	0.08	0.08	0.08	9	5.25%
				10	5.59%
Customized Binomial Lattice	$17.39	(Customized binomial with changing risk-free rates)			
Naïve Black-Scholes	$26.91	(Black-Scholes model with a naïve 10-year assumption)			
Modified Black-Scholes	$19.55	(Black-Scholes model using expected life of 4 years)			
Cost Reduction	$ 2.16				

fully customized binomial lattice valuation of $17.39 yields $9.52. Table 10.12 illustrates where this differential comes from. About 0.02 percent of the difference comes from vesting and changing risk-free rates over the life of the option, 28.60 percent or $2.64 comes from the employees' suboptimal exercise behavior, and the remaining 71.37 percent or $6.58 comes from the 5.51 percent annualized forfeiture rate. The total variation directly explained comes to $9.22. The remaining variation of $0.30 comes from the nonlinear interactions among the various input variables and cannot be accounted for directly. Table 10.13 shows a sample calculation for the January 2005 grant.

It is shown in this valuation analysis that the fair market value of the employee options can be overvalued by 6.14 percent in Table 10.10 ($813.99 million using the binomial lattice versus $863.96 million using the BSM with adjusted life) if the GBM or BSM is used. This is because the GBM cannot take into account real-life conditions of ESOs that could affect their value. A proprietary customized binomial lattice model was used instead. This customized binomial lattice can account for all the GBM inputs (stock price, strike price, risk-free rate, dividend, and volatility) as well as the other real-life conditions such as vesting periods, forfeiture rates, suboptimal exercise behavior, blackout dates, changing risk-free rates, changing dividends, and changing volatilities.

TABLE 10.12 Contribution to Options Valuation Reduction

Contribution to Options Valuation Reduction

Vesting	$0.00	0.02%	Customized Binomial Lattice	$17.39
Suboptimal Exercise Behavior	$2.64	28.60%	Naïve Black-Scholes	$26.91
Forfeiture	$6.58	71.37%	Savings	***$ 9.52***
Changing Risk-Free Rate	$0.00	0.02%		
Total Value	***$9.22***			

Note: The slight difference between $9.22 and $9.52 is due to the interactions between variables.

Variance with Respect to Black-Scholes

Using the Black-Scholes with naïve assumption of full 10-year maturity	$	26.91
Using the Black-Scholes modified with a 4-year expected average life of the option*	$	19.55
Using the Black-Scholes modified with expected life and reduced by forfeiture rate	$	18.47
Customized binomial lattice with changing risk-free, forfeitures, suboptimal, and vesting	$	17.39
Cost reduction obtained by using the binomial versus Black-Scholes (expected life)	$	2.16 (11.04% reduction)
Average option issues per month in 2005		550,000
Cost reduction per year		$14,240,709

Note: 4 years is used because the option is on a monthly graded-vesting scale for 48 months.

Table 10.14 illustrates the allocation of expenses using a BSM over the next six years, for the grants starting in January 2005. Notice that the total expense is $914,341,298, identical to the total valuation results in Table 10.10. Table 10.15, in contrast, shows the allocation of expenses using a customized binomial lattice approach. Again, notice that the $813,997,676 sum of expenses agrees with the results in Figure 10.10.[14] The difference between a naïve BSM and a customized binomial lattice approach is fairly significant (Table 10.16). The difference between the total valuations is 12.33 percent ($914.34 million versus $813.99 million) and this percentage is fairly constant throughout the expensed years. However, the dollar expenses are front-loaded and the total difference of $100.34 million will not be spread out equally.

TABLE 10.13 Options Valuation Comparison

	Conservative Stock Price	Aggressive Stock Price	Average Price	
Option Value	$ 17.39	$ 19.52	$ 18.46	(Customized binomial lattice)
Naïve Black-Scholes	$ 26.91	$ 30.20	$ 28.55	(Black-Scholes model with a naïve 10-year assumption)
Modified Black-Scholes	$ 19.55	$ 21.95	$ 20.75	(Black-Scholes model using expected life of 4 years)
Cost Reduction	$ 2.16	$ 2.42	$ 2.29	
Cost Reduction per Year	$14,240,709	$15,984,148	$15,110,852	

Note: Assumed average option issues per month in 2005: 550,000.

TABLE 10.14 Expense Allocation (BSM)

Total Expenses 2005	$103,588,842
Total Expenses 2006	$304,675,765
Total Expenses 2007	$300,633,091
Total Expenses 2008	$141,257,655
Total Expenses 2009	$ 54,548,249
Total Expenses 2010	$ 9,637,696
Sum of Annual Expenses	$914,341,298

TABLE 10.15 Expense Allocation (Customized Binomial Lattice)

Total Expenses 2005	$ 92,197,733
Total Expenses 2006	$271,222,335
Total Expenses 2007	$267,662,000
Total Expenses 2008	$125,765,601
Total Expenses 2009	$ 48,567,875
Total Expenses 2010	$ 8,582,132
Sum of Annual Expenses	$813,997,676

TABLE 10.16 Dollar and Percentage Difference in Expenses

	Difference ($)	Difference (%)
Total Expenses 2005	($ 11,391,109)	–12.36%
Total Expenses 2006	($ 33,453,430)	–12.33%
Total Expenses 2007	($ 32,971,091)	–12.32%
Total Expenses 2008	($ 15,492,054)	–12.32%
Total Expenses 2009	($ 5,980,374)	–12.31%
Total Expenses 2010	($ 1,055,564)	–12.30%
Sum of Annual Expenses	($100,343,622)	–12.33%

SUMMARY AND KEY POINTS

- The customized binomial lattice methodology coupled with Monte Carlo simulation provides a much more robust and accurate view of the ESOs.
- GBM and BSM may significantly overvalue the ESOs, which consequently forces the firm to incorrectly overexpense its ESOs.

- The customized binomial lattice is the preferred method and conforms to the new FAS 123 ruling. This customized binomial lattice method results in a fair-market valuation by incorporating into its calculations all the input parameters required by the GBM and BSM, plus additional parameters including vesting period requirements, changing employee suboptimal exercise behavior, changing forfeiture rates, blackouts, changing risk-free rates, changing dividends, and changing volatilities over time. However, such analyses are complex and require great care in their modeling and when obtaining the model inputs, and should be replicated only by trained individuals.

APPENDIX 10A—INTRODUCTION TO THE SOFTWARE

Getting Started

This book comes with a demo version of the Employee Stock Options Valuation software version 1.1 (ESO Valuation). This limited version allows you to briefly explore the software, but some of the equations and calculations will not be visible, and some functionality will be disabled. To get started, insert the CD-ROM and install the software by following the online instructions. An installation guide is also available on the CD should you require additional assistance and documentation. Please refer to "About the CD-ROM" for detailed installation instructions.

The software has three main parts. These are the **ESO Toolkit**, which provides a graphical user interface of the models; the **ESO Functions**, which provide the user direct access to the valuation functions in Excel; and several **Excel Worksheet Auditing Templates**. All three parts are accessible directly by clicking on *Start | Programs | ESO Valuation*. In addition, the ESO Functions can be loaded automatically every time Excel starts. To do this, start Excel and click on *Tools | Add-Ins | Browse* and navigate to the directory in which you installed the software—this is typically "*C:\Program Files\ESO Valuation*" and choose the *ESO Functions 1.1.xla* file. (This feature has been disabled in the demo version.) In order to start the software properly, make sure that your Excel macro settings are set to Medium or lower. That is, when in Excel, click on *Tools | Macro | Security | Security Level | Medium*. When starting the ESO Valuation software, click on *Enable Macros* if and when prompted.

ESO Toolkit

Start the Toolkit by clicking on *Start | Programs | ESO Valuation | ESO Toolkit*. The *Main Menu of Models* (*Main Menu*) shows all 12 modules in the ESO Valuation software as seen in Figure 10A.1. In certain modules, the option may be solved using different approaches (e.g., *Basic European Option* is solved using the binomial lattice approach as well as closed-form models such as the Generalized Black-Scholes model). There is also a section for the user to choose between *Auto Calculate* and *Manual Calculate*. To prevent Excel from recalculating all modules at once every time an input is entered, thereby taking longer than usual, you can turn the *Manual Calculate* on. However, if you turn on manual calculation, remember to click on *Calculate* or hit *Ctrl-R* to recalculate your results; otherwise, the results may not be updated. In addition, when you are in any of the calculation modules, you can click on *Main Menu* or hit *Ctrl-M* to return to this main menu.

For those starting out in options analysis, this ESO Valuation interface is a valuable aid to understand the inner workings of valuing ESOs as well as a helpful presentation tool. For advanced users, all of the mathematical and options functions can be accessed directly through the use of Excel functions. Clicking on the *More Info* buttons will provide a quick synopsis of the input variables required to run a particular model. Clicking on the name of the module will take the user to the model itself.

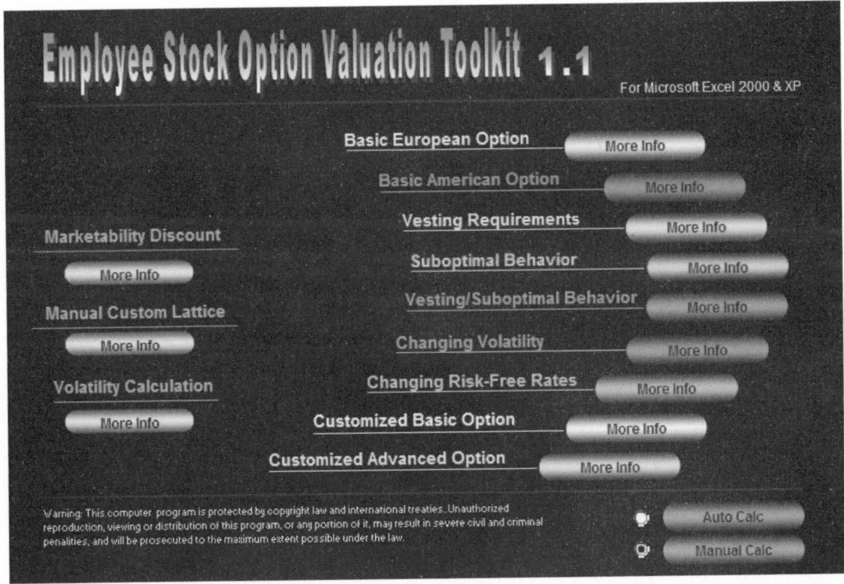

FIGURE 10A.1 ESO Toolkit main index.

For the expert users, the *Manual Custom Lattice* provides an alternative to valuing stock options. This module provides the analyst added modeling flexibility, and the results are readily accessible for auditing purposes (e.g., the formulas are all visible within Excel). See the section on "Manual Custom Lattice" in the *User Manual* for details.

To get started, click on *Basic European Option*. Let us now look at each section in detail. The first is the *Input Parameters* section (see Figure 10A.2). Here, the relevant parameters can be typed in directly or linked in from another spreadsheet. This area is characterized by its colored background. For all modules, a set of sample input parameters exists as a guide.

Assuming all the inputs are correct, the *Intermediate Calculations* section shows the time-step, up jump size, down jump size, and risk-neutral probability calculations for a predetermined five-step binomial lattice (see Figure 10A.3). This section exists only for simple options. For more complex options with exotic inputs and changing inputs, the intermediate calculations are not shown.

The resulting ESO value calculated using the 10-step binomial approach is shown in the *Results* section as seen in Figure 10A.4. The trinomial lattice calculations have been disabled in the demo version. The employee stock purchase plans (ESPP) module has also been disabled.

The 10-step lattice result of $12.09 is calculated based on the manual

Assumptions	
Stock Price ($)	$100.00
Strike Price ($)	$100.00
Maturity in Years	1.00
Risk-Free Rate (%)	5.00%
Dividends (%)	0.00%
Volatility (%)	25.00%

FIGURE 10A.2 Input parameters.

Intermediate Calculations	
Stepping-Time (dt)	0.1000
Up Step-Size (up)	1.0823
Down Step-Size (down)	0.9240
Risk-Neutral Probability (prob)	51.19%

FIGURE 10A.3 Intermediate calculations.

Results	
10-Step Lattice Results	$12.09
Generalized Black-Scholes	$12.34
10-Step Super Lattice	$12.09
Super Lattice Steps	10 Steps

FIGURE 10A.4 ESO valuation results.

10-step lattice shown in the software. In contrast, the Super Lattice result is computed in the software code. The same $12.09 value shows that the software algorithms agree with the manual computations. The benefit of the Super Lattice is that hundreds and even thousands of lattice steps can be computed (extending the same manual computations seen in the 10-step lattice) within a few seconds. The drop-down box seen in Figure 10A.4 beside the Super Lattice Steps provides the user with a choice to change the number of steps to perform using a binomial lattice. For instance, the greater the number of steps, the more granular the lattice becomes and the higher the accuracy of the lattice results. (Manually creating a binomial lattice with 1,000 steps may take years to calculate, as compared to a few seconds using the software.) To obtain more choices in the number of steps, use the ESO Functions instead. Make sure to hit the *Calculate* button or *Ctrl-R* if you turned on *Manual Calculate* on the Main Index page after selecting the relevant steps for the Super Lattice.

In addition, each module has an *Analyze* report button. As an example, Figure 10A.5 shows a sample report that provides more information on the ESO valuation results.

ESO Functions

The same mathematical functions used in the Toolkit can be accessed directly from the user's spreadsheet in Excel. That is, open an existing or blank Excel spreadsheet and start *ESO Valuation Functions* by clicking on *Start | ESO Valuation | ESO Functions 1.1.* Select *Enable Macros* if prompted. When in Excel, click on *Insert | Function* in Excel, select the *All* or *Financial* category, and shoose from among the ESO functions that start with the prefix "ESO." A short description is also provided (see Figure 10A.6). (Expert users might try the Real Options Analysis Toolkit 2.0, which has more than 100 functions.)

For instance, Figure 10A.7 illustrates a user spreadsheet where the *ESO CustomBinomialBasic* function is used to obtain the option value ($31.55). When entering or linking the cells to the function, make sure that all required

Stock Option Analysis Toolkit 

BASIC AMERICAN OPTION WITH DIVIDENDS

This is the Basic American Option with Dividends where the holder of the stock option has the ability to exercise the option at any time up to and including the option's maturity date. This module is calculated using both binomial lattices and a closed-form approximation model. The results illustrate a ten-step binomial recombining lattice for an American call option with continuous dividends. The first lattice is the underlying asset lattice where the starting asset value is simulated based on the Volatility and Number of Steps inputs. The second lattice is the option valuation lattice. Please note that the analysis presented here only uses a ten-step lattice for illustration purposes. For higher levels of precision, use the Super Lattice routine. The higher the number of lattice steps, the higher the level of accuracy.

Note that for stock options whose underlying stock does not pay any dividends, the American stock option and the European stock option are identical in value as theoretically, it is never optimal to exercise early. When there are dividend payments, it may become optimal to exercise early, and the American option has more value than the European option. The results are calculated using the binomial lattice approach as well as a closed-form approximation model. The Generalized Black-Scholes model is included as a benchmark, as these three values should be similar at the limit (with enough steps in the binomial lattice) when no dividends exist in a European option. Only when dividends exist will the binomial lattice and closed-form approximation models be different than the Generalized Black-Scholes model. Finally, for higher levels of dividends, the American closed-form approximation model becomes less robust and the binomial lattice approach (with high number of steps) is more accurate. This is because an exact closed-form model for American options with dividends does not exist.

Based on the analysis, it is found that the Generalized Black-Scholes provides a value of $ 39.94 while the binomial lattice using a 10-Step Super Lattice shows a value of $ 39.71
The American Approximation model yields $ 39.94

The higher the number of steps in a binomial lattice, the higher the level of precision in the results. Usually, 1,000 steps is sufficient to obtain a highly accurate value. The following lists some of the results obtained using the binomial super lattice:

10-Steps	$ 39.71
100-Steps	$ 39.92
300-Steps	$ 39.93
500-Steps	$ 39.93
1,000-Steps	$ 39.94

The results from the binomial lattices converge, indicating that the binomial results are robust.

Function(s) used:
ESOGeneralizedBlackScholesCall
ESOClosedFormAmericanCall

FIGURE 10A.5 *Analyze* report feature.

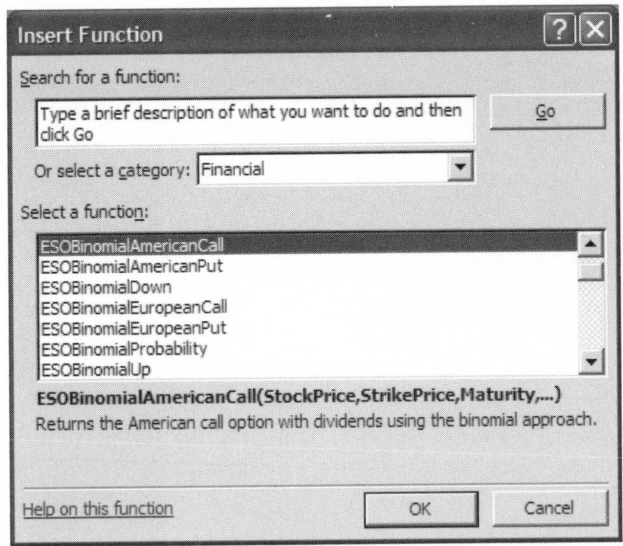

FIGURE 10A.6 ESO functions.

NORMSDIST =ESOCustomBinomialBasic(E4,E5,E6,E7,E9,E8,5,E11,E10,0)

User's Own Model

Stock Price	$50.00
Strike Price	$50.00
Maturity	10.00
Risk-free Rate	5.00%
Dividends	0.00%
Volatility	55.00%
Vesting	4.00
Suboptimal Behavior	1.50
Calculation Opion Value	$31.55

Function Arguments

ESOCustomBinomialBasic

StockPrice	E4	= 50
StrikePrice	E5	= 50
Maturity	E6	= 10
SingleRiskFree	E7	= 0.05
SingleVolatility	E9	= 0.55

= 31.54516996

Returns the American call option with vesting, suboptimal early exercise behavior, forfeiture, changing risk-free rates, and changing volatilities.

StockPrice

Formula result = $31.55

Help on this function OK Cancel

FIGURE 10A.7 Using ESO functions in existing spreadsheets.

inputs are entered (i.e., remember to scroll down the inputs list by using the vertical scroll bar). Using this ESO Functions method, the spreadsheet inputs can be linked to and from multiple sources (databases or other spreadsheets), and the results will be updated automatically. In addition, the inputs used in the model can be seen directly in the cell. Note that this ESO Functions feature has been disabled in the demo version of the software.

Auditing Templates and Spreadsheets

The software also provides formula auditing spreadsheets. Click on *Start | Programs | ESO Valuation | Audit* to access three audit spreadsheets. Figure 10A.8 shows the *Static Binomial* worksheet where the inputs are single values (i.e., input parameters are not changing over time). The other two spreadsheets are the *Basic Changing Binomial* (risk-free rates and volatilities are allowed to change over time, reflecting the algorithms used in the

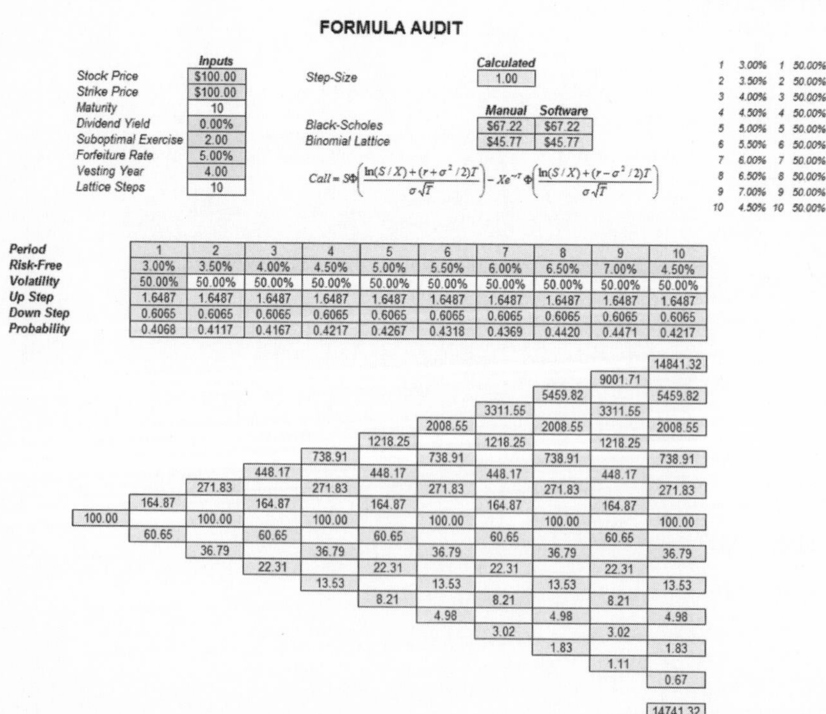

FIGURE 10A.8 Auditing the formulas.

Customized Basic Option module in the Toolkit) and the *Advanced Changing Binomial* (all inputs are allowed to change over time except stock price, strike price, maturity, and vesting period, reflecting the algorithms used in the *Customized Advanced Option* module in the Toolkit). On the computer screen the cells in green are the input cells while the blue cells are the calculated values. The worksheet is protected to prevent users from accidentally changing or deleting a formula. However, the user can click on any cell containing a calculated value and view the formulas that generated the value in the cell, as seen in Figure 10A.8. (This feature has been disabled in the demo version of the software.) The results of interest are the *Manual* and *Software* values. The manual values are those obtained in the manual lattice, and are compared to the results from the software's function cells. These worksheets are to illustrate the algorithms used to calculate the ESO's value. Only a 10-step manual lattice is shown because higher-step lattices (hundreds or thousands of steps) cannot be solved manually, and can be solved only in the software. However, the same algorithm is applied in the software. Thus, understanding the simple 5- and 10-step lattices is sufficient to understand a 1,000-step lattice, as the algorithms applied are identical.

PART Four

Options Valuation Results Tables

APPENDIX

Getting Started with the Options Valuation Results Tables

Part Four provides many solved ESOs using the customized binomial lattice approach. The analysis takes as inputs the following variables: *stock price at grant date, contractual strike price, time to maturity, a single risk-free rate, an optional series of changing risk-free rates over the life of the option, a single dividend rate, an optional series of changing dividend rates over the life of the option, a single volatility, an optional series of changing volatilities, forfeiture rate, suboptimal exercise behavior multiple, vesting period, blackout periods, and number of lattice steps.*

These input variables have nonlinear relationships with the option value and intravariable interactions also exist. That is, a low suboptimal exercise behavior multiple has little effect on a long-vesting option, but the impact increases at a decreasing rate the lower the vesting period while holding the suboptimal exercise behavior multiple constant. Therefore, these tables are required in order to capture these intricate and sometimes complex relationships and interactions among variables.

The idea behind these tables is not *to provide the reader with the exact options valuation answers. Rather, it provides senior management a first-pass look at rough approximations of valuation.* That is, instead of spending tens of thousands of dollars on consultants tasked simply to identify the potential impacts of expensing the options or to see if using the customized binomial lattices will in fact reduce or increase the valuation of the options, these tables provide a fast and accurate, but rough guide to the potential impacts a company may face when considering the valuation of its ESOs.

For instance, suppose your company's stock price at some future grant date is expected to be $22 and historical volatility indicates that it is hovering around 35 percent, and your firm's stocks pay no dividends. Further suppose that the employee turnover rate at your firm is hovering around 10 percent per year and vesting is only 1 month. The closest table will be the *Maturity of 3 Years and Vesting of 1 Month on a $20 Stock Price* located in the next few pages. Of course without the relevant data you cannot correctly pinpoint the suboptimal exercise behavior multiple, but research has shown that the multiple typically tends to hover anywhere between 1.2 and 2.4. So, select 1.6 as the starting point. Looking at the table, a forfeiture rate of say 10 percent and a suboptimal exercise behavior multiple of 1.6 indicates a customized binomial lattice valuation of $4.52, as compared to the naïve GBM result of $5.59. The difference is a reduction of $1.07 or 19.2 percent per option. Of course you can take *haircuts* on the naïve GBM by multiplying it by one less the forfeiture rate or $5.59(1 – 10%) yielding $5.03. Compared to the binomial lattice result, there is still a reduction of $0.51 or 10.2 percent. If your firm issues, say, on average about 15 million options per year (this is pretty standard for a Fortune 100 firm) the reduction in expenses would be roughly between $7.66 and $16.05 million in valuation per year. Another quick way to look at this is to take the discount on last year's stock options valuation. For instance, suppose your firm granted $100 million in options last year; a 10.2 to 19.2 percent reduction implies a $10.2 to $19.2 million expense reduction going forward.

With these new rough values, it would seem that more detailed analysis is justified. However, if these tables did not exist, clearly one would be unable to even grasp the magnitude of potentially over- or underexpensing the options. Of course one can create more cursory analysis of these tables. Table A.1 illustrates a quick summary of the impact of potential expense reduction across different suboptimal exercise behavior multiples for a 10 percent forfeiture rate. Clearly nothing replaces more detailed analysis but this options table method provides quick justification to either pursue or terminate potentially more complex and protracted customized binomial analysis.

Note: These tables were generated using a proprietary customized binomial lattice algorithm with 1,000 steps. In addition, the tables are calculated for 35 percent and 70 percent stock volatilities. The stock prices used range from $20 to $80, with $20 increments. Because in most cases, vesting, suboptimal exercise behavior, and forfeiture rates play a significant role in the option's final fair-market value, these three variables are allowed to change in these tables. If your firm's stock is between two sets of tables, calculate the average options valuation price as a rough proxy of the true value.

TABLE A.1 Scenario Analysis on the Option Results Tables (10% Annual Forfeiture)

Suboptimal Behavior	1.2	1.4	1.6	1.8	2.0	2.2	2.4	2.6	2.8	3.0
Options Valuation	$2.85	$3.99	$4.52	$4.75	$4.88	$4.94	$4.98	$5.00	$5.01	$5.02
Naïve BSM	$5.59	$5.59	$5.59	$5.59	$5.59	$5.59	$5.59	$5.59	$5.59	$5.59
Difference $	($2.74)	($1.60)	($1.07)	($0.83)	($0.71)	($0.64)	($0.61)	($0.59)	($0.58)	($0.57)
Difference %	–49.08%	–28.57%	–19.19%	–14.94%	–12.63%	–11.52%	–10.96%	–10.57%	–10.31%	–10.12%
Modified BSM	$5.03	$5.03	$5.03	$5.03	$5.03	$5.03	$5.03	$5.03	$5.03	$5.03
Difference $	($2.18)	($1.04)	($0.51)	($0.28)	($0.15)	($0.09)	($0.05)	($0.03)	($0.02)	($0.01)
Difference %	–43.43%	–20.64%	–10.21%	–5.49%	–2.92%	–1.69%	–1.07%	–0.64%	–0.34%	–0.13%

THIRTY-FIVE PERCENT VOLATILITY AND 3-YEAR MATURITY ESOs WITH VARYING STOCK PRICE, SUBOPTIMAL BEHAVIOR, VESTING PERIOD, AND FORFEITURE RATES

This section provides ESO valuation results on an underlying stock with 35 percent volatility and a 3-year maturity. The analysis is divided into 1-month and 1-year vesting periods, and accounts for stock prices at grant date of $20, $40, $60, and $80.

MATURITY OF 3 YEARS AND VESTING OF 1 MONTH ON A $20 STOCK PRICE

Stock Price and Strike Price of $20, Maturity of 3 Years, Risk-Free Rate of 3.5%, 35% Volatility, 0% Dividends,
Vesting of 1 Month, Employee Suboptimal Exercise Behavior from 1.2 to 3.0, and Forfeiture Rate from 0% to 40%.
Generalized Black-Scholes: $5.59

Customized Binomial Lattice	Suboptimal (1.2)	Suboptimal (1.4)	Suboptimal (1.6)	Suboptimal (1.8)	Suboptimal (2.0)	Suboptimal (2.2)	Suboptimal (2.4)	Suboptimal (2.6)	Suboptimal (2.8)	Suboptimal (3.0)
Forfeiture (0%)	$3.01	$4.32	$4.94	$5.23	$5.39	$5.46	$5.50	$5.53	$5.55	$5.56
Forfeiture (5%)	$2.92	$4.15	$4.72	$4.98	$5.12	$5.19	$5.23	$5.25	$5.27	$5.28
Forfeiture (10%)	$2.85	$3.99	$4.52	$4.75	$4.88	$4.94	$4.98	$5.00	$5.01	$5.02
Forfeiture (15%)	$2.77	$3.85	$4.33	$4.55	$4.66	$4.72	$4.75	$4.77	$4.78	$4.79
Forfeiture (20%)	$2.70	$3.71	$4.16	$4.35	$4.46	$4.51	$4.53	$4.55	$4.56	$4.57
Forfeiture (25%)	$2.64	$3.59	$4.00	$4.18	$4.27	$4.32	$4.34	$4.36	$4.37	$4.37
Forfeiture (30%)	$2.58	$3.47	$3.85	$4.01	$4.10	$4.14	$4.16	$4.17	$4.18	$4.19
Forfeiture (35%)	$2.52	$3.36	$3.71	$3.86	$3.94	$3.98	$4.00	$4.01	$4.02	$4.02
Forfeiture (40%)	$2.47	$3.26	$3.58	$3.72	$3.79	$3.83	$3.84	$3.85	$3.86	$3.87

Percentage Difference between Binomial and Black–Scholes Model	Suboptimal (1.2)	Suboptimal (1.4)	Suboptimal (1.6)	Suboptimal (1.8)	Suboptimal (2.0)	Suboptimal (2.2)	Suboptimal (2.4)	Suboptimal (2.6)	Suboptimal (2.8)	Suboptimal (3.0)
Forfeiture (0%)	–46.20%	–22.77%	–11.63%	–6.48%	–3.64%	–2.28%	–1.58%	–1.10%	–0.76%	–0.53%
Forfeiture (5%)	–47.69%	–25.78%	–15.57%	–10.89%	–8.33%	–7.10%	–6.47%	–6.04%	–5.74%	–5.54%
Forfeiture (10%)	–49.08%	–28.57%	–19.19%	–14.94%	–12.63%	–11.52%	–10.96%	–10.57%	–10.31%	–10.12%
Forfeiture (15%)	–50.39%	–31.16%	–22.53%	–18.67%	–16.57%	–15.58%	–15.08%	–14.73%	–14.49%	–14.32%
Forfeiture (20%)	–51.62%	–33.57%	–25.62%	–22.10%	–20.21%	–19.32%	–18.86%	–18.55%	–18.33%	–18.18%
Forfeiture (25%)	–52.77%	–35.81%	–28.48%	–25.27%	–23.56%	–22.75%	–22.34%	–22.06%	–21.87%	–21.74%
Forfeiture (30%)	–53.86%	–37.89%	–31.14%	–28.21%	–26.65%	–25.92%	–25.55%	–25.30%	–25.13%	–25.01%
Forfeiture (35%)	–54.89%	–39.84%	–33.60%	–30.92%	–29.51%	–28.85%	–28.52%	–28.29%	–28.13%	–28.03%
Forfeiture (40%)	–55.86%	–41.66%	–35.89%	–33.44%	–32.16%	–31.56%	–31.26%	–31.05%	–30.92%	–30.82%

MATURITY OF 3 YEARS AND VESTING OF 1 MONTH ON A $40 STOCK PRICE

Stock Price and Strike Price of $40, Maturity of 3 Years, Risk-Free Rate of 3.5%, 35% Volatility, 0% Dividends, Vesting of 1 Month, Employee Suboptimal Exercise Behavior from 1.2 to 3.0, and Forfeiture Rate from 0% to 40%.
Generalized Black-Scholes: $11.18

Customized Binomial Lattice	Suboptimal (1.2)	Suboptimal (1.4)	Suboptimal (1.6)	Suboptimal (1.8)	Suboptimal (2.0)	Suboptimal (2.2)	Suboptimal (2.4)	Suboptimal (2.6)	Suboptimal (2.8)	Suboptimal (3.0)
Forfeiture (0%)	$6.01	$8.63	$9.88	$10.45	$10.77	$10.92	$11.00	$11.06	$11.09	$11.12
Forfeiture (5%)	$5.85	$8.30	$9.44	$9.96	$10.25	$10.38	$10.45	$10.50	$10.54	$10.56
Forfeiture (10%)	$5.69	$7.98	$9.03	$9.51	$9.77	$9.89	$9.95	$10.00	$10.03	$10.05
Forfeiture (15%)	$5.55	$7.69	$8.66	$9.09	$9.32	$9.44	$9.49	$9.53	$9.56	$9.58
Forfeiture (20%)	$5.41	$7.43	$8.31	$8.71	$8.92	$9.02	$9.07	$9.10	$9.13	$9.14
Forfeiture (25%)	$5.28	$7.18	$7.99	$8.35	$8.54	$8.63	$8.68	$8.71	$8.73	$8.75
Forfeiture (30%)	$5.16	$6.94	$7.70	$8.02	$8.20	$8.28	$8.32	$8.35	$8.37	$8.38
Forfeiture (35%)	$5.04	$6.72	$7.42	$7.72	$7.88	$7.95	$7.99	$8.02	$8.03	$8.04
Forfeiture (40%)	$4.93	$6.52	$7.17	$7.44	$7.58	$7.65	$7.68	$7.71	$7.72	$7.73

Percentage Difference between Binomial and Black–Scholes Model	Suboptimal (1.2)	Suboptimal (1.4)	Suboptimal (1.6)	Suboptimal (1.8)	Suboptimal (2.0)	Suboptimal (2.2)	Suboptimal (2.4)	Suboptimal (2.6)	Suboptimal (2.8)	Suboptimal (3.0)
Forfeiture (0%)	–46.20%	–22.77%	–11.63%	–6.48%	–3.64%	–2.28%	–1.58%	–1.10%	–0.76%	–0.53%
Forfeiture (5%)	–47.69%	–25.78%	–15.57%	–10.89%	–8.33%	–7.10%	–6.47%	–6.04%	–5.74%	–5.54%
Forfeiture (10%)	–49.08%	–28.57%	–19.19%	–14.94%	–12.63%	–11.52%	–10.96%	–10.57%	–10.31%	–10.12%
Forfeiture (15%)	–50.39%	–31.16%	–22.53%	–18.67%	–16.57%	–15.58%	–15.08%	–14.73%	–14.49%	–14.32%
Forfeiture (20%)	–51.62%	–33.57%	–25.62%	–22.10%	–20.21%	–19.32%	–18.86%	–18.55%	–18.33%	–18.18%
Forfeiture (25%)	–52.77%	–35.81%	–28.48%	–25.27%	–23.56%	–22.75%	–22.34%	–22.06%	–21.87%	–21.74%
Forfeiture (30%)	–53.86%	–37.89%	–31.14%	–28.21%	–26.65%	–25.92%	–25.55%	–25.30%	–25.13%	–25.01%
Forfeiture (35%)	–54.89%	–39.84%	–33.60%	–30.92%	–29.51%	–28.85%	–28.52%	–28.29%	–28.13%	–28.03%
Forfeiture (40%)	–55.86%	–41.66%	–35.89%	–33.44%	–32.16%	–31.56%	–31.26%	–31.05%	–30.92%	–30.82%

MATURITY OF 3 YEARS AND VESTING OF 1 MONTH ON A $60 STOCK PRICE

Stock Price and Strike Price of $60, Maturity of 3 Years, Risk-Free Rate of 3.5%, 35% Volatility, 0% Dividends, Vesting of 1 Month, Employee Suboptimal Exercise Behavior from 1.2 to 3.0, and Forfeiture Rate from 0% to 40%.
Generalized Black-Scholes: $16.77

Customized Binomial Lattice	Suboptimal (1.2)	Suboptimal (1.4)	Suboptimal (1.6)	Suboptimal (1.8)	Suboptimal (2.0)	Suboptimal (2.2)	Suboptimal (2.4)	Suboptimal (2.6)	Suboptimal (2.8)	Suboptimal (3.0)
Forfeiture (0%)	$9.02	$12.95	$14.82	$15.68	$16.16	$16.38	$16.50	$16.58	$16.64	$16.68
Forfeiture (5%)	$8.77	$12.44	$14.16	$14.94	$15.37	$15.58	$15.68	$15.75	$15.80	$15.84
Forfeiture (10%)	$8.54	$11.98	$13.55	$14.26	$14.65	$14.83	$14.93	$14.99	$15.04	$15.07
Forfeiture (15%)	$8.32	$11.54	$12.99	$13.64	$13.99	$14.15	$14.24	$14.30	$14.34	$14.36
Forfeiture (20%)	$8.11	$11.14	$12.47	$13.06	$13.38	$13.53	$13.60	$13.66	$13.69	$13.72
Forfeiture (25%)	$7.92	$10.76	$11.99	$12.53	$12.82	$12.95	$13.02	$13.07	$13.10	$13.12
Forfeiture (30%)	$7.74	$10.41	$11.55	$12.04	$12.30	$12.42	$12.48	$12.52	$12.55	$12.57
Forfeiture (35%)	$7.56	$10.09	$11.13	$11.58	$11.82	$11.93	$11.99	$12.02	$12.05	$12.07
Forfeiture (40%)	$7.40	$9.78	$10.75	$11.16	$11.38	$11.48	$11.53	$11.56	$11.58	$11.60

Percentage Difference between Binomial and Black–Scholes Model	Suboptimal (1.2)	Suboptimal (1.4)	Suboptimal (1.6)	Suboptimal (1.8)	Suboptimal (2.0)	Suboptimal (2.2)	Suboptimal (2.4)	Suboptimal (2.6)	Suboptimal (2.8)	Suboptimal (3.0)
Forfeiture (0%)	–46.20%	–22.77%	–11.63%	–6.48%	–3.64%	–2.28%	–1.58%	–1.10%	–0.76%	–0.53%
Forfeiture (5%)	–47.69%	–25.78%	–15.57%	–10.89%	–8.33%	–7.10%	–6.47%	–6.04%	–5.74%	–5.54%
Forfeiture (10%)	–49.08%	–28.57%	–19.19%	–14.94%	–12.63%	–11.52%	–10.96%	–10.57%	–10.31%	–10.12%
Forfeiture (15%)	–50.39%	–31.16%	–22.53%	–18.67%	–16.57%	–15.58%	–15.08%	–14.73%	–14.49%	–14.32%
Forfeiture (20%)	–51.62%	–33.57%	–25.62%	–22.10%	–20.21%	–19.32%	–18.86%	–18.55%	–18.33%	–18.18%
Forfeiture (25%)	–52.77%	–35.81%	–28.48%	–25.27%	–23.56%	–22.75%	–22.34%	–22.06%	–21.87%	–21.74%
Forfeiture (30%)	–53.86%	–37.89%	–31.14%	–28.21%	–26.65%	–25.92%	–25.55%	–25.30%	–25.13%	–25.01%
Forfeiture (35%)	–54.89%	–39.84%	–33.60%	–30.92%	–29.51%	–28.85%	–28.52%	–28.29%	–28.13%	–28.03%
Forfeiture (40%)	–55.86%	–41.66%	–35.89%	–33.44%	–32.16%	–31.56%	–31.26%	–31.05%	–30.92%	–30.82%

MATURITY OF 3 YEARS AND VESTING OF 1 MONTH ON AN $80 STOCK PRICE

Stock Price and Strike Price of $80, Maturity of 3 Years, Risk-Free Rate of 3.5%, 35% Volatility, 0% Dividends, Vesting of 1 Month, Employee Suboptimal Exercise Behavior from 1.2 to 3.0, and Forfeiture Rate from 0% to 40%.
Generalized Black-Scholes: $22.36

Customized Binomial Lattice	Suboptimal (1.2)	Suboptimal (1.4)	Suboptimal (1.6)	Suboptimal (1.8)	Suboptimal (2.0)	Suboptimal (2.2)	Suboptimal (2.4)	Suboptimal (2.6)	Suboptimal (2.8)	Suboptimal (3.0)
Forfeiture (0%)	$12.03	$17.27	$19.76	$20.91	$21.54	$21.85	$22.00	$22.11	$22.18	$22.24
Forfeiture (5%)	$11.69	$16.59	$18.88	$19.92	$20.49	$20.77	$20.91	$21.00	$21.07	$21.12
Forfeiture (10%)	$11.38	$15.97	$18.07	$19.02	$19.53	$19.78	$19.91	$19.99	$20.05	$20.09
Forfeiture (15%)	$11.09	$15.39	$17.32	$18.18	$18.65	$18.87	$18.98	$19.06	$19.12	$19.15
Forfeiture (20%)	$10.82	$14.85	$16.63	$17.41	$17.84	$18.04	$18.14	$18.21	$18.26	$18.29
Forfeiture (25%)	$10.56	$14.35	$15.99	$16.71	$17.09	$17.27	$17.36	$17.42	$17.47	$17.50
Forfeiture (30%)	$10.32	$13.88	$15.39	$16.05	$16.40	$16.56	$16.64	$16.70	$16.74	$16.76
Forfeiture (35%)	$10.09	$13.45	$14.84	$15.44	$15.76	$15.91	$15.98	$16.03	$16.07	$16.09
Forfeiture (40%)	$9.87	$13.04	$14.33	$14.88	$15.17	$15.30	$15.37	$15.41	$15.44	$15.47

Percentage Difference between Binomial and Black-Scholes Model	Suboptimal (1.2)	Suboptimal (1.4)	Suboptimal (1.6)	Suboptimal (1.8)	Suboptimal (2.0)	Suboptimal (2.2)	Suboptimal (2.4)	Suboptimal (2.6)	Suboptimal (2.8)	Suboptimal (3.0)
Forfeiture (0%)	−46.20%	−22.77%	−11.63%	−6.48%	−3.64%	−2.28%	−1.58%	−1.10%	−0.76%	−0.53%
Forfeiture (5%)	−47.69%	−25.78%	−15.57%	−10.89%	−8.33%	−7.10%	−6.47%	−6.04%	−5.74%	−5.54%
Forfeiture (10%	−49.08%	−28.57%	−19.19%	−14.94%	−12.63%	−11.52%	−10.96%	−10.57%	−10.31%	−10.12%
Forfeiture (15%)	−50.39%	−31.16%	−22.53%	−18.67%	−16.57%	−15.58%	−15.08%	−14.73%	−14.49%	−14.32%
Forfeiture (20%)	−51.62%	−33.57%	−25.62%	−22.10%	−20.21%	−19.32%	−18.86%	−18.55%	−18.33%	−18.18%
Forfeiture (25%)	−52.77%	−35.81%	−28.48%	−25.27%	−23.56%	−22.75%	−22.34%	−22.06%	−21.87%	−21.74%
Forfeiture (30%)	−53.86%	−37.89%	−31.14%	−28.21%	−26.65%	−25.92%	−25.55%	−25.30%	−25.13%	−25.01%
Forfeiture (35%)	−54.89%	−39.84%	−33.60%	−30.92%	−29.51%	−28.85%	−28.52%	−28.29%	−28.13%	−28.03%
Forfeiture (40%)	−55.86%	−41.66%	−35.89%	−33.44%	−32.16%	−31.56%	−31.26%	−31.05%	−30.92%	−30.82%

MATURITY OF 3 YEARS AND VESTING OF 1 YEAR ON A $20 STOCK PRICE

Stock Price and Strike Price of $20, Maturity of 3 Years, Risk–Free Rate of 3.5%, 35% Volatility, 0% Dividends, Vesting of 1 Year, Employee Suboptimal Exercise Behavior from 1.2 to 3.0, and Forfeiture Rate from 0% to 40%.
Generalized Black–Scholes: $5.59

Customized Binomial Lattice	Suboptimal (1.2)	Suboptimal (1.4)	Suboptimal (1.6)	Suboptimal (1.8)	Suboptimal (2.0)	Suboptimal (2.2)	Suboptimal (2.4)	Suboptimal (2.6)	Suboptimal (2.8)	Suboptimal (3.0)
Forfeiture (0%)	$4.12	$4.74	$5.10	$5.29	$5.41	$5.47	$5.50	$5.53	$5.55	$5.56
Forfeiture (5%)	$3.89	$4.45	$4.77	$4.94	$5.05	$5.10	$5.14	$5.16	$5.17	$5.18
Forfeiture (10%)	$3.67	$4.18	$4.47	$4.62	$4.72	$4.77	$4.79	$4.81	$4.83	$4.84
Forfeiture (15%)	$3.46	$3.93	$4.19	$4.32	$4.41	$4.46	$4.48	$4.50	$4.51	$4.52
Forfeiture (20%)	$3.27	$3.69	$3.93	$4.05	$4.13	$4.17	$4.19	$4.20	$4.22	$4.22
Forfeiture (25%)	$3.09	$3.47	$3.68	$3.79	$3.86	$3.90	$3.92	$3.93	$3.94	$3.95
Forfeiture (30%)	$2.92	$3.27	$3.46	$3.56	$3.62	$3.65	$3.67	$3.68	$3.69	$3.70
Forfeiture (35%)	$2.76	$3.07	$3.25	$3.34	$3.39	$3.42	$3.44	$3.45	$3.46	$3.46
Forfeiture (40%)	$2.61	$2.90	$3.05	$3.13	$3.18	$3.21	$3.23	$3.24	$3.24	$3.25

Percentage Difference between Binomial and Black–Scholes Model	Suboptimal (1.2)	Suboptimal (1.4)	Suboptimal (1.6)	Suboptimal (1.8)	Suboptimal (2.0)	Suboptimal (2.2)	Suboptimal (2.4)	Suboptimal (2.6)	Suboptimal (2.8)	Suboptimal (3.0)
Forfeiture (0%)	–26.25%	–15.19%	–8.81%	–5.38%	–3.24%	–2.12%	–1.50%	–1.06%	–0.75%	–0.52%
Forfeiture (5%)	–30.43%	–20.40%	–14.66%	–11.58%	–9.67%	–8.67%	–8.12%	–7.72%	–7.44%	–7.24%
Forfeiture (10%)	–34.35%	–25.25%	–20.08%	–17.32%	–15.61%	–14.71%	–14.21%	–13.86%	–13.61%	–13.43%
Forfeiture (15%)	–38.03%	–29.76%	–25.10%	–22.62%	–21.09%	–20.29%	–19.84%	–19.53%	–19.31%	–19.15%
Forfeiture (20%)	–41.48%	–33.97%	–29.77%	–27.54%	–26.17%	–25.44%	–25.05%	–24.77%	–24.57%	–24.42%
Forfeiture (25%)	–44.72%	–37.90%	–34.10%	–32.10%	–30.86%	–30.22%	–29.86%	–29.61%	–29.43%	–29.30%
Forfeiture (30%)	–47.77%	–41.56%	–38.13%	–36.33%	–35.22%	–34.64%	–34.32%	–34.10%	–33.94%	–33.82%
Forfeiture (35%)	–50.64%	–44.98%	–41.88%	–40.26%	–39.26%	–38.74%	–38.46%	–38.25%	–38.11%	–38.01%
Forfeiture (40%)	–53.33%	–48.18%	–45.38%	–43.92%	–43.02%	–42.55%	–42.29%	–42.11%	–41.98%	–41.89%

MATURITY OF 3 YEARS AND VESTING OF 1 YEAR ON A $40 STOCK PRICE

Stock Price and Strike Price of $40, Maturity of 3 Years, Risk-Free Rate of 3.5%, 35% Volatility, 0% Dividends, Vesting of 1 Year, Employee Suboptimal Exercise Behavior from 1.2 to 3.0, and Forfeiture Rate from 0% to 40%.
Generalized Black-Scholes: $11.18

Customized Binomial Lattice	Suboptimal (1.2)	Suboptimal (1.4)	Suboptimal (1.6)	Suboptimal (1.8)	Suboptimal (2.0)	Suboptimal (2.2)	Suboptimal (2.4)	Suboptimal (2.6)	Suboptimal (2.8)	Suboptimal (3.0)
Forfeiture (0%)	$8.24	$9.48	$10.19	$10.58	$10.81	$10.94	$11.01	$11.06	$11.09	$11.12
Forfeiture (5%)	$7.78	$8.90	$9.54	$9.88	$10.10	$10.21	$10.27	$10.31	$10.35	$10.37
Forfeiture (10%	$7.34	$8.36	$8.93	$9.24	$9.43	$9.53	$9.59	$9.63	$9.66	$9.68
Forfeiture (15%)	$6.93	$7.85	$8.37	$8.65	$8.82	$8.91	$8.96	$8.99	$9.02	$9.04
Forfeiture (20%)	$6.54	$7.38	$7.85	$8.10	$8.25	$8.33	$8.38	$8.41	$8.43	$8.45
Forfeiture (25%)	$6.18	$6.94	$7.37	$7.59	$7.73	$7.80	$7.84	$7.87	$7.89	$7.90
Forfeiture (30%)	$5.84	$6.53	$6.92	$7.12	$7.24	$7.31	$7.34	$7.37	$7.38	$7.40
Forfeiture (35%)	$5.52	$6.15	$6.50	$6.68	$6.79	$6.85	$6.88	$6.90	$6.92	$6.93
Forfeiture (40%)	$5.22	$5.79	$6.11	$6.27	$6.37	$6.42	$6.45	$6.47	$6.48	$6.50

Percentage Difference between Binomial and Black-Scholes Model	Suboptimal (1.2)	Suboptimal (1.4)	Suboptimal (1.6)	Suboptimal (1.8)	Suboptimal (2.0)	Suboptimal (2.2)	Suboptimal (2.4)	Suboptimal (2.6)	Suboptimal (2.8)	Suboptimal (3.0)
Forfeiture (0%)	–26.25%	–15.19%	–8.81%	–5.38%	–3.24%	–2.12%	–1.50%	–1.06%	–0.75%	–0.52%
Forfeiture (5%)	–30.43%	–20.40%	–14.66%	–11.58%	–9.67%	–8.67%	–8.12%	–7.72%	–7.44%	–7.24%
Forfeiture (10%)	–34.35%	–25.25%	–20.08%	–17.32%	–15.61%	–14.71%	–14.21%	–13.86%	–13.61%	–13.43%
Forfeiture (15%)	–38.03%	–29.76%	–25.10%	–22.62%	–21.09%	–20.29%	–19.84%	–19.53%	–19.31%	–19.15%
Forfeiture (20%)	–41.48%	–33.97%	–29.77%	–27.54%	–26.17%	–25.44%	–25.05%	–24.77%	–24.57%	–24.42%
Forfeiture (25%)	–44.72%	–37.90%	–34.10%	–32.10%	–30.86%	–30.22%	–29.86%	–29.61%	–29.43%	–29.30%
Forfeiture (30%)	–47.77%	–41.56%	–38.13%	–36.33%	–35.22%	–34.64%	–34.32%	–34.10%	–33.94%	–33.82%
Forfeiture (35%)	–50.64%	–44.98%	–41.88%	–40.26%	–39.26%	–38.74%	–38.46%	–38.25%	–38.11%	–38.01%
Forfeiture (40%)	–53.33%	–48.18%	–45.38%	–43.92%	–43.02%	–42.55%	–42.29%	–42.11%	–41.98%	–41.89%

MATURITY OF 3 YEARS AND VESTING OF 1 YEAR ON A $60 STOCK PRICE

Stock Price and Strike Price of $60, Maturity of 3 Years, Risk-Free Rate of 3.5%, 35% Volatility, 0% Dividends, Vesting of 1 Year, Employee Suboptimal Exercise Behavior from 1.2 to 3.0, and Forfeiture Rate from 0% to 40%.
Generalized Black-Scholes: $16.77

Customized Binomial Lattice	Suboptimal (1.2)	Suboptimal (1.4)	Suboptimal (1.6)	Suboptimal (1.8)	Suboptimal (2.0)	Suboptimal (2.2)	Suboptimal (2.4)	Suboptimal (2.6)	Suboptimal (2.8)	Suboptimal (3.0)
Forfeiture (0%)	$12.37	$14.22	$15.29	$15.87	$16.22	$16.41	$16.51	$16.59	$16.64	$16.68
Forfeiture (5%)	$11.66	$13.35	$14.31	$14.82	$15.14	$15.31	$15.41	$15.47	$15.52	$15.55
Forfeiture (10%)	$11.01	$12.53	$13.40	$13.86	$14.15	$14.30	$14.38	$14.44	$14.48	$14.51
Forfeiture (15%)	$10.39	$11.78	$12.56	$12.97	$13.23	$13.37	$13.44	$13.49	$13.53	$13.56
Forfeiture (20%)	$9.81	$11.07	$11.78	$12.15	$12.38	$12.50	$12.57	$12.61	$12.65	$12.67
Forfeiture (25%)	$9.27	$10.41	$11.05	$11.38	$11.59	$11.70	$11.76	$11.80	$11.83	$11.85
Forfeiture (30%)	$8.76	$9.80	$10.37	$10.68	$10.86	$10.96	$11.01	$11.05	$11.08	$11.10
Forfeiture (35%)	$8.28	$9.22	$9.74	$10.02	$10.18	$10.27	$10.32	$10.35	$10.38	$10.39
Forfeiture (40%)	$7.82	$8.69	$9.16	$9.40	$9.55	$9.63	$9.68	$9.71	$9.73	$9.74

Percentage Difference between Binomial and Black-Scholes Model	Suboptimal (1.2)	Suboptimal (1.4)	Suboptimal (1.6)	Suboptimal (1.8)	Suboptimal (2.0)	Suboptimal (2.2)	Suboptimal (2.4)	Suboptimal (2.6)	Suboptimal (2.8)	Suboptimal (3.0)
Forfeiture (0%)	–26.25%	–15.19%	–8.81%	–5.38%	–3.24%	–2.12%	–1.50%	–1.06%	–0.75%	–0.52%
Forfeiture (5%)	–30.43%	–20.40%	–14.66%	–11.58%	–9.67%	–8.67%	–8.12%	–7.72%	–7.44%	–7.24%
Forfeiture (10%)	–34.35%	–25.25%	–20.08%	–17.32%	–15.61%	–14.71%	–14.21%	–13.86%	–13.61%	–13.43%
Forfeiture (15%)	–38.03%	–29.76%	–25.10%	–22.62%	–21.09%	–20.29%	–19.84%	–19.53%	–19.31%	–19.15%
Forfeiture (20%)	–41.48%	–33.97%	–29.77%	–27.54%	–26.17%	–25.44%	–25.05%	–24.77%	–24.57%	–24.42%
Forfeiture (25%)	–44.72%	–37.90%	–34.10%	–32.10%	–30.86%	–30.22%	–29.86%	–29.61%	–29.43%	–29.30%
Forfeiture (30%)	–47.77%	–41.56%	–38.13%	–36.33%	–35.22%	–34.64%	–34.32%	–34.10%	–33.94%	–33.82%
Forfeiture (35%)	–50.64%	–44.98%	–41.88%	–40.26%	–39.26%	–38.74%	–38.46%	–38.25%	–38.11%	–38.01%
Forfeiture (40%)	–53.33%	–48.18%	–45.38%	–43.92%	–43.02%	–42.55%	–42.29%	–42.11%	–41.98%	–41.89%

MATURITY OF 3 YEARS AND VESTING OF 1 YEAR ON AN $80 STOCK PRICE

Stock Price and Strike Price of $80, Maturity of 3 Years, Risk-Free Rate of 3.5%, 35% Volatility, 0% Dividends, Vesting of 1 Year, Employee Suboptimal Exercise Behavior from 1.2 to 3.0, and Forfeiture Rate from 0% to 40%.
Generalized Black-Scholes: $22.36

Customized Binomial Lattice	Suboptimal (1.2)	Suboptimal (1.4)	Suboptimal (1.6)	Suboptimal (1.8)	Suboptimal (2.0)	Suboptimal (2.2)	Suboptimal (2.4)	Suboptimal (2.6)	Suboptimal (2.8)	Suboptimal (3.0)
Forfeiture (0%)	$16.49	$18.96	$20.39	$21.15	$21.63	$21.88	$22.02	$22.12	$22.19	$22.24
Forfeiture (5%)	$15.55	$17.79	$19.08	$19.77	$20.19	$20.42	$20.54	$20.63	$20.69	$20.74
Forfeiture (10%)	$14.68	$16.71	$17.87	$18.48	$18.87	$19.07	$19.18	$19.26	$19.31	$19.35
Forfeiture (15%)	$13.85	$15.70	$16.74	$17.30	$17.64	$17.82	$17.92	$17.99	$18.04	$18.08
Forfeiture (20%)	$13.08	$14.76	$15.70	$16.20	$16.51	$16.67	$16.76	$16.82	$16.86	$16.90
Forfeiture (25%)	$12.36	$13.88	$14.73	$15.18	$15.46	$15.60	$15.68	$15.74	$15.78	$15.80
Forfeiture (30%)	$11.68	$13.06	$13.83	$14.23	$14.48	$14.61	$14.68	$14.73	$14.77	$14.79
Forfeiture (35%)	$11.04	$12.30	$12.99	$13.35	$13.58	$13.69	$13.76	$13.80	$13.84	$13.86
Forfeiture (40%)	$10.43	$11.58	$12.21	$12.54	$12.74	$12.84	$12.90	$12.94	$12.97	$12.99

Percentage Difference between Binomial and Black-Scholes Model	Suboptimal (1.2)	Suboptimal (1.4)	Suboptimal (1.6)	Suboptimal (1.8)	Suboptimal (2.0)	Suboptimal (2.2)	Suboptimal (2.4)	Suboptimal (2.6)	Suboptimal (2.8)	Suboptimal (3.0)
Forfeiture (0%)	–26.25%	–15.19%	–8.81%	–5.38%	–3.24%	–2.12%	–1.50%	–1.06%	–0.75%	–0.52%
Forfeiture (5%)	–30.43%	–20.40%	–14.66%	–11.58%	–9.67%	–8.67%	–8.12%	–7.72%	–7.44%	–7.24%
Forfeiture (10%)	–34.35%	–25.25%	–20.08%	–17.32%	–15.61%	–14.71%	–14.21%	–13.86%	–13.61%	–13.43%
Forfeiture (15%)	–38.03%	–29.76%	–25.10%	–22.62%	–21.09%	–20.29%	–19.84%	–19.53%	–19.31%	–19.15%
Forfeiture (20%)	–41.48%	–33.97%	–29.77%	–27.54%	–26.17%	–25.44%	–25.05%	–24.77%	–24.57%	–24.42%
Forfeiture (25%)	–44.72%	–37.90%	–34.10%	–32.10%	–30.86%	–30.22%	–29.86%	–29.61%	–29.43%	–29.30%
Forfeiture (30%)	–47.77%	–41.56%	–38.13%	–36.33%	–35.22%	–34.64%	–34.32%	–34.10%	–33.94%	–33.82%
Forfeiture (35%)	–50.64%	–44.98%	–41.88%	–40.26%	–39.26%	–38.74%	–38.46%	–38.25%	–38.11%	–38.01%
Forfeiture (40%)	–53.33%	–48.18%	–45.38%	–43.92%	–43.02%	–42.55%	–42.29%	–42.11%	–41.98%	–41.89%

SEVENTY PERCENT VOLATILITY AND 3-YEAR MATURITY ESOs WITH VARYING STOCK PRICE, SUBOPTIMAL BEHAVIOR, VESTING PERIOD, AND FORFEITURE RATES

This section provides ESO valuation results on an underlying stock with 70 percent volatility and a 3-year maturity. The analysis is divided into 1-month and 1-year vesting periods, and accounts for stock prices at grant date of $20, $40, $60, and $80.

MATURITY OF 3 YEARS AND VESTING OF 1 MONTH ON A $20 STOCK PRICE

Stock Price and Strike Price of $20, Maturity of 3 Years, Risk-Free Rate of 3.5%, 70% Volatility, 0% Dividends, Vesting of 1 Month, Employee Suboptimal Exercise Behavior from 1.2 to 3.0, and Forfeiture Rate from 0% to 40%.
Generalized Black-Scholes: $9.68

Customized Binomial Lattice	Suboptimal (1.2)	Suboptimal (1.4)	Suboptimal (1.6)	Suboptimal (1.8)	Suboptimal (2.0)	Suboptimal (2.2)	Suboptimal (2.4)	Suboptimal (2.6)	Suboptimal (2.8)	Suboptimal (3.0)
Forfeiture (0%)	$3.65	$5.34	$6.74	$7.54	$8.15	$8.47	$8.73	$8.93	$9.10	$9.23
Forfeiture (5%)	$3.59	$5.21	$6.53	$7.27	$7.84	$8.13	$8.37	$8.55	$8.70	$8.82
Forfeiture (10%)	$3.53	$5.08	$6.33	$7.03	$7.55	$7.82	$8.03	$8.20	$8.34	$8.45
Forfeiture (15%)	$3.48	$4.96	$6.14	$6.80	$7.28	$7.53	$7.72	$7.88	$8.00	$8.10
Forfeiture (20%)	$3.43	$4.85	$5.97	$6.58	$7.03	$7.26	$7.44	$7.58	$7.69	$7.78
Forfeiture (25%)	$3.38	$4.75	$5.81	$6.38	$6.79	$7.00	$7.17	$7.30	$7.40	$7.48
Forfeiture (30%)	$3.33	$4.65	$5.65	$6.19	$6.58	$6.77	$6.92	$7.04	$7.14	$7.21
Forfeiture (35%)	$3.29	$4.56	$5.51	$6.01	$6.37	$6.55	$6.69	$6.80	$6.89	$6.95
Forfeiture (40%)	$3.24	$4.47	$5.37	$5.85	$6.18	$6.35	$6.48	$6.58	$6.66	$6.72

Percentage Difference between Binomial and Black-Scholes Model	Suboptimal (1.2)	Suboptimal (1.4)	Suboptimal (1.6)	Suboptimal (1.8)	Suboptimal (2.0)	Suboptimal (2.2)	Suboptimal (2.4)	Suboptimal (2.6)	Suboptimal (2.8)	Suboptimal (3.0)
Forfeiture (0%)	−62.31%	−44.87%	−30.41%	−22.12%	−15.81%	−12.53%	−9.87%	−7.73%	−6.04%	−4.69%
Forfeiture (5%)	−62.93%	−46.25%	−32.61%	−24.88%	−19.05%	−16.04%	−13.61%	−11.66%	−10.12%	−8.91%
Forfeiture (10%)	−63.52%	−47.53%	−34.66%	−27.44%	−22.05%	−19.28%	−17.06%	−15.29%	−13.89%	−12.79%
Forfeiture (15%)	−64.08%	−48.75%	−36.57%	−29.83%	−24.83%	−22.29%	−20.25%	−18.64%	−17.36%	−16.37%
Forfeiture (20%)	−64.61%	−49.89%	−38.36%	−32.06%	−27.42%	−25.08%	−23.21%	−21.74%	−20.58%	−19.67%
Forfeiture (25%)	−65.12%	−50.97%	−40.04%	−34.14%	−29.83%	−27.67%	−25.96%	−24.61%	−23.55%	−22.73%
Forfeiture (30%)	−65.61%	−51.99%	−41.62%	−36.08%	−32.08%	−30.08%	−28.51%	−27.28%	−26.31%	−25.57%
Forfeiture (35%)	−66.07%	−52.96%	−43.11%	−37.90%	−34.18%	−32.34%	−30.89%	−29.76%	−28.88%	−28.20%
Forfeiture (40%)	−66.52%	−53.88%	−44.51%	−39.62%	−36.15%	−34.44%	−33.10%	−32.07%	−31.27%	−30.65%

MATURITY OF 3 YEARS AND VESTING OF 1 MONTH ON A $40 STOCK PRICE

Stock Price and Strike Price of $40, Maturity of 3 Years, Risk-Free Rate of 3.5%, 70% Volatility, 0% Dividends, Vesting of 1 Month, Employee Suboptimal Exercise Behavior from 1.2 to 3.0, and Forfeiture Rate from 0% to 40%.
Generalized Black-Scholes: $19.37

Customized Binomial Lattice	Suboptimal (1.2)	Suboptimal (1.4)	Suboptimal (1.6)	Suboptimal (1.8)	Suboptimal (2.0)	Suboptimal (2.2)	Suboptimal (2.4)	Suboptimal (2.6)	Suboptimal (2.8)	Suboptimal (3.0)
Forfeiture (0%)	$7.30	$10.68	$13.48	$15.08	$16.31	$16.94	$17.46	$17.87	$18.20	$18.46
Forfeiture (5%)	$7.18	$10.41	$13.05	$14.55	$15.68	$16.26	$16.73	$17.11	$17.41	$17.64
Forfeiture (10%)	$7.07	$10.16	$12.66	$14.05	$15.10	$15.63	$16.06	$16.41	$16.68	$16.89
Forfeiture (15%)	$6.96	$9.93	$12.28	$13.59	$14.56	$15.05	$15.45	$15.76	$16.00	$16.20
Forfeiture (20%)	$6.85	$9.71	$11.94	$13.16	$14.06	$14.51	$14.87	$15.16	$15.38	$15.56
Forfeiture (25%)	$6.76	$9.50	$11.61	$12.76	$13.59	$14.01	$14.34	$14.60	$14.81	$14.96
Forfeiture (30%)	$6.66	$9.30	$11.31	$12.38	$13.15	$13.54	$13.85	$14.09	$14.27	$14.42
Forfeiture (35%)	$6.57	$9.11	$11.02	$12.03	$12.75	$13.10	$13.39	$13.60	$13.77	$13.91
Forfeiture (40%)	$6.48	$8.93	$10.75	$11.69	$12.37	$12.70	$12.96	$13.16	$13.31	$13.43

Percentage Difference between Binomial and Black-Scholes Model	Suboptimal (1.2)	Suboptimal (1.4)	Suboptimal (1.6)	Suboptimal (1.8)	Suboptimal (2.0)	Suboptimal (2.2)	Suboptimal (2.4)	Suboptimal (2.6)	Suboptimal (2.8)	Suboptimal (3.0)
Forfeiture (0%)	–62.31%	–44.87%	–30.41%	–22.12%	–15.81%	–12.53%	–9.87%	–7.73%	–6.04%	–4.69%
Forfeiture (5%)	–62.93%	–46.25%	–32.61%	–24.88%	–19.05%	–16.04%	–13.61%	–11.66%	–10.12%	–8.91%
Forfeiture (10%)	–63.52%	–47.53%	–34.66%	–27.44%	–22.05%	–19.28%	–17.06%	–15.29%	–13.89%	–12.79%
Forfeiture (15%)	–64.08%	–48.75%	–36.57%	–29.83%	–24.83%	–22.29%	–20.25%	–18.64%	–17.36%	–16.37%
Forfeiture (20%)	–64.61%	–49.89%	–38.36%	–32.06%	–27.42%	–25.08%	–23.21%	–21.74%	–20.58%	–19.67%
Forfeiture (25%)	–65.12%	–50.97%	–40.04%	–34.14%	–29.83%	–27.67%	–25.96%	–24.61%	–23.55%	–22.73%
Forfeiture (30%)	–65.61%	–51.99%	–41.62%	–36.08%	–32.08%	–30.08%	–28.51%	–27.28%	–26.31%	–25.57%
Forfeiture (35%)	–66.07%	–52.96%	–43.11%	–37.90%	–34.18%	–32.34%	–30.89%	–29.76%	–28.88%	–28.20%
Forfeiture (40%)	–66.52%	–53.88%	–44.51%	–39.62%	–36.15%	–34.44%	–33.10%	–32.07%	–31.27%	–30.65%

MATURITY OF 3 YEARS AND VESTING OF 1 MONTH ON A $60 STOCK PRICE

Stock Price and Strike Price of $60, Maturity of 3 Years, Risk-Free Rate of 3.5%, 70% Volatility, 0% Dividends, Vesting of 1 Month, Employee Suboptimal Exercise Behavior from 1.2 to 3.0, and Forfeiture Rate from 0% to 40%.
Generalized Black-Scholes: $29.05

Customized Binomial Lattice	Suboptimal (1.2)	Suboptimal (1.4)	Suboptimal (1.6)	Suboptimal (1.8)	Suboptimal (2.0)	Suboptimal (2.2)	Suboptimal (2.4)	Suboptimal (2.6)	Suboptimal (2.8)	Suboptimal (3.0)
Forfeiture (0%)	$10.95	$16.02	$20.22	$22.63	$24.46	$25.41	$26.18	$26.80	$27.30	$27.69
Forfeiture (5%)	$10.77	$15.62	$19.58	$21.82	$23.52	$24.39	$25.10	$25.66	$26.11	$26.46
Forfeiture (10%)	$10.60	$15.24	$18.98	$21.08	$22.65	$23.45	$24.10	$24.61	$25.02	$25.34
Forfeiture (15%)	$10.44	$14.89	$18.43	$20.39	$21.84	$22.58	$23.17	$23.64	$24.01	$24.30
Forfeiture (20%)	$10.28	$14.56	$17.91	$19.74	$21.09	$21.77	$22.31	$22.74	$23.07	$23.34
Forfeiture (25%)	$10.13	$14.24	$17.42	$19.13	$20.38	$21.01	$21.51	$21.90	$22.21	$22.45
Forfeiture (30%)	$9.99	$13.95	$16.96	$18.57	$19.73	$20.31	$20.77	$21.13	$21.41	$21.62
Forfeiture (35%)	$9.86	$13.67	$16.53	$18.04	$19.12	$19.66	$20.08	$20.41	$20.66	$20.86
Forfeiture (40%)	$9.73	$13.40	$16.12	$17.54	$18.55	$19.05	$19.43	$19.74	$19.97	$20.15

Percentage Difference between Binomial and Black-Scholes Model	Suboptimal (1.2)	Suboptimal (1.4)	Suboptimal (1.6)	Suboptimal (1.8)	Suboptimal (2.0)	Suboptimal (2.2)	Suboptimal (2.4)	Suboptimal (2.6)	Suboptimal (2.8)	Suboptimal (3.0)
Forfeiture (0%)	–62.31%	–44.87%	–30.41%	–22.12%	–15.81%	–12.53%	–9.87%	–7.73%	–6.04%	–4.69%
Forfeiture (5%)	–62.93%	–46.25%	–32.61%	–24.88%	–19.05%	–16.04%	–13.61%	–11.66%	–10.12%	–8.91%
Forfeiture (10%)	–63.52%	–47.53%	–34.66%	–27.44%	–22.05%	–19.28%	–17.06%	–15.29%	–13.89%	–12.79%
Forfeiture (15%)	–64.08%	–48.75%	–36.57%	–29.83%	–24.83%	–22.29%	–20.25%	–18.64%	–17.36%	–16.37%
Forfeiture (20%)	–64.61%	–49.89%	–38.36%	–32.06%	–27.42%	–25.08%	–23.21%	–21.74%	–20.58%	–19.67%
Forfeiture (25%)	–65.12%	–50.97%	–40.04%	–34.14%	–29.83%	–27.67%	–25.96%	–24.61%	–23.55%	–22.73%
Forfeiture (30%)	–65.61%	–51.99%	–41.62%	–36.08%	–32.08%	–30.08%	–28.51%	–27.28%	–26.31%	–25.57%
Forfeiture (35%)	–66.07%	–52.96%	–43.11%	–37.90%	–34.18%	–32.34%	–30.89%	–29.76%	–28.88%	–28.20%
Forfeiture (40%)	–66.52%	–53.88%	–44.51%	–39.62%	–36.15%	–34.44%	–33.10%	–32.07%	–31.27%	–30.65%

MATURITY OF 3 YEARS AND VESTING OF 1 MONTH ON AN $80 STOCK PRICE

Stock Price and Strike Price of $80, Maturity of 3 Years, Risk-Free Rate of 3.5%, 70% Volatility, 0% Dividends, Vesting of 1 Month, Employee Suboptimal Exercise Behavior from 1.2 to 3.0, and Forfeiture Rate from 0% to 40%.
Generalized Black-Scholes: $38.74

Customized Binomial Lattice	Suboptimal (1.2)	Suboptimal (1.4)	Suboptimal (1.6)	Suboptimal (1.8)	Suboptimal (2.0)	Suboptimal (2.2)	Suboptimal (2.4)	Suboptimal (2.6)	Suboptimal (2.8)	Suboptimal (3.0)
Forfeiture (0%)	$14.60	$21.35	$26.95	$30.17	$32.61	$33.88	$34.91	$35.74	$36.40	$36.92
Forfeiture (5%)	$14.36	$20.82	$26.10	$29.10	$31.36	$32.52	$33.46	$34.22	$34.81	$35.28
Forfeiture (10%)	$14.13	$20.32	$25.31	$28.11	$30.20	$31.27	$32.13	$32.81	$33.36	$33.78
Forfeiture (15%)	$13.92	$19.85	$24.57	$27.18	$29.12	$30.10	$30.89	$31.52	$32.01	$32.40
Forfeiture (20%)	$13.71	$19.41	$23.88	$26.32	$28.11	$29.02	$29.74	$30.32	$30.76	$31.11
Forfeiture (25%)	$13.51	$18.99	$23.22	$25.51	$27.18	$28.02	$28.68	$29.20	$29.61	$29.93
Forfeiture (30%)	$13.32	$18.60	$22.61	$24.76	$26.31	$27.08	$27.69	$28.17	$28.54	$28.83
Forfeiture (35%)	$13.14	$18.22	$22.04	$24.05	$25.49	$26.21	$26.77	$27.21	$27.55	$27.81
Forfeiture (40%)	$12.97	$17.87	$21.50	$23.39	$24.73	$25.40	$25.91	$26.31	$26.62	$26.86

Percentage Difference between Binomial and Black-Scholes Model	Suboptimal (1.2)	Suboptimal (1.4)	Suboptimal (1.6)	Suboptimal (1.8)	Suboptimal (2.0)	Suboptimal (2.2)	Suboptimal (2.4)	Suboptimal (2.6)	Suboptimal (2.8)	Suboptimal (3.0)
Forfeiture (0%)	−62.31%	−44.87%	−30.41%	−22.12%	−15.81%	−12.53%	−9.87%	−7.73%	−6.04%	−4.69%
Forfeiture (5%)	−62.93%	−46.25%	−32.61%	−24.88%	−19.05%	−16.04%	−13.61%	−11.66%	−10.12%	−8.91%
Forfeiture (10%)	−63.52%	−47.53%	−34.66%	−27.44%	−22.05%	−19.28%	−17.06%	−15.29%	−13.89%	−12.79%
Forfeiture (15%)	−64.08%	−48.75%	−36.57%	−29.83%	−24.83%	−22.29%	−20.25%	−18.64%	−17.36%	−16.37%
Forfeiture (20%)	−64.61%	−49.89%	−38.36%	−32.06%	−27.42%	−25.08%	−23.21%	−21.74%	−20.58%	−19.67%
Forfeiture (25%)	−65.12%	−50.97%	−40.04%	−34.14%	−29.83%	−27.67%	−25.96%	−24.61%	−23.55%	−22.73%
Forfeiture (30%)	−65.61%	−51.99%	−41.62%	−36.08%	−32.08%	−30.08%	−28.51%	−27.28%	−26.31%	−25.57%
Forfeiture (35%)	−66.07%	−52.96%	−43.11%	−37.90%	−34.18%	−32.34%	−30.89%	−29.76%	−28.88%	−28.20%
Forfeiture (40%)	−66.52%	−53.88%	−44.51%	−39.62%	−36.15%	−34.44%	−33.10%	−32.07%	−31.27%	−30.65%

MATURITY OF 3 YEARS AND VESTING OF 1 YEAR ON A $20 STOCK PRICE

Stock Price and Strike Price of $20, Maturity of 3 Years, Risk-Free Rate of 3.5%, 70% Volatility, 0% Dividends, Vesting of 1 Year, Employee Suboptimal Exercise Behavior from 1.2 to 3.0, and Forfeiture Rate from 0% to 40%.
Generalized Black-Scholes: $9.68

Customized Binomial Lattice	Suboptimal (1.2)	Suboptimal (1.4)	Suboptimal (1.6)	Suboptimal (1.8)	Suboptimal (2.0)	Suboptimal (2.2)	Suboptimal (2.4)	Suboptimal (2.6)	Suboptimal (2.8)	Suboptimal (3.0)
Forfeiture (0%)	$6.73	$7.44	$8.04	$8.41	$8.72	$8.89	$9.04	$9.16	$9.26	$9.34
Forfeiture (5%)	$6.38	$7.03	$7.57	$7.91	$8.19	$8.34	$8.47	$8.58	$8.67	$8.74
Forfeiture (10%)	$6.04	$6.64	$7.13	$7.44	$7.69	$7.83	$7.94	$8.04	$8.12	$8.19
Forfeiture (15%)	$5.73	$6.27	$6.72	$7.00	$7.23	$7.35	$7.46	$7.54	$7.62	$7.68
Forfeiture (20%)	$5.43	$5.93	$6.34	$6.59	$6.80	$6.91	$7.00	$7.08	$7.14	$7.20
Forfeiture (25%)	$5.14	$5.60	$5.98	$6.21	$6.39	$6.49	$6.58	$6.65	$6.71	$6.75
Forfeiture (30%)	$4.88	$5.30	$5.64	$5.85	$6.02	$6.11	$6.18	$6.25	$6.30	$6.34
Forfeiture (35%)	$4.62	$5.01	$5.33	$5.51	$5.67	$5.75	$5.82	$5.87	$5.92	$5.96
Forfeiture (40%)	$4.38	$4.74	$5.03	$5.20	$5.34	$5.41	$5.47	$5.52	$5.57	$5.60

Percentage Difference between Binomial and Black-Scholes Model	Suboptimal (1.2)	Suboptimal (1.4)	Suboptimal (1.6)	Suboptimal (1.8)	Suboptimal (2.0)	Suboptimal (2.2)	Suboptimal (2.4)	Suboptimal (2.6)	Suboptimal (2.8)	Suboptimal (3.0)
Forfeiture (0%)	–30.46%	–23.15%	–16.95%	–13.13%	–9.94%	–8.19%	–6.69%	–5.44%	–4.39%	–3.53%
Forfeiture (5%)	–34.13%	–27.43%	–21.79%	–18.34%	–15.46%	–13.88%	–12.54%	–11.42%	–10.48%	–9.71%
Forfeiture (10%)	–37.60%	–31.46%	–26.32%	–23.19%	–20.59%	–19.17%	–17.97%	–16.96%	–16.12%	–15.44%
Forfeiture (15%)	–40.87%	–35.24%	–30.56%	–27.72%	–25.37%	–24.09%	–23.01%	–22.11%	–21.36%	–20.74%
Forfeiture (20%)	–43.96%	–38.79%	–34.53%	–31.95%	–29.83%	–28.68%	–27.71%	–26.89%	–26.22%	–25.67%
Forfeiture (25%)	–46.88%	–42.13%	–38.24%	–35.91%	–33.99%	–32.95%	–32.07%	–31.34%	–30.74%	–30.25%
Forfeiture (30%)	–49.65%	–45.28%	–41.73%	–39.61%	–37.87%	–36.93%	–36.14%	–35.49%	–34.95%	–34.50%
Forfeiture (35%)	–52.26%	–48.24%	–45.00%	–43.07%	–41.50%	–40.65%	–39.94%	–39.35%	–38.86%	–38.47%
Forfeiture (40%)	–54.73%	–51.03%	–48.07%	–46.32%	–44.89%	–44.13%	–43.48%	–42.95%	–42.52%	–42.16%

MATURITY OF 3 YEARS AND VESTING OF 1 YEAR ON A $40 STOCK PRICE

Stock Price and Strike Price of $40, Maturity of 3 Years, Risk-Free Rate of 3.5%, 70% Volatility, 0% Dividends, Vesting of 1 Year, Employee Suboptimal Exercise Behavior from 1.2 to 3.0, and Forfeiture Rate from 0% to 40%.
Generalized Black-Scholes: $19.37

Customized Binomial Lattice	Suboptimal (1.2)	Suboptimal (1.4)	Suboptimal (1.6)	Suboptimal (1.8)	Suboptimal (2.0)	Suboptimal (2.2)	Suboptimal (2.4)	Suboptimal (2.6)	Suboptimal (2.8)	Suboptimal (3.0)
Forfeiture (0%)	$13.47	$14.88	$16.08	$16.82	$17.44	$17.78	$18.07	$18.31	$18.52	$18.68
Forfeiture (5%)	$12.76	$14.05	$15.15	$15.82	$16.37	$16.68	$16.94	$17.16	$17.34	$17.49
Forfeiture (10%)	$12.09	$13.28	$14.27	$14.88	$15.38	$15.65	$15.89	$16.08	$16.25	$16.38
Forfeiture (15%)	$11.45	$12.54	$13.45	$14.00	$14.45	$14.70	$14.91	$15.09	$15.23	$15.35
Forfeiture (20%)	$10.85	$11.85	$12.68	$13.18	$13.59	$13.81	$14.00	$14.16	$14.29	$14.40
Forfeiture (25%)	$10.29	$11.21	$11.96	$12.41	$12.78	$12.99	$13.16	$13.30	$13.41	$13.51
Forfeiture (30%)	$9.75	$10.60	$11.29	$11.70	$12.03	$12.21	$12.37	$12.49	$12.60	$12.68
Forfeiture (35%)	$9.25	$10.02	$10.65	$11.03	$11.33	$11.49	$11.63	$11.75	$11.84	$11.92
Forfeiture (40%)	$8.77	$9.48	$10.06	$10.40	$10.67	$10.82	$10.95	$11.05	$11.13	$11.20

Percentage Difference between Binomial and Black-Scholes Model	Suboptimal (1.2)	Suboptimal (1.4)	Suboptimal (1.6)	Suboptimal (1.8)	Suboptimal (2.0)	Suboptimal (2.2)	Suboptimal (2.4)	Suboptimal (2.6)	Suboptimal (2.8)	Suboptimal (3.0)
Forfeiture (0%)	–30.46%	–23.15%	–16.95%	–13.13%	–9.94%	–8.19%	–6.69%	–5.44%	–4.39%	–3.53%
Forfeiture (5%)	–34.13%	–27.43%	–21.79%	–18.34%	15.46%	–13.88%	–12.54%	–11.42%	–10.48%	–9.71%
Forfeiture (10%)	–37.60%	–31.46%	–26.32%	–23.19%	20.59%	–19.17%	–17.97%	–16.96%	–16.12%	–15.44%
Forfeiture (15%)	–40.87%	–35.24%	–30.56%	–27.72%	25.37%	–24.09%	–23.01%	–22.11%	–21.36%	–20.74%
Forfeiture (20%)	–43.96%	–38.79%	–34.53%	–31.95%	29.83%	–28.68%	–27.71%	–26.89%	–26.22%	–25.67%
Forfeiture (25%)	–46.88%	–42.13%	–38.24%	–35.91%	33.99%	–32.95%	–32.07%	–31.34%	–30.74%	–30.25%
Forfeiture (30%)	–49.65%	–45.28%	–41.73%	–39.61%	37.87%	–36.93%	–36.14%	–35.49%	–34.95%	–34.50%
Forfeiture (35%)	–52.26%	–48.24%	–45.00%	–43.07%	41.50%	–40.65%	–39.94%	–39.35%	–38.86%	–38.47%
Forfeiture (40%)	–54.73%	–51.03%	–48.07%	–46.32%	44.89%	–44.13%	–43.48%	–42.95%	–42.52%	–42.16%

MATURITY OF 3 YEARS AND VESTING OF 1 YEAR ON A $60 STOCK PRICE

Stock Price and Strike Price of $60, Maturity of 3 Years, Risk-Free Rate of 3.5%, 70% Volatility, 0% Dividends, Vesting of 1 Year, Employee Suboptimal Exercise Behavior from 1.2 to 3.0, and Forfeiture Rate from 0% to 40%.
Generalized Black-Scholes: $29.05

Customized Binomial Lattice	Suboptimal (1.2)	Suboptimal (1.4)	Suboptimal (1.6)	Suboptimal (1.8)	Suboptimal (2.0)	Suboptimal (2.2)	Suboptimal (2.4)	Suboptimal (2.6)	Suboptimal (2.8)	Suboptimal (3.0)
Forfeiture (0%)	$20.20	$22.33	$24.13	$25.24	$26.16	$26.67	$27.11	$27.47	$27.78	$28.03
Forfeiture (5%)	$19.14	$21.08	$22.72	$23.72	$24.56	$25.02	$25.41	$25.74	$26.01	$26.23
Forfeiture (10%)	$18.13	$19.91	$21.40	$22.31	$23.07	$23.48	$23.83	$24.12	$24.37	$24.57
Forfeiture (15%)	$17.18	$18.81	$20.17	$21.00	$21.68	$22.05	$22.37	$22.63	$22.85	$23.03
Forfeiture (20%)	$16.28	$17.78	$19.02	$19.77	$20.39	$20.72	$21.00	$21.24	$21.43	$21.59
Forfeiture (25%)	$15.43	$16.81	$17.94	$18.62	$19.18	$19.48	$19.73	$19.95	$20.12	$20.26
Forfeiture (30%)	$14.63	$15.90	$16.93	$17.54	$18.05	$18.32	$18.55	$18.74	$18.90	$19.03
Forfeiture (35%)	$13.87	$15.04	$15.98	$16.54	$17.00	$17.24	$17.45	$17.62	$17.76	$17.88
Forfeiture (40%)	$13.15	$14.23	$15.09	$15.60	$16.01	$16.23	$16.42	$16.57	$16.70	$16.80

Percentage Difference between Binomial and Black-Scholes Model	Suboptimal (1.2)	Suboptimal (1.4)	Suboptimal (1.6)	Suboptimal (1.8)	Suboptimal (2.0)	Suboptimal (2.2)	Suboptimal (2.4)	Suboptimal (2.6)	Suboptimal (2.8)	Suboptimal (3.0)
Forfeiture (0%)	–30.46%	–23.15%	–16.95%	–13.13%	–9.94%	–8.19%	–6.69%	–5.44%	–4.39%	–3.53%
Forfeiture (5%)	–34.13%	–27.43%	–21.79%	–18.34%	–15.46%	–13.88%	–12.54%	–11.42%	–10.48%	–9.71%
Forfeiture (10%)	–37.60%	–31.46%	–26.32%	–23.19%	–20.59%	–19.17%	–17.97%	–16.96%	–16.12%	–15.44%
Forfeiture (15%)	–40.87%	–35.24%	–30.56%	–27.72%	–25.37%	–24.09%	–23.01%	–22.11%	–21.36%	–20.74%
Forfeiture (20%)	–43.96%	–38.79%	–34.53%	–31.95%	–29.83%	–28.68%	–27.71%	–26.89%	–26.22%	–25.67%
Forfeiture (25%)	–46.88%	–42.13%	–38.24%	–35.91%	–33.99%	–32.95%	–32.07%	–31.34%	–30.74%	–30.25%
Forfeiture (30%)	–49.65%	–45.28%	–41.73%	–39.61%	–37.87%	–36.93%	–36.14%	–35.49%	–34.95%	–34.50%
Forfeiture (35%)	–52.26%	–48.24%	–45.00%	–43.07%	–41.50%	–40.65%	–39.94%	–39.35%	–38.86%	–38.47%
Forfeiture (40%)	–54.73%	–51.03%	–48.07%	–46.32%	–44.89%	–44.13%	–43.48%	–42.95%	–42.52%	–42.16%

MATURITY OF 3 YEARS AND VESTING OF 1 YEAR ON AN $80 STOCK PRICE

Stock Price and Strike Price of $80, Maturity of 3 Years, Risk-Free Rate of 3.5%, 70% Volatility, 0% Dividends, Vesting of 1 Year,
Employee Suboptimal Exercise Behavior from 1.2 to 3.0, and Forfeiture Rate from 0% to 40%.
Generalized Black-Scholes: $38.74

Customized Binomial Lattice	Suboptimal (1.2)	Suboptimal (1.4)	Suboptimal (1.6)	Suboptimal (1.8)	Suboptimal (2.0)	Suboptimal (2.2)	Suboptimal (2.4)	Suboptimal (2.6)	Suboptimal (2.8)	Suboptimal (3.0)
Forfeiture (0%)	$26.94	$29.77	$32.17	$33.65	$34.89	$35.56	$36.14	$36.63	$37.03	$37.37
Forfeiture (5%)	$25.52	$28.11	$30.29	$31.63	$32.75	$33.36	$33.88	$34.31	$34.68	$34.97
Forfeiture (10%)	$24.17	$26.55	$28.54	$29.75	$30.76	$31.31	$31.78	$32.17	$32.49	$32.76
Forfeiture (15%)	$22.90	$25.09	$26.90	$28.00	$28.91	$29.40	$29.82	$30.17	$30.46	$30.70
Forfeiture (20%)	$21.71	$23.71	$25.36	$26.36	$27.18	$27.63	$28.00	$28.32	$28.58	$28.79
Forfeiture (25%)	$20.57	$22.41	$23.92	$24.83	$25.57	$25.97	$26.31	$26.59	$26.83	$27.02
Forfeiture (30%)	$19.50	$21.20	$22.57	$23.39	$24.07	$24.43	$24.73	$24.99	$25.20	$25.37
Forfeiture (35%)	$18.49	$20.05	$21.31	$22.05	$22.66	$22.99	$23.26	$23.49	$23.68	$23.83
Forfeiture (40%)	$17.54	$18.97	$20.12	$20.79	$21.35	$21.64	$21.89	$22.10	$22.27	$22.40

Percentage Difference between Binomial and Black-Scholes Model	Suboptimal (1.2)	Suboptimal (1.4)	Suboptimal (1.6)	Suboptimal (1.8)	Suboptimal (2.0)	Suboptimal (2.2)	Suboptimal (2.4)	Suboptimal (2.6)	Suboptimal (2.8)	Suboptimal (3.0)
Forfeiture (0%)	–30.46%	–23.15%	–16.95%	–13.13%	–9.94%	–8.19%	–6.69%	–5.44%	–4.39%	–3.53%
Forfeiture (5%)	–34.13%	–27.43%	–21.79%	–18.34%	–15.46%	–13.88%	–12.54%	–11.42%	–10.48%	–9.71%
Forfeiture (10%)	–37.60%	–31.46%	–26.32%	–23.19%	–20.59%	–19.17%	–17.97%	–16.96%	–16.12%	–15.44%
Forfeiture (15%)	–40.87%	–35.24%	–30.56%	–27.72%	–25.37%	–24.09%	–23.01%	–22.11%	–21.36%	–20.74%
Forfeiture (20%)	–43.96%	–38.79%	–34.53%	–31.95%	–29.83%	–28.68%	–27.71%	–26.89%	–26.22%	–25.67%
Forfeiture (25%)	–46.88%	–42.13%	–38.24%	–35.91%	–33.99%	–32.95%	–32.07%	–31.34%	–30.74%	–30.25%
Forfeiture (30%)	–49.65%	–45.28%	–41.73%	–39.61%	–37.87%	–36.93%	–36.14%	–35.49%	–34.95%	–34.50%
Forfeiture (35%)	–52.26%	–48.24%	–45.00%	–43.07%	–41.50%	–40.65%	–39.94%	–39.35%	–38.86%	–38.47%
Forfeiture (40%)	–54.73%	–51.03%	–48.07%	–46.32%	–44.89%	–44.13%	–43.48%	–42.95%	–42.52%	–42.16%

THIRTY-FIVE PERCENT VOLATILITY AND 5-YEAR MATURITY ESOs WITH VARYING STOCK PRICE, SUBOPTIMAL BEHAVIOR, VESTING PERIOD, AND FORFEITURE RATES

This section provides ESO valuation results on an underlying stock with 35 percent volatility and a 5-year maturity. The analysis is divided into 1-month, 1-year, and 3-year vesting periods, and accounts for stock prices at grant date of $20, $40, $60, and $80.

MATURITY OF 5 YEARS AND VESTING OF 1 MONTH ON A $20 STOCK PRICE

Stock Price and Strike Price of $20, Maturity of 5 Years, Risk-Free Rate of 3.5%, 35% Volatility, 0% Dividends, Vesting of 1 Month, Employee Suboptimal Exercise Behavior from 1.2 to 3.0, and Forfeiture Rate from 0% to 40%.
Generalized Black-Scholes: $7.34

Customized Binomial Lattice	Suboptimal (1.2)	Suboptimal (1.4)	Suboptimal (1.6)	Suboptimal (1.8)	Suboptimal (2.0)	Suboptimal (2.2)	Suboptimal (2.4)	Suboptimal (2.6)	Suboptimal (2.8)	Suboptimal (3.0)
Forfeiture (0%)	$3.27	$4.85	$5.75	$6.33	$6.71	$6.86	$7.01	$7.09	$7.15	$7.20
Forfeiture (5%)	$3.15	$4.59	$5.38	$5.89	$6.21	$6.34	$6.47	$6.54	$6.59	$6.62
Forfeiture (10%)	$3.04	$4.36	$5.06	$5.50	$5.78	$5.89	$6.00	$6.05	$6.10	$6.13
Forfeiture (15%)	$2.94	$4.15	$4.77	$5.16	$5.40	$5.50	$5.59	$5.63	$5.67	$5.70
Forfeiture (20%)	$2.85	$3.96	$4.52	$4.86	$5.07	$5.15	$5.23	$5.27	$5.30	$5.32
Forfeiture (25%)	$2.77	$3.80	$4.30	$4.60	$4.77	$4.85	$4.91	$4.94	$4.97	$4.99
Forfeiture (30%)	$2.69	$3.64	$4.09	$4.36	$4.51	$4.57	$4.63	$4.66	$4.68	$4.70
Forfeiture (35%)	$2.62	$3.50	$3.91	$4.15	$4.28	$4.33	$4.38	$4.41	$4.43	$4.44
Forfeiture (40%)	$2.56	$3.38	$3.75	$3.96	$4.07	$4.12	$4.16	$4.18	$4.20	$4.21

Percentage Difference between Binomial and Black-Scholes Model	Suboptimal (1.2)	Suboptimal (1.4)	Suboptimal (1.6)	Suboptimal (1.8)	Suboptimal (2.0)	Suboptimal (2.2)	Suboptimal (2.4)	Suboptimal (2.6)	Suboptimal (2.8)	Suboptimal (3.0)
Forfeiture (0%)	-55.39%	-33.83%	-21.70%	-13.67%	-8.54%	-6.44%	-4.43%	-3.36%	-2.55%	-1.93%
Forfeiture (5%)	-57.05%	-37.41%	-26.68%	-19.71%	-15.32%	-13.53%	-11.83%	-10.93%	-10.25%	-9.74%
Forfeiture (10%)	-58.54%	-40.59%	-31.06%	-24.99%	-21.22%	-19.70%	-18.26%	-17.49%	-16.92%	-16.49%
Forfeiture (15%)	-59.90%	-43.43%	-34.94%	-29.63%	-26.38%	-25.08%	-23.86%	-23.21%	-22.73%	-22.37%
Forfeiture (20%)	-61.14%	-45.98%	-38.38%	-33.73%	-30.92%	-29.81%	-28.76%	-28.21%	-27.81%	-27.50%
Forfeiture (25%)	-62.27%	-48.27%	-41.46%	-37.36%	-34.92%	-33.97%	-33.08%	-32.61%	-32.26%	-32.01%
Forfeiture (30%)	-63.31%	-50.35%	-44.21%	-40.60%	-38.48%	-37.65%	-36.89%	-36.49%	-36.20%	-35.98%
Forfeiture (35%)	-64.28%	-52.23%	-46.69%	-43.49%	-41.64%	-40.92%	-40.27%	-39.93%	-39.68%	-39.49%
Forfeiture (40%)	-65.17%	-53.95%	-48.93%	-46.09%	-44.47%	-43.85%	-43.28%	-42.99%	-42.77%	-42.62%

MATURITY OF 5 YEARS AND VESTING OF 1 MONTH ON A $40 STOCK PRICE

Stock Price and Strike Price of $40, Maturity of 5 Years, Risk-Free Rate of 3.5%, 35% Volatility, 0% Dividends, Vesting of 1 Month, Employee Suboptimal Exercise Behavior from 1.2 to 3.0, and Forfeiture Rate from 0% to 40%.
Generalized Black-Scholes: $14.67

Customized Binomial Lattice	Suboptimal (1.2)	Suboptimal (1.4)	Suboptimal (1.6)	Suboptimal (1.8)	Suboptimal (2.0)	Suboptimal (2.2)	Suboptimal (2.4)	Suboptimal (2.6)	Suboptimal (2.8)	Suboptimal (3.0)
Forfeiture (0%)	$6.55	$9.71	$11.49	$12.67	$13.42	$13.73	$14.02	$14.18	$14.30	$14.39
Forfeiture (5%)	$6.30	$9.18	$10.76	$11.78	$12.43	$12.69	$12.94	$13.07	$13.17	$13.25
Forfeiture (10%)	$6.08	$8.72	$10.12	$11.01	$11.56	$11.78	$12.00	$12.11	$12.19	$12.25
Forfeiture (15%)	$5.88	$8.30	$9.55	$10.33	$10.80	$10.99	$11.17	$11.27	$11.34	$11.39
Forfeiture (20%)	$5.70	$7.93	$9.04	$9.73	$10.14	$10.30	$10.45	$10.53	$10.59	$10.64
Forfeiture (25%)	$5.54	$7.59	$8.59	$9.19	$9.55	$9.69	$9.82	$9.89	$9.94	$9.98
Forfeiture (30%)	$5.38	$7.29	$8.19	$8.72	$9.03	$9.15	$9.26	$9.32	$9.36	$9.40
Forfeiture (35%)	$5.24	$7.01	$7.82	$8.29	$8.56	$8.67	$8.77	$8.82	$8.85	$8.88
Forfeiture (40%)	$5.11	$6.76	$7.49	$7.91	$8.15	$8.24	$8.32	$8.37	$8.40	$8.42

Percentage Difference between Binomial and Black-Scholes Model	Suboptimal (1.2)	Suboptimal (1.4)	Suboptimal (1.6)	Suboptimal (1.8)	Suboptimal (2.0)	Suboptimal (2.2)	Suboptimal (2.4)	Suboptimal (2.6)	Suboptimal (2.8)	Suboptimal (3.0)
Forfeiture (0%)	−55.39%	−33.83%	−21.70%	−13.67%	−8.54%	−6.44%	−4.43%	−3.36%	−2.55%	−1.93%
Forfeiture (5%)	−57.05%	−37.41%	−26.68%	−19.71%	−15.32%	−13.53%	−11.83%	−10.93%	−10.25%	−9.74%
Forfeiture (10%)	−58.54%	−40.59%	−31.06%	−24.99%	−21.22%	−19.70%	−18.26%	−17.49%	−16.92%	−16.49%
Forfeiture (15%)	−59.90%	−43.43%	−34.94%	−29.63%	−26.38%	−25.08%	−23.86%	−23.21%	−22.73%	−22.37%
Forfeiture (20%)	−61.14%	−45.98%	−38.38%	−33.73%	−30.92%	−29.81%	−28.76%	−28.21%	−27.81%	−27.50%
Forfeiture (25%)	−62.27%	−48.27%	−41.46%	−37.36%	−34.92%	−33.97%	−33.08%	−32.61%	−32.26%	−32.01%
Forfeiture (30%)	−63.31%	−50.35%	−44.21%	−40.60%	−38.48%	−37.65%	−36.89%	−36.49%	−36.20%	−35.98%
Forfeiture (35%)	−64.28%	−52.23%	−46.69%	−43.49%	−41.64%	−40.92%	−40.27%	−39.93%	−39.68%	−39.49%
Forfeiture (40%)	−65.17%	−53.95%	−48.93%	−46.09%	−44.47%	−43.85%	−43.28%	−42.99%	−42.77%	−42.62%

MATURITY OF 5 YEARS AND VESTING OF 1 MONTH ON A $60 STOCK PRICE

Stock Price and Strike Price of $60, Maturity of 5 Years, Risk-Free Rate of 3.5%, 35% Volatility, 0% Dividends, Vesting of 1 Month, Employee Suboptimal Exercise Behavior from 1.2 to 3.0, and Forfeiture Rate from 0% to 40%.
Generalized Black-Scholes: $22.01

Customized Binomial Lattice	Suboptimal (1.2)	Suboptimal (1.4)	Suboptimal (1.6)	Suboptimal (1.8)	Suboptimal (2.0)	Suboptimal (2.2)	Suboptimal (2.4)	Suboptimal (2.6)	Suboptimal (2.8)	Suboptimal (3.0)
Forfeiture (0%)	$9.82	$14.56	$17.24	$19.00	$20.13	$20.59	$21.04	$21.27	$21.45	$21.59
Forfeiture (5%)	$9.46	$13.78	$16.14	$17.67	$18.64	$19.03	$19.41	$19.61	$19.76	$19.87
Forfeiture (10%)	$9.13	$13.08	$15.18	$16.51	$17.34	$17.68	$17.99	$18.16	$18.29	$18.38
Forfeiture (15%)	$8.83	$12.45	$14.32	$15.49	$16.21	$16.49	$16.76	$16.90	$17.01	$17.09
Forfeiture (20%)	$8.55	$11.89	$13.56	$14.59	$15.21	$15.45	$15.68	$15.80	$15.89	$15.96
Forfeiture (25%)	$8.30	$11.39	$12.89	$13.79	$14.32	$14.54	$14.73	$14.83	$14.91	$14.97
Forfeiture (30%)	$8.08	$10.93	$12.28	$13.08	$13.54	$13.72	$13.89	$13.98	$14.04	$14.09
Forfeiture (35%)	$7.86	$10.51	$11.73	$12.44	$12.85	$13.00	$13.15	$13.22	$13.28	$13.32
Forfeiture (40%)	$7.67	$10.14	$11.24	$11.87	$12.22	$12.36	$12.49	$12.55	$12.60	$12.63

Percentage Difference between Binomial and Black-Scholes Model	Suboptimal (1.2)	Suboptimal (1.4)	Suboptimal (1.6)	Suboptimal (1.8)	Suboptimal (2.0)	Suboptimal (2.2)	Suboptimal (2.4)	Suboptimal (2.6)	Suboptimal (2.8)	Suboptimal (3.0)
Forfeiture (0%)	−55.39%	−33.83%	−21.70%	−13.67%	−8.54%	−6.44%	−4.43%	−3.36%	−2.55%	−1.93%
Forfeiture (5%)	−57.05%	−37.41%	−26.68%	−19.71%	−15.32%	−13.53%	−11.83%	−10.93%	−10.25%	−9.74%
Forfeiture (10%)	−58.54%	−40.59%	−31.06%	−24.99%	−21.22%	−19.70%	−18.26%	−17.49%	−16.92%	−16.49%
Forfeiture (15%)	−59.90%	−43.43%	−34.94%	−29.63%	−26.38%	−25.08%	−23.86%	−23.21%	−22.73%	−22.37%
Forfeiture (20%)	−61.14%	−45.98%	−38.38%	−33.73%	−30.92%	−29.81%	−28.76%	−28.21%	−27.81%	−27.50%
Forfeiture (25%)	−62.27%	−48.27%	−41.46%	−37.36%	−34.92%	−33.97%	−33.08%	−32.61%	−32.26%	−32.01%
Forfeiture (30%)	−63.31%	−50.35%	−44.21%	−40.60%	−38.48%	−37.65%	−36.89%	−36.49%	−36.20%	−35.98%
Forfeiture (35%)	−64.28%	−52.23%	−46.69%	−43.49%	−41.64%	−40.92%	−40.27%	−39.93%	−39.68%	−39.49%
Forfeiture (40%)	−65.17%	−53.95%	−48.93%	−46.09%	−44.47%	−43.85%	−43.28%	−42.99%	−42.77%	−42.62%

MATURITY OF 5 YEARS AND VESTING OF 1 MONTH ON AN $80 STOCK PRICE

Stock Price and Strike Price of $80, Maturity of 5 Years, Risk-Free Rate of 3.5%, 35% Volatility, 0% Dividends, Vesting of 1 Month, Employee Suboptimal Exercise Behavior from 1.2 to 3.0, and Forfeiture Rate from 0% to 40%.
Generalized Black-Scholes: $29.35

Customized Binomial Lattice	Suboptimal (1.2)	Suboptimal (1.4)	Suboptimal (1.6)	Suboptimal (1.8)	Suboptimal (2.0)	Suboptimal (2.2)	Suboptimal (2.4)	Suboptimal (2.6)	Suboptimal (2.8)	Suboptimal (3.0)
Forfeiture (0%)	$13.09	$19.42	$22.98	$25.34	$26.84	$27.46	$28.05	$28.36	$28.60	$28.78
Forfeiture (5%)	$12.61	$18.37	$21.52	$23.57	$24.85	$25.38	$25.88	$26.14	$26.34	$26.49
Forfeiture (10%)	$12.17	$17.44	$20.23	$22.02	$23.12	$23.57	$23.99	$24.22	$24.38	$24.51
Forfeiture (15%)	$11.77	$16.60	$19.10	$20.65	$21.61	$21.99	$22.35	$22.54	$22.68	$22.78
Forfeiture (20%)	$11.41	$15.86	$18.08	$19.45	$20.28	$20.60	$20.91	$21.07	$21.19	$21.28
Forfeiture (25%)	$11.07	$15.18	$17.18	$18.38	$19.10	$19.38	$19.64	$19.78	$19.88	$19.96
Forfeiture (30%)	$10.77	$14.57	$16.37	$17.43	$18.06	$18.30	$18.52	$18.64	$18.73	$18.79
Forfeiture (35%)	$10.48	$14.02	$15.65	$16.59	$17.13	$17.34	$17.53	$17.63	$17.70	$17.76
Forfeiture (40%)	$10.22	$13.51	$14.99	$15.82	$16.30	$16.48	$16.65	$16.73	$16.80	$16.84

Percentage Difference between Binomial and Black-Scholes Model	Suboptimal (1.2)	Suboptimal (1.4)	Suboptimal (1.6)	Suboptimal (1.8)	Suboptimal (2.0)	Suboptimal (2.2)	Suboptimal (2.4)	Suboptimal (2.6)	Suboptimal (2.8)	Suboptimal (3.0)
Forfeiture (0%)	−55 .39%	−33.83%	−21.70%	−13.67%	−8.54%	−6.44%	−4.43%	−3.36%	−2.55%	−1.93%
Forfeiture (5%)	−57 .05%	−37.41%	−26.68%	−19.71%	−15.32%	−13.53%	−11.83%	−10.93%	−10.25%	−9.74%
Forfeiture (10%)	−58 .54%	−40.59%	−31.06%	−24.99%	−21.22%	−19.70%	−18.26%	−17.49%	−16.92%	−16.49%
Forfeiture (15%)	−59 .90%	−43.43%	−34.94%	−29.63%	−26.38%	−25.08%	−23.86%	−23.21%	−22.73%	−22.37%
Forfeiture (20%)	−61 .14%	−45.98%	−38.38%	−33.73%	−30.92%	−29.81%	−28.76%	−28.21%	−27.81%	−27.50%
Forfeiture (25%)	−62 .27%	−48.27%	−41.46%	−37.36%	−34.92%	−33.97%	−33.08%	−32.61%	−32.26%	−32.01%
Forfeiture (30%)	−63 .31%	−50.35%	−44.2%1	−40.60%	−38.48%	−37.65%	−36.89%	−36.49%	−36.20%	−35.98%
Forfeiture (35%)	−64 .28%	−52.23%	−46.69%	−43.49%	−41.64%	−40.92%	−40.27%	−39.93%	−39.68%	−39.49%
Forfeiture (40%)	−65 .17%	−53.95%	−48.93%	−46.09%	−44.47%	−43.85%	−43.28%	−42.99%	−42.77%	−42.62%

MATURITY OF 5 YEARS AND VESTING OF 1 YEAR ON A $20 STOCK PRICE

Stock Price and Strike Price of $20, Maturity of 5 Years, Risk-Free Rate of 3.5%, 35% Volatility, 0% Dividends, Vesting of 1 Year, Employee Suboptimal Exercise Behavior from 1.2 to 3.0, and Forfeiture Rate from 0% to 40%.
Generalized Black-Scholes: $7.34

Customized Binomial Lattice	Suboptimal (1.2)	Suboptimal (1.4)	Suboptimal (1.6)	Suboptimal (1.8)	Suboptimal (2.0)	Suboptimal (2.2)	Suboptimal (2.4)	Suboptimal (2.6)	Suboptimal (2.8)	Suboptimal (3.0)
Forfeiture (0%)	$4.42	$5.34	$5.96	$6.42	$6.74	$6.88	$7.02	$7.09	$7.15	$7.20
Forfeiture (5%)	$4.14	$4.94	$5.48	$5.87	$6.14	$6.26	$6.38	$6.44	$6.49	$6.53
Forfeiture (10%)	$3.88	$4.59	$5.05	$5.38	$5.62	$5.72	$5.82	$5.87	$5.91	$5.94
Forfeiture (15%)	$3.64	$4.26	$4.66	$4.95	$5.15	$5.24	$5.32	$5.37	$5.40	$5.43
Forfeiture (20%)	$3.42	$3.97	$4.32	$4.57	$4.74	$4.81	$4.88	$4.92	$4.95	$4.97
Forfeiture (25%)	$3.21	$3.70	$4.01	$4.22	$4.37	$4.43	$4.49	$4.52	$4.55	$4.57
Forfeiture (30%)	$3.02	$3.46	$3.72	$3.91	$4.04	$4.09	$4.14	$4.17	$4.19	$4.21
Forfeiture (35%)	$2.85	$3.23	$3.47	$3.63	$3.74	$3.79	$3.83	$3.85	$3.87	$3.88
Forfeiture (40%)	$2.68	$3.03	$3.23	$3.38	$3.47	$3.51	$3.55	$3.57	$3.58	$3.59

Percentage Difference between Binomial and Black-Scholes Model	Suboptimal (1.2)	Suboptimal (1.4)	Suboptimal (1.6)	Suboptimal (1.8)	Suboptimal (2.0)	Suboptimal (2.2)	Suboptimal (2.4)	Suboptimal (2.6)	Suboptimal (2.8)	Suboptimal (3.0)
Forfeiture (0%)	-39.70%	-27.24%	-18.84%	-12.56%	-8.15%	-6.24%	-4.36%	-3.32%	-2.53%	-1.93%
Forfeiture (5%)	-43.58%	-32.64%	-25.38%	-20.01%	-16.26%	-14.65%	-13.06%	-12.19%	-11.53%	-11.03%
Forfeiture (10%)	-47.13%	-37.51%	-31.21%	-26.61%	-23.42%	-22.06%	-20.71%	-19.98%	-19.43%	-19.00%
Forfeiture (15%)	-50.40%	-41.92%	-36.44%	-32.48%	-29.76%	-28.60%	-27.47%	-26.85%	-26.38%	-26.03%
Forfeiture (20%)	-53.42%	-45.91%	-41.14%	-37.73%	-35.40%	-34.41%	-33.45%	-32.93%	-32.53%	-32.23%
Forfeiture (25%)	-56.21%	-49.56%	-45.39%	-42.44%	-40.44%	-39.60%	-38.78%	-38.33%	-38.00%	-37.75%
Forfeiture (30%)	-58.80%	-52.88%	-49.23%	-46.68%	-44.95%	-44.23%	-43.53%	-43.16%	-42.87%	-42.66%
Forfeiture (35%)	-61.21%	-55.94%	-52.73%	-50.51%	-49.02%	-48.40%	-47.80%	-47.48%	-47.24%	-47.06%
Forfeiture (40%)	-63.45%	-58.74%	-55.92%	-53.98%	-52.70%	-52.16%	-51.65%	-51.37%	-51.17%	-51.02%

MATURITY OF 5 YEARS AND VESTING OF 1 YEAR ON A $40 STOCK PRICE

Stock Price and Strike Price of $40, Maturity of 5 Years, Risk-Free Rate of 3.5%, 35% Volatility, 0% Dividends, Vesting of 1 Year, Employee Suboptimal Exercise Behavior from 1.2 to 3.0, and Forfeiture Rate from 0% to 40%.
Generalized Black-Scholes: $14.67

Customized Binomial Lattice	Suboptimal (1.2)	Suboptimal (1.4)	Suboptimal (1.6)	Suboptimal (1.8)	Suboptimal (2.0)	Suboptimal (2.2)	Suboptimal (2.4)	Suboptimal (2.6)	Suboptimal (2.8)	Suboptimal (3.0)
Forfeiture (0%)	$8.85	$10.68	$11.91	$12.83	$13.48	$13.76	$14.04	$14.19	$14.30	$14.39
Forfeiture (5%)	$8.28	$9.88	$10.95	$11.74	$12.29	$12.52	$12.76	$12.89	$12.98	$13.06
Forfeiture (10%)	$7.76	$9.17	$10.09	$10.77	$11.24	$11.44	$11.64	$11.74	$11.82	$11.89
Forfeiture (15%)	$7.28	$8.52	$9.33	$9.91	$10.31	$10.48	$10.64	$10.73	$10.80	$10.86
Forfeiture (20%)	$6.84	$7.94	$8.64	$9.14	$9.48	$9.62	$9.77	$9.84	$9.90	$9.94
Forfeiture (25%)	$6.43	$7.40	$8.01	$8.45	$8.74	$8.86	$8.98	$9.05	$9.10	$9.14
Forfeiture (30%)	$6.05	$6.91	$7.45	$7.83	$8.08	$8.18	$8.29	$8.34	$8.38	$8.41
Forfeiture (35%)	$5.69	$6.47	$6.94	$7.26	$7.48	$7.57	$7.66	$7.71	$7.74	$7.77
Forfeiture (40%)	$5.36	$6.06	$6.47	$6.75	$6.94	$7.02	$7.10	$7.14	$7.17	$7.19

Percentage Difference between Binomial and Black-Scholes Model	Suboptimal (1.2)	Suboptimal (1.4)	Suboptimal (1.6)	Suboptimal (1.8)	Suboptimal (2.0)	Suboptimal (2.2)	Suboptimal (2.4)	Suboptimal (2.6)	Suboptimal (2.8)	Suboptimal (3.0)
Forfeiture (0%)	-39.70%	-27.24%	-18.84%	-12.56%	-8.15%	-6.24%	-4.36%	-3.32%	-2.53%	-1.93%
Forfeiture (5%)	-43.58%	-32.64%	-25.38%	-20.01%	-16.26%	-14.65%	-13.06%	-12.19%	-11.53%	-11.03%
Forfeiture (10%)	-47.13%	-37.51%	-31.21%	-26.61%	-23.42%	-22.06%	-20.71%	-19.98%	-19.43%	-19.00%
Forfeiture (15%)	-50.40%	-41.92%	-36.44%	-32.48%	-29.76%	-28.60%	-27.47%	-26.85%	-26.38%	-26.03%
Forfeiture (20%)	-53.42%	-45.91%	-41.14%	-37.73%	-35.40%	-34.41%	-33.45%	-32.93%	-32.53%	-32.23%
Forfeiture (25%)	-56.21%	-49.56%	-45.39%	-42.44%	-40.44%	-39.60%	-38.78%	-38.33%	-38.00%	-37.75%
Forfeiture (30%)	-58.80%	-52.88%	-49.23%	-46.68%	-44.95%	-44.23%	-43.53%	-43.16%	-42.87%	-42.66%
Forfeiture (35%)	-61.21%	-55.94%	-52.73%	-50.51%	-49.02%	-48.40%	-47.80%	-47.48%	-47.24%	-47.06%
Forfeiture (40%)	-63.45%	-58.74%	-55.92%	-53.98%	-52.70%	-52.16%	-51.65%	-51.37%	-51.17%	-51.02%

MATURITY OF 5 YEARS AND VESTING OF 1 YEAR ON A $60 STOCK PRICE

Stock Price and Strike Price of $60, Maturity of 5 Years, Risk-Free Rate of 3.5%, 35% Volatility, 0% Dividends, Vesting of 1 Year, Employee Suboptimal Exercise Behavior from 1.2 to 3.0, and Forfeiture Rate from 0% to 40%.
Generalized Black-Scholes: $22.01

Customized Binomial Lattice	Suboptimal (1.2)	Suboptimal (1.4)	Suboptimal (1.6)	Suboptimal (1.8)	Suboptimal (2.0)	Suboptimal (2.2)	Suboptimal (2.4)	Suboptimal (2.6)	Suboptimal (2.8)	Suboptimal (3.0)
Forfeiture (0%)	$13.27	$16.02	$17.87	$19.25	$20.22	$20.64	$21.05	$21.28	$21.46	$21.59
Forfeiture (5%)	$12.42	$14.83	$16.43	$17.61	$18.43	$18.79	$19.14	$19.33	$19.47	$19.58
Forfeiture (10%)	$11.64	$13.76	$15.14	$16.15	$16.86	$17.16	$17.45	$17.61	$17.74	$17.83
Forfeiture (15%)	$10.92	$12.79	$13.99	$14.86	$15.46	$15.72	$15.97	$16.10	$16.21	$16.28
Forfeiture (20%)	$10.25	$11.91	$12.96	$13.71	$14.22	$14.44	$14.65	$14.76	$14.85	$14.92
Forfeiture (25%)	$9.64	$11.10	$12.02	$12.67	$13.11	$13.30	$13.48	$13.57	$13.65	$13.70
Forfeiture (30%)	$9.07	$10.37	$11.17	$11.74	$12.12	$12.28	$12.43	$12.51	$12.57	$12.62
Forfeiture (35%)	$8.54	$9.70	$10.41	$10.89	$11.22	$11.36	$11.49	$11.56	$11.61	$11.65
Forfeiture (40%)	$8.05	$9.08	$9.70	$10.13	$10.41	$10.53	$10.64	$10.70	$10.75	$10.78

Percentage Difference between Binomial and Black-Scholes Model	Suboptimal (1.2)	Suboptimal (1.4)	Suboptimal (1.6)	Suboptimal (1.8)	Suboptimal (2.0)	Suboptimal (2.2)	Suboptimal (2.4)	Suboptimal (2.6)	Suboptimal (2.8)	Suboptimal (3.0)
Forfeiture (0%)	−39.70%	−27.24%	−18.84%	−12.56%	−8.15%	−6.24%	−4.36%	−3.32%	−2.53%	−1.93%
Forfeiture (5%)	−43.58%	−32.64%	−25.38%	−20.01%	−16.26%	−14.65%	−13.06%	−12.19%	−11.53%	−11.03%
Forfeiture (10%)	−47.13%	−37.51%	−31.21%	−26.61%	−23.42%	−22.06%	−20.71%	−19.98%	−19.43%	−19.00%
Forfeiture (15%)	−50.40%	−41.92%	−36.44%	−32.48%	−29.76%	−28.60%	−27.47%	−26.85%	−26.38%	−26.03%
Forfeiture (20%)	−53.42%	−45.91%	−41.14%	−37.73%	−35.40%	−34.41%	−33.45%	−32.93%	−32.53%	−32.23%
Forfeiture (25%)	−56.21%	−49.56%	−45.39%	−42.44%	−40.44%	−39.60%	−38.78%	−38.33%	−38.00%	−37.75%
Forfeiture (30%)	−58.80%	−52.88%	−49.23%	−46.68%	−44.95%	−44.23%	−43.53%	−43.16%	−42.87%	−42.66%
Forfeiture (35%)	−61.21%	−55.94%	−52.73%	−50.51%	−49.02%	−48.40%	−47.80%	−47.48%	−47.24%	−47.06%
Forfeiture (40%)	−63.45%	−58.74%	−55.92%	−53.98%	−52.70%	−52.16%	−51.65%	−51.37%	−51.17%	−51.02%

MATURITY OF 5 YEARS AND VESTING OF 1 YEAR ON AN $80 STOCK PRICE

Stock Price and Strike Price of $80, Maturity of 5 Years, Risk-Free Rate of 3.5%, 35% Volatility, 0% Dividends, Vesting of 1 Year, Employee Suboptimal Exercise Behavior from 1.2 to 3.0, and Forfeiture Rate from 0% to 40%.
Generalized Black-Scholes: $29.35

Customized Binomial Lattice	Suboptimal (1.2)	Suboptimal (1.4)	Suboptimal (1.6)	Suboptimal (1.8)	Suboptimal (2.0)	Suboptimal (2.2)	Suboptimal (2.4)	Suboptimal (2.6)	Suboptimal (2.8)	Suboptimal (3.0)
Forfeiture (0%)	$17.70	$21.35	$23.82	$25.66	$26.96	$27.52	$28.07	$28.38	$28.61	$28.78
Forfeiture (5%)	$16.56	$19.77	$21.90	$23.48	$24.58	$25.05	$25.52	$25.77	$25.96	$26.11
Forfeiture (10%)	$15.52	$18.34	$20.19	$21.54	$22.48	$22.88	$23.27	$23.49	$23.65	$23.77
Forfeiture (15%)	$14.56	$17.05	$18.65	$19.82	$20.62	$20.96	$21.29	$21.47	$21.61	$21.71
Forfeiture (20%)	$13.67	$15.87	$17.27	$18.28	$18.96	$19.25	$19.53	$19.69	$19.80	$19.89
Forfeiture (25%)	$12.85	$14.80	$16.03	$16.89	$17.48	$17.73	$17.97	$18.10	$18.20	$18.27
Forfeiture (30%)	$12.09	$13.83	$14.90	$15.65	$16.16	$16.37	$16.57	$16.68	$16.77	$16.83
Forfeiture (35%)	$11.39	$12.93	$13.87	$14.53	$14.96	$15.14	$15.32	$15.41	$15.48	$15.54
Forfeiture (40%)	$10.73	$12.11	$12.94	$13.51	$13.88	$14.04	$14.19	$14.27	$14.33	$14.38

Percentage Difference between Binomial and Black-Scholes Model	Suboptimal (1.2)	Suboptimal (1.4)	Suboptimal (1.6)	Suboptimal (1.8)	Suboptimal (2.0)	Suboptimal (2.2)	Suboptimal (2.4)	Suboptimal (2.6)	Suboptimal (2.8)	Suboptimal (3.0)
Forfeiture (0%)	-39.70%	-27.24%	-18.84%	-12.56%	-8.15%	-6.24%	-4.36%	-3.32%	-2.53%	-1.93%
Forfeiture (5%)	-43.58%	-32.64%	-25.38%	-20.01%	-16.26%	-14.65%	-13.06%	-12.19%	-11.53%	-11.03%
Forfeiture (10%)	-47.13%	-37.51%	-31.21%	-26.61%	-23.42%	-22.06%	-20.71%	-19.98%	-19.43%	-19.00%
Forfeiture (15%)	-50.40%	-41.92%	-36.44%	-32.48%	-29.76%	-28.60%	-27.47%	-26.85%	-26.38%	-26.03%
Forfeiture (20%)	-53.42%	-45.91%	-41.14%	-37.73%	-35.40%	-34.41%	-33.45%	-32.93%	-32.53%	-32.23%
Forfeiture (25%)	-56.21%	-49.56%	-45.39%	-42.44%	-40.44%	-39.60%	-38.78%	-38.33%	-38.00%	-37.75%
Forfeiture (30%)	-58.80%	-52.88%	-49.23%	-46.68%	-44.95%	-44.23%	-43.53%	-43.16%	-42.87%	-42.66%
Forfeiture (35%)	-61.21%	-55.94%	-52.73%	-50.51%	-49.02%	-48.40%	-47.80%	-47.48%	-47.24%	-47.06%
Forfeiture (40%)	-63.45%	-58.74%	-55.92%	-53.98%	-52.70%	-52.16%	-51.65%	-51.37%	-51.17%	-51.02%

MATURITY OF 5 YEARS AND VESTING OF 3 YEARS ON A $20 STOCK PRICE

Stock Price and Strike Price of $20, Maturity of 5 Years, Risk-Free Rate of 3.5%, 35% Volatility, 0% Dividends, Vesting of 3 Years, Employee Suboptimal Exercise Behavior from 1.2 to 3.0, and Forfeiture Rate from 0% to 40%.
Generalized Black-Scholes: $7.34

Customized Binomial Lattice	Suboptimal (1.2)	Suboptimal (1.4)	Suboptimal (1.6)	Suboptimal (1.8)	Suboptimal (2.0)	Suboptimal (2.2)	Suboptimal (2.4)	Suboptimal (2.6)	Suboptimal (2.8)	Suboptimal (3.0)
Forfeiture (0%)	$6.24	$6.59	$6.81	$6.96	$7.07	$7.11	$7.17	$7.20	$7.22	$7.25
Forfeiture (5%)	$5.35	$5.64	$5.81	$5.94	$6.02	$6.06	$6.11	$6.13	$6.15	$6.17
Forfeiture (10%)	$4.59	$4.83	$4.97	$5.07	$5.14	$5.17	$5.21	$5.23	$5.24	$5.26
Forfeiture (15%)	$3.94	$4.13	$4.25	$4.33	$4.39	$4.41	$4.44	$4.46	$4.47	$4.48
Forfeiture (20%)	$3.38	$3.54	$3.63	$3.70	$3.74	$3.77	$3.79	$3.80	$3.81	$3.82
Forfeiture (25%)	$2.90	$3.03	$3.11	$3.16	$3.20	$3.22	$3.23	$3.25	$3.25	$3.26
Forfeiture (30%)	$2.49	$2.59	$2.66	$2.70	$2.73	$2.75	$2.76	$2.77	$2.78	$2.79
Forfeiture (35%)	$2.13	$2.22	$2.27	$2.31	$2.34	$2.35	$2.36	$2.37	$2.37	$2.38
Forfeiture (40%)	$1.83	$1.90	$1.95	$1.98	$2.00	$2.01	$2.02	$2.02	$2.03	$2.03

Percentage Difference between Binomial and Black-Scholes Model	Suboptimal (1.2)	Suboptimal (1.4)	Suboptimal (1.6)	Suboptimal (1.8)	Suboptimal (2.0)	Suboptimal (2.2)	Suboptimal (2.4)	Suboptimal (2.6)	Suboptimal (2.8)	Suboptimal (3.0)
Forfeiture (0%)	−14.92%	−10.12%	−7.23%	−5.18%	−3.71%	−3.04%	−2.33%	−1.90%	−1.54%	−1.25%
Forfeiture (5%)	−27.05%	−23.11%	−20.76%	−19.09%	−17.90%	−17.36%	−16.78%	−16.42%	−16.14%	−15.89%
Forfeiture (10%)	−37.44%	−34.21%	−32.29%	−30.94%	−29.96%	−29.52%	−29.05%	−28.76%	−28.53%	−28.33%
Forfeiture (15%)	−46.34%	−43.69%	−42.12%	−41.02%	−40.23%	−39.87%	−39.49%	−39.25%	−39.06%	−38.90%
Forfeiture (20%)	−53.97%	−51.79%	−50.51%	−49.61%	−48.97%	−48.68%	−48.37%	−48.18%	−48.02%	−47.89%
Forfeiture (25%)	−60.51%	−58.72%	−57.67%	−56.94%	−56.42%	−56.18%	−55.92%	−55.77%	−55.64%	−55.53%
Forfeiture (30%)	−66.12%	−64.64%	−63.79%	−63.19%	−62.76%	−62.57%	−62.36%	−62.23%	−62.13%	−62.04%
Forfeiture (35%)	−70.92%	−69.71%	−69.01%	−68.52%	−68.17%	−68.02%	−67.85%	−67.74%	−67.66%	−67.59%
Forfeiture (40%)	−75.04%	−74.05%	−73.47%	−73.08%	−72.79%	−72.66%	−72.52%	−72.44%	−72.37%	−72.31%

MATURITY OF 5 YEARS AND VESTING OF 3 YEARS ON A $40 STOCK PRICE

Stock Price and Strike Price of $40, Maturity of 5 Years, Risk-Free Rate of 3.5%, 35% Volatility, 0% Dividends, Vesting of 3 Years,
Employee Suboptimal Exercise Behavior from 1.2 to 3.0, and Forfeiture Rate from 0% to 40%.
Generalized Black-Scholes: $14.67

Customized Binomial Lattice	Suboptimal (1.2)	Suboptimal (1.4)	Suboptimal (1.6)	Suboptimal (1.8)	Suboptimal (2.0)	Suboptimal (2.2)	Suboptimal (2.4)	Suboptimal (2.6)	Suboptimal (2.8)	Suboptimal (3.0)
Forfeiture (0%)	$12.48	$13.19	$13.61	$13.91	$14.13	$14.23	$14.33	$14.40	$14.45	$14.49
Forfeiture (5%)	$10.70	$11.28	$11.63	$11.87	$12.05	$12.13	$12.21	$12.26	$12.31	$12.34
Forfeiture (10%)	$9.18	$9.65	$9.94	$10.14	$10.28	$10.34	$10.41	$10.45	$10.49	$10.52
Forfeiture (15%)	$7.87	$8.26	$8.49	$8.66	$8.77	$8.82	$8.88	$8.91	$8.94	$8.97
Forfeiture (20%)	$6.75	$7.07	$7.26	$7.39	$7.49	$7.53	$7.58	$7.61	$7.63	$7.65
Forfeiture (25%)	$5.80	$6.06	$6.21	$6.32	$6.40	$6.43	$6.47	$6.49	$6.51	$6.53
Forfeiture (30%)	$4.97	$5.19	$5.31	$5.40	$5.46	$5.49	$5.52	$5.54	$5.56	$5.57
Forfeiture (35%)	$4.27	$4.44	$4.55	$4.62	$4.67	$4.69	$4.72	$4.73	$4.75	$4.76
Forfeiture (40%)	$3.66	$3.81	$3.89	$3.95	$3.99	$4.01	$4.03	$4.04	$4.05	$4.06

Percentage Difference between Binomial and Black-Scholes Model	Suboptimal (1.2)	Suboptimal (1.4)	Suboptimal (1.6)	Suboptimal (1.8)	Suboptimal (2.0)	Suboptimal (2.2)	Suboptimal (2.4)	Suboptimal (2.6)	Suboptimal (2.8)	Suboptimal (3.0)
Forfeiture (0%)	−14.92%	−10.12%	−7.23%	−5.18%	−3.71%	−3.04%	−2.33%	−1.90%	−1.54%	−1.25%
Forfeiture (5%)	−27.05%	−23.11%	−20.76%	−19.09%	−17.90%	−17.36%	−16.78%	−16.42%	−16.14%	−15.89%
Forfeiture (10%)	−37.44%	−34.21%	−32.29%	−30.94%	−29.96%	−29.52%	−29.05%	−28.76%	−28.53%	−28.33%
Forfeiture (15%)	−46.34%	−43.69%	−42.12%	−41.02%	−40.23%	−39.87%	−39.49%	−39.25%	−39.06%	−38.90%
Forfeiture (20%)	−53.97%	−51.79%	−50.51%	−49.61%	−48.97%	−48.68%	−48.37%	−48.18%	−48.02%	−47.89%
Forfeiture (25%)	−60.51%	−58.72%	−57.67%	−56.94%	−56.42%	−56.18%	−55.92%	−55.77%	−55.64%	−55.53%
Forfeiture (30%)	−66.12%	−64.64%	−63.79%	−63.19%	−62.76%	−62.57%	−62.36%	−62.23%	−62.13%	−62.04%
Forfeiture (35%)	−70.92%	−69.71%	−69.01%	−68.52%	−68.17%	−68.02%	−67.85%	−67.74%	−67.66%	−67.59%
Forfeiture (40%)	−75.04%	−74.05%	−73.47%	−73.08%	−72.79%	−72.66%	−72.52%	−72.44%	−72.37%	−72.31%

MATURITY OF 5 YEARS AND VESTING OF 3 YEARS ON A $60 STOCK PRICE

Stock Price and Strike Price of $60, Maturity of 5 Years, Risk-Free Rate of 3.5%, 35% Volatility, 0% Dividends, Vesting of 3 Years, Employee Suboptimal Exercise Behavior from 1.2 to 3.0, and Forfeiture Rate from 0% to 40%.
Generalized Black-Scholes: $22.01

Customized Binomial Lattice	Suboptimal (1.2)	Suboptimal (1.4)	Suboptimal (1.6)	Suboptimal (1.8)	Suboptimal (2.0)	Suboptimal (2.2)	Suboptimal (2.4)	Suboptimal (2.6)	Suboptimal (2.8)	Suboptimal (3.0)
Forfeiture (0%)	$18.73	$19.78	$20.42	$20.87	$21.20	$21.34	$21.50	$21.59	$21.67	$21.74
Forfeiture (5%)	$16.06	$16.92	$17.44	$17.81	$18.07	$18.19	$18.32	$18.40	$18.46	$18.51
Forfeiture (10%)	$13.77	$14.48	$14.90	$15.20	$15.42	$15.51	$15.62	$15.68	$15.73	$15.78
Forfeiture (15%)	$11.81	$12.39	$12.74	$12.98	$13.16	$13.24	$13.32	$13.37	$13.41	$13.45
Forfeiture (20%)	$10.13	$10.61	$10.89	$11.09	$11.23	$11.30	$11.37	$11.41	$11.44	$11.47
Forfeiture (25%)	$8.69	$9.09	$9.32	$9.48	$9.59	$9.65	$9.70	$9.74	$9.76	$9.79
Forfeiture (30%)	$7.46	$7.78	$7.97	$8.10	$8.20	$8.24	$8.29	$8.31	$8.34	$8.36
Forfeiture (35%)	$6.40	$6.67	$6.82	$6.93	$7.01	$7.04	$7.08	$7.10	$7.12	$7.13
Forfeiture (40%)	$5.49	$5.71	$5.84	$5.93	$5.99	$6.02	$6.05	$6.07	$6.08	$6.09

Percentage Difference between Binomial and Black-Scholes Model	Suboptimal (1.2)	Suboptimal (1.4)	Suboptimal (1.6)	Suboptimal (1.8)	Suboptimal (2.0)	Suboptimal (2.2)	Suboptimal (2.4)	Suboptimal (2.6)	Suboptimal (2.8)	Suboptimal (3.0)
Forfeiture (0%)	–14.92%	–10.12%	–7.23%	–5.18%	–3.71%	–3.04%	–2.33%	–1.90%	–1.54%	–1.25%
Forfeiture (5%)	–27.05%	–23.11%	–20.76%	–19.09%	–17.90%	–17.36%	–16.78%	–16.42%	–16.14%	–15.89%
Forfeiture (10%)	–37.44%	–34.21%	–32.29%	–30.94%	–29.96%	–29.52%	–29.05%	–28.76%	–28.53%	–28.33%
Forfeiture (15%)	–46.34%	–43.69%	–42.12%	–41.02%	–40.23%	–39.87%	–39.49%	–39.25%	–39.06%	–38.90%
Forfeiture (20%)	–53.97%	–51.79%	–50.51%	–49.61%	–48.97%	–48.68%	–48.37%	–48.18%	–48.02%	–47.89%
Forfeiture (25%)	–60.51%	–58.72%	–57.67%	–56.94%	–56.42%	–56.18%	–55.92%	–55.77%	–55.64%	–55.53%
Forfeiture (30%)	–66.12%	–64.64%	–63.79%	–63.19%	–62.76%	–62.57%	–62.36%	–62.23%	–62.13%	–62.04%
Forfeiture (35%)	–70.92%	–69.71%	–69.01%	–68.52%	–68.17%	–68.02%	–67.85%	–67.74%	–67.66%	–67.59%
Forfeiture (40%)	–75.04%	–74.05%	–73.47%	–73.08%	–72.79%	–72.66%	–72.52%	–72.44%	–72.37%	–72.31%

MATURITY OF 5 YEARS AND VESTING OF 3 YEARS ON AN $80 STOCK PRICE

Stock Price and Strike Price of $80, Maturity of 5 Years, Risk-Free Rate of 3.5%, 35% Volatility, 0% Dividends, Vesting of 3 Years, Employee Suboptimal Exercise Behavior from 1.2 to 3.0, and Forfeiture Rate from 0% to 40%.
Generalized Black-Scholes: $29.35

Customized Binomial Lattice	Suboptimal (1.2)	Suboptimal (1.4)	Suboptimal (1.6)	Suboptimal (1.8)	Suboptimal (2.0)	Suboptimal (2.2)	Suboptimal (2.4)	Suboptimal (2.6)	Suboptimal (2.8)	Suboptimal (3.0)
Forfeiture (0%)	$24.97	$26.38	$27.23	$27.83	$28.26	$28.46	$28.67	$28.79	$28.90	$28.98
Forfeiture (5%)	$21.41	$22.57	$23.26	$23.75	$24.10	$24.26	$24.43	$24.53	$24.61	$24.68
Forfeiture (10%)	$18.36	$19.31	$19.87	$20.27	$20.56	$20.68	$20.82	$20.91	$20.98	$21.03
Forfeiture (15%)	$15.75	$16.53	$16.99	$17.31	$17.54	$17.65	$17.76	$17.83	$17.88	$17.93
Forfeiture (20%)	$13.51	$14.15	$14.52	$14.79	$14.98	$15.06	$15.15	$15.21	$15.26	$15.29
Forfeiture (25%)	$11.59	$12.12	$12.42	$12.64	$12.79	$12.86	$12.94	$12.98	$13.02	$13.05
Forfeiture (30%)	$9.95	$10.38	$10.63	$10.80	$10.93	$10.99	$11.05	$11.08	$11.11	$11.14
Forfeiture (35%)	$8.53	$8.89	$9.10	$9.24	$9.34	$9.39	$9.44	$9.47	$9.49	$9.51
Forfeiture (40%)	$7.32	$7.62	$7.79	$7.90	$7.99	$8.02	$8.06	$8.09	$8.11	$8.13

Percentage Difference between Binomial and Black-Scholes Model	Suboptimal (1.2)	Suboptimal (1.4)	Suboptimal (1.6)	Suboptimal (1.8)	Suboptimal (2.0)	Suboptimal (2.2)	Suboptimal (2.4)	Suboptimal (2.6)	Suboptimal (2.8)	Suboptimal (3.0)
Forfeiture (0%)	−14.92%	−10.12%	−7.23%	−5.18%	−3.71%	−3.04%	−2.33%	−1.90%	−1.54%	−1.25%
Forfeiture (5%)	−27.05%	−23.11%	−20.76%	−19.09%	−17.90%	−17.36%	−16.78%	−16.42%	−16.14%	−15.89%
Forfeiture (10%)	−37.44%	−34.21%	−32.29%	−30.94%	−29.96%	−29.52%	−29.05%	−28.76%	−28.53%	−28.33%
Forfeiture (15%)	−46.34%	−43.69%	−42.12%	−41.02%	−40.23%	−39.87%	−39.49%	−39.25%	−39.06%	−38.90%
Forfeiture (20%)	−53.97%	−51.79%	−50.51%	−49.61%	−48.97%	−48.68%	−48.37%	−48.18%	−48.02%	−47.89%
Forfeiture (25%)	−60.51%	−58.72%	−57.67%	−56.94%	−56.42%	−56.18%	−55.92%	−55.77%	−55.64%	−55.53%
Forfeiture (30%)	−66.12%	−64.64%	−63.79%	−63.19%	−62.76%	−62.57%	−62.36%	−62.23%	−62.13%	−62.04%
Forfeiture (35%)	−70.92%	−69.71%	−69.01%	−68.52%	−68.17%	−68.02%	−67.85%	−67.74%	−67.66%	−67.59%
Forfeiture (40%)	−75.04%	−74.05%	−73.47%	−73.08%	−72.79%	−72.66%	−72.52%	−72.44%	−72.37%	−72.31%

SEVENTY PERCENT VOLATILITY AND 5-YEAR MATURITY ESOs WITH VARYING STOCK PRICE, SUBOPTIMAL BEHAVIOR, VESTING PERIOD, AND FORFEITURE RATES

This section provides ESO valuation results on an underlying stock with 70 percent volatility and a 5-year maturity. The analysis is divided into 1-month, 1-year, and 3-year vesting periods, and accounts for stock prices at grant date of $20, $40, $60, and $80.

MATURITY OF 5 YEARS AND VESTING OF 1 MONTH ON A $20 STOCK PRICE

Stock Price and Strike Price of $20, Maturity of 5 Years, Risk-Free Rate of 3.5%, 70% Volatility, 0% Dividends, Vesting of 1 Month, Employee Suboptimal Exercise Behavior from 1.2 to 3.0, and Forfeiture Rate from 0% to 40%.
Generalized Black-Scholes: $12.07

Customized Binomial Lattice	Suboptimal (1.2)	Suboptimal (1.4)	Suboptimal (1.6)	Suboptimal (1.8)	Suboptimal (2.0)	Suboptimal (2.2)	Suboptimal (2.4)	Suboptimal (2.6)	Suboptimal (2.8)	Suboptimal (3.0)
Forfeiture (0%)	$3.82	$5.60	$7.20	$8.09	$9.17	$9.47	$9.99	$10.42	$10.60	$10.91
Forfeiture (5%)	$3.74	$5.42	$6.90	$7.71	$8.68	$8.95	$9.41	$9.78	$9.94	$10.21
Forfeiture (10%)	$3.67	$5.26	$6.63	$7.37	$8.25	$8.49	$8.89	$9.22	$9.36	$9.59
Forfeiture (15%)	$3.60	$5.11	$6.39	$7.07	$7.86	$8.07	$8.43	$8.72	$8.84	$9.05
Forfeiture (20%)	$3.54	$4.98	$6.17	$6.80	$7.51	$7.70	$8.02	$8.28	$8.38	$8.56
Forfeiture (25%)	$3.48	$4.85	$5.97	$6.55	$7.20	$7.37	$7.66	$7.88	$7.98	$8.13
Forfeiture (30%)	$3.43	$4.73	$5.79	$6.32	$6.92	$7.07	$7.33	$7.53	$7.61	$7.74
Forfeiture (35%)	$3.37	$4.63	$5.62	$6.11	$6.66	$6.80	$7.03	$7.21	$7.28	$7.40
Forfeiture (40%)	$3.32	$4.52	$5.46	$5.92	$6.42	$6.55	$6.76	$6.91	$6.98	$7.09

Percentage Difference between Binomial and Black-Scholes Model	Suboptimal (1.2)	Suboptimal (1.4)	Suboptimal (1.6)	Suboptimal (1.8)	Suboptimal (2.0)	Suboptimal (2.2)	Suboptimal (2.4)	Suboptimal (2.6)	Suboptimal (2.8)	Suboptimal (3.0)
Forfeiture (0%)	−68.33%	−53.62%	−40.39%	− 33.03%	− 24.06%	−21.57%	−17.26%	−13.72%	−12.20%	−9.61%
Forfeiture (5%)	−68.99%	−55.09%	−42.84%	− 36.13%	− 28.09%	−25.88%	−22.08%	−18.98%	−17.67%	−15.43%
Forfeiture (10%)	−69.59%	−56.43%	−45.05%	− 38.92%	− 31.67%	−29.71%	−26.34%	−23.63%	−22.48%	−20.55%
Forfeiture (15%)	−70.15%	−57.66%	−47.05%	− 41.43%	− 34.88%	−33.12%	−30.14%	−27.75%	−26.75%	−25.07%
Forfeiture (20%)	−70.68%	−58.79%	−48.87%	− 43.70%	− 37.76%	−36.18%	−33.53%	−31.42%	−30.54%	−29.08%
Forfeiture (25%)	−71.17%	−59.83%	−50.53%	− 45.76%	− 40.36%	−38.94%	−36.57%	−34.70%	−33.93%	−32.65%
Forfeiture (30%)	−71.63%	−60.79%	−52.06%	− 47.65%	− 42.71%	−41.43%	−39.31%	−37.65%	−36.97%	−35.85%
Forfeiture (35%)	−72.06%	−61.68%	−53.46%	− 49.37%	− 44.86%	−43.70%	−41.78%	−40.31%	−39.71%	−38.72%
Forfeiture (40%)	−72.47%	−62.52%	−54.76%	− 50.95%	− 46.81%	−45.76%	−44.04%	−42.72%	−42.18%	−41.31%

MATURITY OF 5 YEARS AND VESTING OF 1 MONTH ON A $40 STOCK PRICE

Stock Price and Strike Price of $40, Maturity of 5 Years, Risk-Free Rate of 3.5%, 70% Volatility, 0% Dividends, Vesting of 1 Month, Employee Suboptimal Exercise Behavior from 1.2 to 3.0, and Forfeiture Rate from 0% to 40%.
Generalized Black-Scholes: $24.14

Customized Binomial Lattice	Suboptimal (1.2)	Suboptimal (1.4)	Suboptimal (1.6)	Suboptimal (1.8)	Suboptimal (2.0)	Suboptimal (2.2)	Suboptimal (2.4)	Suboptimal (2.6)	Suboptimal (2.8)	Suboptimal (3.0)
Forfeiture (0%)	$7.65	$11.20	$14.39	$16.17	$18.33	$18.94	$19.98	$20.83	$21.20	$21.82
Forfeiture (5%)	$7.49	$10.84	$13.80	$15.42	$17.36	$17.90	$18.81	$19.56	$19.88	$20.42
Forfeiture (10%)	$7.34	$10.52	$13.27	$14.75	$16.50	$16.97	$17.78	$18.44	$18.72	$19.18
Forfeiture (15%)	$7.21	$10.22	$12.78	$14.14	$15.72	$16.15	$16.87	$17.44	$17.69	$18.09
Forfeiture (20%)	$7.08	$9.95	$12.34	$13.59	$15.03	$15.41	$16.05	$16.56	$16.77	$17.12
Forfeiture (25%)	$6.96	$9.70	$11.94	$13.09	$14.40	$14.74	$15.32	$15.77	$15.95	$16.26
Forfeiture (30%)	$6.85	$9.47	$11.57	$12.64	$13.83	$14.14	$14.65	$15.05	$15.22	$15.49
Forfeiture (35%)	$6.75	$9.25	$11.24	$12.22	$13.31	$13.59	$14.06	$14.41	$14.56	$14.80
Forfeiture (40%)	$6.65	$9.05	$10.92	$11.84	$12.84	$13.10	$13.51	$13.83	$13.96	$14.17

Percentage Difference between Binomial and Black-Scholes Model	Suboptimal (1.2)	Suboptimal (1.4)	Suboptimal (1.6)	Suboptimal (1.8)	Suboptimal (2.0)	Suboptimal (2.2)	Suboptimal (2.4)	Suboptimal (2.6)	Suboptimal (2.8)	Suboptimal (3.0)
Forfeiture (0%)	−68.33%	−53.62%	−40.39%	−33.03%	−24.06%	−21.57%	−17.26%	−13.72%	−12.20%	−9.61%
Forfeiture (5%)	−68.99%	−55.09%	−42.84%	−36.13%	−28.09%	−25.88%	−22.08%	−18.98%	−17.67%	−15.43%
Forfeiture (10%)	−69.59%	−56.43%	−45.05%	−38.92%	−31.67%	−29.71%	−26.34%	−23.63%	−22.48%	−20.55%
Forfeiture (15%)	−70.15%	−57.66%	−47.05%	−41.43%	−34.88%	−33.12%	−30.14%	−27.75%	−26.75%	−25.07%
Forfeiture (20%)	−70.68%	−58.79%	−48.87%	−43.70%	−37.76%	−36.18%	−33.53%	−31.42%	−30.54%	−29.08%
Forfeiture (25%)	−71.17%	−59.83%	−50.53%	−45.76%	−40.36%	−38.94%	−36.57%	−34.70%	−33.93%	−32.65%
Forfeiture (30%)	−71.63%	−60.79%	−52.06%	−47.65%	−42.71%	−41.43%	−39.31%	−37.65%	−36.97%	−35.85%
Forfeiture (35%)	−72.06%	−61.68%	−53.46%	−49.37%	−44.86%	−43.70%	−41.78%	−40.31%	−39.71%	−38.72%
Forfeiture (40%)	−72.47%	−62.52%	−54.76%	−50.95%	−46.81%	−45.76%	−44.04%	−42.72%	−42.18%	−41.31%

MATURITY OF 5 YEARS AND VESTING OF 1 MONTH ON A $60 STOCK PRICE

Stock Price and Strike Price of $60, Maturity of 5 Years, Risk-Free Rate of 3.5%, 70% Volatility, 0% Dividends, Vesting of 1 Month, Employee Suboptimal Exercise Behavior from 1.2 to 3.0, and Forfeiture Rate from 0% to 40%.
Generalized Black-Scholes: $36.22

Customized Binomial Lattice	Suboptimal (1.2)	Suboptimal (1.4)	Suboptimal (1.6)	Suboptimal (1.8)	Suboptimal (2.0)	Suboptimal (2.2)	Suboptimal (2.4)	Suboptimal (2.6)	Suboptimal (2.8)	Suboptimal (3.0)
Forfeiture (0%)	$11.47	$16.80	$21.59	$24.26	$27.50	$28.40	$29.97	$31.25	$31.80	$32.74
Forfeiture (5%)	$11.23	$16.26	$20.70	$23.13	$26.04	$26.84	$28.22	$29.34	$29.82	$30.63
Forfeiture (10%)	$11.01	$15.78	$19.90	$22.12	$24.75	$25.46	$26.68	$27.66	$28.07	$28.77
Forfeiture (15%)	$10.81	$15.33	$19.18	$21.21	$23.58	$24.22	$25.30	$26.17	$26.53	$27.14
Forfeiture (20%)	$10.62	$14.93	$18.52	$20.39	$22.54	$23.11	$24.07	$24.84	$25.15	$25.69
Forfeiture (25%)	$10.44	$14.55	$17.91	$19.64	$21.60	$22.11	$22.97	$23.65	$23.93	$24.39
Forfeiture (30%)	$10.28	$14.20	$17.36	$18.96	$20.75	$21.21	$21.98	$22.58	$22.83	$23.23
Forfeiture (35%)	$10.12	$13.88	$16.85	$18.34	$19.97	$20.39	$21.08	$21.62	$21.84	$22.19
Forfeiture (40%)	$9.97	$13.57	$16.38	$17.76	$19.26	$19.64	$20.27	$20.74	$20.94	$21.26

Percentage Difference between Binomial and Black-Scholes Model	Suboptimal (1.2)	Suboptimal (1.4)	Suboptimal (1.6)	Suboptimal (1.8)	Suboptimal (2.0)	Suboptimal (2.2)	Suboptimal (2.4)	Suboptimal (2.6)	Suboptimal (2.8)	Suboptimal (3.0)
Forfeiture (0%)	–68.33%	–53.62%	–40.39%	–33.03%	–24.06%	–21.57%	–17.26%	–13.72%	–12.20%	–9.61%
Forfeiture (5%)	–68.99%	–55.09%	–42.84%	–36.13%	–28.09%	–25.88%	–22.08%	–18.98%	–17.67%	–15.43%
Forfeiture (10%)	–69.59%	–56.43%	–45.05%	–38.92%	–31.67%	–29.71%	–26.34%	–23.63%	–22.48%	–20.55%
Forfeiture (15%)	–70.15%	–57.66%	–47.05%	–41.43%	–34.88%	–33.12%	–30.14%	–27.75%	–26.75%	–25.07%
Forfeiture (20%)	–70.68%	–58.79%	–48.87%	–43.70%	–37.76%	–36.18%	–33.53%	–31.42%	–30.54%	–29.08%
Forfeiture (25%)	–71.17%	–59.83%	–50.53%	–45.76%	–40.36%	–38.94%	–36.57%	–34.70%	–33.93%	–32.65%
Forfeiture (30%)	–71.63%	–60.79%	–52.06%	–47.65%	–42.71%	–41.43%	–39.31%	–37.65%	–36.97%	–35.85%
Forfeiture (35%)	–72.06%	–61.68%	–53.46%	–49.37%	–44.86%	–43.70%	–41.78%	–40.31%	–39.71%	–38.72%
Forfeiture (40%)	–72.47%	–62.52%	–54.76%	–50.95%	–46.81%	–45.76%	–44.04%	–42.72%	–42.18%	–41.31%

MATURITY OF 5 YEARS AND VESTING OF 1 MONTH ON AN $80 STOCK PRICE

Stock Price and Strike Price of $80, Maturity of 5 Years, Risk-Free Rate of 3.5%, 70% Volatility, 0% Dividends, Vesting of 1 Month, Employee Suboptimal Exercise Behavior from 1.2 to 3.0, and Forfeiture Rate from 0% to 40%.
Generalized Black-Scholes: $48.29

Customized Binomial Lattice	Suboptimal (1.2)	Suboptimal (1.4)	Suboptimal (1.6)	Suboptimal (1.8)	Suboptimal (2.0)	Suboptimal (2.2)	Suboptimal (2.4)	Suboptimal (2.6)	Suboptimal (2.8)	Suboptimal (3.0)
Forfeiture (0%)	$15.29	$22.40	$28.79	$32.34	$36.67	$37.87	$39.96	$41.67	$42.40	$43.65
Forfeiture (5%)	$14.98	$21.69	$27.60	$30.84	$34.73	$35.79	$37.63	$39.12	$39.76	$40.84
Forfeiture (10%)	$14.68	$21.04	$26.53	$29.49	$32.99	$33.94	$35.57	$36.88	$37.43	$38.37
Forfeiture (15%)	$14.41	$20.45	$25.57	$28.28	$31.45	$32.29	$33.74	$34.89	$35.37	$36.18
Forfeiture (20%)	$14.16	$19.90	$24.69	$27.19	$30.05	$30.82	$32.10	$33.12	$33.54	$34.25
Forfeiture (25%)	$13.92	$19.40	$23.89	$26.19	$28.80	$29.48	$30.63	$31.53	$31.90	$32.52
Forfeiture (30%)	$13.70	$18.93	$23.15	$25.28	$27.66	$28.28	$29.31	$30.11	$30.44	$30.98
Forfeiture (35%)	$13.49	$18.50	$22.47	$24.45	$26.63	$27.19	$28.11	$28.82	$29.11	$29.59
Forfeiture (40%)	$13.29	$18.10	$21.84	$23.68	$25.68	$26.19	$27.02	$27.66	$27.92	$28.34

Percentage Difference between Binomial and Black-Scholes Model	Suboptimal (1.2)	Suboptimal (1.4)	Suboptimal (1.6)	Suboptimal (1.8)	Suboptimal (2.0)	Suboptimal (2.2)	Suboptimal (2.4)	Suboptimal (2.6)	Suboptimal (2.8)	Suboptimal (3.0)
Forfeiture (0%)	−68.33%	−53.62%	−40.39%	−33.03%	−24.06%	−21.57%	−17.26%	−13.72%	−12.20%	−9.61%
Forfeiture (5%)	−68.99%	−55.09%	−42.84%	−36.13%	−28.09%	−25.88%	−22.08%	−18.98%	−17.67%	−15.43%
Forfeiture (10%)	−69.59%	−56.43%	−45.05%	−38.92%	−31.67%	−29.71%	−26.34%	−23.63%	−22.48%	−20.55%
Forfeiture (15%)	−70.15%	−57.66%	−47.05%	−41.43%	−34.88%	−33.12%	−30.14%	−27.75%	−26.75%	−25.07%
Forfeiture (20%)	−70.68%	−58.79%	−48.87%	−43.70%	−37.76%	−36.18%	−33.53%	−31.42%	−30.54%	−29.08%
Forfeiture (25%)	−71.17%	−59.83%	−50.53%	−45.76%	−40.36%	−38.94%	−36.57%	−34.70%	−33.93%	−32.65%
Forfeiture (30%)	−71.63%	−60.79%	−52.06%	−47.65%	−42.71%	−41.43%	−39.31%	−37.65%	−36.97%	−35.85%
Forfeiture (35%)	−72.06%	−61.68%	−53.46%	−49.37%	−44.86%	−43.70%	−41.78%	−40.31%	−39.71%	−38.72%
Forfeiture (40%)	−72.47%	−62.52%	−54.76%	−50.95%	−46.81%	−45.76%	−44.04%	−42.72%	−42.18%	−41.31%

MATURITY OF 5 YEARS AND VESTING OF 1 YEAR ON A $20 STOCK PRICE

Stock Price and Strike Price of $20, Maturity of 5 Years, Risk-Free Rate of 3.5%, 70% Volatility, 0% Dividends, Vesting of 1 Year, Employee Suboptimal Exercise Behavior from 1.2 to 3.0, and Forfeiture Rate from 0% to 40%.
Generalized Black-Scholes: $12.07

Customized Binomial Lattice	Suboptimal (1.2)	Suboptimal (1.4)	Suboptimal (1.6)	Suboptimal (1.8)	Suboptimal (2.0)	Suboptimal (2.2)	Suboptimal (2.4)	Suboptimal (2.6)	Suboptimal (2.8)	Suboptimal (3.0)
Forfeiture (0%)	$6.94	$7.83	$8.64	$9.14	$9.80	$10.00	$10.35	$10.66	$10.80	$11.05
Forfeiture (5%)	$6.55	$7.35	$8.06	$8.50	$9.08	$9.25	$9.56	$9.82	$9.94	$10.15
Forfeiture (10%)	$6.19	$6.90	$7.54	$7.92	$8.43	$8.58	$8.84	$9.07	$9.17	$9.35
Forfeiture (15%)	$5.85	$6.49	$7.06	$7.40	$7.84	$7.97	$8.20	$8.40	$8.48	$8.63
Forfeiture (20%)	$5.53	$6.11	$6.61	$6.91	$7.30	$7.41	$7.62	$7.79	$7.86	$7.99
Forfeiture (25%)	$5.23	$5.76	$6.21	$6.47	$6.82	$6.91	$7.09	$7.23	$7.30	$7.41
Forfeiture (30%)	$4.95	$5.43	$5.83	$6.07	$6.37	$6.45	$6.61	$6.73	$6.79	$6.89
Forfeiture (35%)	$4.68	$5.12	$5.48	$5.69	$5.96	$6.03	$6.17	$6.28	$6.33	$6.41
Forfeiture (40%)	$4.44	$4.83	$5.16	$5.34	$5.58	$5.65	$5.76	$5.86	$5.90	$5.98

Percentage Difference between Binomial and Black-Scholes Model	Suboptimal (1.2)	Suboptimal (1.4)	Suboptimal (1.6)	Suboptimal (1.8)	Suboptimal (2.0)	Suboptimal (2.2)	Suboptimal (2.4)	Suboptimal (2.6)	Suboptimal (2.8)	Suboptimal (3.0)
Forfeiture (0%)	−42.53%	−35.15%	−28.45%	−24.32%	−18.79%	−17.20%	−14.23%	−11.66%	−10.50%	−8.49%
Forfeiture (5%)	−45.75%	−39.14%	−33.21%	−29.58%	−24.77%	−23.39%	−20.83%	−18.63%	−17.63%	−15.92%
Forfeiture (10%)	−48.76%	−42.82%	−37.56%	−34.37%	−30.16%	−28.97%	−26.76%	−24.86%	−24.01%	−22.54%
Forfeiture (15%)	−51.58%	−46.23%	−41.54%	−38.73%	−35.05%	−34.01%	−32.09%	−30.46%	−29.73%	−28.47%
Forfeiture (20%)	−54.22%	−49.39%	−45.21%	−42.72%	−39.49%	−38.58%	−36.92%	−35.51%	−34.88%	−33.80%
Forfeiture (25%)	−56.69%	−52.33%	−48.59%	−46.38%	−43.54%	−42.75%	−41.30%	−40.07%	−39.53%	−38.61%
Forfeiture (30%)	−59.02%	−55.06%	−51.71%	−49.75%	−47.24%	−46.55%	−45.29%	−44.22%	−43.75%	−42.95%
Forfeiture (35%)	−61.20%	−57.61%	−54.61%	−52.86%	−50.64%	−50.03%	−48.93%	−48.00%	−47.59%	−46.90%
Forfeiture (40%)	−63.26%	−59.99%	−57.29%	−55.73%	−53.77%	−53.23%	−52.26%	−51.45%	−51.10%	−50.50%

MATURITY OF 5 YEARS AND VESTING OF 1 YEAR ON A $40 STOCK PRICE

Stock Price and Strike Price of $40, Maturity of 5 Years, Risk-Free Rate of 3.5%, 70% Volatility, 0% Dividends, Vesting of 1 Year, Employee Suboptimal Exercise Behavior from 1.2 to 3.0, and Forfeiture Rate from 0% to 40%.
Generalized Black-Scholes: $24.14

Customized Binomial Lattice	Suboptimal (1.2)	Suboptimal (1.4)	Suboptimal (1.6)	Suboptimal (1.8)	Suboptimal (2.0)	Suboptimal (2.2)	Suboptimal (2.4)	Suboptimal (2.6)	Suboptimal (2.8)	Suboptimal (3.0)
Forfeiture (0%)	$13.88	$15.66	$17.28	$18.27	$19.61	$19.99	$20.71	$21.33	$21.61	$22.10
Forfeiture (5%)	$13.10	$14.69	$16.13	$17.00	$18.16	$18.50	$19.11	$19.65	$19.89	$20.30
Forfeiture (10%)	$12.37	$13.80	$15.08	$15.85	$16.86	$17.15	$17.68	$18.14	$18.35	$18.70
Forfeiture (15%)	$11.69	$12.98	$14.11	$14.79	$15.68	$15.93	$16.40	$16.79	$16.97	$17.27
Forfeiture (20%)	$11.05	$12.22	$13.23	$13.83	$14.61	$14.83	$15.23	$15.57	$15.72	$15.98
Forfeiture (25%)	$10.46	$11.51	$12.41	$12.95	$13.63	$13.82	$14.17	$14.47	$14.60	$14.82
Forfeiture (30%)	$9.89	$10.85	$11.66	$12.13	$12.74	$12.90	$13.21	$13.47	$13.58	$13.77
Forfeiture (35%)	$9.37	$10.23	$10.96	$11.38	$11.92	$12.06	$12.33	$12.55	$12.65	$12.82
Forfeiture (40%)	$8.87	$9.66	$10.31	$10.69	$11.16	$11.29	$11.53	$11.72	$11.81	$11.95

Percentage Difference between Binomial and Black-Scholes Model	Suboptimal (1.2)	Suboptimal (1.4)	Suboptimal (1.6)	Suboptimal (1.8)	Suboptimal (2.0)	Suboptimal (2.2)	Suboptimal (2.4)	Suboptimal (2.6)	Suboptimal (2.8)	Suboptimal (3.0)
Forfeiture (0%)	−42.53%	−35.15%	−28.45%	−24.32%	−18.79%	−17.20%	−14.23%	−11.66%	−10.50%	−8.49%
Forfeiture (5%)	−45.75%	−39.14%	−33.21%	−29.58%	−24.77%	−23.39%	−20.83%	−18.63%	−17.63%	−15.92%
Forfeiture (10%)	−48.76%	−42.82%	−37.56%	−34.37%	−30.16%	−28.97%	−26.76%	−24.86%	−24.01%	−22.54%
Forfeiture (15%)	−51.58%	−46.23%	−41.54%	−38.73%	−35.05%	−34.01%	−32.09%	−30.46%	−29.73%	−28.47%
Forfeiture (20%)	−54.22%	−49.39%	−45.21%	−42.72%	−39.49%	−38.58%	−36.92%	−35.51%	−34.88%	−33.80%
Forfeiture (25%)	−56.69%	−52.33%	−48.59%	−46.38%	−43.54%	−42.75%	−41.30%	−40.07%	−39.53%	−38.61%
Forfeiture (30%)	−59.02%	−55.06%	−51.71%	−49.75%	−47.24%	−46.55%	−45.29%	−44.22%	−43.75%	−42.95%
Forfeiture (35%)	−61.20%	−57.61%	−54.61%	−52.86%	−50.64%	−50.03%	−48.93%	−48.00%	−47.59%	−46.90%
Forfeiture (40%)	−63.26%	−59.99%	−57.29%	−55.73%	−53.77%	−53.23%	−52.26%	−51.45%	−51.10%	−50.50%

MATURITY OF 5 YEARS AND VESTING OF 1 YEAR ON A $60 STOCK PRICE

Stock Price and Strike Price of $60, Maturity of 5 Years, Risk-Free Rate of 3.5%, 70% Volatility, 0% Dividends, Vesting of 1 Year, Employee Suboptimal Exercise Behavior from 1.2 to 3.0, and Forfeiture Rate from 0% to 40%.
Generalized Black-Scholes: $36.22

Customized Binomial Lattice	Suboptimal (1.2)	Suboptimal (1.4)	Suboptimal (1.6)	Suboptimal (1.8)	Suboptimal (2.0)	Suboptimal (2.2)	Suboptimal (2.4)	Suboptimal (2.6)	Suboptimal (2.8)	Suboptimal (3.0)
Forfeiture (0%)	$20.81	$23.49	$25.91	$27.41	$29.41	$29.99	$31.06	$31.99	$32.41	$33.14
Forfeiture (5%)	$19.65	$22.04	$24.19	$25.50	$27.25	$27.75	$28.67	$29.47	$29.83	$30.45
Forfeiture (10%)	$18.56	$20.71	$22.62	$23.77	$25.29	$25.73	$26.53	$27.21	$27.52	$28.05
Forfeiture (15%)	$17.54	$19.47	$21.17	$22.19	$23.52	$23.90	$24.59	$25.19	$25.45	$25.90
Forfeiture (20%)	$16.58	$18.33	$19.84	$20.74	$21.91	$22.24	$22.85	$23.36	$23.59	$23.98
Forfeiture (25%)	$15.68	$17.27	$18.62	$19.42	$20.45	$20.73	$21.26	$21.70	$21.90	$22.23
Forfeiture (30%)	$14.84	$16.28	$17.49	$18.20	$19.11	$19.36	$19.82	$20.20	$20.37	$20.66
Forfeiture (35%)	$14.05	$15.35	$16.44	$17.07	$17.88	$18.10	$18.50	$18.83	$18.98	$19.23
Forfeiture (40%)	$13.31	$14.49	$15.47	$16.03	$16.74	$16.94	$17.29	$17.58	$17.71	$17.93

Percentage Difference between Binomial and Black-Scholes Model	Suboptimal (1.2)	Suboptimal (1.4)	Suboptimal (1.6)	Suboptimal (1.8)	Suboptimal (2.0)	Suboptimal (2.2)	Suboptimal (2.4)	Suboptimal (2.6)	Suboptimal (2.8)	Suboptimal (3.0)
Forfeiture (0%)	–42.53%	–35.15%	–28.45%	–24.32%	–18.79%	–17.20%	–14.23%	–11.66%	–10.50%	–8.49%
Forfeiture (5%)	–45.75%	–39.14%	–33.21%	–29.58%	–24.77%	–23.39%	–20.83%	–18.63%	–17.63%	–15.92%
Forfeiture (10%)	–48.76%	–42.82%	–37.56%	–34.37%	–30.16%	–28.97%	–26.76%	–24.86%	–24.01%	–22.54%
Forfeiture (15%)	–51.58%	–46.23%	–41.54%	–38.73%	–35.05%	–34.01%	–32.09%	–30.46%	–29.73%	–28.47%
Forfeiture (20%)	–54.22%	–49.39%	–45.21%	–42.72%	–39.49%	–38.58%	–36.92%	–35.51%	–34.88%	–33.80%
Forfeiture (25%)	–56.69%	–52.33%	–48.59%	–46.38%	–43.54%	–42.75%	–41.30%	–40.07%	–39.53%	–38.61%
Forfeiture (30%)	–59.02%	–55.06%	–51.71%	–49.75%	–47.24%	–46.55%	–45.29%	–44.22%	–43.75%	–42.95%
Forfeiture (35%)	–61.20%	–57.61%	–54.61%	–52.86%	–50.64%	–50.03%	–48.93%	–48.00%	–47.59%	–46.90%
Forfeiture (40%)	–63.26%	–59.99%	–57.29%	–55.73%	–53.77%	–53.23%	–52.26%	–51.45%	–51.10%	–50.50%

MATURITY OF 5 YEARS AND VESTING OF 1 YEAR ON AN $80 STOCK PRICE

Stock Price and Strike Price of $80, Maturity of 5 Years, Risk-Free Rate of 3.5%, 70% Volatility, 0% Dividends, Vesting of 1 Year, Employee Suboptimal Exercise Behavior from 1.2 to 3.0, and Forfeiture Rate from 0% to 40%.
Generalized Black-Scholes: $48.29

Customized Binomial Lattice	Suboptimal (1.2)	Suboptimal (1.4)	Suboptimal (1.6)	Suboptimal (1.8)	Suboptimal (2.0)	Suboptimal (2.2)	Suboptimal (2.4)	Suboptimal (2.6)	Suboptimal (2.8)	Suboptimal (3.0)
Forfeiture (0%)	$27.75	$31.31	$34.55	$36.54	$39.21	$39.98	$41.42	$42.66	$43.22	$44.19
Forfeiture (5%)	$26.19	$29.39	$32.25	$34.00	$36.33	$36.99	$38.23	$39.29	$39.77	$40.60
Forfeiture (10%)	$24.74	$27.61	$30.15	$31.69	$33.72	$34.30	$35.37	$36.28	$36.70	$37.40
Forfeiture (15%)	$23.38	$25.96	$28.23	$29.59	$31.36	$31.87	$32.79	$33.58	$33.93	$34.54
Forfeiture (20%)	$22.11	$24.44	$26.46	$27.66	$29.22	$29.66	$30.46	$31.14	$31.45	$31.97
Forfeiture (25%)	$20.91	$23.02	$24.82	$25.89	$27.26	$27.65	$28.35	$28.94	$29.20	$29.65
Forfeiture (30%)	$19.79	$21.70	$23.32	$24.26	$25.47	$25.81	$26.42	$26.93	$27.16	$27.55
Forfeiture (35%)	$18.73	$20.47	$21.92	$22.76	$23.83	$24.13	$24.66	$25.11	$25.31	$25.64
Forfeiture (40%)	$17.74	$19.32	$20.62	$21.38	$22.33	$22.58	$23.05	$23.44	$23.61	$23.90

Percentage Difference between Binomial and Black-Scholes Model	Suboptimal (1.2)	Suboptimal (1.4)	Suboptimal (1.6)	Suboptimal (1.8)	Suboptimal (2.0)	Suboptimal (2.2)	Suboptimal (2.4)	Suboptimal (2.6)	Suboptimal (2.8)	Suboptimal (3.0)
Forfeiture (0%)	−42.53%	−35.15%	−28.45%	−24.32%	−18.79%	−17.20%	−14.23%	−11.66%	−10.50%	−8.49%
Forfeiture (5%)	−45.75%	−39.14%	−33.21%	−29.58%	−24.77%	−23.39%	−20.83%	−18.63%	−17.63%	−15.92%
Forfeiture (10%)	−48.76%	−42.82%	−37.56%	−34.37%	−30.16%	−28.97%	−26.76%	−24.86%	−24.01%	−22.54%
Forfeiture (15%)	−51.58%	−46.23%	−41.54%	−38.73%	−35.05%	−34.01%	−32.09%	−30.46%	−29.73%	−28.47%
Forfeiture (20%)	−54.22%	−49.39%	−45.21%	−42.72%	−39.49%	−38.58%	−36.92%	−35.51%	−34.88%	−33.80%
Forfeiture (25%)	−56.69%	−52.33%	−48.59%	−46.38%	−43.54%	−42.75%	−41.30%	−40.07%	−39.53%	−38.61%
Forfeiture (30%)	−59.02%	−55.06%	−51.71%	−49.75%	−47.24%	−46.55%	−45.29%	−44.22%	−43.75%	−42.95%
Forfeiture (35%)	−61.20%	−57.61%	−54.61%	−52.86%	−50.64%	−50.03%	−48.93%	−48.00%	−47.59%	−46.90%
Forfeiture (40%)	−63.26%	−59.99%	−57.29%	−55.73%	−53.77%	−53.23%	−52.26%	−51.45%	−51.10%	−50.50%

MATURITY OF 5 YEARS AND VESTING OF 3 YEARS ON A $20 STOCK PRICE

Stock Price and Strike Price of $20, Maturity of 5 Years, Risk-Free Rate of 3.5%, 70% Volatility, 0% Dividends, Vesting of 3 Years, Employee Suboptimal Exercise Behavior from 1.2 to 3.0, and Forfeiture Rate from 0% to 40%.
Generalized Black-Scholes: $12.07

Customized Binomial Lattice	Suboptimal (1.2)	Suboptimal (1.4)	Suboptimal (1.6)	Suboptimal (1.8)	Suboptimal (2.0)	Suboptimal (2.2)	Suboptimal (2.4)	Suboptimal (2.6)	Suboptimal (2.8)	Suboptimal (3.0)
Forfeiture (0%)	$10.28	$10.66	$10.97	$11.15	$11.37	$11.43	$11.54	$11.64	$11.68	$11.75
Forfeiture (5%)	$8.83	$9.15	$9.40	$9.55	$9.73	$9.78	$9.87	$9.95	$9.98	$10.04
Forfeiture (10%)	$7.59	$7.85	$8.06	$8.18	$8.33	$8.37	$8.44	$8.50	$8.53	$8.58
Forfeiture (15%)	$6.52	$6.73	$6.91	$7.01	$7.13	$7.16	$7.22	$7.27	$7.29	$7.33
Forfeiture (20%)	$5.60	$5.78	$5.92	$6.00	$6.10	$6.13	$6.18	$6.22	$6.24	$6.27
Forfeiture (25%)	$4.81	$4.96	$5.08	$5.15	$5.23	$5.25	$5.29	$5.32	$5.34	$5.36
Forfeiture (30%)	$4.14	$4.26	$4.36	$4.41	$4.48	$4.50	$4.53	$4.55	$4.57	$4.59
Forfeiture (35%)	$3.55	$3.66	$3.74	$3.78	$3.84	$3.85	$3.88	$3.90	$3.91	$3.93
Forfeiture (40%)	$3.05	$3.14	$3.21	$3.24	$3.29	$3.30	$3.32	$3.34	$3.35	$3.36

Percentage Difference between Binomial and Black-Scholes Model	Suboptimal (1.2)	Suboptimal (1.4)	Suboptimal (1.6)	Suboptimal (1.8)	Suboptimal (2.0)	Suboptimal (2.2)	Suboptimal (2.4)	Suboptimal (2.6)	Suboptimal (2.8)	Suboptimal (3.0)
Forfeiture (0%)	–14.87%	–11.71%	–9.13%	–7.65%	–5.80%	–5.29%	–4.37%	–3.60%	–3.25%	–2.67%
Forfeiture (5%)	–26.86%	–24.25%	–22.13%	–20.92%	–19.40%	–18.99%	–18.25%	–17.62%	–17.34%	–16.87%
Forfeiture (10%)	–37.16%	–35.00%	–33.25%	–32.26%	–31.02%	–30.69%	–30.08%	–29.57%	–29.34%	–28.96%
Forfeiture (15%)	–46.01%	–44.21%	–42.78%	–41.97%	–40.95%	–40.68%	–40.19%	–39.77%	–39.59%	–39.28%
Forfeiture (20%)	–53.61%	–52.12%	–50.94%	–50.27%	–49.44%	–49.22%	–48.82%	–48.48%	–48.33%	–48.08%
Forfeiture (25%)	–60.13%	–58.90%	–57.93%	–57.38%	–56.70%	–56.52%	–56.19%	–55.92%	–55.80%	–55.59%
Forfeiture (30%)	–65.74%	–64.72%	–63.92%	–63.47%	–62.91%	–62.76%	–62.50%	–62.27%	–62.17%	–62.01%
Forfeiture (35%)	–70.56%	–69.71%	–69.05%	–68.68%	–68.22%	–68.10%	–67.88%	–67.70%	–67.62%	–67.49%
Forfeiture (40%)	–74.70%	–74.00%	–73.45%	–73.14%	–72.77%	–72.67%	–72.49%	–72.34%	–72.28%	–72.17%

MATURITY OF 5 YEARS AND VESTING OF 3 YEARS ON A $40 STOCK PRICE

Stock Price and Strike Price of $40, Maturity of 5 Years, Risk-Free Rate of 3.5%, 70% Volatility, 0% Dividends, Vesting of 3 Years, Employee Suboptimal Exercise Behavior from 1.2 to 3.0, and Forfeiture Rate from 0% to 40%.
Generalized Black-Scholes: $24.14

Customized Binomial Lattice	Suboptimal (1.2)	Suboptimal (1.4)	Suboptimal (1.6)	Suboptimal (1.8)	Suboptimal (2.0)	Suboptimal (2.2)	Suboptimal (2.4)	Suboptimal (2.6)	Suboptimal (2.8)	Suboptimal (3.0)
Forfeiture (0%)	$20.56	$21.32	$21.94	$22.30	$22.75	$22.87	$23.09	$23.27	$23.36	$23.50
Forfeiture (5%)	$17.66	$18.29	$18.80	$19.09	$19.46	$19.56	$19.74	$19.89	$19.96	$20.07
Forfeiture (10%)	$15.17	$15.69	$16.12	$16.35	$16.65	$16.73	$16.88	$17.00	$17.06	$17.15
Forfeiture (15%)	$13.04	$13.47	$13.82	$14.01	$14.26	$14.32	$14.44	$14.54	$14.59	$14.66
Forfeiture (20%)	$11.20	$11.56	$11.85	$12.01	$12.21	$12.26	$12.36	$12.44	$12.47	$12.54
Forfeiture (25%)	$9.63	$9.92	$10.16	$10.29	$10.45	$10.50	$10.58	$10.64	$10.67	$10.72
Forfeiture (30%)	$8.27	$8.52	$8.71	$8.82	$8.96	$8.99	$9.06	$9.11	$9.13	$9.17
Forfeiture (35%)	$7.11	$7.31	$7.47	$7.56	$7.67	$7.70	$7.75	$7.80	$7.82	$7.85
Forfeiture (40%)	$6.11	$6.28	$6.41	$6.48	$6.57	$6.60	$6.64	$6.68	$6.69	$6.72

Percentage Difference between Binomial and Black-Scholes Model	Suboptimal (1.2)	Suboptimal (1.4)	Suboptimal (1.6)	Suboptimal (1.8)	Suboptimal (2.0)	Suboptimal (2.2)	Suboptimal (2.4)	Suboptimal (2.6)	Suboptimal (2.8)	Suboptimal (3.0)
Forfeiture (0%)	−14.87%	−11.71%	−9.13%	−7.65%	−5.80%	−5.29%	−4.37%	−3.60%	−3.25%	−2.67%
Forfeiture (5%)	−26.86%	−24.25%	−22.13%	−20.92%	−19.40%	−18.99%	−18.25%	−17.62%	−17.34%	−16.87%
Forfeiture (10%)	−37.16%	−35.00%	−33.25%	−32.26%	−31.02%	−30.69%	−30.08%	−29.57%	−29.34%	−28.96%
Forfeiture (15%)	−46.01%	−44.21%	−42.78%	−41.97%	−40.95%	−40.68%	−40.19%	−39.77%	−39.59%	−39.28%
Forfeiture (20%)	−53.61%	−52.12%	−50.94%	−50.27%	−49.44%	−49.22%	−48.82%	−48.48%	−48.33%	−48.08%
Forfeiture (25%)	−60.13%	−58.90%	−57.93%	−57.38%	−56.70%	−56.52%	−56.19%	−55.92%	−55.80%	−55.59%
Forfeiture (30%)	−65.74%	−64.72%	−63.92%	−63.47%	−62.91%	−62.76%	−62.50%	−62.27%	−62.17%	−62.01%
Forfeiture (35%)	−70.56%	−69.71%	−69.05%	−68.68%	−68.22%	−68.10%	−67.88%	−67.70%	−67.62%	−67.49%
Forfeiture (40%)	−74.70%	−74.00%	−73.45%	−73.14%	−72.77%	−72.67%	−72.49%	−72.34%	−72.28%	−72.17%

MATURITY OF 5 YEARS AND VESTING OF 3 YEARS ON A $60 STOCK PRICE

Stock Price and Strike Price of $60, Maturity of 5 Years, Risk-Free Rate of 3.5%, 70% Volatility, 0% Dividends, Vesting of 3 Years, Employee Suboptimal Exercise Behavior from 1.2 to 3.0, and Forfeiture Rate from 0% to 40%.
Generalized Black-Scholes: $36.22

Customized Binomial Lattice	Suboptimal (1.2)	Suboptimal (1.4)	Suboptimal (1.6)	Suboptimal (1.8)	Suboptimal (2.0)	Suboptimal (2.2)	Suboptimal (2.4)	Suboptimal (2.6)	Suboptimal (2.8)	Suboptimal (3.0)
Forfeiture (0%)	$30.83	$31.98	$32.91	$33.44	$34.12	$34.30	$34.63	$34.91	$35.04	$35.25
Forfeiture (5%)	$26.49	$27.44	$28.20	$28.64	$29.19	$29.34	$29.61	$29.84	$29.94	$30.11
Forfeiture (10%)	$22.76	$23.54	$24.17	$24.53	$24.98	$25.10	$25.32	$25.51	$25.59	$25.73
Forfeiture (15%)	$19.55	$20.20	$20.72	$21.02	$21.38	$21.48	$21.66	$21.81	$21.88	$21.99
Forfeiture (20%)	$16.80	$17.34	$17.77	$18.01	$18.31	$18.39	$18.54	$18.66	$18.71	$18.80
Forfeiture (25%)	$14.44	$14.88	$15.24	$15.44	$15.68	$15.75	$15.87	$15.96	$16.01	$16.08
Forfeiture (30%)	$12.41	$12.78	$13.07	$13.23	$13.43	$13.49	$13.58	$13.66	$13.70	$13.76
Forfeiture (35%)	$10.66	$10.97	$11.21	$11.34	$11.51	$11.55	$11.63	$11.70	$11.73	$11.78
Forfeiture (40%)	$9.16	$9.42	$9.62	$9.73	$9.86	$9.90	$9.96	$10.02	$10.04	$10.08

Percentage Difference between Binomial and Black-Scholes Model	Suboptimal (1.2)	Suboptimal (1.4)	Suboptimal (1.6)	Suboptimal (1.8)	Suboptimal (2.0)	Suboptimal (2.2)	Suboptimal (2.4)	Suboptimal (2.6)	Suboptimal (2.8)	Suboptimal (3.0)
Forfeiture (0%)	–14.87%	–11.71%	–9.13%	–7.65%	–5.80%	–5.29%	–4.37%	–3.60%	–3.25%	–2.67%
Forfeiture (5%)	–26.86%	–24.25%	–22.13%	–20.92%	–19.40%	–18.99%	–18.25%	–17.62%	–17.34%	–16.87%
Forfeiture (10%)	–37.16%	–35.00%	–33.25%	–32.26%	–31.02%	–30.69%	–30.08%	–29.57%	–29.34%	–28.96%
Forfeiture (15%)	–46.01%	–44.21%	–42.78%	–41.97%	–40.95%	–40.68%	–40.19%	–39.77%	–39.59%	–39.28%
Forfeiture (20%)	–53.61%	–52.12%	–50.94%	–50.27%	–49.44%	–49.22%	–48.82%	–48.48%	–48.33%	–48.08%
Forfeiture (25%)	–60.13%	–58.90%	–57.93%	–57.38%	–56.70%	–56.52%	–56.19%	–55.92%	–55.80%	–55.59%
Forfeiture (30%)	–65.74%	–64.72%	–63.92%	–63.47%	–62.91%	–62.76%	–62.50%	–62.27%	–62.17%	–62.01%
Forfeiture (35%)	–70.56%	–69.71%	–69.05%	–68.68%	–68.22%	–68.10%	–67.88%	–67.70%	–67.62%	–67.49%
Forfeiture (40%)	–74.70%	–74.00%	–73.45%	–73.14%	–72.77%	–72.67%	–72.49%	–72.34%	–72.28%	–72.17%

MATURITY OF 5 YEARS AND VESTING OF 3 YEARS ON AN $80 STOCK PRICE

Stock Price and Strike Price of $80, Maturity of 5 Years, Risk-Free Rate of 3.5%, 70% Volatility, 0% Dividends, Vesting of 3 Years, Employee Suboptimal Exercise Behavior from 1.2 to 3.0, and Forfeiture Rate from 0% to 40%.
Generalized Black-Scholes: $48.29

Customized Binomial Lattice	Suboptimal (1.2)	Suboptimal (1.4)	Suboptimal (1.6)	Suboptimal (1.8)	Suboptimal (2.0)	Suboptimal (2.2)	Suboptimal (2.4)	Suboptimal (2.6)	Suboptimal (2.8)	Suboptimal (3.0)
Forfeiture (0%)	$41.11	$42.64	$43.88	$44.59	$45.49	$45.73	$46.18	$46.55	$46.72	$47.00
Forfeiture (5%)	$35.32	$36.58	$37.60	$38.19	$38.92	$39.12	$39.48	$39.78	$39.92	$40.14
Forfeiture (10%)	$30.34	$31.39	$32.23	$32.71	$33.31	$33.47	$33.76	$34.01	$34.12	$34.30
Forfeiture (15%)	$26.07	$26.94	$27.63	$28.02	$28.51	$28.64	$28.88	$29.08	$29.17	$29.32
Forfeiture (20%)	$22.40	$23.12	$23.69	$24.01	$24.41	$24.52	$24.71	$24.88	$24.95	$25.07
Forfeiture (25%)	$19.25	$19.85	$20.32	$20.58	$20.91	$21.00	$21.15	$21.29	$21.35	$21.44
Forfeiture (30%)	$16.54	$17.04	$17.42	$17.64	$17.91	$17.98	$18.11	$18.22	$18.27	$18.35
Forfeiture (35%)	$14.22	$14.63	$14.95	$15.12	$15.34	$15.40	$15.51	$15.60	$15.64	$15.70
Forfeiture (40%)	$12.22	$12.56	$12.82	$12.97	$13.15	$13.20	$13.28	$13.35	$13.39	$13.44

Percentage Difference between Binomial and Black-Scholes Model	Suboptimal (1.2)	Suboptimal (1.4)	Suboptimal (1.6)	Suboptimal (1.8)	Suboptimal (2.0)	Suboptimal (2.2)	Suboptimal (2.4)	Suboptimal (2.6)	Suboptimal (2.8)	Suboptimal (3.0)
Forfeiture (0%)	–14.87%	–11.71%	–9.13%	–7.65%	–5.80%	–5.29%	–4.37%	–3.60%	–3.25%	–2.67%
Forfeiture (5%)	–26.86%	–24.25%	–22.13%	–20.92%	–19.40%	–18.99%	–18.25%	–17.62%	–17.34%	–16.87%
Forfeiture (10%)	–37.16%	–35.00%	–33.25%	–32.26%	–31.02%	–30.69%	–30.08%	–29.57%	–29.34%	–28.96%
Forfeiture (15%)	–46.01%	–44.21%	–42.78%	–41.97%	–40.95%	–40.68%	–40.19%	–39.77%	–39.59%	–39.28%
Forfeiture (20%)	–53.61%	–52.12%	–50.94%	–50.27%	–49.44%	–49.22%	–48.82%	–48.48%	–48.33%	–48.08%
Forfeiture (25%)	–60.13%	–58.90%	–57.93%	–57.38%	–56.70%	–56.52%	–56.19%	–55.92%	–55.80%	–55.59%
Forfeiture (30%)	–65.74%	–64.72%	–63.92%	–63.47%	–62.91%	–62.76%	–62.50%	–62.27%	–62.17%	–62.01%
Forfeiture (35%)	–70.56%	–69.71%	–69.05%	–68.68%	–68.22%	–68.10%	–67.88%	–67.70%	–67.62%	–67.49%
Forfeiture (40%)	–74.70%	–74.00%	–73.45%	–73.14%	–72.77%	–72.67%	–72.49%	–72.34%	–72.28%	–72.17%

THIRTY-FIVE PERCENT VOLATILITY AND 7-YEAR MATURITY ESOs WITH VARYING STOCK PRICE, SUBOPTIMAL BEHAVIOR, VESTING PERIOD, AND FORFEITURE RATES

This section provides ESO valuation results on an underlying stock with 35 percent volatility and a 7-year maturity. The analysis is divided into 1-month, 1-year, 3-year, and 5-year vesting periods, and accounts for stock prices at grant date of $20, $40, $60, and $80.

MATURITY OF 7 YEARS AND VESTING OF 1 MONTH ON A $20 STOCK PRICE

Stock Price and Strike Price of $20, Maturity of 7 Years, Risk-Free Rate of 3.5%, 35% Volatility, 0% Dividends, Vesting of 1 Month, Employee Suboptimal Exercise Behavior from 1.2 to 3.0, and Forfeiture Rate from 0% to 40%.
Generalized Black-Scholes: $8.74

Customized Binomial Lattice	Suboptimal (1.2)	Suboptimal (1.4)	Suboptimal (1.6)	Suboptimal (1.8)	Suboptimal (2.0)	Suboptimal (2.2)	Suboptimal (2.4)	Suboptimal (2.6)	Suboptimal (2.8)	Suboptimal (3.0)
Forfeiture (0%)	$3.47	$5.19	$6.42	$7.11	$7.50	$7.80	$8.03	$8.20	$8.33	$8.40
Forfeiture (5%)	$3.31	$4.85	$5.90	$6.48	$6.80	$7.04	$7.22	$7.36	$7.46	$7.51
Forfeiture (10%)	$3.18	$4.55	$5.46	$5.95	$6.21	$6.41	$6.55	$6.66	$6.75	$6.79
Forfeiture (15%)	$3.06	$4.30	$5.09	$5.50	$5.72	$5.88	$6.00	$6.09	$6.15	$6.19
Forfeiture (20%)	$2.95	$4.08	$4.77	$5.12	$5.30	$5.44	$5.53	$5.61	$5.66	$5.69
Forfeiture (25%)	$2.85	$3.89	$4.49	$4.79	$4.95	$5.06	$5.14	$5.20	$5.24	$5.26
Forfeiture (30%)	$2.77	$3.72	$4.25	$4.51	$4.64	$4.73	$4.80	$4.85	$4.88	$4.90
Forfeiture (35%)	$2.69	$3.56	$4.04	$4.26	$4.37	$4.45	$4.51	$4.55	$4.58	$4.59
Forfeiture (40%)	$2.62	$3.42	$3.85	$4.05	$4.14	$4.21	$4.25	$4.29	$4.31	$4.32

Percentage Difference between Binomial and Black-Scholes Model	Suboptimal (1.2)	Suboptimal (1.4)	Suboptimal (1.6)	Suboptimal (1.8)	Suboptimal (2.0)	Suboptimal (2.2)	Suboptimal (2.4)	Suboptimal (2.6)	Suboptimal (2.8)	Suboptimal (3.0)
Forfeiture (0%)	–60.32%	–40.61%	–26.52%	–18.58%	–14.14%	–10.73%	–8.13%	–6.16%	–4.67%	–3.88%
Forfeiture (5%)	–62.10%	–44.52%	–32.45%	–25.83%	–22.20%	–19.43%	–17.34%	–15.77%	–14.59%	–13.98%
Forfeiture (10%)	–63.65%	–47.87%	–37.46%	–31.90%	–28.90%	–26.65%	–24.96%	–23.70%	–22.77%	–22.27%
Forfeiture (15%)	–65.02%	–50.76%	–41.72%	–37.03%	–34.54%	–32.69%	–31.32%	–30.30%	–29.55%	–29.16%
Forfeiture (20%)	–66.24%	–53.29%	–45.38%	–41.39%	–39.31%	–37.78%	–36.66%	–35.83%	–35.23%	–34.92%
Forfeiture (25%)	–67.34%	–55.51%	–48.54%	–45.13%	–43.38%	–42.11%	–41.19%	–40.52%	–40.03%	–39.77%
Forfeiture (30%)	–68.33%	–57.47%	–51.31%	–48.37%	–46.89%	–45.83%	–45.06%	–44.51%	–44.11%	–43.91%
Forfeiture (35%)	–69.23%	–59.22%	–53.74%	–51.20%	–49.93%	–49.04%	–48.40%	–47.95%	–47.62%	–47.45%
Forfeiture (40%)	–70.05%	–60.80%	–55.90%	–53.68%	–52.60%	–51.84%	–51.31%	–50.93%	–50.66%	–50.52%

MATURITY OF 7 YEARS AND VESTING OF 1 MONTH ON A $40 STOCK PRICE

Stock Price and Strike Price of $40, Maturity of 7 Years, Risk-Free Rate of 3.5%, 35% Volatility, 0% Dividends, Vesting of 1 Month, Employee Suboptimal Exercise Behavior from 1.2 to 3.0, and Forfeiture Rate from 0% to 40%.
Generalized Black-Scholes: $17.47

Customized Binomial Lattice	Suboptimal (1.2)	Suboptimal (1.4)	Suboptimal (1.6)	Suboptimal (1.8)	Suboptimal (2.0)	Suboptimal (2.2)	Suboptimal (2.4)	Suboptimal (2.6)	Suboptimal (2.8)	Suboptimal (3.0)
Forfeiture (0%)	$6.93	$10.38	$12.84	$14.22	$15.00	$15.60	$16.05	$16.40	$16.66	$16.79
Forfeiture (5%)	$6.62	$9.69	$11.80	$12.96	$13.59	$14.08	$14.44	$14.72	$14.92	$15.03
Forfeiture (10%)	$6.35	$9.11	$10.93	$11.90	$12.42	$12.81	$13.11	$13.33	$13.49	$13.58
Forfeiture (15%)	$6.11	$8.60	$10.18	$11.00	$11.44	$11.76	$12.00	$12.18	$12.31	$12.38
Forfeiture (20%)	$5.90	$8.16	$9.54	$10.24	$10.60	$10.87	$11.07	$11.21	$11.32	$11.37
Forfeiture (25%)	$5.71	$7.77	$8.99	$9.59	$9.89	$10.11	$10.27	$10.39	$10.48	$10.52
Forfeiture (30%)	$5.53	$7.43	$8.51	$9.02	$9.28	$9.46	$9.60	$9.69	$9.76	$9.80
Forfeiture (35%)	$5.38	$7.12	$8.08	$8.53	$8.75	$8.90	$9.01	$9.09	$9.15	$9.18
Forfeiture (40%)	$5.23	$6.85	$7.71	$8.09	$8.28	$8.41	$8.51	$8.57	$8.62	$8.64

Percentage Difference between Binomial and Black-Scholes Model	Suboptimal (1.2)	Suboptimal (1.4)	Suboptimal (1.6)	Suboptimal (1.8)	Suboptimal (2.0)	Suboptimal (2.2)	Suboptimal (2.4)	Suboptimal (2.6)	Suboptimal (2.8)	Suboptimal (3.0)
Forfeiture (0%)	−60.32%	−40.61%	−26.52%	−18.58%	−14.14%	−10.73%	−8.13%	−6.16%	−4.67%	−3.88%
Forfeiture (5%)	−62.10%	−44.52%	−32.45%	−25.83%	−22.20%	−19.43%	−17.34%	−15.77%	−14.59%	−13.98%
Forfeiture (10%)	−63.65%	−47.87%	−37.46%	−31.90%	−28.90%	−26.65%	−24.96%	−23.70%	−22.77%	−22.27%
Forfeiture (15%)	−65.02%	−50.76%	−41.72%	−37.03%	−34.54%	−32.69%	−31.32%	−30.30%	−29.55%	−29.16%
Forfeiture (20%)	−66.24%	−53.29%	−45.38%	−41.39%	−39.31%	−37.78%	−36.66%	−35.83%	−35.23%	−34.92%
Forfeiture (25%)	−67.34%	−55.51%	−48.54%	−45.13%	−43.38%	−42.11%	−41.19%	−40.52%	−40.03%	−39.77%
Forfeiture (30%)	−68.33%	−57.47%	−51.31%	−48.37%	−46.89%	−45.83%	−45.06%	−44.51%	−44.11%	−43.91%
Forfeiture (35%)	−69.23%	−59.22%	−53.74%	−51.20%	−49.93%	−49.04%	−48.40%	−47.95%	−47.62%	−47.45%
Forfeiture (40%)	−70.05%	−60.80%	−55.90%	−53.68%	−52.60%	−51.84%	−51.31%	−50.93%	−50.66%	−50.52%

MATURITY OF 7 YEARS AND VESTING OF 1 MONTH ON A $60 STOCK PRICE

Stock Price and Strike Price of $60, Maturity of 7 Years, Risk-Free Rate of 3.5%, 35% Volatility, 0% Dividends, Vesting of 1 Month, Employee Suboptimal Exercise Behavior from 1.2 to 3.0, and Forfeiture Rate from 0% to 40%.
Generalized Black-Scholes: $26.21

Customized Binomial Lattice	Suboptimal (1.2)	Suboptimal (1.4)	Suboptimal (1.6)	Suboptimal (1.8)	Suboptimal (2.0)	Suboptimal (2.2)	Suboptimal (2.4)	Suboptimal (2.6)	Suboptimal (2.8)	Suboptimal (3.0)
Forfeiture (0%)	$10.40	$15.56	$19.26	$21.34	$22.50	$23.39	$24.08	$24.59	$24.98	$25.19
Forfeiture (5%)	$9.93	$14.54	$17.70	$19.44	$20.39	$21.11	$21.66	$22.07	$22.38	$22.54
Forfeiture (10%)	$9.53	$13.66	$16.39	$17.85	$18.63	$19.22	$19.66	$19.99	$20.24	$20.37
Forfeiture (15%)	$9.17	$12.90	$15.27	$16.50	$17.16	$17.64	$18.00	$18.27	$18.46	$18.57
Forfeiture (20%)	$8.85	$12.24	$14.31	$15.36	$15.91	$16.31	$16.60	$16.82	$16.97	$17.06
Forfeiture (25%)	$8.56	$11.66	$13.48	$14.38	$14.84	$15.17	$15.41	$15.59	$15.72	$15.78
Forfeiture (30%)	$8.30	$11.15	$12.76	$13.53	$13.92	$14.20	$14.40	$14.54	$14.65	$14.70
Forfeiture (35%)	$8.06	$10.69	$12.12	$12.79	$13.12	$13.35	$13.52	$13.64	$13.73	$13.77
Forfeiture (40%)	$7.85	$10.27	$11.56	$12.14	$12.42	$12.62	$12.76	$12.86	$12.93	$12.97

Percentage Difference between Binomial and Black-Scholes Model	Suboptimal (1.2)	Suboptimal (1.4)	Suboptimal (1.6)	Suboptimal (1.8)	Suboptimal (2.0)	Suboptimal (2.2)	Suboptimal (2.4)	Suboptimal (2.6)	Suboptimal (2.8)	Suboptimal (3.0)
Forfeiture (0%)	–60.32%	–40.61%	–26.52%	–18.58%	–14.14%	–10.73%	–8.13%	–6.16%	–4.67%	–3.88%
Forfeiture (5%)	–62.10%	–44.52%	–32.45%	–25.83%	–22.20%	–19.43%	–17.34%	–15.77%	–14.59%	–13.98%
Forfeiture (10%)	–63.65%	–47.87%	–37.46%	–31.90%	–28.90%	–26.65%	–24.96%	–23.70%	–22.77%	–22.27%
Forfeiture (15%)	–65.02%	–50.76%	–41.72%	–37.03%	–34.54%	–32.69%	–31.32%	–30.30%	–29.55%	–29.16%
Forfeiture (20%)	–66.24%	–53.29%	–45.38%	–41.39%	–39.31%	–37.78%	–36.66%	–35.83%	–35.23%	–34.92%
Forfeiture (25%)	–67.34%	–55.51%	–48.54%	–45.13%	–43.38%	–42.11%	–41.19%	–40.52%	–40.03%	–39.77%
Forfeiture (30%)	–68.33%	–57.47%	–51.31%	–48.37%	–46.89%	–45.83%	–45.06%	–44.51%	–44.11%	–43.91%
Forfeiture (35%)	–69.23%	–59.22%	–53.74%	–51.20%	–49.93%	–49.04%	–48.40%	–47.95%	–47.62%	–47.45%
Forfeiture (40%)	–70.05%	–60.80%	–55.90%	–53.68%	–52.60%	–51.84%	–51.31%	–50.93%	–50.66%	–50.52%

MATURITY OF 7 YEARS AND VESTING OF 1 MONTH ON AN $80 STOCK PRICE

Stock Price and Strike Price of $80, Maturity of 7 Years, Risk-Free Rate of 3.5%, 35% Volatility, 0% Dividends, Vesting of 1 Month, Employee Suboptimal Exercise Behavior from 1.2 to 3.0, and Forfeiture Rate from 0% to 40%.
Generalized Black-Scholes: $34.94

Customized Binomial Lattice	Suboptimal (1.2)	Suboptimal (1.4)	Suboptimal (1.6)	Suboptimal (1.8)	Suboptimal (2.0)	Suboptimal (2.2)	Suboptimal (2.4)	Suboptimal (2.6)	Suboptimal (2.8)	Suboptimal (3.0)
Forfeiture (0%)	$13.86	$20.75	$25.67	$28.45	$30.00	$31.19	$32.10	$32.79	$33.31	$33.59
Forfeiture (5%)	$13.24	$19.39	$23.60	$25.92	$27.19	$28.15	$28.88	$29.43	$29.84	$30.06
Forfeiture (10%)	$12.70	$18.22	$21.85	$23.79	$24.84	$25.63	$26.22	$26.66	$26.99	$27.16
Forfeiture (15%)	$12.22	$17.20	$20.37	$22.00	$22.87	$23.52	$24.00	$24.35	$24.62	$24.75
Forfeiture (20%)	$11.80	$16.32	$19.09	$20.48	$21.21	$21.74	$22.13	$22.42	$22.63	$22.74
Forfeiture (25%)	$11.41	$15.55	$17.98	$19.17	$19.78	$20.23	$20.55	$20.78	$20.96	$21.04
Forfeiture (30%)	$11.07	$14.86	$17.01	$18.04	$18.56	$18.93	$19.20	$19.39	$19.53	$19.60
Forfeiture (35%)	$10.75	$14.25	$16.16	$17.05	$17.49	$17.81	$18.03	$18.19	$18.30	$18.36
Forfeiture (40%)	$10.46	$13.70	$15.41	$16.19	$16.56	$16.83	$17.01	$17.15	$17.24	$17.29

Percentage Difference between Binomial and Black-Scholes Model	Suboptimal (1.2)	Suboptimal (1.4)	Suboptimal (1.6)	Suboptimal (1.8)	Suboptimal (2.0)	Suboptimal (2.2)	Suboptimal (2.4)	Suboptimal (2.6)	Suboptimal (2.8)	Suboptimal (3.0)
Forfeiture (0%)	–60.32%	–40.61%	–26.52%	–18.58%	–14.14%	–10.73%	–8.13%	–6.16%	–4.67%	–3.88%
Forfeiture (5%)	–62.10%	–44.52%	–32.45%	–25.83%	–22.20%	–19.43%	–17.34%	–15.77%	–14.59%	–13.98%
Forfeiture (10%)	–63.65%	–47.87%	–37.46%	–31.90%	–28.90%	–26.65%	–24.96%	–23.70%	–22.77%	–22.27%
Forfeiture (15%)	–65.02%	–50.76%	–41.72%	–37.03%	–34.54%	–32.69%	–31.32%	–30.30%	–29.55%	–29.16%
Forfeiture (20%)	–66.24%	–53.29%	–45.38%	–41.39%	–39.31%	–37.78%	–36.66%	–35.83%	–35.23%	–34.92%
Forfeiture (25%)	–67.34%	–55.51%	–48.54%	–45.13%	–43.38%	–42.11%	–41.19%	–40.52%	–40.03%	–39.77%
Forfeiture (30%)	–68.33%	–57.47%	–51.31%	–48.37%	–46.89%	–45.83%	–45.06%	–44.51%	–44.11%	–43.91%
Forfeiture (35%)	–69.23%	–59.22%	–53.74%	–51.20%	–49.93%	–49.04%	–48.40%	–47.95%	–47.62%	–47.45%
Forfeiture (40%)	–70.05%	–60.80%	–55.90%	–53.68%	–52.60%	–51.84%	–51.31%	–50.93%	–50.66%	–50.52%

MATURITY OF 7 YEARS AND VESTING OF 1 YEAR ON A $20 STOCK PRICE

Stock Price and Strike Price of $20, Maturity of 7 Years, Risk-Free Rate of 3.5%, 35% Volatility, 0% Dividends, Vesting of 1 Year, Employee Suboptimal Exercise Behavior from 1.2 to 3.0, and Forfeiture Rate from 0% to 40%.
Generalized Black-Scholes: $8.74

Customized Binomial Lattice	Suboptimal (1.2)	Suboptimal (1.4)	Suboptimal (1.6)	Suboptimal (1.8)	Suboptimal (2.0)	Suboptimal (2.2)	Suboptimal (2.4)	Suboptimal (2.6)	Suboptimal (2.8)	Suboptimal (3.0)
Forfeiture (0%)	$4.61	$5.69	$6.61	$7.19	$7.54	$7.82	$8.03	$8.20	$8.33	$8.40
Forfeiture (5%)	$4.29	$5.21	$5.97	$6.45	$6.73	$6.96	$7.13	$7.26	$7.37	$7.42
Forfeiture (10%)	$3.99	$4.79	$5.43	$5.82	$6.06	$6.24	$6.38	$6.48	$6.56	$6.61
Forfeiture (15%)	$3.73	$4.42	$4.96	$5.29	$5.48	$5.62	$5.74	$5.82	$5.89	$5.92
Forfeiture (20%)	$3.49	$4.09	$4.55	$4.82	$4.98	$5.10	$5.19	$5.26	$5.31	$5.34
Forfeiture (25%)	$3.27	$3.79	$4.18	$4.41	$4.54	$4.64	$4.72	$4.78	$4.82	$4.84
Forfeiture (30%)	$3.07	$3.53	$3.86	$4.06	$4.17	$4.25	$4.31	$4.36	$4.39	$4.41
Forfeiture (35%)	$2.88	$3.29	$3.58	$3.74	$3.83	$3.90	$3.95	$3.99	$4.02	$4.03
Forfeiture (40%)	$2.71	$3.07	$3.32	$3.46	$3.54	$3.60	$3.64	$3.67	$3.69	$3.71

Percentage Difference between Binomial and Black-Scholes Model	Suboptimal (1.2)	Suboptimal (1.4)	Suboptimal (1.6)	Suboptimal (1.8)	Suboptimal (2.0)	Suboptimal (2.2)	Suboptimal (2.4)	Suboptimal (2.6)	Suboptimal (2.8)	Suboptimal (3.0)
Forfeiture (0%)	–47.18%	–34.85%	–24.38%	–17.69%	–13.70%	–10.53%	–8.04%	–6.12%	–4.65%	–3.87%
Forfeiture (5%)	–50.92%	–40.37%	–31.63%	–26.15%	–22.90%	–20.35%	–18.36%	–16.83%	–15.67%	–15.06%
Forfeiture (10%)	–54.27%	–45.20%	–37.86%	–33.33%	–30.68%	–28.62%	–27.01%	–25.79%	–24.87%	–24.38%
Forfeiture (15%)	–57.30%	–49.46%	–43.26%	–39.49%	–37.32%	–35.63%	–34.34%	–33.36%	–32.62%	–32.23%
Forfeiture (20%)	–60.05%	–53.23%	–47.97%	–44.82%	–43.02%	–41.64%	–40.59%	–39.80%	–39.20%	–38.89%
Forfeiture (25%)	–62.56%	–56.61%	–52.11%	–49.47%	–47.97%	–46.84%	–45.97%	–45.33%	–44.85%	–44.60%
Forfeiture (30%)	–64.86%	–59.64%	–55.78%	–53.55%	–52.30%	–51.36%	–50.65%	–50.12%	–49.73%	–49.53%
Forfeiture (35%)	–66.98%	–62.39%	–59.06%	–57.16%	–56.11%	–55.32%	–54.74%	–54.30%	–53.98%	–53.82%
Forfeiture (40%)	–68.94%	–64.88%	–61.99%	–60.38%	–59.49%	–58.83%	–58.34%	–57.98%	–57.72%	–57.58%

MATURITY OF 7 YEARS AND VESTING OF 1 YEAR ON A $40 STOCK PRICE

Stock Price and Strike Price of $40, Maturity of 7 Years, Risk-Free Rate of 3.5%, 35% Volatility, 0% Dividends, Vesting of 1 Year, Employee Suboptimal Exercise Behavior from 1.2 to 3.0, and Forfeiture Rate from 0% to 40%.
Generalized Black-Scholes: $17.47

Customized Binomial Lattice	Suboptimal (1.2)	Suboptimal (1.4)	Suboptimal (1.6)	Suboptimal (1.8)	Suboptimal (2.0)	Suboptimal (2.2)	Suboptimal (2.4)	Suboptimal (2.6)	Suboptimal (2.8)	Suboptimal (3.0)
Forfeiture (0%)	$9.23	$11.38	$13.21	$14.38	$15.08	$15.63	$16.07	$16.40	$16.66	$16.79
Forfeiture (5%)	$8.57	$10.42	$11.94	$12.90	$13.47	$13.92	$14.26	$14.53	$14.73	$14.84
Forfeiture (10%)	$7.99	$9.57	$10.86	$11.65	$12.11	$12.47	$12.75	$12.96	$13.13	$13.21
Forfeiture (15%)	$7.46	$8.83	$9.91	$10.57	$10.95	$11.25	$11.47	$11.64	$11.77	$11.84
Forfeiture (20%)	$6.98	$8.17	$9.09	$9.64	$9.95	$10.20	$10.38	$10.52	$10.62	$10.68
Forfeiture (25%)	$6.54	$7.58	$8.37	$8.83	$9.09	$9.29	$9.44	$9.55	$9.64	$9.68
Forfeiture (30%)	$6.14	$7.05	$7.73	$8.12	$8.33	$8.50	$8.62	$8.71	$8.78	$8.82
Forfeiture (35%)	$5.77	$6.57	$7.15	$7.48	$7.67	$7.81	$7.91	$7.98	$8.04	$8.07
Forfeiture (40%)	$5.43	$6.14	$6.64	$6.92	$7.08	$7.19	$7.28	$7.34	$7.39	$7.41

Percentage Difference between Binomial and Black-Scholes Model	Suboptimal (1.2)	Suboptimal (1.4)	Suboptimal (1.6)	Suboptimal (1.8)	Suboptimal (2.0)	Suboptimal (2.2)	Suboptimal (2.4)	Suboptimal (2.6)	Suboptimal (2.8)	Suboptimal (3.0)
Forfeiture (0%)	–47.18%	–34.85%	–24.38%	–17.69%	–13.70%	–10.53%	–8.04%	–6.12%	–4.65%	–3.87%
Forfeiture (5%)	–50.92%	–40.37%	–31.63%	–26.15%	–22.90%	–20.35%	–18.36%	–16.83%	–15.67%	–15.06%
Forfeiture (10%)	–54.27%	–45.20%	–37.86%	–33.33%	–30.68%	–28.62%	–27.01%	–25.79%	–24.87%	–24.38%
Forfeiture (15%)	–57.30%	–49.46%	–43.26%	–39.49%	–37.32%	–35.63%	–34.34%	–33.36%	–32.62%	–32.23%
Forfeiture (20%)	–60.05%	–53.23%	–47.97%	–44.82%	–43.02%	–41.64%	–40.59%	–39.80%	–39.20%	–38.89%
Forfeiture (25%)	–62.56%	–56.61%	–52.11%	–49.47%	–47.97%	–46.84%	–45.97%	–45.33%	–44.85%	–44.60%
Forfeiture (30%)	–64.86%	–59.64%	–55.78%	–53.55%	–52.30%	–51.36%	–50.65%	–50.12%	–49.73%	–49.53%
Forfeiture (35%)	–66.98%	–62.39%	–59.06%	–57.16%	–56.11%	–55.32%	–54.74%	–54.30%	–53.98%	–53.82%
Forfeiture (40%)	–68.94%	–64.88%	–61.99%	–60.38%	–59.49%	–58.83%	–58.34%	–57.98%	–57.72%	–57.58%

MATURITY OF 7 YEARS AND VESTING OF 1 YEAR ON A $60 STOCK PRICE

Stock Price and Strike Price of $60, Maturity of 7 Years, Risk-Free Rate of 3.5%, 35% Volatility, 0% Dividends, Vesting of 1 Year, Employee Suboptimal Exercise Behavior from 1.2 to 3.0, and Forfeiture Rate from 0% to 40%.
Generalized Black-Scholes: $26.21

Customized Binomial Lattice	Suboptimal (1.2)	Suboptimal (1.4)	Suboptimal (1.6)	Suboptimal (1.8)	Suboptimal (2.0)	Suboptimal (2.2)	Suboptimal (2.4)	Suboptimal (2.6)	Suboptimal (2.8)	Suboptimal (3.0)
Forfeiture (0%)	$13.84	$17.07	$19.82	$21.57	$22.62	$23.45	$24.10	$24.60	$24.99	$25.19
Forfeiture (5%)	$12.86	$15.63	$17.92	$19.35	$20.20	$20.87	$21.40	$21.79	$22.10	$22.26
Forfeiture (10%)	$11.98	$14.36	$16.28	$17.47	$18.17	$18.71	$19.13	$19.45	$19.69	$19.82
Forfeiture (15%)	$11.19	$13.25	$14.87	$15.86	$16.43	$16.87	$17.21	$17.47	$17.66	$17.76
Forfeiture (20%)	$10.47	$12.26	$13.64	$14.46	$14.93	$15.29	$15.57	$15.78	$15.93	$16.01
Forfeiture (25%)	$9.81	$11.37	$12.55	$13.24	$13.63	$13.93	$14.16	$14.33	$14.45	$14.52
Forfeiture (30%)	$9.21	$10.58	$11.59	$12.17	$12.50	$12.75	$12.93	$13.07	$13.17	$13.23
Forfeiture (35%)	$8.65	$9.86	$10.73	$11.23	$11.50	$11.71	$11.86	$11.98	$12.06	$12.10
Forfeiture (40%)	$8.14	$9.20	$9.96	$10.38	$10.62	$10.79	$10.92	$11.01	$11.08	$11.12

Percentage Difference between Binomial and Black-Scholes Model	Suboptimal (1.2)	Suboptimal (1.4)	Suboptimal (1.6)	Suboptimal (1.8)	Suboptimal (2.0)	Suboptimal (2.2)	Suboptimal (2.4)	Suboptimal (2.6)	Suboptimal (2.8)	Suboptimal (3.0)
Forfeiture (0%)	-47.18%	-34.85%	-24.38%	-17.69%	-13.70%	-10.53%	-8.04%	-6.12%	-4.65%	-3.87%
Forfeiture (5%)	-50.92%	-40.37%	-31.63%	-26.15%	-22.90%	-20.35%	-18.36%	-16.83%	-15.67%	-15.06%
Forfeiture (10%)	-54.27%	-45.20%	-37.86%	-33.33%	-30.68%	-28.62%	-27.01%	-25.79%	-24.87%	-24.38%
Forfeiture (15%)	-57.30%	-49.46%	-43.26%	-39.49%	-37.32%	-35.63%	-34.34%	-33.36%	-32.62%	-32.23%
Forfeiture (20%)	-60.05%	-53.23%	-47.97%	-44.82%	-43.02%	-41.64%	-40.59%	-39.80%	-39.20%	-38.89%
Forfeiture (25%)	-62.56%	-56.61%	-52.11%	-49.47%	-47.97%	-46.84%	-45.97%	-45.33%	-44.85%	-44.60%
Forfeiture (30%)	-64.86%	-59.64%	-55.78%	-53.55%	-52.30%	-51.36%	-50.65%	-50.12%	-49.73%	-49.53%
Forfeiture (35%)	-66.98%	-62.39%	-59.06%	-57.16%	-56.11%	-55.32%	-54.74%	-54.30%	-53.98%	-53.82%
Forfeiture (40%)	-68.94%	-64.88%	-61.99%	-60.38%	-59.49%	-58.83%	-58.34%	-57.98%	-57.72%	-57.58%

MATURITY OF 7 YEARS AND VESTING OF 1 YEAR ON AN $80 STOCK PRICE

Stock Price and Strike Price of $80, Maturity of 7 Years, Risk-Free Rate of 3.5%, 35% Volatility, 0% Dividends, Vesting of 1 Year, Employee Suboptimal Exercise Behavior from 1.2 to 3.0, and Forfeiture Rate from 0% to 40%.
Generalized Black-Scholes: $34.94

Customized Binomial Lattice	Suboptimal (1.2)	Suboptimal (1.4)	Suboptimal (1.6)	Suboptimal (1.8)	Suboptimal (2.0)	Suboptimal (2.2)	Suboptimal (2.4)	Suboptimal (2.6)	Suboptimal (2.8)	Suboptimal (3.0)
Forfeiture (0%)	$18.45	$22.77	$26.42	$28.76	$30.15	$31.26	$32.13	$32.80	$33.32	$33.59
Forfeiture (5%)	$17.15	$20.83	$23.89	$25.81	$26.94	$27.83	$28.53	$29.06	$29.47	$29.68
Forfeiture (10%)	$15.98	$19.15	$21.71	$23.30	$24.22	$24.94	$25.50	$25.93	$26.25	$26.42
Forfeiture (15%)	$14.92	$17.66	$19.83	$21.14	$21.90	$22.49	$22.94	$23.29	$23.54	$23.68
Forfeiture (20%)	$13.96	$16.34	$18.18	$19.28	$19.91	$20.39	$20.76	$21.04	$21.24	$21.35
Forfeiture (25%)	$13.08	$15.16	$16.73	$17.66	$18.18	$18.58	$18.88	$19.10	$19.27	$19.36
Forfeiture (30%)	$12.28	$14.10	$15.45	$16.23	$16.67	$17.00	$17.25	$17.43	$17.57	$17.64
Forfeiture (35%)	$11.54	$13.14	$14.31	$14.97	$15.34	$15.61	$15.82	$15.97	$16.08	$16.14
Forfeiture (40%)	$10.85	$12.27	$13.28	$13.85	$14.16	$14.39	$14.56	$14.68	$14.77	$14.82

Percentage Difference between Binomial and Black-Scholes Model	Suboptimal (1.2)	Suboptimal (1.4)	Suboptimal (1.6)	Suboptimal (1.8)	Suboptimal (2.0)	Suboptimal (2.2)	Suboptimal (2.4)	Suboptimal (2.6)	Suboptimal (2.8)	Suboptimal (3.0)
Forfeiture (0%)	−47.18%	−34.85%	−24.38%	−17.69%	−13.70%	−10.53%	−8.04%	−6.12%	−4.65%	−3.87%
Forfeiture (5%)	−50.92%	−40.37%	−31.63%	−26.15%	−22.90%	−20.35%	−18.36%	−16.83%	−15.67%	−15.06%
Forfeiture (10%)	−54.27%	−45.20%	−37.86%	−33.33%	−30.68%	−28.62%	−27.01%	−25.79%	−24.87%	−24.38%
Forfeiture (15%)	−57.30%	−49.46%	−43.26%	−39.49%	−37.32%	−35.63%	−34.34%	−33.36%	−32.62%	−32.23%
Forfeiture (20%)	−60.05%	−53.23%	−47.97%	−44.82%	−43.02%	−41.64%	−40.59%	−39.80%	−39.20%	−38.89%
Forfeiture (25%)	−62.56%	−56.61%	−52.11%	−49.47%	−47.97%	−46.84%	−45.97%	−45.33%	−44.85%	−44.60%
Forfeiture (30%)	−64.86%	−59.64%	−55.78%	−53.55%	−52.30%	−51.36%	−50.65%	−50.12%	−49.73%	−49.53%
Forfeiture (35%)	−66.98%	−62.39%	−59.06%	−57.16%	−56.11%	−55.32%	−54.74%	−54.30%	−53.98%	−53.82%
Forfeiture (40%)	−68.94%	−64.88%	−61.99%	−60.38%	−59.49%	−58.83%	−58.34%	−57.98%	−57.72%	−57.58%

MATURITY OF 7 YEARS AND VESTING OF 3 YEARS ON A $20 STOCK PRICE

Stock Price and Strike Price of $20, Maturity of 7 Years, Risk-Free Rate of 3.5%, 35% Volatility, 0% Dividends, Vesting of 3 Years, Employee Suboptimal Exercise Behavior from 1.2 to 3.0, and Forfeiture Rate from 0% to 40%.
Generalized Black-Scholes: $8.74

Customized Binomial Lattice	Suboptimal (1.2)	Suboptimal (1.4)	Suboptimal (1.6)	Suboptimal (1.8)	Suboptimal (2.0)	Suboptimal (2.2)	Suboptimal (2.4)	Suboptimal (2.6)	Suboptimal (2.8)	Suboptimal (3.0)
Forfeiture (0%)	$6.50	$7.06	$7.51	$7.80	$7.97	$8.12	$8.24	$8.34	$8.42	$8.47
Forfeiture (5%)	$5.54	$5.99	$6.34	$6.56	$6.70	$6.81	$6.90	$6.98	$7.04	$7.08
Forfeiture (10%)	$4.73	$5.08	$5.36	$5.53	$5.64	$5.73	$5.80	$5.86	$5.90	$5.93
Forfeiture (15%)	$4.04	$4.32	$4.54	$4.67	$4.76	$4.82	$4.88	$4.92	$4.96	$4.98
Forfeiture (20%)	$3.46	$3.68	$3.85	$3.96	$4.02	$4.07	$4.12	$4.15	$4.18	$4.19
Forfeiture (25%)	$2.96	$3.13	$3.27	$3.35	$3.40	$3.44	$3.48	$3.50	$3.53	$3.54
Forfeiture (30%)	$2.53	$2.67	$2.78	$2.84	$2.88	$2.92	$2.94	$2.96	$2.98	$2.99
Forfeiture (35%)	$2.17	$2.28	$2.36	$2.42	$2.45	$2.47	$2.49	$2.51	$2.52	$2.53
Forfeiture (40%)	$1.86	$1.95	$2.01	$2.05	$2.08	$2.10	$2.11	$2.13	$2.14	$2.14

Percentage Difference between Binomial and Black-Scholes Model	Suboptimal (1.2)	Suboptimal (1.4)	Suboptimal (1.6)	Suboptimal (1.8)	Suboptimal (2.0)	Suboptimal (2.2)	Suboptimal (2.4)	Suboptimal (2.6)	Suboptimal (2.8)	Suboptimal (3.0)
Forfeiture (0%)	−25.60%	−19.21%	−14.06%	−10.76%	−8.72%	−7.05%	−5.65%	−4.53%	−3.60%	−3.09%
Forfeiture (5%)	−36.53%	−31.48%	−27.45%	−24.89%	−23.32%	−22.03%	−20.96%	−20.10%	−19.39%	−18.99%
Forfeiture (10%)	−45.81%	−41.80%	−38.65%	−36.66%	−35.44%	−34.45%	−33.62%	−32.96%	−32.41%	−32.11%
Forfeiture (15%)	−53.70%	−50.51%	−48.04%	−46.49%	−45.54%	−44.78%	−44.14%	−43.62%	−43.20%	−42.97%
Forfeiture (20%)	−60.42%	−57.88%	−55.93%	−54.72%	−53.98%	−53.39%	−52.89%	−52.50%	−52.17%	−51.99%
Forfeiture (25%)	−66.14%	−64.11%	−62.58%	−61.63%	−61.05%	−60.59%	−60.20%	−59.90%	−59.64%	−59.50%
Forfeiture (30%)	−71.03%	−69.40%	−68.19%	−67.44%	−66.99%	−66.63%	−66.33%	−66.09%	−65.89%	−65.78%
Forfeiture (35%)	−75.20%	−73.89%	−72.93%	−72.34%	−71.99%	−71.70%	−71.47%	−71.28%	−71.13%	−71.04%
Forfeiture (40%)	−78.76%	−77.71%	−76.94%	−76.48%	−76.20%	−75.98%	−75.79%	−75.65%	−75.53%	−75.46%

MATURITY OF 7 YEARS AND VESTING OF 3 YEARS ON A $40 STOCK PRICE

Stock Price and Strike Price of $40, Maturity of 7 Years, Risk-Free Rate of 3.5%, 35% Volatility, 0% Dividends, Vesting of 3 Years, Employee Suboptimal Exercise Behavior from 1.2 to 3.0, and Forfeiture Rate from 0% to 40%.
Generalized Black-Scholes: $17.47

Customized Binomial Lattice	Suboptimal (1.2)	Suboptimal (1.4)	Suboptimal (1.6)	Suboptimal (1.8)	Suboptimal (2.0)	Suboptimal (2.2)	Suboptimal (2.4)	Suboptimal (2.6)	Suboptimal (2.8)	Suboptimal (3.0)
Forfeiture (0%)	$13.00	$14.11	$15.01	$15.59	$15.95	$16.24	$16.48	$16.68	$16.84	$16.93
Forfeiture (5%)	$11.09	$11.97	$12.67	$13.12	$13.40	$13.62	$13.81	$13.96	$14.08	$14.15
Forfeiture (10%)	$9.47	$10.17	$10.72	$11.07	$11.28	$11.45	$11.60	$11.71	$11.81	$11.86
Forfeiture (15%)	$8.09	$8.65	$9.08	$9.35	$9.51	$9.65	$9.76	$9.85	$9.92	$9.96
Forfeiture (20%)	$6.92	$7.36	$7.70	$7.91	$8.04	$8.14	$8.23	$8.30	$8.36	$8.39
Forfeiture (25%)	$5.92	$6.27	$6.54	$6.70	$6.80	$6.89	$6.95	$7.01	$7.05	$7.08
Forfeiture (30%)	$5.06	$5.35	$5.56	$5.69	$5.77	$5.83	$5.88	$5.92	$5.96	$5.98
Forfeiture (35%)	$4.33	$4.56	$4.73	$4.83	$4.89	$4.94	$4.98	$5.02	$5.04	$5.06
Forfeiture (40%)	$3.71	$3.89	$4.03	$4.11	$4.16	$4.20	$4.23	$4.25	$4.28	$4.29

Percentage Difference between Binomial and Black-Scholes Model	Suboptimal (1.2)	Suboptimal (1.4)	Suboptimal (1.6)	Suboptimal (1.8)	Suboptimal (2.0)	Suboptimal (2.2)	Suboptimal (2.4)	Suboptimal (2.6)	Suboptimal (2.8)	Suboptimal (3.0)
Forfeiture (0%)	–25.60%	–19.21%	–14.06%	–10.76%	–8.72%	–7.05%	–5.65%	–4.53%	–3.60%	–3.09%
Forfeiture (5%)	–36.53%	–31.48%	–27.45%	–24.89%	–23.32%	–22.03%	–20.96%	–20.10%	–19.39%	–18.99%
Forfeiture (10%)	–45.81%	–41.80%	–38.65%	–36.66%	–35.44%	–34.45%	–33.62%	–32.96%	–32.41%	–32.11%
Forfeiture (15%)	–53.70%	–50.51%	–48.04%	–46.49%	–45.54%	–44.78%	–44.14%	–43.62%	–43.20%	–42.97%
Forfeiture (20%)	–60.42%	–57.88%	–55.93%	–54.72%	–53.98%	–53.39%	–52.89%	–52.50%	–52.17%	–51.99%
Forfeiture (25%)	–66.14%	–64.11%	–62.58%	–61.63%	–61.05%	–60.59%	–60.20%	–59.90%	–59.64%	–59.50%
Forfeiture (30%)	–71.03%	–69.40%	–68.19%	–67.44%	–66.99%	–66.63%	–66.33%	–66.09%	–65.89%	–65.78%
Forfeiture (35%)	–75.20%	–73.89%	–72.93%	–72.34%	–71.99%	–71.70%	–71.47%	–71.28%	–71.13%	–71.04%
Forfeiture (40%)	–78.76%	–77.71%	–76.94%	–76.48%	–76.20%	–75.98%	–75.79%	–75.65%	–75.53%	–75.46%

MATURITY OF 7 YEARS AND VESTING OF 3 YEARS ON A $60 STOCK PRICE

Stock Price and Strike Price of $60, Maturity of 7 Years, Risk–Free Rate of 3.5%, 35% Volatility, 0% Dividends, Vesting of 3 Years, Employee Suboptimal Exercise Behavior from 1.2 to 3.0, and Forfeiture Rate from 0% to 40%.

Generalized Black-Scholes: $26.21

Customized Binomial Lattice	Suboptimal (1.2)	Suboptimal (1.4)	Suboptimal (1.6)	Suboptimal (1.8)	Suboptimal (2.0)	Suboptimal (2.2)	Suboptimal (2.4)	Suboptimal (2.6)	Suboptimal (2.8)	Suboptimal (3.0)
Forfeiture (0%)	$19.50	$21.17	$22.52	$23.39	$23.92	$24.36	$24.72	$25.02	$25.26	$25.40
Forfeiture (5%)	$16.63	$17.96	$19.01	$19.68	$20.10	$20.43	$20.71	$20.94	$21.13	$21.23
Forfeiture (10%)	$14.20	$15.25	$16.08	$16.60	$16.92	$17.18	$17.39	$17.57	$17.71	$17.79
Forfeiture (15%)	$12.13	$12.97	$13.62	$14.02	$14.27	$14.47	$14.64	$14.77	$14.88	$14.95
Forfeiture (20%)	$10.37	$11.04	$11.55	$11.87	$12.06	$12.22	$12.35	$12.45	$12.53	$12.58
Forfeiture (25%)	$8.87	$9.40	$9.81	$10.06	$10.21	$10.33	$10.43	$10.51	$10.58	$10.61
Forfeiture (30%)	$7.59	$8.02	$8.34	$8.53	$8.65	$8.75	$8.82	$8.89	$8.94	$8.97
Forfeiture (35%)	$6.50	$6.84	$7.09	$7.25	$7.34	$7.42	$7.48	$7.53	$7.57	$7.59
Forfeiture (40%)	$5.57	$5.84	$6.04	$6.16	$6.24	$6.30	$6.34	$6.38	$6.41	$6.43

Percentage Difference between Binomial and Black-Scholes Model	Suboptimal (1.2)	Suboptimal (1.4)	Suboptimal (1.6)	Suboptimal (1.8)	Suboptimal (2.0)	Suboptimal (2.2)	Suboptimal (2.4)	Suboptimal (2.6)	Suboptimal (2.8)	Suboptimal (3.0)
Forfeiture (0%)	–25.60%	–19.21%	–14.06%	–10.76%	–8.72%	–7.05%	–5.65%	–4.53%	–3.60%	–3.09%
Forfeiture (5%)	–36.53%	–31.48%	–27.45%	–24.89%	–23.32%	–22.03%	–20.96%	–20.10%	–19.39%	–18.99%
Forfeiture (10%)	–45.81%	–41.80%	–38.65%	–36.66%	–35.44%	–34.45%	–33.62%	–32.96%	–32.41%	–32.11%
Forfeiture (15%)	–53.70%	–50.51%	–48.04%	–46.49%	–45.54%	–44.78%	–44.14%	–43.62%	–43.20%	–42.97%
Forfeiture (20%)	–60.42%	–57.88%	–55.93%	–54.72%	–53.98%	–53.39%	–52.89%	–52.50%	–52.17%	–51.99%
Forfeiture (25%)	–66.14%	–64.11%	–62.58%	–61.63%	–61.05%	–60.59%	–60.20%	–59.90%	–59.64%	–59.50%
Forfeiture (30%)	–71.03%	–69.40%	–68.19%	–67.44%	–66.99%	–66.63%	–66.33%	–66.09%	–65.89%	–65.78%
Forfeiture (35%)	–75.20%	–73.89%	–72.93%	–72.34%	–71.99%	–71.70%	–71.47%	–71.28%	–71.13%	–71.04%
Forfeiture (40%)	–78.76%	–77.71%	–76.94%	–76.48%	–76.20%	–75.98%	–75.79%	–75.65%	–75.53%	–75.46%

MATURITY OF 7 YEARS AND VESTING OF 3 YEARS ON AN $80 STOCK PRICE

Stock Price and Strike Price of $80, Maturity of 7 Years, Risk-Free Rate of 3.5%, 35% Volatility, 0% Dividends, Vesting of 3 Years, Employee Suboptimal Exercise Behavior from 1.2 to 3.0, and Forfeiture Rate from 0% to 40%.
Generalized Black-Scholes: $34.94

Customized Binomial Lattice	Suboptimal (1.2)	Suboptimal (1.4)	Suboptimal (1.6)	Suboptimal (1.8)	Suboptimal (2.0)	Suboptimal (2.2)	Suboptimal (2.4)	Suboptimal (2.6)	Suboptimal (2.8)	Suboptimal (3.0)
Forfeiture (0%)	$26.00	$28.23	$30.03	$31.18	$31.90	$32.48	$32.97	$33.36	$33.68	$33.86
Forfeiture (5%)	$22.18	$23.94	$25.35	$26.24	$26.79	$27.24	$27.62	$27.92	$28.17	$28.31
Forfeiture (10%)	$18.94	$20.34	$21.44	$22.13	$22.56	$22.90	$23.19	$23.42	$23.62	$23.72
Forfeiture (15%)	$16.18	$17.29	$18.16	$18.70	$19.03	$19.30	$19.52	$19.70	$19.85	$19.93
Forfeiture (20%)	$13.83	$14.72	$15.40	$15.82	$16.08	$16.29	$16.46	$16.60	$16.71	$16.78
Forfeiture (25%)	$11.83	$12.54	$13.08	$13.41	$13.61	$13.77	$13.91	$14.01	$14.10	$14.15
Forfeiture (30%)	$10.12	$10.69	$11.12	$11.38	$11.53	$11.66	$11.77	$11.85	$11.92	$11.96
Forfeiture (35%)	$8.67	$9.12	$9.46	$9.66	$9.79	$9.89	$9.97	$10.03	$10.09	$10.12
Forfeiture (40%)	$7.42	$7.79	$8.06	$8.22	$8.32	$8.39	$8.46	$8.51	$8.55	$8.58

Percentage Difference between Binomial and Black-Scholes Model	Suboptimal (1.2)	Suboptimal (1.4)	Suboptimal (1.6)	Suboptimal (1.8)	Suboptimal (2.0)	Suboptimal (2.2)	Suboptimal (2.4)	Suboptimal (2.6)	Suboptimal (2.8)	Suboptimal (3.0)
Forfeiture (0%)	–25.60%	–19.21%	–14.06%	–10.76%	–8.72%	–7.05%	–5.65%	–4.53%	–3.60%	–3.09%
Forfeiture (5%)	–36.53%	–31.48%	–27.45%	–24.89%	–23.32%	–22.03%	–20.96%	–20.10%	–19.39%	–18.99%
Forfeiture (10%)	–45.81%	–41.80%	–38.65%	–36.66%	–35.44%	–34.45%	–33.62%	–32.96%	–32.41%	–32.11%
Forfeiture (15%)	–53.70%	–50.51%	–48.04%	–46.49%	–45.54%	–44.78%	–44.14%	–43.62%	–43.20%	–42.97%
Forfeiture (20%)	–60.42%	–57.88%	–55.93%	–54.72%	–53.98%	–53.39%	–52.89%	–52.50%	–52.17%	–51.99%
Forfeiture (25%)	–66.14%	–64.11%	–62.58%	–61.63%	–61.05%	–60.59%	–60.20%	–59.90%	–59.64%	–59.50%
Forfeiture (30%)	–71.03%	–69.40%	–68.19%	–67.44%	–66.99%	–66.63%	–66.33%	–66.09%	–65.89%	–65.78%
Forfeiture (35%)	–75.20%	–73.89%	–72.93%	–72.34%	–71.99%	–71.70%	–71.47%	–71.28%	–71.13%	–71.04%
Forfeiture (40%)	–78.76%	–77.71%	–76.94%	–76.48%	–76.20%	–75.98%	–75.79%	–75.65%	–75.53%	–75.46%

MATURITY OF 7 YEARS AND VESTING OF 5 YEARS ON A $20 STOCK PRICE

Stock Price and Strike Price of $20, Maturity of 7 Years, Risk–Free Rate of 3.5%, 35% Volatility, 0% Dividends, Vesting of 5 Years, Employee Suboptimal Exercise Behavior from 1.2 to 3.0, and Forfeiture Rate from 0% to 40%.
Generalized Black–Scholes: $8.74

Customized Binomial Lattice	Suboptimal (1.2)	Suboptimal (1.4)	Suboptimal (1.6)	Suboptimal (1.8)	Suboptimal (2.0)	Suboptimal (2.2)	Suboptimal (2.4)	Suboptimal (2.6)	Suboptimal (2.8)	Suboptimal (3.0)
Forfeiture (0%)	$7.84	$8.10	$8.27	$8.38	$8.44	$8.49	$8.53	$8.56	$8.59	$8.61
Forfeiture (5%)	$6.09	$6.28	$6.41	$6.49	$6.53	$6.57	$6.60	$6.62	$6.64	$6.66
Forfeiture (10%)	$4.73	$4.87	$4.97	$5.02	$5.06	$5.08	$5.10	$5.12	$5.14	$5.15
Forfeiture (15%)	$3.68	$3.78	$3.85	$3.89	$3.92	$3.93	$3.95	$3.96	$3.98	$3.98
Forfeiture (20%)	$2.86	$2.93	$2.98	$3.01	$3.03	$3.05	$3.06	$3.07	$3.08	$3.08
Forfeiture (25%)	$2.22	$2.27	$2.31	$2.34	$2.35	$2.36	$2.37	$2.38	$2.38	$2.39
Forfeiture (30%)	$1.72	$1.77	$1.79	$1.81	$1.82	$1.83	$1.83	$1.84	$1.84	$1.85
Forfeiture (35%)	$1.34	$1.37	$1.39	$1.40	$1.41	$1.42	$1.42	$1.43	$1.43	$1.43
Forfeiture (40%)	$1.04	$1.06	$1.08	$1.09	$1.09	$1.10	$1.10	$1.10	$1.11	$1.11

Percentage Difference between Binomial and Black-Scholes Model	Suboptimal (1.2)	Suboptimal (1.4)	Suboptimal (1.6)	Suboptimal (1.8)	Suboptimal (2.0)	Suboptimal (2.2)	Suboptimal (2.4)	Suboptimal (2.6)	Suboptimal (2.8)	Suboptimal (3.0)
Forfeiture (0%)	−10.22%	−7.32%	−5.30%	−4.12%	−3.42%	−2.86%	−2.39%	−2.00%	−1.67%	−1.47%
Forfeiture (5%)	−30.27%	−28.12%	−26.63%	−25.76%	−25.24%	−24.84%	−24.49%	−24.20%	−23.95%	−23.81%
Forfeiture (10%)	−45.84%	−44.24%	−43.14%	−42.50%	−42.12%	−41.82%	−41.56%	−41.35%	−41.17%	−41.07%
Forfeiture (15%)	−57.93%	−56.74%	−55.93%	−55.46%	−55.18%	−54.96%	−54.77%	−54.61%	−54.48%	−54.40%
Forfeiture (20%)	−67.32%	−66.44%	−65.84%	−65.49%	−65.29%	−65.12%	−64.98%	−64.87%	−64.77%	−64.71%
Forfeiture (25%)	−74.61%	−73.96%	−73.51%	−73.26%	−73.11%	−72.99%	−72.88%	−72.80%	−72.72%	−72.68%
Forfeiture (30%)	−80.28%	−79.79%	−79.46%	−79.27%	−79.16%	−79.07%	−79.00%	−78.94%	−78.88%	−78.85%
Forfeiture (35%)	−84.68%	−84.32%	−84.07%	−83.94%	−83.85%	−83.79%	−83.73%	−83.68%	−83.64%	−83.62%
Forfeiture (40%)	−88.10%	−87.83%	−87.65%	−87.55%	−87.49%	−87.44%	−87.40%	−87.36%	−87.33%	−87.31%

MATURITY OF 7 YEARS AND VESTING OF 5 YEARS ON A $40 STOCK PRICE

Stock Price and Strike Price of $40, Maturity of 7 Years, Risk-Free Rate of 3.5%, 35% Volatility, 0% Dividends, Vesting of 5 Years, Employee Suboptimal Exercise Behavior from 1.2 to 3.0, and Forfeiture Rate from 0% to 40%.
Generalized Black-Scholes: $17.47

Customized Binomial Lattice	Suboptimal (1.2)	Suboptimal (1.4)	Suboptimal (1.6)	Suboptimal (1.8)	Suboptimal (2.0)	Suboptimal (2.2)	Suboptimal (2.4)	Suboptimal (2.6)	Suboptimal (2.8)	Suboptimal (3.0)
Forfeiture (0%)	$15.68	$16.19	$16.54	$16.75	$16.87	$16.97	$17.05	$17.12	$17.18	$17.21
Forfeiture (5%)	$12.18	$12.56	$12.82	$12.97	$13.06	$13.13	$13.19	$13.24	$13.29	$13.31
Forfeiture (10%)	$9.46	$9.74	$9.93	$10.05	$10.11	$10.16	$10.21	$10.25	$10.28	$10.30
Forfeiture (15%)	$7.35	$7.56	$7.70	$7.78	$7.83	$7.87	$7.90	$7.93	$7.95	$7.97
Forfeiture (20%)	$5.71	$5.86	$5.97	$6.03	$6.06	$6.09	$6.12	$6.14	$6.16	$6.17
Forfeiture (25%)	$4.44	$4.55	$4.63	$4.67	$4.70	$4.72	$4.74	$4.75	$4.77	$4.77
Forfeiture (30%)	$3.45	$3.53	$3.59	$3.62	$3.64	$3.66	$3.67	$3.68	$3.69	$3.70
Forfeiture (35%)	$2.68	$2.74	$2.78	$2.81	$2.82	$2.83	$2.84	$2.85	$2.86	$2.86
Forfeiture (40%)	$2.08	$2.13	$2.16	$2.18	$2.19	$2.19	$2.20	$2.21	$2.21	$2.22

Percentage Difference between Binomial and Black-Scholes Model	Suboptimal (1.2)	Suboptimal (1.4)	Suboptimal (1.6)	Suboptimal (1.8)	Suboptimal (2.0)	Suboptimal (2.2)	Suboptimal (2.4)	Suboptimal (2.6)	Suboptimal (2.8)	Suboptimal (3.0)
Forfeiture (0%)	–10.22%	–7.32%	–5.30%	–4.12%	–3.42%	–2.86%	–2.39%	–2.00%	–1.67%	–1.47%
Forfeiture (5%)	–30.27%	–28.12%	–26.63%	–25.76%	–25.24%	–24.84%	–24.49%	–24.20%	–23.95%	–23.81%
Forfeiture (10%)	–45.84%	–44.24%	–43.14%	–42.50%	–42.12%	–41.82%	–41.56%	–41.35%	–41.17%	–41.07%
Forfeiture (15%)	–57.93%	–56.74%	–55.93%	–55.46%	–55.18%	–54.96%	–54.77%	–54.61%	–54.48%	–54.40%
Forfeiture (20%)	–67.32%	–66.44%	–65.84%	–65.49%	–65.29%	–65.12%	–64.98%	–64.87%	–64.77%	–64.71%
Forfeiture (25%)	–74.61%	–73.96%	–73.51%	–73.26%	–73.11%	–72.99%	–72.88%	–72.80%	–72.72%	–72.68%
Forfeiture (30%)	–80.28%	–79.79%	–79.46%	–79.27%	–79.16%	–79.07%	–79.00%	–78.94%	–78.88%	–78.85%
Forfeiture (35%)	–84.68%	–84.32%	–84.07%	–83.94%	–83.85%	–83.79%	–83.73%	–83.68%	–83.64%	–83.62%
Forfeiture (40%)	–88.10%	–87.83%	–87.65%	–87.55%	–87.49%	–87.44%	–87.40%	–87.36%	–87.33%	–87.31%

MATURITY OF 7 YEARS AND VESTING OF 5 YEARS ON A $60 STOCK PRICE

Stock Price and Strike Price of $60, Maturity of 7 Years, Risk-Free Rate of 3.5%, 35% Volatility, 0% Dividends, Vesting of 5 Years, Employee Suboptimal Exercise Behavior from 1.2 to 3.0, and Forfeiture Rate from 0% to 40%.
Generalized Black-Scholes: $26.21

Customized Binomial Lattice	Suboptimal (1.2)	Suboptimal (1.4)	Suboptimal (1.6)	Suboptimal (1.8)	Suboptimal (2.0)	Suboptimal (2.2)	Suboptimal (2.4)	Suboptimal (2.6)	Suboptimal (2.8)	Suboptimal (3.0)
Forfeiture (0%)	$23.53	$24.29	$24.82	$25.13	$25.31	$25.46	$25.58	$25.68	$25.77	$25.82
Forfeiture (5%)	$18.27	$18.84	$19.23	$19.46	$19.59	$19.70	$19.79	$19.86	$19.93	$19.97
Forfeiture (10%)	$14.19	$14.61	$14.90	$15.07	$15.17	$15.25	$15.31	$15.37	$15.42	$15.44
Forfeiture (15%)	$11.03	$11.34	$11.55	$11.67	$11.75	$11.80	$11.85	$11.89	$11.93	$11.95
Forfeiture (20%)	$8.57	$8.80	$8.95	$9.04	$9.10	$9.14	$9.18	$9.21	$9.23	$9.25
Forfeiture (25%)	$6.65	$6.82	$6.94	$7.01	$7.05	$7.08	$7.11	$7.13	$7.15	$7.16
Forfeiture (30%)	$5.17	$5.30	$5.38	$5.43	$5.46	$5.48	$5.50	$5.52	$5.53	$5.54
Forfeiture (35%)	$4.02	$4.11	$4.17	$4.21	$4.23	$4.25	$4.26	$4.28	$4.29	$4.29
Forfeiture (40%)	$3.12	$3.19	$3.24	$3.26	$3.28	$3.29	$3.30	$3.31	$3.32	$3.32

Percentage Difference between Binomial and Black-Scholes Model	Suboptimal (1.2)	Suboptimal (1.4)	Suboptimal (1.6)	Suboptimal (1.8)	Suboptimal (2.0)	Suboptimal (2.2)	Suboptimal (2.4)	Suboptimal (2.6)	Suboptimal (2.8)	Suboptimal (3.0)
Forfeiture (0%)	–10.22%	–7.32%	–5.30%	–4.12%	–3.42%	–2.86%	–2.39%	–2.00%	–1.67%	–1.47%
Forfeiture (5%)	–30.27%	–28.12%	–26.63%	–25.76%	–25.24%	–24.84%	–24.49%	–24.20%	–23.95%	–23.81%
Forfeiture (10%)	–45.84%	–44.24%	–43.14%	–42.50%	–42.12%	–41.82%	–41.56%	–41.35%	–41.17%	–41.07%
Forfeiture (15%)	–57.93%	–56.74%	–55.93%	–55.46%	–55.18%	–54.96%	–54.77%	–54.61%	–54.48%	–54.40%
Forfeiture (20%)	–67.32%	–66.44%	–65.84%	–65.49%	–65.29%	–65.12%	–64.98%	–64.87%	–64.77%	–64.71%
Forfeiture (25%)	–74.61%	–73.96%	–73.51%	–73.26%	–73.11%	–72.99%	–72.88%	–72.80%	–72.72%	–72.68%
Forfeiture (30%)	–80.28%	–79.79%	–79.46%	–79.27%	–79.16%	–79.07%	–79.00%	–78.94%	–78.88%	–78.85%
Forfeiture (35%)	–84.68%	–84.32%	–84.07%	–83.94%	–83.85%	–83.79%	–83.73%	–83.68%	–83.64%	–83.62%
Forfeiture (40%)	–88.10%	–87.83%	–87.65%	–87.55%	–87.49%	–87.44%	–87.40%	–87.36%	–87.33%	–87.31%

MATURITY OF 7 YEARS AND VESTING OF 5 YEARS ON AN $80 STOCK PRICE

Stock Price and Strike Price of $80, Maturity of 7 Years, Risk-Free Rate of 3.5%, 35% Volatility, 0% Dividends, Vesting of 5 Years, Employee Suboptimal Exercise Behavior from 1.2 to 3.0, and Forfeiture Rate from 0% to 40%.
Generalized Black-Scholes: $34.94

Customized Binomial Lattice	Suboptimal (1.2)	Suboptimal (1.4)	Suboptimal (1.6)	Suboptimal (1.8)	Suboptimal (2.0)	Suboptimal (2.2)	Suboptimal (2.4)	Suboptimal (2.6)	Suboptimal (2.8)	Suboptimal (3.0)
Forfeiture (0%)	$31.37	$32.38	$33.09	$33.50	$33.75	$33.94	$34.11	$34.24	$34.36	$34.43
Forfeiture (5%)	$24.37	$25.12	$25.64	$25.94	$26.12	$26.26	$26.39	$26.49	$26.57	$26.62
Forfeiture (10%)	$18.93	$19.48	$19.87	$20.09	$20.22	$20.33	$20.42	$20.49	$20.56	$20.59
Forfeiture (15%)	$14.70	$15.12	$15.40	$15.56	$15.66	$15.74	$15.80	$15.86	$15.91	$15.93
Forfeiture (20%)	$11.42	$11.73	$11.94	$12.06	$12.13	$12.19	$12.24	$12.28	$12.31	$12.33
Forfeiture (25%)	$8.87	$9.10	$9.25	$9.34	$9.40	$9.44	$9.48	$9.50	$9.53	$9.55
Forfeiture (30%)	$6.89	$7.06	$7.18	$7.24	$7.28	$7.31	$7.34	$7.36	$7.38	$7.39
Forfeiture (35%)	$5.35	$5.48	$5.56	$5.61	$5.64	$5.67	$5.68	$5.70	$5.72	$5.72
Forfeiture (40%)	$4.16	$4.25	$4.32	$4.35	$4.37	$4.39	$4.40	$4.42	$4.43	$4.43

Percentage Difference between Binomial and Black-Scholes Model	Suboptimal (1.2)	Suboptimal (1.4)	Suboptimal (1.6)	Suboptimal (1.8)	Suboptimal (2.0)	Suboptimal (2.2)	Suboptimal (2.4)	Suboptimal (2.6)	Suboptimal (2.8)	Suboptimal (3.0)
Forfeiture (0%)	−10.22%	−7.32%	−5.30%	−4.12%	−3.42%	−2.86%	−2.39%	−2.00%	−1.67%	−1.47%
Forfeiture (5%)	−30.27%	−28.12%	−26.63%	−25.76%	−25.24%	−24.84%	−24.49%	−24.20%	−23.95%	−23.81%
Forfeiture (10%)	−45.84%	−44.24%	−43.14%	−42.50%	−42.12%	−41.82%	−41.56%	−41.35%	−41.17%	−41.07%
Forfeiture (15%)	−57.93%	−56.74%	−55.93%	−55.46%	−55.18%	−54.96%	−54.77%	−54.61%	−54.48%	−54.40%
Forfeiture (20%)	−67.32%	−66.44%	−65.84%	−65.49%	−65.29%	−65.12%	−64.98%	−64.87%	−64.77%	−64.71%
Forfeiture (25%)	−74.61%	−73.96%	−73.51%	−73.26%	−73.11%	−72.99%	−72.88%	−72.80%	−72.72%	−72.68%
Forfeiture (30%)	−80.28%	−79.79%	−79.46%	−79.27%	−79.16%	−79.07%	−79.00%	−78.94%	−78.88%	−78.85%
Forfeiture (35%)	−84.68%	−84.32%	−84.07%	−83.94%	−83.85%	−83.79%	−83.73%	−83.68%	−83.64%	−83.62%
Forfeiture (40%)	−88.10%	−87.83%	−87.65%	−87.55%	−87.49%	−87.44%	−87.40%	−87.36%	−87.33%	−87.31%

SEVENTY PERCENT VOLATILITY AND 7-YEAR MATURITY ESOs WITH VARYING STOCK PRICE, SUBOPTIMAL BEHAVIOR, VESTING PERIOD, AND FORFEITURE RATES

This section provides ESO valuation results on an underlying stock with 70 percent volatility and a 7-year maturity. The analysis is divided into 1-month, 1-year, 3-year, and 5-year vesting periods, and accounts for stock prices at grant date of $20, $40, $60, and $80.

MATURITY OF 7 YEARS AND VESTING OF 1 MONTH ON A $20 STOCK PRICE

Stock Price and Strike Price of $20, Maturity of 7 Years, Risk-Free Rate of 3.5%, 70% Volatility, 0% Dividends, Vesting of 1 Month, Employee Suboptimal Exercise Behavior from 1.2 to 3.0, and Forfeiture Rate from 0% to 40%.
Generalized Black-Scholes: $13.76

Customized Binomial Lattice	Suboptimal (1.2)	Suboptimal (1.4)	Suboptimal (1.6)	Suboptimal (1.8)	Suboptimal (2.0)	Suboptimal (2.2)	Suboptimal (2.4)	Suboptimal (2.6)	Suboptimal (2.8)	Suboptimal (3.0)
Forfeiture (0%)	$4.29	$5.77	$7.76	$8.85	$9.34	$10.18	$10.55	$11.19	$11.47	$11.71
Forfeiture (5%)	$4.17	$5.56	$7.37	$8.35	$8.77	$9.50	$9.82	$10.36	$10.59	$10.80
Forfeiture (10%)	$4.07	$5.37	$7.03	$7.90	$8.28	$8.92	$9.19	$9.65	$9.85	$10.02
Forfeiture (15%)	$3.98	$5.20	$6.73	$7.52	$7.85	$8.41	$8.65	$9.05	$9.21	$9.36
Forfeiture (20%)	$3.89	$5.05	$6.47	$7.18	$7.48	$7.97	$8.18	$8.52	$8.66	$8.79
Forfeiture (25%)	$3.82	$4.91	$6.23	$6.88	$7.15	$7.59	$7.77	$8.07	$8.19	$8.29
Forfeiture (30%)	$3.75	$4.79	$6.02	$6.61	$6.85	$7.24	$7.40	$7.66	$7.77	$7.86
Forfeiture (35%)	$3.68	$4.67	$5.82	$6.37	$6.59	$6.94	$7.08	$7.31	$7.40	$7.48
Forfeiture (40%)	$3.62	$4.57	$5.65	$6.15	$6.35	$6.66	$6.79	$6.99	$7.07	$7.14

Percentage Difference between Binomial and Black-Scholes Model	Suboptimal (1.2)	Suboptimal (1.4)	Suboptimal (1.6)	Suboptimal (1.8)	Suboptimal (2.0)	Suboptimal (2.2)	Suboptimal (2.4)	Suboptimal (2.6)	Suboptimal (2.8)	Suboptimal (3.0)
Forfeiture (0%)	−68.83%	−58.04%	−43.61%	−35.64%	−32.13%	−25.98%	−23.30%	−18.65%	−16.65%	−14.84%
Forfeiture (5%)	−69.66%	−59.59%	−46.43%	−39.34%	−36.26%	−30.92%	−28.63%	−24.70%	−23.02%	−21.51%
Forfeiture (10%)	−70.40%	−60.95%	−48.89%	−42.54%	−39.82%	−35.17%	−33.19%	−29.83%	−28.41%	−27.15%
Forfeiture (15%)	−71.07%	−62.17%	−51.06%	−45.34%	−42.92%	−38.84%	−37.12%	−34.24%	−33.03%	−31.96%
Forfeiture (20%)	−71.69%	−63.27%	−52.98%	−47.81%	−45.65%	−42.04%	−40.54%	−38.05%	−37.01%	−36.11%
Forfeiture (25%)	−72.25%	−64.27%	−54.71%	−50.00%	−48.05%	−44.85%	−43.53%	−41.37%	−40.48%	−39.70%
Forfeiture (30%)	−72.77%	−65.18%	−56.26%	−51.95%	−50.20%	−47.34%	−46.18%	−44.28%	−43.52%	−42.85%
Forfeiture (35%)	−73.25%	−66.02%	−57.67%	−53.72%	−52.13%	−49.56%	−48.53%	−46.87%	−46.20%	−45.62%
Forfeiture (40%)	−73.71%	−66.80%	−58.95%	−55.31%	−53.87%	−51.55%	−50.63%	−49.16%	−48.58%	−48.08%

MATURITY OF 7 YEARS AND VESTING OF 1 MONTH ON A $40 STOCK PRICE

Stock Price and Strike Price of $40, Maturity of 7 Years, Risk-Free Rate of 3.5%, 70% Volatility, 0% Dividends, Vesting of 1 Month, Employee Suboptimal Exercise Behavior from 1.2 to 3.0, and Forfeiture Rate from 0% to 40%.
Generalized Black-Scholes: $27.51

Customized Binomial Lattice	Suboptimal (1.2)	Suboptimal (1.4)	Suboptimal (1.6)	Suboptimal (1.8)	Suboptimal (2.0)	Suboptimal (2.2)	Suboptimal (2.4)	Suboptimal (2.6)	Suboptimal (2.8)	Suboptimal (3.0)
Forfeiture (0%)	$8.58	$11.54	$15.51	$17.71	$18.67	$20.37	$21.10	$22.38	$22.93	$23.43
Forfeiture (5%)	$8.35	$11.12	$14.74	$16.69	$17.54	$19.00	$19.63	$20.72	$21.18	$21.60
Forfeiture (10%)	$8.14	$10.74	$14.06	$15.81	$16.56	$17.84	$18.38	$19.30	$19.69	$20.04
Forfeiture (15%)	$7.96	$10.41	$13.47	$15.04	$15.70	$16.83	$17.30	$18.09	$18.42	$18.72
Forfeiture (20%)	$7.79	$10.10	$12.94	$14.36	$14.95	$15.95	$16.36	$17.04	$17.33	$17.58
Forfeiture (25%)	$7.63	$9.83	$12.46	$13.76	$14.29	$15.17	$15.53	$16.13	$16.38	$16.59
Forfeiture (30%)	$7.49	$9.58	$12.03	$13.22	$13.70	$14.49	$14.81	$15.33	$15.54	$15.72
Forfeiture (35%)	$7.36	$9.35	$11.65	$12.73	$13.17	$13.88	$14.16	$14.62	$14.80	$14.96
Forfeiture (40%)	$7.23	$9.13	$11.29	$12.29	$12.69	$13.33	$13.58	$13.99	$14.15	$14.28

Percentage Difference between Binomial and Black-Scholes Model	Suboptimal (1.2)	Suboptimal (1.4)	Suboptimal (1.6)	Suboptimal (1.8)	Suboptimal (2.0)	Suboptimal (2.2)	Suboptimal (2.4)	Suboptimal (2.6)	Suboptimal (2.8)	Suboptimal (3.0)
Forfeiture (0%)	–68.83%	–58.04%	–43.61%	–35.64%	–32.13%	–25.98%	–23.30%	–18.65%	–16.65%	–14.84%
Forfeiture (5%)	–69.66%	–59.59%	–46.43%	–39.34%	–36.26%	–30.92%	–28.63%	–24.70%	–23.02%	–21.51%
Forfeiture (10%)	–70.40%	–60.95%	–48.89%	–42.54%	–39.82%	–35.17%	–33.19%	–29.83%	–28.41%	–27.15%
Forfeiture (15%)	–71.07%	–62.17%	–51.06%	–45.34%	–42.92%	–38.84%	–37.12%	–34.24%	–33.03%	–31.96%
Forfeiture (20%)	–71.69%	–63.27%	–52.98%	–47.81%	–45.65%	–42.04%	–40.54%	–38.05%	–37.01%	–36.11%
Forfeiture (25%)	–72.25%	–64.27%	–54.71%	–50.00%	–48.05%	–44.85%	–43.53%	–41.37%	–40.48%	–39.70%
Forfeiture (30%)	–72.77%	–65.18%	–56.26%	–51.95%	–50.20%	–47.34%	–46.18%	–44.28%	–43.52%	–42.85%
Forfeiture (35%)	–73.25%	–66.02%	–57.67%	–53.72%	–52.13%	–49.56%	–48.53%	–46.87%	–46.20%	–45.62%
Forfeiture (40%)	–73.71%	–66.80%	–58.95%	–55.31%	–53.87%	–51.55%	–50.63%	–49.16%	–48.58%	–48.08%

MATURITY OF 7 YEARS AND VESTING OF 1 MONTH ON A $60 STOCK PRICE

Stock Price and Strike Price of $60, Maturity of 7 Years, Risk-Free Rate of 3.5%, 70% Volatility, 0% Dividends, Vesting of 1 Month, Employee Suboptimal Exercise Behavior from 1.2 to 3.0, and Forfeiture Rate from 0% to 40%.
Generalized Black-Scholes: $41.27

Customized Binomial Lattice	Suboptimal (1.2)	Suboptimal (1.4)	Suboptimal (1.6)	Suboptimal (1.8)	Suboptimal (2.0)	Suboptimal (2.2)	Suboptimal (2.4)	Suboptimal (2.6)	Suboptimal (2.8)	Suboptimal (3.0)
Forfeiture (0%)	$12.86	$17.31	$23.27	$26.56	$28.01	$30.55	$31.65	$33.57	$34.40	$35.14
Forfeiture (5%)	$12.52	$16.68	$22.11	$25.04	$26.31	$28.51	$29.45	$31.08	$31.77	$32.39
Forfeiture (10%)	$12.22	$16.11	$21.09	$23.71	$24.84	$26.75	$27.57	$28.96	$29.54	$30.07
Forfeiture (15%)	$11.94	$15.61	$20.20	$22.56	$23.55	$25.24	$25.95	$27.14	$27.64	$28.08
Forfeiture (20%)	$11.68	$15.16	$19.40	$21.54	$22.43	$23.92	$24.54	$25.57	$25.99	$26.37
Forfeiture (25%)	$11.45	$14.74	$18.69	$20.64	$21.44	$22.76	$23.30	$24.20	$24.56	$24.88
Forfeiture (30%)	$11.24	$14.37	$18.05	$19.83	$20.55	$21.73	$22.21	$22.99	$23.31	$23.59
Forfeiture (35%)	$11.04	$14.02	$17.47	$19.10	$19.76	$20.82	$21.24	$21.93	$22.20	$22.44
Forfeiture (40%)	$10.85	$13.70	$16.94	$18.44	$19.04	$19.99	$20.37	$20.98	$21.22	$21.43

Percentage Difference between Binomial and Black-Scholes Model	Suboptimal (1.2)	Suboptimal (1.4)	Suboptimal (1.6)	Suboptimal (1.8)	Suboptimal (2.0)	Suboptimal (2.2)	Suboptimal (2.4)	Suboptimal (2.6)	Suboptimal (2.8)	Suboptimal (3.0)
Forfeiture (0%)	–68.83%	–58.04%	–43.61%	–35.64%	–32.13%	–25.98%	–23.30%	–18.65%	–16.65%	–14.84%
Forfeiture (5%)	–69.66%	–59.59%	–46.43%	–39.34%	–36.26%	–30.92%	–28.63%	–24.70%	–23.02%	–21.51%
Forfeiture (10%)	–70.40%	–60.95%	–48.89%	–42.54%	–39.82%	–35.17%	–33.19%	–29.83%	–28.41%	–27.15%
Forfeiture (15%)	–71.07%	–62.17%	–51.06%	–45.34%	–42.92%	–38.84%	–37.12%	–34.24%	–33.03%	–31.96%
Forfeiture (20%)	–71.69%	–63.27%	–52.98%	–47.81%	–45.65%	–42.04%	–40.54%	–38.05%	–37.01%	–36.11%
Forfeiture (25%)	–72.25%	–64.27%	–54.71%	–50.00%	–48.05%	–44.85%	–43.53%	–41.37%	–40.48%	–39.70%
Forfeiture (30%)	–72.77%	–65.18%	–56.26%	–51.95%	–50.20%	–47.34%	–46.18%	–44.28%	–43.52%	–42.85%
Forfeiture (35%)	–73.25%	–66.02%	–57.67%	–53.72%	–52.13%	–49.56%	–48.53%	–46.87%	–46.20%	–45.62%
Forfeiture (40%)	–73.71%	–66.80%	–58.95%	–55.31%	–53.87%	–51.55%	–50.63%	–49.16%	–48.58%	–48.08%

MATURITY OF 7 YEARS AND VESTING OF 1 MONTH ON AN $80 STOCK PRICE

Stock Price and Strike Price of $80, Maturity of 7 Years, Risk-Free Rate of 3.5%, 70% Volatility, 0% Dividends, Vesting of 1 Month, Employee Suboptimal Exercise Behavior from 1.2 to 3.0, and Forfeiture Rate from 0% to 40%.
Generalized Black-Scholes: $55.02

Customized Binomial Lattice	Suboptimal (1.2)	Suboptimal (1.4)	Suboptimal (1.6)	Suboptimal (1.8)	Suboptimal (2.0)	Suboptimal (2.2)	Suboptimal (2.4)	Suboptimal (2.6)	Suboptimal (2.8)	Suboptimal (3.0)
Forfeiture (0%)	$17.15	$23.09	$31.03	$35.42	$37.35	$40.73	$42.20	$44.76	$45.86	$46.86
Forfeiture (5%)	$16.70	$22.24	$29.48	$33.38	$35.07	$38.01	$39.27	$41.44	$42.36	$43.19
Forfeiture (10%)	$16.29	$21.49	$28.12	$31.62	$33.11	$35.67	$36.76	$38.61	$39.39	$40.09
Forfeiture (15%)	$15.92	$20.81	$26.93	$30.08	$31.41	$33.65	$34.60	$36.19	$36.85	$37.44
Forfeiture (20%)	$15.58	$20.21	$25.87	$28.72	$29.91	$31.89	$32.72	$34.09	$34.66	$35.16
Forfeiture (25%)	$15.27	$19.66	$24.92	$27.51	$28.58	$30.35	$31.07	$32.26	$32.75	$33.18
Forfeiture (30%)	$14.98	$19.16	$24.07	$26.44	$27.40	$28.98	$29.62	$30.66	$31.08	$31.45
Forfeiture (35%)	$14.72	$18.70	$23.29	$25.47	$26.34	$27.75	$28.32	$29.24	$29.60	$29.92
Forfeiture (40%)	$14.47	$18.27	$22.59	$24.59	$25.38	$26.66	$27.16	$27.97	$28.29	$28.57

Percentage Difference between Binomial and Black-Scholes Model	Suboptimal (1.2)	Suboptimal (1.4)	Suboptimal (1.6)	Suboptimal (1.8)	Suboptimal (2.0)	Suboptimal (2.2)	Suboptimal (2.4)	Suboptimal (2.6)	Suboptimal (2.8)	Suboptimal (3.0)
Forfeiture (0%)	–68.83%	–58.04%	–43.61%	–35.64%	–32.13%	–25.98%	–23.30%	–18.65%	–16.65%	–14.84%
Forfeiture (5%)	–69.66%	–59.59%	–46.43%	–39.34%	–36.26%	–30.92%	–28.63%	–24.70%	–23.02%	–21.51%
Forfeiture (10%)	–70.40%	–60.95%	–48.89%	–42.54%	–39.82%	–35.17%	–33.19%	–29.83%	–28.41%	–27.15%
Forfeiture (15%)	–71.07%	–62.17%	–51.06%	–45.34%	–42.92%	–38.84%	–37.12%	–34.24%	–33.03%	–31.96%
Forfeiture (20%)	–71.69%	–63.27%	–52.98%	–47.81%	–45.65%	–42.04%	–40.54%	–38.05%	–37.01%	–36.11%
Forfeiture (25%)	–72.25%	–64.27%	–54.71%	–50.00%	–48.05%	–44.85%	–43.53%	–41.37%	–40.48%	–39.70%
Forfeiture (30%)	–72.77%	–65.18%	–56.26%	–51.95%	–50.20%	–47.34%	–46.18%	–44.28%	–43.52%	–42.85%
Forfeiture (35%)	–73.25%	–66.02%	–57.67%	–53.72%	–52.13%	–49.56%	–48.53%	–46.87%	–46.20%	–45.62%
Forfeiture (40%)	–73.71%	–66.80%	–58.95%	–55.31%	–53.87%	–51.55%	–50.63%	–49.16%	–48.58%	–48.08%

MATURITY OF 7 YEARS AND VESTING OF 1 YEAR ON A $20 STOCK PRICE

Stock Price and Strike Price of $20, Maturity of 7 Years, Risk-Free Rate of 3.5%,70% Volatility, 0% Dividends, Vesting of 1 Year, Employee Suboptimal Exercise Behavior from 1.2 to 3.0, and Forfeiture Rate from 0% to 40%.
Generalized Black-Scholes: $13.76

Customized Binomial Lattice	Suboptimal (1.2)	Suboptimal (1.4)	Suboptimal (1.6)	Suboptimal (1.8)	Suboptimal (2.0)	Suboptimal (2.2)	Suboptimal (2.4)	Suboptimal (2.6)	Suboptimal (2.8)	Suboptimal (3.0)
Forfeiture (0%)	$7.27	$8.03	$9.12	$9.79	$10.12	$10.70	$10.97	$11.46	$11.68	$11.88
Forfeiture (5%)	$6.83	$7.50	$8.44	$9.02	$9.29	$9.79	$10.01	$10.42	$10.60	$10.76
Forfeiture (10%)	$6.43	$7.02	$7.84	$8.34	$8.57	$8.99	$9.17	$9.51	$9.67	$9.80
Forfeiture (15%)	$6.06	$6.59	$7.30	$7.73	$7.93	$8.28	$8.44	$8.73	$8.85	$8.97
Forfeiture (20%)	$5.71	$6.18	$6.81	$7.18	$7.36	$7.66	$7.79	$8.03	$8.14	$8.23
Forfeiture (25%)	$5.39	$5.81	$6.37	$6.69	$6.84	$7.10	$7.21	$7.42	$7.51	$7.59
Forfeiture (30%)	$5.09	$5.47	$5.96	$6.24	$6.38	$6.60	$6.70	$6.87	$6.95	$7.01
Forfeiture (35%)	$4.81	$5.15	$5.59	$5.84	$5.95	$6.15	$6.23	$6.38	$6.44	$6.50
Forfeiture (40%)	$4.55	$4.86	$5.25	$5.47	$5.57	$5.74	$5.81	$5.94	$5.99	$6.04

Percentage Difference between Binomial and Black-Scholes Model	Suboptimal (1.2)	Suboptimal (1.4)	Suboptimal (1.6)	Suboptimal (1.8)	Suboptimal (2.0)	Suboptimal (2.2)	Suboptimal (2.4)	Suboptimal (2.6)	Suboptimal (2.8)	Suboptimal (3.0)
Forfeiture (0%)	−47.13%	−41.59%	−33.73%	−28.82%	−26.47%	−22.20%	−20.28%	−16.71%	−15.08%	−13.62%
Forfeiture (5%)	−50.31%	−45.44%	−38.63%	−34.44%	−32.44%	−28.85%	−27.25%	−24.29%	−22.94%	−21.74%
Forfeiture (10%)	−53.24%	−48.94%	−43.01%	−39.41%	−37.70%	−34.66%	−33.32%	−30.85%	−29.73%	−28.74%
Forfeiture (15%)	−55.95%	−52.13%	−46.94%	−43.83%	−42.36%	−39.78%	−38.64%	−36.57%	−35.64%	−34.82%
Forfeiture (20%)	−58.46%	−55.05%	−50.49%	−47.79%	−46.53%	−44.32%	−43.36%	−41.61%	−40.83%	−40.15%
Forfeiture (25%)	−60.80%	−57.75%	−53.72%	−51.36%	−50.27%	−48.37%	−47.55%	−46.07%	−45.42%	−44.84%
Forfeiture (30%)	−62.97%	−60.24%	−56.67%	−54.61%	−53.65%	−52.02%	−51.31%	−50.05%	−49.50%	−49.01%
Forfeiture (35%)	−65.01%	−62.54%	−59.37%	−57.56%	−56.72%	−55.31%	−54.70%	−53.62%	−53.15%	−52.74%
Forfeiture (40%)	−66.91%	−64.69%	−61.86%	−60.26%	−59.53%	−58.29%	−57.77%	−56.84%	−56.44%	−56.09%

MATURITY OF 7 YEARS AND VESTING OF 1 YEAR ON A $40 STOCK PRICE

Stock Price and Strike Price of $40, Maturity of 7 Years, Risk-Free Rate of 3.5%, 70% Volatility, 0% Dividends, Vesting of 1 Year, Employee Suboptimal Exercise Behavior from 1.2 to 3.0, and Forfeiture Rate from 0% to 40%.
Generalized Black-Scholes: $27.51

Customized Binomial Lattice	Suboptimal (1.2)	Suboptimal (1.4)	Suboptimal (1.6)	Suboptimal (1.8)	Suboptimal (2.0)	Suboptimal (2.2)	Suboptimal (2.4)	Suboptimal (2.6)	Suboptimal (2.8)	Suboptimal (3.0)
Forfeiture (0%)	$14.55	$16.07	$18.23	$19.58	$20.23	$21.40	$21.93	$22.91	$23.36	$23.77
Forfeiture (5%)	$13.67	$15.01	$16.88	$18.04	$18.59	$19.57	$20.02	$20.83	$21.20	$21.53
Forfeiture (10%)	$12.86	$14.05	$15.68	$16.67	$17.14	$17.98	$18.35	$19.03	$19.33	$19.60
Forfeiture (15%)	$12.12	$13.17	$14.60	$15.45	$15.86	$16.57	$16.88	$17.45	$17.71	$17.93
Forfeiture (20%)	$11.43	$12.37	$13.62	$14.36	$14.71	$15.32	$15.58	$16.06	$16.28	$16.47
Forfeiture (25%)	$10.79	$11.62	$12.73	$13.38	$13.68	$14.20	$14.43	$14.84	$15.02	$15.17
Forfeiture (30%)	$10.19	$10.94	$11.92	$12.49	$12.75	$13.20	$13.39	$13.74	$13.89	$14.03
Forfeiture (35%)	$9.63	$10.31	$11.18	$11.68	$11.91	$12.30	$12.46	$12.76	$12.89	$13.00
Forfeiture (40%)	$9.10	$9.72	$10.49	$10.93	$11.13	$11.47	$11.62	$11.87	$11.98	$12.08

Percentage Difference between Binomial and Black-Scholes Model	Suboptimal (1.2)	Suboptimal (1.4)	Suboptimal (1.6)	Suboptimal (1.8)	Suboptimal (2.0)	Suboptimal (2.2)	Suboptimal (2.4)	Suboptimal (2.6)	Suboptimal (2.8)	Suboptimal (3.0)
Forfeiture (0%)	–47.13%	–41.59%	–33.73%	–28.82%	–26.47%	–22.20%	–20.28%	–16.71%	–15.08%	–13.62%
Forfeiture (5%)	–50.31%	–45.44%	–38.63%	–34.44%	–32.44%	–28.85%	–27.25%	–24.29%	–22.94%	–21.74%
Forfeiture (10%)	–53.24%	–48.94%	–43.01%	–39.41%	–37.70%	–34.66%	–33.32%	–30.85%	–29.73%	–28.74%
Forfeiture (15%)	–55.95%	–52.13%	–46.94%	–43.83%	–42.36%	–39.78%	–38.64%	–36.57%	–35.64%	–34.82%
Forfeiture (20%)	–58.46%	–55.05%	–50.49%	–47.79%	–46.53%	–44.32%	–43.36%	–41.61%	–40.83%	–40.15%
Forfeiture (25%)	–60.80%	–57.75%	–53.72%	–51.36%	–50.27%	–48.37%	–47.55%	–46.07%	–45.42%	–44.84%
Forfeiture (30%)	–62.97%	–60.24%	–56.67%	–54.61%	–53.65%	–52.02%	–51.31%	–50.05%	–49.50%	–49.01%
Forfeiture (35%)	–65.01%	–62.54%	–59.37%	–57.56%	–56.72%	–55.31%	–54.70%	–53.62%	–53.15%	–52.74%
Forfeiture (40%)	–66.91%	–64.69%	–61.86%	–60.26%	–59.53%	–58.29%	–57.77%	–56.84%	–56.44%	–56.09%

MATURITY OF 7 YEARS AND VESTING OF 1 YEAR ON A $60 STOCK PRICE

Stock Price and Strike Price of $60, Maturity of 7 Years, Risk-Free Rate of 3.5%, 70% Volatility, 0% Dividends, Vesting of 1 Year, Employee Suboptimal Exercise Behavior from 1.2 to 3.0, and Forfeiture Rate from 0% to 40%.
Generalized Black-Scholes: $41.27

Customized Binomial Lattice	Suboptimal (1.2)	Suboptimal (1.4)	Suboptimal (1.6)	Suboptimal (1.8)	Suboptimal (2.0)	Suboptimal (2.2)	Suboptimal (2.4)	Suboptimal (2.6)	Suboptimal (2.8)	Suboptimal (3.0)
Forfeiture (0%)	$21.82	$24.10	$27.35	$29.37	$30.35	$32.11	$32.90	$34.37	$35.04	$35.65
Forfeiture (5%)	$20.50	$22.51	$25.32	$27.05	$27.88	$29.36	$30.02	$31.25	$31.80	$32.29
Forfeiture (10%)	$19.29	$21.07	$23.52	$25.01	$25.71	$26.96	$27.52	$28.54	$29.00	$29.41
Forfeiture (15%)	$18.18	$19.76	$21.90	$23.18	$23.79	$24.85	$25.32	$26.18	$26.56	$26.90
Forfeiture (20%)	$17.14	$18.55	$20.43	$21.55	$22.07	$22.98	$23.38	$24.10	$24.42	$24.70
Forfeiture (25%)	$16.18	$17.44	$19.10	$20.07	$20.52	$21.31	$21.64	$22.26	$22.53	$22.76
Forfeiture (30%)	$15.28	$16.41	$17.88	$18.73	$19.13	$19.80	$20.09	$20.61	$20.84	$21.04
Forfeiture (35%)	$14.44	$15.46	$16.77	$17.52	$17.86	$18.44	$18.69	$19.14	$19.33	$19.50
Forfeiture (40%)	$13.65	$14.57	$15.74	$16.40	$16.70	$17.21	$17.43	$17.81	$17.98	$18.12

Percentage Difference between Binomial and Black-Scholes Model	Suboptimal (1.2)	Suboptimal (1.4)	Suboptimal (1.6)	Suboptimal (1.8)	Suboptimal (2.0)	Suboptimal (2.2)	Suboptimal (2.4)	Suboptimal (2.6)	Suboptimal (2.8)	Suboptimal (3.0)
Forfeiture (0%)	–47.13%	–41.59%	–33.73%	–28.82%	–26.47%	–22.20%	–20.28%	–16.71%	–15.08%	–13.62%
Forfeiture (5%)	–50.31%	–45.44%	–38.63%	–34.44%	–32.44%	–28.85%	–27.25%	–24.29%	–22.94%	–21.74%
Forfeiture (10%)	–53.24%	–48.94%	–43.01%	–39.41%	–37.70%	–34.66%	–33.32%	–30.85%	–29.73%	–28.74%
Forfeiture (15%)	–55.95%	–52.13%	–46.94%	–43.83%	–42.36%	–39.78%	–38.64%	–36.57%	–35.64%	–34.82%
Forfeiture (20%)	–58.46%	–55.05%	–50.49%	–47.79%	–46.53%	–44.32%	–43.36%	–41.61%	–40.83%	–40.15%
Forfeiture (25%)	–60.80%	–57.75%	–53.72%	–51.36%	–50.27%	–48.37%	–47.55%	–46.07%	–45.42%	–44.84%
Forfeiture (30%)	–62.97%	–60.24%	–56.67%	–54.61%	–53.65%	–52.02%	–51.31%	–50.05%	–49.50%	–49.01%
Forfeiture (35%)	–65.01%	–62.54%	–59.37%	–57.56%	–56.72%	–55.31%	–54.70%	–53.62%	–53.15%	–52.74%
Forfeiture (40%)	–66.91%	–64.69%	–61.86%	–60.26%	–59.53%	–58.29%	–57.77%	–56.84%	–56.44%	–56.09%

MATURITY OF 7 YEARS AND VESTING OF 1 YEAR ON AN $80 STOCK PRICE

Stock Price and Strike Price of $80, Maturity of 7 Years, Risk-Free Rate of 3.5%, 70% Volatility, 0% Dividends, Vesting of 1 Year, Employee Suboptimal Exercise Behavior from 1.2 to 3.0, and Forfeiture Rate from 0% to 40%.
Generalized Black-Scholes: $55.02

Customized Binomial Lattice	Suboptimal (1.2)	Suboptimal (1.4)	Suboptimal (1.6)	Suboptimal (1.8)	Suboptimal (2.0)	Suboptimal (2.2)	Suboptimal (2.4)	Suboptimal (2.6)	Suboptimal (2.8)	Suboptimal (3.0)
Forfeiture (0%)	$29.09	$32.14	$36.46	$39.16	$40.46	$42.81	$43.87	$45.83	$46.72	$47.53
Forfeiture (5%)	$27.34	$30.02	$33.77	$36.07	$37.17	$39.15	$40.03	$41.66	$42.40	$43.06
Forfeiture (10%)	$25.73	$28.10	$31.36	$33.34	$34.28	$35.95	$36.69	$38.05	$38.66	$39.21
Forfeiture (15%)	$24.24	$26.34	$29.20	$30.91	$31.71	$33.14	$33.76	$34.90	$35.41	$35.86
Forfeiture (20%)	$22.86	$24.73	$27.24	$28.73	$29.42	$30.64	$31.17	$32.13	$32.56	$32.93
Forfeiture (25%)	$21.57	$23.25	$25.46	$26.76	$27.36	$28.41	$28.86	$29.67	$30.03	$30.35
Forfeiture (30%)	$20.37	$21.88	$23.84	$24.98	$25.50	$26.40	$26.79	$27.48	$27.79	$28.06
Forfeiture (35%)	$19.25	$20.61	$22.36	$23.35	$23.81	$24.59	$24.93	$25.52	$25.78	$26.00
Forfeiture (40%)	$18.20	$19.43	$20.99	$21.87	$22.27	$22.95	$23.24	$23.75	$23.97	$24.16

Percentage Difference between Binomial and Black-Scholes Model	Suboptimal (1.2)	Suboptimal (1.4)	Suboptimal (1.6)	Suboptimal (1.8)	Suboptimal (2.0)	Suboptimal (2.2)	Suboptimal (2.4)	Suboptimal (2.6)	Suboptimal (2.8)	Suboptimal (3.0)
Forfeiture (0%)	–47.13%	–41.59%	–33.73%	–28.82%	–26.47%	–22.20%	–20.28%	–16.71%	–15.08%	–13.62%
Forfeiture (5%)	–50.31%	–45.44%	–38.63%	–34.44%	–32.44%	–28.85%	–27.25%	–24.29%	–22.94%	–21.74%
Forfeiture (10%)	–53.24%	–48.94%	–43.01%	–39.41%	–37.70%	–34.66%	–33.32%	–30.85%	–29.73%	–28.74%
Forfeiture (15%)	–55.95%	–52.13%	–46.94%	–43.83%	–42.36%	–39.78%	–38.64%	–36.57%	–35.64%	–34.82%
Forfeiture (20%)	–58.46%	–55.05%	–50.49%	–47.79%	–46.53%	–44.32%	–43.36%	–41.61%	–40.83%	–40.15%
Forfeiture (25%)	–60.80%	–57.75%	–53.72%	–51.36%	–50.27%	–48.37%	–47.55%	–46.07%	–45.42%	–44.84%
Forfeiture (30%)	–62.97%	–60.24%	–56.67%	–54.61%	–53.65%	–52.02%	–51.31%	–50.05%	–49.50%	–49.01%
Forfeiture (35%)	–65.01%	–62.54%	–59.37%	–57.56%	–56.72%	–55.31%	–54.70%	–53.62%	–53.15%	–52.74%
Forfeiture (40%)	–66.91%	–64.69%	–61.86%	–60.26%	–59.53%	–58.29%	–57.77%	–56.84%	–56.44%	–56.09%

MATURITY OF 7 YEARS AND VESTING OF 3 YEARS ON A $20 STOCK PRICE

Stock Price and Strike Price of $20, Maturity of 7 Years, Risk-Free Rate of 3.5%,70% Volatility, 0% Dividends, Vesting of 3 Years, Employee Suboptimal Exercise Behavior from 1.2 to 3.0, and Forfeiture Rate from 0% to 40%.
Generalized Black-Scholes: $13.76

Customized Binomial Lattice	Suboptimal (1.2)	Suboptimal (1.4)	Suboptimal (1.6)	Suboptimal (1.8)	Suboptimal (2.0)	Suboptimal (2.2)	Suboptimal (2.4)	Suboptimal (2.6)	Suboptimal (2.8)	Suboptimal (3.0)
Forfeiture (0%)	$10.57	$10.97	$11.51	$11.83	$11.99	$12.26	$12.38	$12.60	$12.70	$12.80
Forfeiture (5%)	$9.06	$9.38	$9.81	$10.06	$10.18	$10.39	$10.49	$10.66	$10.74	$10.81
Forfeiture (10%)	$7.76	$8.02	$8.36	$8.56	$8.66	$8.83	$8.90	$9.04	$9.10	$9.15
Forfeiture (15%)	$6.65	$6.86	$7.14	$7.30	$7.37	$7.50	$7.56	$7.67	$7.72	$7.76
Forfeiture (20%)	$5.71	$5.88	$6.10	$6.22	$6.28	$6.39	$6.43	$6.51	$6.55	$6.58
Forfeiture (25%)	$4.89	$5.03	$5.21	$5.31	$5.36	$5.44	$5.47	$5.54	$5.57	$5.60
Forfeiture (30%)	$4.20	$4.31	$4.45	$4.53	$4.57	$4.64	$4.67	$4.72	$4.74	$4.76
Forfeiture (35%)	$3.60	$3.69	$3.81	$3.87	$3.90	$3.96	$3.98	$4.02	$4.04	$4.05
Forfeiture (40%)	$3.09	$3.17	$3.26	$3.31	$3.34	$3.38	$3.39	$3.43	$3.44	$3.45

Percentage Difference between Binomial and Black-Scholes Model	Suboptimal (1.2)	Suboptimal (1.4)	Suboptimal (1.6)	Suboptimal (1.8)	Suboptimal (2.0)	Suboptimal (2.2)	Suboptimal (2.4)	Suboptimal (2.6)	Suboptimal (2.8)	Suboptimal (3.0)
Forfeiture (0%)	−23.14%	−20.22%	−16.32%	−13.98%	−12.87%	−10.89%	−10.02%	−8.39%	−7.64%	−6.98%
Forfeiture (5%)	−34.15%	−31.81%	−28.70%	−26.86%	−25.98%	−24.44%	−23.76%	−22.49%	−21.91%	−21.40%
Forfeiture (10%)	−43.57%	−41.68%	−39.20%	−37.74%	−37.05%	−35.83%	−35.30%	−34.32%	−33.86%	−33.47%
Forfeiture (15%)	−51.62%	−50.10%	−48.11%	−46.95%	−46.40%	−45.45%	−45.03%	−44.26%	−43.91%	−43.61%
Forfeiture (20%)	−58.52%	−57.28%	−55.69%	−54.76%	−54.33%	−53.58%	−53.25%	−52.65%	−52.37%	−52.13%
Forfeiture (25%)	−64.42%	−63.42%	−62.13%	−61.40%	−61.05%	−60.46%	−60.20%	−59.73%	−59.51%	−59.32%
Forfeiture (30%)	−69.47%	−68.66%	−67.62%	−67.03%	−66.76%	−66.29%	−66.09%	−65.71%	−65.54%	−65.40%
Forfeiture (35%)	−73.81%	−73.14%	−72.31%	−71.83%	−71.61%	−71.24%	−71.08%	−70.79%	−70.65%	−70.54%
Forfeiture (40%)	−77.52%	−76.98%	−76.30%	−75.92%	−75.74%	−75.45%	−75.32%	−75.09%	−74.98%	−74.89%

MATURITY OF 7 YEARS AND VESTING OF 3 YEARS ON A $40 STOCK PRICE

Stock Price and Strike Price of $40, Maturity of 7 Years, Risk-Free Rate of 3.5%, 70% Volatility, 0% Dividends, Vesting of 3 Years, Employee Suboptimal Exercise Behavior from 1.2 to 3.0, and Forfeiture Rate from 0% to 40%.
Generalized Black-Scholes: $27.51

Customized Binomial Lattice	Suboptimal (1.2)	Suboptimal (1.4)	Suboptimal (1.6)	Suboptimal (1.8)	Suboptimal (2.0)	Suboptimal (2.2)	Suboptimal (2.4)	Suboptimal (2.6)	Suboptimal (2.8)	Suboptimal (3.0)
Forfeiture (0%)	$21.15	$21.95	$23.02	$23.67	$23.97	$24.51	$24.75	$25.20	$25.41	$25.59
Forfeiture (5%)	$18.12	$18.76	$19.62	$20.12	$20.36	$20.79	$20.98	$21.32	$21.48	$21.62
Forfeiture (10%)	$15.53	$16.04	$16.73	$17.13	$17.32	$17.65	$17.80	$18.07	$18.20	$18.30
Forfeiture (15%)	$13.31	$13.73	$14.28	$14.59	$14.75	$15.01	$15.12	$15.33	$15.43	$15.52
Forfeiture (20%)	$11.41	$11.75	$12.19	$12.45	$12.57	$12.77	$12.86	$13.03	$13.10	$13.17
Forfeiture (25%)	$9.79	$10.07	$10.42	$10.62	$10.72	$10.88	$10.95	$11.08	$11.14	$11.19
Forfeiture (30%)	$8.40	$8.62	$8.91	$9.07	$9.15	$9.27	$9.33	$9.43	$9.48	$9.52
Forfeiture (35%)	$7.21	$7.39	$7.62	$7.75	$7.81	$7.91	$7.96	$8.04	$8.07	$8.11
Forfeiture (40%)	$6.18	$6.33	$6.52	$6.62	$6.67	$6.76	$6.79	$6.85	$6.88	$6.91

Percentage Difference between Binomial and Black-Scholes Model	Suboptimal (1.2)	Suboptimal (1.4)	Suboptimal (1.6)	Suboptimal (1.8)	Suboptimal (2.0)	Suboptimal (2.2)	Suboptimal (2.4)	Suboptimal (2.6)	Suboptimal (2.8)	Suboptimal (3.0)
Forfeiture (0%)	–23.14%	–20.22%	–16.32%	–13.98%	–12.87%	–10.89%	–10.02%	–8.39%	–7.64%	–6.98%
Forfeiture (5%)	–34.15%	–31.81%	–28.70%	–26.86%	–25.98%	–24.44%	–23.76%	–22.49%	–21.91%	–21.40%
Forfeiture (10%)	–43.57%	–41.68%	–39.20%	–37.74%	–37.05%	–35.83%	–35.30%	–34.32%	–33.86%	–33.47%
Forfeiture (15%)	–51.62%	–50.10%	–48.11%	–46.95%	–46.40%	–45.45%	–45.03%	–44.26%	–43.91%	–43.61%
Forfeiture (20%)	–58.52%	–57.28%	–55.69%	–54.76%	–54.33%	–53.58%	–53.25%	–52.65%	–52.37%	–52.13%
Forfeiture (25%)	–64.42%	–63.42%	–62.13%	–61.40%	–61.05%	–60.46%	–60.20%	–59.73%	–59.51%	–59.32%
Forfeiture (30%)	–69.47%	–68.66%	–67.62%	–67.03%	–66.76%	–66.29%	–66.09%	–65.71%	–65.54%	–65.40%
Forfeiture (35%)	–73.81%	–73.14%	–72.31%	–71.83%	–71.61%	–71.24%	–71.08%	–70.79%	–70.65%	–70.54%
Forfeiture (40%)	–77.52%	–76.98%	–76.30%	–75.92%	–75.74%	–75.45%	–75.32%	–75.09%	–74.98%	–74.89%

MATURITY OF 7 YEARS AND VESTING OF 3 YEARS ON A $60 STOCK PRICE

Stock Price and Strike Price of $60, Maturity of 7 Years, Risk-Free Rate of 3.5%, 70% Volatility, 0% Dividends, Vesting of 3 Years, Employee Suboptimal Exercise Behavior from 1.2 to 3.0, and Forfeiture Rate from 0% to 40%.
Generalized Black-Scholes: $41.27

Customized Binomial Lattice	Suboptimal (1.2)	Suboptimal (1.4)	Suboptimal (1.6)	Suboptimal (1.8)	Suboptimal (2.0)	Suboptimal (2.2)	Suboptimal (2.4)	Suboptimal (2.6)	Suboptimal (2.8)	Suboptimal (3.0)
Forfeiture (0%)	$31.72	$32.92	$34.53	$35.50	$35.96	$36.77	$37.13	$37.80	$38.11	$38.39
Forfeiture (5%)	$27.17	$28.14	$29.42	$30.19	$30.55	$31.18	$31.46	$31.99	$32.23	$32.44
Forfeiture (10%)	$23.29	$24.07	$25.09	$25.69	$25.98	$26.48	$26.70	$27.11	$27.29	$27.46
Forfeiture (15%)	$19.96	$20.59	$21.41	$21.89	$22.12	$22.51	$22.68	$23.00	$23.15	$23.27
Forfeiture (20%)	$17.12	$17.63	$18.29	$18.67	$18.85	$19.16	$19.29	$19.54	$19.66	$19.75
Forfeiture (25%)	$14.68	$15.10	$15.63	$15.93	$16.07	$16.32	$16.42	$16.62	$16.71	$16.79
Forfeiture (30%)	$12.60	$12.93	$13.36	$13.60	$13.72	$13.91	$14.00	$14.15	$14.22	$14.28
Forfeiture (35%)	$10.81	$11.08	$11.43	$11.62	$11.71	$11.87	$11.94	$12.06	$12.11	$12.16
Forfeiture (40%)	$9.28	$9.50	$9.78	$9.94	$10.01	$10.13	$10.18	$10.28	$10.32	$10.36

Percentage Difference between Binomial and Black-Scholes Model	Suboptimal (1.2)	Suboptimal (1.4)	Suboptimal (1.6)	Suboptimal (1.8)	Suboptimal (2.0)	Suboptimal (2.2)	Suboptimal (2.4)	Suboptimal (2.6)	Suboptimal (2.8)	Suboptimal (3.0)
Forfeiture (0%)	−23.14%	−20.22%	−16.32%	−13.98%	−12.87%	−10.89%	−10.02%	−8.39%	−7.64%	−6.98%
Forfeiture (5%)	−34.15%	−31.81%	−28.70%	−26.86%	−25.98%	−24.44%	−23.76%	−22.49%	−21.91%	−21.40%
Forfeiture (10%)	−43.57%	−41.68%	−39.20%	−37.74%	−37.05%	−35.83%	−35.30%	−34.32%	−33.86%	−33.47%
Forfeiture (15%)	−51.62%	−50.10%	−48.11%	−46.95%	−46.40%	−45.45%	−45.03%	−44.26%	−43.91%	−43.61%
Forfeiture (20%)	−58.52%	−57.28%	−55.69%	−54.76%	−54.33%	−53.58%	−53.25%	−52.65%	−52.37%	−52.13%
Forfeiture (25%)	−64.42%	−63.42%	−62.13%	−61.40%	−61.05%	−60.46%	−60.20%	−59.73%	−59.51%	−59.32%
Forfeiture (30%)	−69.47%	−68.66%	−67.62%	−67.03%	−66.76%	−66.29%	−66.09%	−65.71%	−65.54%	−65.40%
Forfeiture (35%)	−73.81%	−73.14%	−72.31%	−71.83%	−71.61%	−71.24%	−71.08%	−70.79%	−70.65%	−70.54%
Forfeiture (40%)	−77.52%	−76.98%	−76.30%	−75.92%	−75.74%	−75.45%	−75.32%	−75.09%	−74.98%	−74.89%

MATURITY OF 7 YEARS AND VESTING OF 3 YEARS ON AN $80 STOCK PRICE

Stock Price and Strike Price of $80, Maturity of 7 Years, Risk-Free Rate of 3.5%, 70% Volatility, 0% Dividends, Vesting of 3 Years, Employee Suboptimal Exercise Behavior from 1.2 to 3.0, and Forfeiture Rate from 0% to 40%.
Generalized Black-Scholes: $55.02

Customized Binomial Lattice	Suboptimal (1.2)	Suboptimal (1.4)	Suboptimal (1.6)	Suboptimal (1.8)	Suboptimal (2.0)	Suboptimal (2.2)	Suboptimal (2.4)	Suboptimal (2.6)	Suboptimal (2.8)	Suboptimal (3.0)
Forfeiture (0%)	$42.29	$43.90	$46.04	$47.33	$47.94	$49.03	$49.51	$50.40	$50.82	$51.18
Forfeiture (5%)	$36.23	$37.52	$39.23	$40.25	$40.73	$41.58	$41.95	$42.65	$42.97	$43.25
Forfeiture (10%)	$31.05	$32.09	$33.45	$34.26	$34.64	$35.31	$35.60	$36.14	$36.39	$36.61
Forfeiture (15%)	$26.62	$27.46	$28.55	$29.19	$29.49	$30.02	$30.24	$30.67	$30.86	$31.03
Forfeiture (20%)	$22.83	$23.51	$24.38	$24.89	$25.13	$25.54	$25.72	$26.06	$26.21	$26.34
Forfeiture (25%)	$19.58	$20.13	$20.84	$21.24	$21.43	$21.76	$21.90	$22.16	$22.28	$22.38
Forfeiture (30%)	$16.80	$17.25	$17.81	$18.14	$18.29	$18.55	$18.66	$18.87	$18.96	$19.04
Forfeiture (35%)	$14.41	$14.78	$15.24	$15.50	$15.62	$15.83	$15.91	$16.08	$16.15	$16.21
Forfeiture (40%)	$12.37	$12.67	$13.04	$13.25	$13.35	$13.51	$13.58	$13.71	$13.77	$13.81

Percentage Difference between Binomial and Black-Scholes Model	Suboptimal (1.2)	Suboptimal (1.4)	Suboptimal (1.6)	Suboptimal (1.8)	Suboptimal (2.0)	Suboptimal (2.2)	Suboptimal (2.4)	Suboptimal (2.6)	Suboptimal (2.8)	Suboptimal (3.0)
Forfeiture (0%)	−23.14%	−20.22%	−16.32%	−13.98%	−12.87%	−10.89%	−10.02%	−8.39%	−7.64%	−6.98%
Forfeiture (5%)	−34.15%	−31.81%	−28.70%	−26.86%	−25.98%	−24.44%	−23.76%	−22.49%	−21.91%	−21.40%
Forfeiture (10%)	−43.57%	−41.68%	−39.20%	−37.74%	−37.05%	−35.83%	−35.30%	−34.32%	−33.86%	−33.47%
Forfeiture (15%)	−51.62%	−50.10%	−48.11%	−46.95%	−46.40%	−45.45%	−45.03%	−44.26%	−43.91%	−43.61%
Forfeiture (20%)	−58.52%	−57.28%	−55.69%	−54.76%	−54.33%	−53.58%	−53.25%	−52.65%	−52.37%	−52.13%
Forfeiture (25%)	−64.42%	−63.42%	−62.13%	−61.40%	−61.05%	−60.46%	−60.20%	−59.73%	−59.51%	−59.32%
Forfeiture (30%)	−69.47%	−68.66%	−67.62%	−67.03%	−66.76%	−66.29%	−66.09%	−65.71%	−65.54%	−65.40%
Forfeiture (35%)	−73.81%	−73.14%	−72.31%	−71.83%	−71.61%	−71.24%	−71.08%	−70.79%	−70.65%	−70.54%
Forfeiture (40%)	−77.52%	−76.98%	−76.30%	−75.92%	−75.74%	−75.45%	−75.32%	−75.09%	−74.98%	−74.89%

MATURITY OF 7 YEARS AND VESTING OF 5 YEARS ON A $20 STOCK PRICE

Stock Price and Strike Price of $20, Maturity of 7 Years, Risk-Free Rate of 3.5%, 70% Volatility, 0% Dividends, Vesting of 5 Years, Employee Suboptimal Exercise Behavior from 1.2 to 3.0, and Forfeiture Rate from 0% to 40%.
Generalized Black-Scholes: $13.76

Customized Binomial Lattice	Suboptimal (1.2)	Suboptimal (1.4)	Suboptimal (1.6)	Suboptimal (1.8)	Suboptimal (2.0)	Suboptimal (2.2)	Suboptimal (2.4)	Suboptimal (2.6)	Suboptimal (2.8)	Suboptimal (3.0)
Forfeiture (0%)	$12.56	$12.75	$13.00	$13.13	$13.19	$13.29	$13.33	$13.41	$13.45	$13.47
Forfeiture (5%)	$9.76	$9.91	$10.09	$10.19	$10.24	$10.31	$10.34	$10.40	$10.42	$10.44
Forfeiture (10%)	$7.59	$7.70	$7.84	$7.91	$7.94	$8.00	$8.02	$8.06	$8.08	$8.10
Forfeiture (15%)	$5.90	$5.99	$6.08	$6.14	$6.16	$6.20	$6.22	$6.25	$6.27	$6.28
Forfeiture (20%)	$4.59	$4.65	$4.73	$4.77	$4.78	$4.81	$4.83	$4.85	$4.86	$4.87
Forfeiture (25%)	$3.57	$3.61	$3.67	$3.70	$3.71	$3.74	$3.74	$3.76	$3.77	$3.77
Forfeiture (30%)	$2.77	$2.81	$2.85	$2.87	$2.88	$2.90	$2.91	$2.92	$2.92	$2.93
Forfeiture (35%)	$2.16	$2.18	$2.21	$2.23	$2.24	$2.25	$2.25	$2.26	$2.27	$2.27
Forfeiture (40%)	$1.68	$1.70	$1.72	$1.73	$1.74	$1.75	$1.75	$1.76	$1.76	$1.76

Percentage Difference between Binomial and Black-Scholes Model	Suboptimal (1.2)	Suboptimal (1.4)	Suboptimal (1.6)	Suboptimal (1.8)	Suboptimal (2.0)	Suboptimal (2.2)	Suboptimal (2.4)	Suboptimal (2.6)	Suboptimal (2.8)	Suboptimal (3.0)
Forfeiture (0%)	-8.71%	-7.28%	-5.53%	-4.55%	-4.11%	-3.37%	-3.06%	-2.50%	-2.25%	-2.05%
Forfeiture (5%)	-29.02%	-27.95%	-26.64%	-25.92%	-25.60%	-25.05%	-24.82%	-24.41%	-24.23%	-24.08%
Forfeiture (10%)	-44.81%	-44.01%	-43.04%	-42.50%	-42.26%	-41.86%	-41.69%	-41.39%	-41.26%	-41.15%
Forfeiture (15%)	-57.08%	-56.49%	-55.77%	-55.37%	-55.19%	-54.89%	-54.77%	-54.55%	-54.45%	-54.37%
Forfeiture (20%)	-66.63%	-66.19%	-65.65%	-65.36%	-65.22%	-65.00%	-64.91%	-64.75%	-64.68%	-64.62%
Forfeiture (25%)	-74.06%	-73.72%	-73.32%	-73.10%	-73.01%	-72.84%	-72.78%	-72.66%	-72.60%	-72.56%
Forfeiture (30%)	-79.83%	-79.58%	-79.28%	-79.12%	-79.05%	-78.93%	-78.88%	-78.79%	-78.75%	-78.72%
Forfeiture (35%)	-84.32%	-84.13%	-83.91%	-83.79%	-83.73%	-83.65%	-83.61%	-83.55%	-83.52%	-83.49%
Forfeiture (40%)	-87.81%	-87.67%	-87.50%	-87.41%	-87.37%	-87.31%	-87.28%	-87.23%	-87.21%	-87.19%

MATURITY OF 7 YEARS AND VESTING OF 5 YEARS ON A $40 STOCK PRICE

Stock Price and Strike Price of $40, Maturity of 7 Years, Risk-Free Rate of 3.5%,70% Volatility, 0% Dividends, Vesting of 5 Years, Employee Suboptimal Exercise Behavior from 1.2 to 3.0, and Forfeiture Rate from 0% to 40%.
Generalized Black-Scholes: $27.51

Customized Binomial Lattice	Suboptimal (1.2)	Suboptimal (1.4)	Suboptimal (1.6)	Suboptimal (1.8)	Suboptimal (2.0)	Suboptimal (2.2)	Suboptimal (2.4)	Suboptimal (2.6)	Suboptimal (2.8)	Suboptimal (3.0)
Forfeiture (0%)	$25.11	$25.51	$25.99	$26.26	$26.38	$26.59	$26.67	$26.82	$26.89	$26.95
Forfeiture (5%)	$19.53	$19.82	$20.18	$20.38	$20.47	$20.62	$20.68	$20.79	$20.85	$20.89
Forfeiture (10%)	$15.18	$15.40	$15.67	$15.82	$15.88	$16.00	$16.04	$16.12	$16.16	$16.19
Forfeiture (15%)	$11.81	$11.97	$12.17	$12.28	$12.33	$12.41	$12.44	$12.50	$12.53	$12.55
Forfeiture (20%)	$9.18	$9.30	$9.45	$9.53	$9.57	$9.63	$9.65	$9.70	$9.72	$9.73
Forfeiture (25%)	$7.14	$7.23	$7.34	$7.40	$7.43	$7.47	$7.49	$7.52	$7.54	$7.55
Forfeiture (30%)	$5.55	$5.62	$5.70	$5.74	$5.76	$5.80	$5.81	$5.84	$5.85	$5.85
Forfeiture (35%)	$4.31	$4.37	$4.43	$4.46	$4.47	$4.50	$4.51	$4.53	$4.54	$4.54
Forfeiture (40%)	$3.35	$3.39	$3.44	$3.46	$3.47	$3.49	$3.50	$3.51	$3.52	$3.52

Percentage Difference between Binomial and Black-Scholes Model	Suboptimal (1.2)	Suboptimal (1.4)	Suboptimal (1.6)	Suboptimal (1.8)	Suboptimal (2.0)	Suboptimal (2.2)	Suboptimal (2.4)	Suboptimal (2.6)	Suboptimal (2.8)	Suboptimal (3.0)
Forfeiture (0%)	–8.71%	–7.28%	–5.53%	–4.55%	–4.11%	–3.37%	–3.06%	–2.50%	–2.25%	–2.05%
Forfeiture (5%)	–29.02%	–27.95%	–26.64%	–25.92%	–25.60%	–25.05%	–24.82%	–24.41%	–24.23%	–24.08%
Forfeiture (10%)	–44.81%	–44.01%	–43.04%	–42.50%	–42.26%	–41.86%	–41.69%	–41.39%	–41.26%	–41.15%
Forfeiture (15%)	–57.08%	–56.49%	–55.77%	–55.37%	–55.19%	–54.89%	–54.77%	–54.55%	–54.45%	–54.37%
Forfeiture (20%)	–66.63%	–66.19%	–65.65%	–65.36%	–65.22%	–65.00%	–64.91%	–64.75%	–64.68%	–64.62%
Forfeiture (25%)	–74.06%	–73.72%	–73.32%	–73.10%	–73.01%	–72.84%	–72.78%	–72.66%	–72.60%	–72.56%
Forfeiture (30%)	–79.83%	–79.58%	–79.28%	–79.12%	–79.05%	–78.93%	–78.88%	–78.79%	–78.75%	–78.72%
Forfeiture (35%)	–84.32%	–84.13%	–83.91%	–83.79%	–83.73%	–83.65%	–83.61%	–83.55%	–83.52%	–83.49%
Forfeiture (40%)	–87.81%	–87.67%	–87.50%	–87.41%	–87.37%	–87.31%	–87.28%	–87.23%	–87.21%	–87.19%

MATURITY OF 7 YEARS AND VESTING OF 5 YEARS ON A $60 STOCK PRICE

Stock Price and Strike Price of $60, Maturity of 7 Years, Risk-Free Rate of 3.5%, 70% Volatility, 0% Dividends, Vesting of 5 Years, Employee Suboptimal Exercise Behavior from 1.2 to 3.0, and Forfeiture Rate from 0% to 40%.
Generalized Black-Scholes: $41.27

Customized Binomial Lattice	Suboptimal (1.2)	Suboptimal (1.4)	Suboptimal (1.6)	Suboptimal (1.8)	Suboptimal (2.0)	Suboptimal (2.2)	Suboptimal (2.4)	Suboptimal (2.6)	Suboptimal (2.8)	Suboptimal (3.0)
Forfeiture (0%)	$37.67	$38.26	$38.99	$39.39	$39.57	$39.88	$40.00	$40.23	$40.34	$40.42
Forfeiture (5%)	$29.29	$29.73	$30.27	$30.57	$30.71	$30.93	$31.02	$31.19	$31.27	$31.33
Forfeiture (10%)	$22.78	$23.11	$23.51	$23.73	$23.83	$23.99	$24.06	$24.19	$24.24	$24.29
Forfeiture (15%)	$17.71	$17.96	$18.25	$18.42	$18.49	$18.61	$18.66	$18.76	$18.80	$18.83
Forfeiture (20%)	$13.77	$13.95	$14.18	$14.30	$14.35	$14.44	$14.48	$14.55	$14.58	$14.60
Forfeiture (25%)	$10.71	$10.84	$11.01	$11.10	$11.14	$11.21	$11.23	$11.28	$11.31	$11.32
Forfeiture (30%)	$8.32	$8.43	$8.55	$8.62	$8.65	$8.70	$8.72	$8.75	$8.77	$8.78
Forfeiture (35%)	$6.47	$6.55	$6.64	$6.69	$6.71	$6.75	$6.76	$6.79	$6.80	$6.81
Forfeiture (40%)	$5.03	$5.09	$5.16	$5.19	$5.21	$5.24	$5.25	$5.27	$5.28	$5.28

Percentage Difference between Binomial and Black-Scholes Model	Suboptimal (1.2)	Suboptimal (1.4)	Suboptimal (1.6)	Suboptimal (1.8)	Suboptimal (2.0)	Suboptimal (2.2)	Suboptimal (2.4)	Suboptimal (2.6)	Suboptimal (2.8)	Suboptimal (3.0)
Forfeiture (0%)	–8.71%	–7.28%	–5.53%	–4.55%	–4.11%	–3.37%	–3.06%	–2.50%	–2.25%	–2.05%
Forfeiture (5%)	–29.02%	–27.95%	–26.64%	–25.92%	–25.60%	–25.05%	–24.82%	–24.41%	–24.23%	–24.08%
Forfeiture (10%)	–44.81%	–44.01%	–43.04%	–42.50%	–42.26%	–41.86%	–41.69%	–41.39%	–41.26%	–41.15%
Forfeiture (15%)	–57.08%	–56.49%	–55.77%	–55.37%	–55.19%	–54.89%	–54.77%	–54.55%	–54.45%	–54.37%
Forfeiture (20%)	–66.63%	–66.19%	–65.65%	–65.36%	–65.22%	–65.00%	–64.91%	–64.75%	–64.68%	–64.62%
Forfeiture (25%)	–74.06%	–73.72%	–73.32%	–73.10%	–73.01%	–72.84%	–72.78%	–72.66%	–72.60%	–72.56%
Forfeiture (30%)	–79.83%	–79.58%	–79.28%	–79.12%	–79.05%	–78.93%	–78.88%	–78.79%	–78.75%	–78.72%
Forfeiture (35%)	–84.32%	–84.13%	–83.91%	–83.79%	–83.73%	–83.65%	–83.61%	–83.55%	–83.52%	–83.49%
Forfeiture (40%)	–87.81%	–87.67%	–87.50%	–87.41%	–87.37%	–87.31%	–87.28%	–87.23%	–87.21%	–87.19%

MATURITY OF 7 YEARS AND VESTING OF 5 YEARS ON AN $80 STOCK PRICE

Stock Price and Strike Price of $80, Maturity of 7 Years, Risk-Free Rate of 3.5%, 70% Volatility, 0% Dividends, Vesting of 5 Years, Employee Suboptimal Exercise Behavior from 1.2 to 3.0, and Forfeiture Rate from 0% to 40%.
Generalized Black-Scholes: $55.02

Customized Binomial Lattice	Suboptimal (1.2)	Suboptimal (1.4)	Suboptimal (1.6)	Suboptimal (1.8)	Suboptimal (2.0)	Suboptimal (2.2)	Suboptimal (2.4)	Suboptimal (2.6)	Suboptimal (2.8)	Suboptimal (3.0)
Forfeiture (0%)	$50.23	$51.02	$51.98	$52.52	$52.76	$53.17	$53.34	$53.65	$53.78	$53.90
Forfeiture (5%)	$39.06	$39.64	$40.36	$40.76	$40.94	$41.24	$41.36	$41.59	$41.69	$41.77
Forfeiture (10%)	$30.37	$30.81	$31.34	$31.64	$31.77	$31.99	$32.08	$32.25	$32.32	$32.38
Forfeiture (15%)	$23.61	$23.94	$24.34	$24.56	$24.66	$24.82	$24.89	$25.01	$25.06	$25.11
Forfeiture (20%)	$18.36	$18.61	$18.90	$19.06	$19.14	$19.26	$19.31	$19.40	$19.44	$19.47
Forfeiture (25%)	$14.28	$14.46	$14.68	$14.80	$14.85	$14.94	$14.98	$15.04	$15.07	$15.10
Forfeiture (30%)	$11.10	$11.24	$11.40	$11.49	$11.53	$11.60	$11.62	$11.67	$11.69	$11.71
Forfeiture (35%)	$8.63	$8.73	$8.85	$8.92	$8.95	$9.00	$9.02	$9.05	$9.07	$9.08
Forfeiture (40%)	$6.71	$6.79	$6.88	$6.93	$6.95	$6.98	$7.00	$7.02	$7.04	$7.05

Percentage Difference between Binomial and Black-Scholes Model	Suboptimal (1.2)	Suboptimal (1.4)	Suboptimal (1.6)	Suboptimal (1.8)	Suboptimal (2.0)	Suboptimal (2.2)	Suboptimal (2.4)	Suboptimal (2.6)	Suboptimal (2.8)	Suboptimal (3.0)
Forfeiture (0%)	−8.71%	−7.28%	−5.53%	−4.55%	−4.11%	−3.37%	−3.06%	−2.50%	−2.25%	−2.05%
Forfeiture (5%)	−29.02%	−27.95%	−26.64%	−25.92%	−25.60%	−25.05%	−24.82%	−24.41%	−24.23%	−24.08%
Forfeiture (10%)	−44.81%	−44.01%	−43.04%	−42.50%	−42.26%	−41.86%	−41.69%	−41.39%	−41.26%	−41.15%
Forfeiture (15%)	−57.08%	−56.49%	−55.77%	−55.37%	−55.19%	−54.89%	−54.77%	−54.55%	−54.45%	−54.37%
Forfeiture (20%)	−66.63%	−66.19%	−65.65%	−65.36%	−65.22%	−65.00%	−64.91%	−64.75%	−64.68%	−64.62%
Forfeiture (25%)	−74.06%	−73.72%	−73.32%	−73.10%	−73.01%	−72.84%	−72.78%	−72.66%	−72.60%	−72.56%
Forfeiture (30%)	−79.83%	−79.58%	−79.28%	−79.12%	−79.05%	−78.93%	−78.88%	−78.79%	−78.75%	−78.72%
Forfeiture (35%)	−84.32%	−84.13%	−83.91%	−83.79%	−83.73%	−83.65%	−83.61%	−83.55%	−83.52%	−83.49%
Forfeiture (40%)	−87.81%	−87.67%	−87.50%	−87.41%	−87.37%	−87.31%	−87.28%	−87.23%	−87.21%	−87.19%

THIRTY-FIVE PERCENT VOLATILITY AND 10-YEAR MATURITY ESOs WITH VARYING STOCK PRICE, SUBOPTIMAL BEHAVIOR, VESTING PERIOD, AND FORFEITURE RATES

This section provides ESO valuation results on an underlying stock with 35 percent volatility and a 10-year maturity. The analysis is divided into 1-month, 1-year, 3-year, 4-year, 5-year, and 7-year vesting periods, and accounts for stock prices at grant date of $20, $40, $60, and $80.

MATURITY OF 10 YEARS AND VESTING OF 1 MONTH ON A $20 STOCK PRICE

Stock Price and Strike Price of $20, Maturity of 10 Years, Risk-Free Rate of 3.5%, 35% Volatility, 0% Dividends, Vesting of 1 Month, Employee Suboptimal Exercise Behavior from 1.2 to 3.0, and Forfeiture Rate from 0% to 40%.
Generalized Black-Scholes: $10.43

Customized Binomial Lattice	Suboptimal (1.2)	Suboptimal (1.4)	Suboptimal (1.6)	Suboptimal (1.8)	Suboptimal (2.0)	Suboptimal (2.2)	Suboptimal (2.4)	Suboptimal (2.6)	Suboptimal (2.8)	Suboptimal (3.0)
Forfeiture (0%)	$3.63	$5.42	$6.81	$7.62	$8.27	$8.78	$9.17	$9.38	$9.55	$9.70
Forfeiture (5%)	$3.44	$5.00	$6.15	$6.80	$7.30	$7.69	$7.98	$8.14	$8.27	$8.37
Forfeiture (10%)	$3.27	$4.65	$5.62	$6.14	$6.54	$6.84	$7.06	$7.18	$7.28	$7.35
Forfeiture (15%)	$3.13	$4.36	$5.19	$5.62	$5.93	$6.17	$6.34	$6.43	$6.50	$6.56
Forfeiture (20%)	$3.01	$4.12	$4.83	$5.18	$5.44	$5.63	$5.76	$5.83	$5.89	$5.93
Forfeiture (25%)	$2.91	$3.91	$4.52	$4.83	$5.04	$5.19	$5.29	$5.35	$5.39	$5.42
Forfeiture (30%)	$2.82	$3.73	$4.27	$4.52	$4.70	$4.82	$4.90	$4.95	$4.98	$5.01
Forfeiture (35%)	$2.73	$3.57	$4.04	$4.26	$4.41	$4.51	$4.58	$4.61	$4.64	$4.66
Forfeiture (40%)	$2.65	$3.42	$3.85	$4.04	$4.16	$4.25	$4.30	$4.33	$4.35	$4.37

Percentage Difference between Binomial and Black-Scholes Model	Suboptimal (1.2)	Suboptimal (1.4)	Suboptimal (1.6)	Suboptimal (1.8)	Suboptimal (2.0)	Suboptimal (2.2)	Suboptimal (2.4)	Suboptimal (2.6)	Suboptimal (2.8)	Suboptimal (3.0)
Forfeiture (0%)	-65.21%	-48.03%	-34.68%	-26.89%	-20.70%	-15.85%	-12.09%	-10.07%	-8.39%	-6.98%
Forfeiture (5%)	-67.06%	-52.10%	-41.04%	-34.81%	-30.00%	-26.29%	-23.47%	-21.98%	-20.75%	-19.72%
Forfeiture (10%)	-68.62%	-55.42%	-46.13%	-41.09%	-37.28%	-34.42%	-32.28%	-31.16%	-30.24%	-29.48%
Forfeiture (15%)	-69.94%	-58.19%	-50.28%	-46.14%	-43.10%	-40.86%	-39.21%	-38.36%	-37.66%	-37.10%
Forfeiture (20%)	-71.09%	-60.52%	-53.73%	-50.29%	-47.82%	-46.04%	-44.75%	-44.10%	-43.57%	-43.14%
Forfeiture (25%)	-72.10%	-62.53%	-56.62%	-53.73%	-51.71%	-50.27%	-49.26%	-48.75%	-48.34%	-48.01%
Forfeiture (30%)	-73.00%	-64.27%	-59.10%	-56.64%	-54.96%	-53.80%	-52.98%	-52.58%	-52.26%	-52.01%
Forfeiture (35%)	-73.81%	-65.80%	-61.23%	-59.13%	-57.72%	-56.76%	-56.11%	-55.79%	-55.53%	-55.33%
Forfeiture (40%)	-74.54%	-67.17%	-63.10%	-61.28%	-60.09%	-59.30%	-58.76%	-58.50%	-58.30%	-58.14%

MATURITY OF 10 YEARS AND VESTING OF 1 MONTH ON A $40 STOCK PRICE

Stock Price and Strike Price of $40, Maturity of 10 Years, Risk-Free Rate of 3.5%, 35% Volatility, 0% Dividends, Vesting of 1 Month, Employee Suboptimal Exercise Behavior from 1.2 to 3.0, and Forfeiture Rate from 0% to 40%.
Generalized Black-Scholes: $20.86

Customized Binomial Lattice	Suboptimal (1.2)	Suboptimal (1.4)	Suboptimal (1.6)	Suboptimal (1.8)	Suboptimal (2.0)	Suboptimal (2.2)	Suboptimal (2.4)	Suboptimal (2.6)	Suboptimal (2.8)	Suboptimal (3.0)
Forfeiture (0%)	$7.26	$10.84	$13.62	$15.25	$16.54	$17.55	$18.34	$18.76	$19.11	$19.40
Forfeiture (5%)	$6.87	$9.99	$12.30	$13.60	$14.60	$15.37	$15.96	$16.27	$16.53	$16.74
Forfeiture (10%)	$6.55	$9.30	$11.24	$12.29	$13.08	$13.68	$14.13	$14.36	$14.55	$14.71
Forfeiture (15%)	$6.27	$8.72	$10.37	$11.23	$11.87	$12.34	$12.68	$12.86	$13.00	$13.12
Forfeiture (20%)	$6.03	$8.23	$9.65	$10.37	$10.88	$11.26	$11.52	$11.66	$11.77	$11.86
Forfeiture (25%)	$5.82	$7.82	$9.05	$9.65	$10.07	$10.37	$10.58	$10.69	$10.78	$10.84
Forfeiture (30%)	$5.63	$7.45	$8.53	$9.04	$9.39	$9.64	$9.81	$9.89	$9.96	$10.01
Forfeiture (35%)	$5.46	$7.13	$8.09	$8.52	$8.82	$9.02	$9.16	$9.22	$9.27	$9.32
Forfeiture (40%)	$5.31	$6.85	$7.70	$8.08	$8.32	$8.49	$8.60	$8.66	$8.70	$8.73

Percentage Difference between Binomial and Black-Scholes Model	Suboptimal (1.2)	Suboptimal (1.4)	Suboptimal (1.6)	Suboptimal (1.8)	Suboptimal (2.0)	Suboptimal (2.2)	Suboptimal (2.4)	Suboptimal (2.6)	Suboptimal (2.8)	Suboptimal (3.0)
Forfeiture (0%)	−65.21%	−48.03%	−34.68%	−26.89%	−20.70%	−15.85%	−12.09%	−10.07%	−8.39%	−6.98%
Forfeiture (5%)	−67.06%	−52.10%	−41.04%	−34.81%	−30.00%	−26.29%	−23.47%	−21.98%	−20.75%	−19.72%
Forfeiture (10%)	−68.62%	−55.42%	−46.13%	−41.09%	−37.28%	−34.42%	−32.28%	−31.16%	−30.24%	−29.48%
Forfeiture (15%)	−69.94%	−58.19%	−50.28%	−46.14%	−43.10%	−40.86%	−39.21%	−38.36%	−37.66%	−37.10%
Forfeiture (20%)	−71.09%	−60.52%	−53.73%	−50.29%	−47.82%	−46.04%	−44.75%	−44.10%	−43.57%	−43.14%
Forfeiture (25%)	−72.10%	−62.53%	−56.62%	−53.73%	−51.71%	−50.27%	−49.26%	−48.75%	−48.34%	−48.01%
Forfeiture (30%)	−73.00%	−64.27%	−59.10%	−56.64%	−54.96%	−53.80%	−52.98%	−52.58%	−52.26%	−52.01%
Forfeiture (35%)	−73.81%	−65.80%	−61.23%	−59.13%	−57.72%	−56.76%	−56.11%	−55.79%	−55.53%	−55.33%
Forfeiture (40%)	−74.54%	−67.17%	−63.10%	−61.28%	−60.09%	−59.30%	−58.76%	−58.50%	−58.30%	−58.14%

MATURITY OF 10 YEARS AND VESTING OF 1 MONTH ON A $60 STOCK PRICE

Stock Price and Strike Price of $60, Maturity of 10 Years, Risk-Free Rate of 3.5%, 35% Volatility, 0% Dividends, Vesting of 1 Month, Employee Suboptimal Exercise Behavior from 1.2 to 3.0, and Forfeiture Rate from 0% to 40%.
Generalized Black-Scholes: $31.29

Customized Binomial Lattice	Suboptimal (1.2)	Suboptimal (1.4)	Suboptimal (1.6)	Suboptimal (1.8)	Suboptimal (2.0)	Suboptimal (2.2)	Suboptimal (2.4)	Suboptimal (2.6)	Suboptimal (2.8)	Suboptimal (3.0)
Forfeiture (0%)	$10.88	$16.26	$20.44	$22.87	$24.81	$26.33	$27.51	$28.14	$28.66	$29.10
Forfeiture (5%)	$10.31	$14.99	$18.45	$20.40	$21.90	$23.06	$23.94	$24.41	$24.80	$25.12
Forfeiture (10%)	$9.82	$13.95	$16.85	$18.43	$19.62	$20.52	$21.19	$21.54	$21.83	$22.06
Forfeiture (15%)	$9.40	$13.08	$15.56	$16.85	$17.80	$18.50	$19.02	$19.29	$19.50	$19.68
Forfeiture (20%)	$9.04	$12.35	$14.48	$15.55	$16.33	$16.88	$17.29	$17.49	$17.66	$17.79
Forfeiture (25%)	$8.73	$11.72	$13.57	$14.48	$15.11	$15.56	$15.88	$16.04	$16.16	$16.27
Forfeiture (30%)	$8.45	$11.18	$12.80	$13.57	$14.09	$14.46	$14.71	$14.84	$14.94	$15.02
Forfeiture (35%)	$8.19	$10.70	$12.13	$12.79	$13.23	$13.53	$13.73	$13.83	$13.91	$13.97
Forfeiture (40%)	$7.96	$10.27	$11.54	$12.11	$12.49	$12.74	$12.90	$12.98	$13.05	$13.10

Percentage Difference between Binomial and Black-Scholes Model	Suboptimal (1.2)	Suboptimal (1.4)	Suboptimal (1.6)	Suboptimal (1.8)	Suboptimal (2.0)	Suboptimal (2.2)	Suboptimal (2.4)	Suboptimal (2.6)	Suboptimal (2.8)	Suboptimal (3.0)
Forfeiture (0%)	–65.21%	–48.03%	–34.68%	–26.89%	–20.70%	–15.85%	–12.09%	–10.07%	–8.39%	–6.98%
Forfeiture (5%)	–67.06%	–52.10%	–41.04%	–34.81%	–30.00%	–26.29%	–23.47%	–21.98%	–20.75%	–19.72%
Forfeiture (10%)	–68.62%	–55.42%	–46.13%	–41.09%	–37.28%	–34.42%	–32.28%	–31.16%	–30.24%	–29.48%
Forfeiture (15%)	–69.94%	–58.19%	–50.28%	–46.14%	–43.10%	–40.86%	–39.21%	–38.36%	–37.66%	–37.10%
Forfeiture (20%)	–71.09%	–60.52%	–53.73%	–50.29%	–47.82%	–46.04%	–44.75%	–44.10%	–43.57%	–43.14%
Forfeiture (25%)	–72.10%	–62.53%	–56.62%	–53.73%	–51.71%	–50.27%	–49.26%	–48.75%	–48.34%	–48.01%
Forfeiture (30%)	–73.00%	–64.27%	–59.10%	–56.64%	–54.96%	–53.80%	–52.98%	–52.58%	–52.26%	–52.01%
Forfeiture (35%)	–73.81%	–65.80%	–61.23%	–59.13%	–57.72%	–56.76%	–56.11%	–55.79%	–55.53%	–55.33%
Forfeiture (40%)	–74.54%	–67.17%	–63.10%	–61.28%	–60.09%	–59.30%	–58.76%	–58.50%	–58.30%	–58.14%

MATURITY OF 10 YEARS AND VESTING OF 1 MONTH ON AN $80 STOCK PRICE

Stock Price and Strike Price of $80, Maturity of 10 Years, Risk-Free Rate of 3.5%, 35% Volatility, 0% Dividends, Vesting of 1 Month, Employee Suboptimal Exercise Behavior from 1.2 to 3.0, and Forfeiture Rate from 0% to 40%.
Generalized Black-Scholes: $41.72

Customized Binomial Lattice	Suboptimal (1.2)	Suboptimal (1.4)	Suboptimal (1.6)	Suboptimal (1.8)	Suboptimal (2.0)	Suboptimal (2.2)	Suboptimal (2.4)	Suboptimal (2.6)	Suboptimal (2.8)	Suboptimal (3.0)
Forfeiture (0%)	$14.51	$21.68	$27.25	$30.50	$33.08	$35.10	$36.67	$37.51	$38.22	$38.80
Forfeiture (5%)	$13.74	$19.98	$24.60	$27.19	$29.20	$30.75	$31.92	$32.55	$33.06	$33.49
Forfeiture (10%)	$13.09	$18.60	$22.47	$24.58	$26.16	$27.36	$28.25	$28.72	$29.10	$29.42
Forfeiture (15%)	$12.54	$17.44	$20.74	$22.47	$23.74	$24.67	$25.36	$25.72	$26.00	$26.24
Forfeiture (20%)	$12.06	$16.47	$19.30	$20.74	$21.77	$22.51	$23.05	$23.32	$23.54	$23.72
Forfeiture (25%)	$11.64	$15.63	$18.10	$19.30	$20.15	$20.74	$21.17	$21.38	$21.55	$21.69
Forfeiture (30%)	$11.26	$14.90	$17.06	$18.09	$18.79	$19.27	$19.61	$19.78	$19.91	$20.02
Forfeiture (35%)	$10.93	$14.27	$16.17	$17.05	$17.64	$18.04	$18.31	$18.44	$18.55	$18.63
Forfeiture (40%)	$10.62	$13.70	$15.39	$16.15	$16.65	$16.98	$17.20	$17.31	$17.40	$17.46

Percentage Difference between Binomial and Black-Scholes Model	Suboptimal (1.2)	Suboptimal (1.4)	Suboptimal (1.6)	Suboptimal (1.8)	Suboptimal (2.0)	Suboptimal (2.2)	Suboptimal (2.4)	Suboptimal (2.6)	Suboptimal (2.8)	Suboptimal (3.0)
Forfeiture (0%)	–65.21%	–48.03%	–34.68%	–26.89%	–20.70%	–15.85%	–12.09%	–10.07%	–8.39%	–6.98%
Forfeiture (5%)	–67.06%	–52.10%	–41.04%	–34.81%	–30.00%	–26.29%	–23.47%	–21.98%	–20.75%	–19.72%
Forfeiture (10%)	–68.62%	–55.42%	–46.13%	–41.09%	–37.28%	–34.42%	–32.28%	–31.16%	–30.24%	–29.48%
Forfeiture (15%)	–69.94%	–58.19%	–50.28%	–46.14%	–43.10%	–40.86%	–39.21%	–38.36%	–37.66%	–37.10%
Forfeiture (20%)	–71.09%	–60.52%	–53.73%	–50.29%	–47.82%	–46.04%	–44.75%	–44.10%	–43.57%	–43.14%
Forfeiture (25%)	–72.10%	–62.53%	–56.62%	–53.73%	–51.71%	–50.27%	–49.26%	–48.75%	–48.34%	–48.01%
Forfeiture (30%)	–73.00%	–64.27%	–59.10%	–56.64%	–54.96%	–53.80%	–52.98%	–52.58%	–52.26%	–52.01%
Forfeiture (35%)	–73.81%	–65.80%	–61.23%	–59.13%	–57.72%	–56.76%	–56.11%	–55.79%	–55.53%	–55.33%
Forfeiture (40%)	–74.54%	–67.17%	–63.10%	–61.28%	–60.09%	–59.30%	–58.76%	–58.50%	–58.30%	–58.14%

MATURITY OF 10 YEARS AND VESTING OF 1 YEAR ON A $20 STOCK PRICE

Stock Price and Strike Price of $20, Maturity of 10 Years, Risk-Free Rate of 3.5%, 35% Volatility, 0% Dividends, Vesting of 1 Year, Employee Suboptimal Exercise Behavior from 1.2 to 3.0, and Forfeiture Rate from 0% to 40%.
Generalized Black-Scholes: $10.43

Customized Binomial Lattice	Suboptimal (1.2)	Suboptimal (1.4)	Suboptimal (1.6)	Suboptimal (1.8)	Suboptimal (2.0)	Suboptimal (2.2)	Suboptimal (2.4)	Suboptimal (2.6)	Suboptimal (2.8)	Suboptimal (3.0)
Forfeiture (0%)	$4.77	$5.94	$7.02	$7.73	$8.31	$8.79	$9.17	$9.38	$9.56	$9.70
Forfeiture (5%)	$4.40	$5.37	$6.24	$6.79	$7.24	$7.61	$7.89	$8.04	$8.17	$8.28
Forfeiture (10%)	$4.07	$4.89	$5.60	$6.04	$6.39	$6.67	$6.88	$7.00	$7.09	$7.17
Forfeiture (15%)	$3.79	$4.48	$5.06	$5.42	$5.69	$5.91	$6.08	$6.16	$6.23	$6.29
Forfeiture (20%)	$3.53	$4.13	$4.61	$4.90	$5.12	$5.29	$5.42	$5.49	$5.54	$5.58
Forfeiture (25%)	$3.30	$3.82	$4.22	$4.46	$4.64	$4.77	$4.88	$4.93	$4.97	$5.00
Forfeiture (30%)	$3.10	$3.54	$3.88	$4.08	$4.23	$4.34	$4.42	$4.46	$4.49	$4.52
Forfeiture (35%)	$2.90	$3.29	$3.59	$3.75	$3.87	$3.96	$4.03	$4.06	$4.08	$4.11
Forfeiture (40%)	$2.73	$3.07	$3.32	$3.46	$3.56	$3.64	$3.69	$3.72	$3.74	$3.75

Percentage Difference between Binomial and Black-Scholes Model	Suboptimal (1.2)	Suboptimal (1.4)	Suboptimal (1.6)	Suboptimal (1.8)	Suboptimal (2.0)	Suboptimal (2.2)	Suboptimal (2.4)	Suboptimal (2.6)	Suboptimal (2.8)	Suboptimal (3.0)
Forfeiture (0%)	–54.26%	–43.00%	–32.65%	–25.93%	–20.30%	–15.68%	–12.03%	–10.05%	–8.38%	–6.98%
Forfeiture (5%)	–57.83%	–48.49%	–40.17%	–34.89%	–30.56%	–27.06%	–24.33%	–22.87%	–21.64%	–20.62%
Forfeiture (10%)	–60.94%	–53.09%	–46.32%	–42.13%	–38.75%	–36.06%	–34.00%	–32.90%	–31.99%	–31.24%
Forfeiture (15%)	–63.68%	–57.02%	–51.45%	–48.07%	–45.40%	–43.31%	–41.73%	–40.90%	–40.22%	–39.66%
Forfeiture (20%)	–66.12%	–60.43%	–55.79%	–53.04%	–50.90%	–49.26%	–48.03%	–47.40%	–46.88%	–46.45%
Forfeiture (25%)	–68.32%	–63.41%	–59.51%	–57.25%	–55.53%	–54.22%	–53.25%	–52.76%	–52.36%	–52.03%
Forfeiture (30%)	–70.32%	–66.05%	–62.75%	–60.87%	–59.46%	–58.41%	–57.64%	–57.25%	–56.94%	–56.69%
Forfeiture (35%)	–72.15%	–68.42%	–65.60%	–64.02%	–62.86%	–62.00%	–61.39%	–61.08%	–60.83%	–60.63%
Forfeiture (40%)	–73.83%	–70.55%	–68.12%	–66.79%	–65.83%	–65.12%	–64.62%	–64.37%	–64.18%	–64.02%

MATURITY OF 10 YEARS AND VESTING OF 1 YEAR ON A $40 STOCK PRICE

Stock Price and Strike Price of $40, Maturity of 10 Years, Risk-Free Rate of 3.5%, 35% Volatility, 0% Dividends, Vesting of 1 Year, Employee Suboptimal Exercise Behavior from 1.2 to 3.0, and Forfeiture Rate from 0% to 40%.
Generalized Black-Scholes: $20.86

Customized Binomial Lattice	Suboptimal (1.2)	Suboptimal (1.4)	Suboptimal (1.6)	Suboptimal (1.8)	Suboptimal (2.0)	Suboptimal (2.2)	Suboptimal (2.4)	Suboptimal (2.6)	Suboptimal (2.8)	Suboptimal (3.0)
Forfeiture (0%)	$9.54	$11.89	$14.05	$15.45	$16.62	$17.59	$18.35	$18.76	$19.11	$19.40
Forfeiture (5%)	$8.80	$10.74	$12.48	$13.58	$14.48	$15.21	$15.78	$16.09	$16.34	$16.56
Forfeiture (10%)	$8.15	$9.78	$11.20	$12.07	$12.78	$13.34	$13.77	$14.00	$14.19	$14.34
Forfeiture (15%)	$7.58	$8.96	$10.13	$10.83	$11.39	$11.82	$12.15	$12.33	$12.47	$12.59
Forfeiture (20%)	$7.07	$8.25	$9.22	$9.80	$10.24	$10.58	$10.84	$10.97	$11.08	$11.17
Forfeiture (25%)	$6.61	$7.63	$8.45	$8.92	$9.28	$9.55	$9.75	$9.85	$9.94	$10.01
Forfeiture (30%)	$6.19	$7.08	$7.77	$8.16	$8.46	$8.68	$8.83	$8.92	$8.98	$9.03
Forfeiture (35%)	$5.81	$6.59	$7.18	$7.50	$7.75	$7.93	$8.05	$8.12	$8.17	$8.21
Forfeiture (40%)	$5.46	$6.14	$6.65	$6.93	$7.13	$7.27	$7.38	$7.43	$7.47	$7.50

Percentage Difference between Binomial and Black-Scholes Model	Suboptimal (1.2)	Suboptimal (1.4)	Suboptimal (1.6)	Suboptimal (1.8)	Suboptimal (2.0)	Suboptimal (2.2)	Suboptimal (2.4)	Suboptimal (2.6)	Suboptimal (2.8)	Suboptimal (3.0)
Forfeiture (0%)	–54.26%	–43.00%	–32.65%	–25.93%	–20.30%	–15.68%	–12.03%	–10.05%	–8.38%	–6.98%
Forfeiture (5%)	–57.83%	–48.49%	–40.17%	–34.89%	–30.56%	–27.06%	–24.33%	–22.87%	–21.64%	–20.62%
Forfeiture (10%)	–60.94%	–53.09%	–46.32%	–42.13%	–38.75%	–36.06%	–34.00%	–32.90%	–31.99%	–31.24%
Forfeiture (15%)	–63.68%	–57.02%	–51.45%	–48.07%	–45.40%	–43.31%	–41.73%	–40.90%	–40.22%	–39.66%
Forfeiture (20%)	–66.12%	–60.43%	–55.79%	–53.04%	–50.90%	–49.26%	–48.03%	–47.40%	–46.88%	–46.45%
Forfeiture (25%)	–68.32%	–63.41%	–59.51%	–57.25%	–55.53%	–54.22%	–53.25%	–52.76%	–52.36%	–52.03%
Forfeiture (30%)	–70.32%	–66.05%	–62.75%	–60.87%	–59.46%	–58.41%	–57.64%	–57.25%	–56.94%	–56.69%
Forfeiture (35%)	–72.15%	–68.42%	–65.60%	–64.02%	–62.86%	–62.00%	–61.39%	–61.08%	–60.83%	–60.63%
Forfeiture (40%)	–73.83%	–70.55%	–68.12%	–66.79%	–65.83%	–65.12%	–64.62%	–64.37%	–64.18%	–64.02%

MATURITY OF 10 YEARS AND VESTING OF 1 YEAR ON A $60 STOCK PRICE

Stock Price and Strike Price of $60, Maturity of 10 Years, Risk-Free Rate of 3.5%, 35% Volatility, 0% Dividends, Vesting of 1 Year, Employee Suboptimal Exercise Behavior from 1.2 to 3.0, and Forfeiture Rate from 0% to 40%.
Generalized Black-Scholes: $31.29

Customized Binomial Lattice	Suboptimal (1.2)	Suboptimal (1.4)	Suboptimal (1.6)	Suboptimal (1.8)	Suboptimal (2.0)	Suboptimal (2.2)	Suboptimal (2.4)	Suboptimal (2.6)	Suboptimal (2.8)	Suboptimal (3.0)
Forfeiture (0%)	$14.31	$17.83	$21.07	$23.18	$24.94	$26.38	$27.52	$28.14	$28.67	$29.10
Forfeiture (5%)	$13.19	$16.12	$18.72	$20.37	$21.73	$22.82	$23.67	$24.13	$24.52	$24.83
Forfeiture (10%)	$12.22	$14.68	$16.79	$18.11	$19.16	$20.00	$20.65	$20.99	$21.28	$21.51
Forfeiture (15%)	$11.36	$13.45	$15.19	$16.25	$17.08	$17.74	$18.23	$18.49	$18.70	$18.88
Forfeiture (20%)	$10.60	$12.38	$13.83	$14.69	$15.36	$15.88	$16.26	$16.46	$16.62	$16.75
Forfeiture (25%)	$9.91	$11.45	$12.67	$13.38	$13.91	$14.32	$14.63	$14.78	$14.91	$15.01
Forfeiture (30%)	$9.29	$10.62	$11.65	$12.24	$12.68	$13.01	$13.25	$13.37	$13.47	$13.55
Forfeiture (35%)	$8.71	$9.88	$10.76	$11.26	$11.62	$11.89	$12.08	$12.18	$12.25	$12.32
Forfeiture (40%)	$8.19	$9.22	$9.97	$10.39	$10.69	$10.91	$11.07	$11.15	$11.21	$11.26

Percentage Difference between Binomial and Black-Scholes Model	Suboptimal (1.2)	Suboptimal (1.4)	Suboptimal (1.6)	Suboptimal (1.8)	Suboptimal (2.0)	Suboptimal (2.2)	Suboptimal (2.4)	Suboptimal (2.6)	Suboptimal (2.8)	Suboptimal (3.0)
Forfeiture (0%)	–54.26%	–43.00%	–32.65%	–25.93%	–20.30%	–15.68%	–12.03%	–10.05%	–8.38%	–6.98%
Forfeiture (5%)	–57.83%	–48.49%	–40.17%	–34.89%	–30.56%	–27.06%	–24.33%	–22.87%	–21.64%	–20.62%
Forfeiture (10%)	–60.94%	–53.09%	–46.32%	–42.13%	–38.75%	–36.06%	–34.00%	–32.90%	–31.99%	–31.24%
Forfeiture (15%)	–63.68%	–57.02%	–51.45%	–48.07%	–45.40%	–43.31%	–41.73%	–40.90%	–40.22%	–39.66%
Forfeiture (20%)	–66.12%	–60.43%	–55.79%	–53.04%	–50.90%	–49.26%	–48.03%	–47.40%	–46.88%	–46.45%
Forfeiture (25%)	–68.32%	–63.41%	–59.51%	–57.25%	–55.53%	–54.22%	–53.25%	–52.76%	–52.36%	–52.03%
Forfeiture (30%)	–70.32%	–66.05%	–62.75%	–60.87%	–59.46%	–58.41%	–57.64%	–57.25%	–56.94%	–56.69%
Forfeiture (35%)	–72.15%	–68.42%	–65.60%	–64.02%	–62.86%	–62.00%	–61.39%	–61.08%	–60.83%	–60.63%
Forfeiture (40%)	–73.83%	–70.55%	–68.12%	–66.79%	–65.83%	–65.12%	–64.62%	–64.37%	–64.18%	–64.02%

MATURITY OF 10 YEARS AND VESTING OF 1 YEAR ON AN $80 STOCK PRICE

Stock Price and Strike Price of $80, Maturity of 10 Years, Risk-Free Rate of 3.5%, 35% Volatility, 0% Dividends, Vesting of 1 Year, Employee Suboptimal Exercise Behavior from 1.2 to 3.0, and Forfeiture Rate from 0% to 40%.
Generalized Black-Scholes: $41.72

Customized Binomial Lattice	Suboptimal (1.2)	Suboptimal (1.4)	Suboptimal (1.6)	Suboptimal (1.8)	Suboptimal (2.0)	Suboptimal (2.2)	Suboptimal (2.4)	Suboptimal (2.6)	Suboptimal (2.8)	Suboptimal (3.0)
Forfeiture (0%)	$19.08	$23.78	$28.09	$30.90	$33.25	$35.17	$36.70	$37.53	$38.22	$38.81
Forfeiture (5%)	$17.59	$21.49	$24.96	$27.16	$28.97	$30.43	$31.57	$32.18	$32.69	$33.11
Forfeiture (10%)	$16.29	$19.57	$22.39	$24.14	$25.55	$26.67	$27.53	$27.99	$28.37	$28.68
Forfeiture (15%)	$15.15	$17.93	$20.25	$21.66	$22.78	$23.65	$24.31	$24.65	$24.94	$25.17
Forfeiture (20%)	$14.13	$16.51	$18.44	$19.59	$20.48	$21.17	$21.68	$21.94	$22.16	$22.34
Forfeiture (25%)	$13.21	$15.26	$16.89	$17.83	$18.55	$19.10	$19.50	$19.71	$19.88	$20.01
Forfeiture (30%)	$12.38	$14.16	$15.54	$16.32	$16.91	$17.35	$17.67	$17.83	$17.96	$18.07
Forfeiture (35%)	$11.62	$13.18	$14.35	$15.01	$15.49	$15.85	$16.11	$16.24	$16.34	$16.42
Forfeiture (40%)	$10.92	$12.29	$13.30	$13.85	$14.26	$14.55	$14.76	$14.86	$14.94	$15.01

Percentage Difference between Binomial and Black-Scholes Model	Suboptimal (1.2)	Suboptimal (1.4)	Suboptimal (1.6)	Suboptimal (1.8)	Suboptimal (2.0)	Suboptimal (2.2)	Suboptimal (2.4)	Suboptimal (2.6)	Suboptimal (2.8)	Suboptimal (3.0)
Forfeiture (0%)	–54.26%	–43.00%	–32.65%	–25.93%	–20.30%	–15.68%	–12.03%	–10.05%	–8.38%	–6.98%
Forfeiture (5%)	–57.83%	–48.49%	–40.17%	–34.89%	–30.56%	–27.06%	–24.33%	–22.87%	–21.64%	–20.62%
Forfeiture (10%)	–60.94%	–53.09%	–46.32%	–42.13%	–38.75%	–36.06%	–34.00%	–32.90%	–31.99%	–31.24%
Forfeiture (15%)	–63.68%	–57.02%	–51.45%	–48.07%	–45.40%	–43.31%	–41.73%	–40.90%	–40.22%	–39.66%
Forfeiture (20%)	–66.12%	–60.43%	–55.79%	–53.04%	–50.90%	–49.26%	–48.03%	–47.40%	–46.88%	–46.45%
Forfeiture (25%)	–68.32%	–63.41%	–59.51%	–57.25%	–55.53%	–54.22%	–53.25%	–52.76%	–52.36%	–52.03%
Forfeiture (30%)	–70.32%	–66.05%	–62.75%	–60.87%	–59.46%	–58.41%	–57.64%	–57.25%	–56.94%	–56.69%
Forfeiture (35%)	–72.15%	–68.42%	–65.60%	–64.02%	–62.86%	–62.00%	–61.39%	–61.08%	–60.83%	–60.63%
Forfeiture (40%)	–73.83%	–70.55%	–68.12%	–66.79%	–65.83%	–65.12%	–64.62%	–64.37%	–64.18%	–64.02%

MATURITY OF 10 YEARS AND VESTING OF 3 YEARS ON A $20 STOCK PRICE

Stock Price and Strike Price of $20, Maturity of 10 Years, Risk-Free Rate of 3.5%, 35% Volatility, 0% Dividends, Vesting of 3 Years, Employee Suboptimal Exercise Behavior from 1.2 to 3.0, and Forfeiture Rate from 0% to 40%.
Generalized Black-Scholes: $10.43

Customized Binomial Lattice	Suboptimal (1.2)	Suboptimal (1.4)	Suboptimal (1.6)	Suboptimal (1.8)	Suboptimal (2.0)	Suboptimal (2.2)	Suboptimal (2.4)	Suboptimal (2.6)	Suboptimal (2.8)	Suboptimal (3.0)
Forfeiture (0%)	$6.70	$7.40	$8.04	$8.46	$8.82	$9.13	$9.39	$9.54	$9.67	$9.78
Forfeiture (5%)	$5.68	$6.21	$6.68	$6.99	$7.26	$7.48	$7.67	$7.77	$7.86	$7.94
Forfeiture (10%)	$4.83	$5.23	$5.59	$5.81	$6.01	$6.17	$6.30	$6.38	$6.45	$6.50
Forfeiture (15%)	$4.11	$4.42	$4.69	$4.86	$5.00	$5.12	$5.22	$5.27	$5.32	$5.36
Forfeiture (20%)	$3.50	$3.74	$3.95	$4.07	$4.18	$4.27	$4.34	$4.38	$4.41	$4.44
Forfeiture (25%)	$2.99	$3.18	$3.33	$3.43	$3.51	$3.57	$3.63	$3.66	$3.68	$3.70
Forfeiture (30%)	$2.55	$2.70	$2.82	$2.89	$2.95	$3.00	$3.04	$3.06	$3.08	$3.10
Forfeiture (35%)	$2.18	$2.30	$2.39	$2.45	$2.49	$2.53	$2.56	$2.58	$2.59	$2.60
Forfeiture (40%)	$1.87	$1.96	$2.03	$2.08	$2.11	$2.14	$2.16	$2.17	$2.18	$2.19

Percentage Difference between Binomial and Black-Scholes Model	Suboptimal (1.2)	Suboptimal (1.4)	Suboptimal (1.6)	Suboptimal (1.8)	Suboptimal (2.0)	Suboptimal (2.2)	Suboptimal (2.4)	Suboptimal (2.6)	Suboptimal (2.8)	Suboptimal (3.0)
Forfeiture (0%)	–35.76%	–29.03%	–22.95%	–18.91%	–15.43%	–12.42%	–9.93%	–8.51%	–7.26%	–6.18%
Forfeiture (5%)	–45.54%	–40.43%	–35.91%	–32.95%	–30.44%	–28.27%	–26.49%	–25.47%	–24.59%	–23.83%
Forfeiture (10%)	–53.73%	–49.82%	–46.44%	–44.25%	–42.41%	–40.84%	–39.56%	–38.83%	–38.20%	–37.65%
Forfeiture (15%)	–60.62%	–57.61%	–55.05%	–53.42%	–52.07%	–50.92%	–49.98%	–49.46%	–49.00%	–48.61%
Forfeiture (20%)	–66.43%	–64.10%	–62.16%	–60.93%	–59.92%	–59.07%	–58.39%	–58.01%	–57.67%	–57.39%
Forfeiture (25%)	–71.36%	–69.53%	–68.04%	–67.12%	–66.36%	–65.73%	–65.23%	–64.94%	–64.70%	–64.49%
Forfeiture (30%)	–75.53%	–74.10%	–72.95%	–72.25%	–71.68%	–71.21%	–70.83%	–70.62%	–70.44%	–70.28%
Forfeiture (35%)	–79.09%	–77.96%	–77.07%	–76.52%	–76.09%	–75.73%	–75.45%	–75.29%	–75.16%	–75.04%
Forfeiture (40%)	–82.11%	–81.21%	–80.52%	–80.10%	–79.77%	–79.50%	–79.29%	–79.17%	–79.07%	–78.98%

MATURITY OF 10 YEARS AND VESTING OF 3 YEARS ON A $40 STOCK PRICE

Stock Price and Strike Price of $40, Maturity of 10 Years, Risk-Free Rate of 3.5%, 35% Volatility, 0% Dividends, Vesting of 3 Years, Employee Suboptimal Exercise Behavior from 1.2 to 3.0, and Forfeiture Rate from 0% to 40%.
Generalized Black-Scholes: $20.86

Customized Binomial Lattice	Suboptimal (1.2)	Suboptimal (1.4)	Suboptimal (1.6)	Suboptimal (1.8)	Suboptimal (2.0)	Suboptimal (2.2)	Suboptimal (2.4)	Suboptimal (2.6)	Suboptimal (2.8)	Suboptimal (3.0)
Forfeiture (0%)	$13.40	$14.80	$16.07	$16.91	$17.64	$18.27	$18.79	$19.08	$19.34	$19.57
Forfeiture (5%)	$11.36	$12.43	$13.37	$13.98	$14.51	$14.96	$15.33	$15.54	$15.73	$15.89
Forfeiture (10%)	$9.65	$10.47	$11.17	$11.63	$12.01	$12.34	$12.61	$12.76	$12.89	$13.01
Forfeiture (15%)	$8.21	$8.84	$9.38	$9.72	$10.00	$10.24	$10.43	$10.54	$10.64	$10.72
Forfeiture (20%)	$7.00	$7.49	$7.89	$8.15	$8.36	$8.54	$8.68	$8.76	$8.83	$8.89
Forfeiture (25%)	$5.97	$6.35	$6.67	$6.86	$7.02	$7.15	$7.25	$7.31	$7.36	$7.41
Forfeiture (30%)	$5.10	$5.40	$5.64	$5.79	$5.91	$6.01	$6.08	$6.13	$6.17	$6.20
Forfeiture (35%)	$4.36	$4.60	$4.78	$4.90	$4.99	$5.06	$5.12	$5.15	$5.18	$5.21
Forfeiture (40%)	$3.73	$3.92	$4.06	$4.15	$4.22	$4.28	$4.32	$4.35	$4.37	$4.38

Percentage Difference between Binomial and Black-Scholes Model	Suboptimal (1.2)	Suboptimal (1.4)	Suboptimal (1.6)	Suboptimal (1.8)	Suboptimal (2.0)	Suboptimal (2.2)	Suboptimal (2.4)	Suboptimal (2.6)	Suboptimal (2.8)	Suboptimal (3.0)
Forfeiture (0%)	−35.76%	−29.03%	−22.95%	−18.91%	−15.43%	−12.42%	−9.93%	−8.51%	−7.26%	−6.18%
Forfeiture (5%)	−45.54%	−40.43%	−35.91%	−32.95%	−30.44%	−28.27%	−26.49%	−25.47%	−24.59%	−23.83%
Forfeiture (10%)	−53.73%	−49.82%	−46.44%	−44.25%	−42.41%	−40.84%	−39.56%	−38.83%	−38.20%	−37.65%
Forfeiture (15%)	−60.62%	−57.61%	−55.05%	−53.42%	−52.07%	−50.92%	−49.98%	−49.46%	−49.00%	−48.61%
Forfeiture (20%)	−66.43%	−64.10%	−62.16%	−60.93%	−59.92%	−59.07%	−58.39%	−58.01%	−57.67%	−57.39%
Forfeiture (25%)	−71.36%	−69.53%	−68.04%	−67.12%	−66.36%	−65.73%	−65.23%	−64.94%	−64.70%	−64.49%
Forfeiture (30%)	−75.53%	−74.10%	−72.95%	−72.25%	−71.68%	−71.21%	−70.83%	−70.62%	−70.44%	−70.28%
Forfeiture (35%)	−79.09%	−77.96%	−77.07%	−76.52%	−76.09%	−75.73%	−75.45%	−75.29%	−75.16%	−75.04%
Forfeiture (40%)	−82.11%	−81.21%	−80.52%	−80.10%	−79.77%	−79.50%	−79.29%	−79.17%	−79.07%	−78.98%

MATURITY OF 10 YEARS AND VESTING OF 3 YEARS ON A $60 STOCK PRICE

Stock Price and Strike Price of $60, Maturity of 10 Years, Risk-Free Rate of 3.5%, 35% Volatility, 0% Dividends, Vesting of 3 Years, Employee Suboptimal Exercise Behavior from 1.2 to 3.0, and Forfeiture Rate from 0% to 40%.
Generalized Black-Scholes: $31.29

Customized Binomial Lattice	Suboptimal (1.2)	Suboptimal (1.4)	Suboptimal (1.6)	Suboptimal (1.8)	Suboptimal (2.0)	Suboptimal (2.2)	Suboptimal (2.4)	Suboptimal (2.6)	Suboptimal (2.8)	Suboptimal (3.0)
Forfeiture (0%)	$20.10	$22.21	$24.11	$25.37	$26.46	$27.40	$28.18	$28.63	$29.02	$29.35
Forfeiture (5%)	$17.04	$18.64	$20.05	$20.98	$21.77	$22.44	$23.00	$23.32	$23.59	$23.83
Forfeiture (10%)	$14.48	$15.70	$16.76	$17.44	$18.02	$18.51	$18.91	$19.14	$19.34	$19.51
Forfeiture (15%)	$12.32	$13.26	$14.06	$14.57	$15.00	$15.36	$15.65	$15.81	$15.96	$16.08
Forfeiture (20%)	$10.50	$11.23	$11.84	$12.22	$12.54	$12.80	$13.02	$13.14	$13.24	$13.33
Forfeiture (25%)	$8.96	$9.53	$10.00	$10.29	$10.52	$10.72	$10.88	$10.97	$11.04	$11.11
Forfeiture (30%)	$7.65	$8.10	$8.46	$8.68	$8.86	$9.01	$9.13	$9.19	$9.25	$9.30
Forfeiture (35%)	$6.54	$6.90	$7.18	$7.34	$7.48	$7.59	$7.68	$7.73	$7.77	$7.81
Forfeiture (40%)	$5.60	$5.88	$6.10	$6.23	$6.33	$6.41	$6.48	$6.52	$6.55	$6.58

Percentage Difference between Binomial and Black-Scholes Model	Suboptimal (1.2)	Suboptimal (1.4)	Suboptimal (1.6)	Suboptimal (1.8)	Suboptimal (2.0)	Suboptimal (2.2)	Suboptimal (2.4)	Suboptimal (2.6)	Suboptimal (2.8)	Suboptimal (3.0)
Forfeiture (0%)	-35.76%	-29.03%	-22.95%	-18.91%	-15.43%	-12.42%	-9.93%	-8.51%	-7.26%	-6.18%
Forfeiture (5%)	-45.54%	-40.43%	-35.91%	-32.95%	-30.44%	-28.27%	-26.49%	-25.47%	-24.59%	-23.83%
Forfeiture (10%)	-53.73%	-49.82%	-46.44%	-44.25%	-42.41%	-40.84%	-39.56%	-38.83%	-38.20%	-37.65%
Forfeiture (15%)	-60.62%	-57.61%	-55.05%	-53.42%	-52.07%	-50.92%	-49.98%	-49.46%	-49.00%	-48.61%
Forfeiture (20%)	-66.43%	-64.10%	-62.16%	-60.93%	-59.92%	-59.07%	-58.39%	-58.01%	-57.67%	-57.39%
Forfeiture (25%)	-71.36%	-69.53%	-68.04%	-67.12%	-66.36%	-65.73%	-65.23%	-64.94%	-64.70%	-64.49%
Forfeiture (30%)	-75.53%	-74.10%	-72.95%	-72.25%	-71.68%	-71.21%	-70.83%	-70.62%	-70.44%	-70.28%
Forfeiture (35%)	-79.09%	-77.96%	-77.07%	-76.52%	-76.09%	-75.73%	-75.45%	-75.29%	-75.16%	-75.04%
Forfeiture (40%)	-82.11%	-81.21%	-80.52%	-80.10%	-79.77%	-79.50%	-79.29%	-79.17%	-79.07%	-78.98%

MATURITY OF 10 YEARS AND VESTING OF 3 YEARS ON AN $80 STOCK PRICE

Stock Price and Strike Price of $80, Maturity of 10 Years, Risk-Free Rate of 3.5%, 35% Volatility, 0% Dividends, Vesting of 3 Years, Employee Suboptimal Exercise Behavior from 1.2 to 3.0, and Forfeiture Rate from 0% to 40%.
Generalized Black-Scholes: $41.72

Customized Binomial Lattice	Suboptimal (1.2)	Suboptimal (1.4)	Suboptimal (1.6)	Suboptimal (1.8)	Suboptimal (2.0)	Suboptimal (2.2)	Suboptimal (2.4)	Suboptimal (2.6)	Suboptimal (2.8)	Suboptimal (3.0)
Forfeiture (0%)	$26.80	$29.61	$32.14	$33.83	$35.28	$36.53	$37.57	$38.17	$38.69	$39.14
Forfeiture (5%)	$22.72	$24.85	$26.73	$27.97	$29.02	$29.92	$30.67	$31.09	$31.46	$31.78
Forfeiture (10%)	$19.30	$20.93	$22.34	$23.26	$24.02	$24.68	$25.22	$25.52	$25.78	$26.01
Forfeiture (15%)	$16.43	$17.68	$18.75	$19.43	$20.00	$20.48	$20.87	$21.09	$21.28	$21.44
Forfeiture (20%)	$14.00	$14.98	$15.79	$16.30	$16.72	$17.07	$17.36	$17.52	$17.66	$17.78
Forfeiture (25%)	$11.95	$12.71	$13.33	$13.72	$14.03	$14.30	$14.51	$14.62	$14.73	$14.81
Forfeiture (30%)	$10.21	$10.80	$11.28	$11.58	$11.81	$12.01	$12.17	$12.26	$12.33	$12.40
Forfeiture (35%)	$8.72	$9.20	$9.57	$9.79	$9.97	$10.12	$10.24	$10.31	$10.36	$10.41
Forfeiture (40%)	$7.46	$7.84	$8.13	$8.30	$8.44	$8.55	$8.64	$8.69	$8.73	$8.77

Percentage Difference between Binomial and Black-Scholes Model	Suboptimal (1.2)	Suboptimal (1.4)	Suboptimal (1.6)	Suboptimal (1.8)	Suboptimal (2.0)	Suboptimal (2.2)	Suboptimal (2.4)	Suboptimal (2.6)	Suboptimal (2.8)	Suboptimal (3.0)
Forfeiture (0%)	−35.76%	−29.03%	−22.95%	−18.91%	−15.43%	−12.42%	−9.93%	−8.51%	−7.26%	−6.18%
Forfeiture (5%)	−45.54%	−40.43%	−35.91%	−32.95%	−30.44%	−28.27%	−26.49%	−25.47%	−24.59%	−23.83%
Forfeiture (10%)	−53.73%	−49.82%	−46.44%	−44.25%	−42.41%	−40.84%	−39.56%	−38.83%	−38.20%	−37.65%
Forfeiture (15%)	−60.62%	−57.61%	−55.05%	−53.42%	−52.07%	−50.92%	−49.98%	−49.46%	−49.00%	−48.61%
Forfeiture (20%)	−66.43%	−64.10%	−62.16%	−60.93%	−59.92%	−59.07%	−58.39%	−58.01%	−57.67%	−57.39%
Forfeiture (25%)	−71.36%	−69.53%	−68.04%	−67.12%	−66.36%	−65.73%	−65.23%	−64.94%	−64.70%	−64.49%
Forfeiture (30%)	−75.53%	−74.10%	−72.95%	−72.25%	−71.68%	−71.21%	−70.83%	−70.62%	−70.44%	−70.28%
Forfeiture (35%)	−79.09%	−77.96%	−77.07%	−76.52%	−76.09%	−75.73%	−75.45%	−75.29%	−75.16%	−75.04%
Forfeiture (40%)	−82.11%	−81.21%	−80.52%	−80.10%	−79.77%	−79.50%	−79.29%	−79.17%	−79.07%	−78.98%

MATURITY OF 10 YEARS AND VESTING OF 4 YEARS ON A $20 STOCK PRICE

Stock Price and Strike Price of $20, Maturity of 10 Years, Risk-Free Rate of 3.5%, 35% Volatility, 0% Dividends, Vesting of 4 Years, Employee Suboptimal Exercise Behavior from 1.2 to 3.0, and Forfeiture Rate from 0% to 40%.
Generalized Black-Scholes: $10.43

Customized Binomial Lattice	Suboptimal (1.2)	Suboptimal (1.4)	Suboptimal (1.6)	Suboptimal (1.8)	Suboptimal (2.0)	Suboptimal (2.2)	Suboptimal (2.4)	Suboptimal (2.6)	Suboptimal (2.8)	Suboptimal (3.0)
Forfeiture (0%)	$7.45	$8.02	$8.52	$8.84	$9.12	$9.37	$9.57	$9.68	$9.78	$9.87
Forfeiture (5%)	$6.04	$6.45	$6.81	$7.04	$7.23	$7.40	$7.54	$7.63	$7.70	$7.76
Forfeiture (10%)	$4.90	$5.20	$5.46	$5.62	$5.76	$5.88	$5.98	$6.04	$6.09	$6.13
Forfeiture (15%)	$3.98	$4.20	$4.39	$4.51	$4.60	$4.69	$4.76	$4.80	$4.83	$4.86
Forfeiture (20%)	$3.23	$3.40	$3.53	$3.62	$3.69	$3.75	$3.80	$3.83	$3.85	$3.87
Forfeiture (25%)	$2.63	$2.75	$2.85	$2.91	$2.97	$3.01	$3.04	$3.06	$3.08	$3.10
Forfeiture (30%)	$2.14	$2.23	$2.31	$2.35	$2.39	$2.42	$2.45	$2.46	$2.47	$2.48
Forfeiture (35%)	$1.74	$1.81	$1.87	$1.90	$1.93	$1.95	$1.97	$1.98	$1.99	$2.00
Forfeiture (40%)	$1.42	$1.47	$1.51	$1.54	$1.56	$1.57	$1.59	$1.59	$1.60	$1.61

Percentage Difference between Binomial and Black-Scholes Model	Suboptimal (1.2)	Suboptimal (1.4)	Suboptimal (1.6)	Suboptimal (1.8)	Suboptimal (2.0)	Suboptimal (2.2)	Suboptimal (2.4)	Suboptimal (2.6)	Suboptimal (2.8)	Suboptimal (3.0)
Forfeiture (0%)	−28.56%	−23.13%	−18.35%	−15.20%	−12.53%	−10.20%	−8.27%	−7.16%	−6.18%	−5.32%
Forfeiture (5%)	−42.13%	−38.17%	−34.74%	−32.51%	−30.63%	−29.00%	−27.66%	−26.88%	−26.20%	−25.61%
Forfeiture (10%)	−53.06%	−50.16%	−47.68%	−46.09%	−44.76%	−43.61%	−42.67%	−42.13%	−41.65%	−41.24%
Forfeiture (15%)	−61.88%	−59.74%	−57.94%	−56.80%	−55.85%	−55.04%	−54.37%	−53.99%	−53.66%	−53.37%
Forfeiture (20%)	−69.02%	−67.43%	−66.12%	−65.29%	−64.61%	−64.03%	−63.56%	−63.29%	−63.05%	−62.85%
Forfeiture (25%)	−74.80%	−73.62%	−72.65%	−72.05%	−71.56%	−71.15%	−70.81%	−70.62%	−70.45%	−70.30%
Forfeiture (30%)	−79.49%	−78.60%	−77.89%	−77.45%	−77.10%	−76.80%	−76.56%	−76.42%	−76.30%	−76.19%
Forfeiture (35%)	−83.30%	−82.63%	−82.10%	−81.78%	−81.52%	−81.30%	−81.13%	−81.03%	−80.94%	−80.87%
Forfeiture (40%)	−86.40%	−85.89%	−85.50%	−85.26%	−85.07%	−84.91%	−84.78%	−84.71%	−84.65%	−84.59%

MATURITY OF 10 YEARS AND VESTING OF 4 YEARS ON A $40 STOCK PRICE

Stock Price and Strike Price of $40, Maturity of 10 Years, Risk-Free Rate of 3.5%, 35% Volatility, 0% Dividends, Vesting of 4 Years, Employee Suboptimal Exercise Behavior from 1.2 to 3.0, and Forfeiture Rate from 0% to 40%.
Generalized Black-Scholes: $20.86

Customized Binomial Lattice	Suboptimal (1.2)	Suboptimal (1.4)	Suboptimal (1.6)	Suboptimal (1.8)	Suboptimal (2.0)	Suboptimal (2.2)	Suboptimal (2.4)	Suboptimal (2.6)	Suboptimal (2.8)	Suboptimal (3.0)
Forfeiture (0%)	$14.90	$16.03	$17.03	$17.69	$18.25	$18.73	$19.13	$19.37	$19.57	$19.75
Forfeiture (5%)	$12.07	$12.90	$13.61	$14.08	$14.47	$14.81	$15.09	$15.25	$15.39	$15.52
Forfeiture (10%)	$9.79	$10.40	$10.91	$11.24	$11.52	$11.76	$11.96	$12.07	$12.17	$12.26
Forfeiture (15%)	$7.95	$8.40	$8.77	$9.01	$9.21	$9.38	$9.52	$9.60	$9.67	$9.73
Forfeiture (20%)	$6.46	$6.79	$7.07	$7.24	$7.38	$7.50	$7.60	$7.66	$7.71	$7.75
Forfeiture (25%)	$5.26	$5.50	$5.70	$5.83	$5.93	$6.02	$6.09	$6.13	$6.16	$6.19
Forfeiture (30%)	$4.28	$4.46	$4.61	$4.70	$4.78	$4.84	$4.89	$4.92	$4.94	$4.97
Forfeiture (35%)	$3.48	$3.62	$3.73	$3.80	$3.85	$3.90	$3.94	$3.96	$3.97	$3.99
Forfeiture (40%)	$2.84	$2.94	$3.03	$3.07	$3.11	$3.15	$3.17	$3.19	$3.20	$3.21

Percentage Difference between Binomial and Black-Scholes Model	Suboptimal (1.2)	Suboptimal (1.4)	Suboptimal (1.6)	Suboptimal (1.8)	Suboptimal (2.0)	Suboptimal (2.2)	Suboptimal (2.4)	Suboptimal (2.6)	Suboptimal (2.8)	Suboptimal (3.0)
Forfeiture (0%)	–28.56%	–23.13%	–18.35%	–15.20%	–12.53%	–10.20%	–8.27%	–7.16%	–6.18%	–5.32%
Forfeiture (5%)	–42.13%	–38.17%	–34.74%	–32.51%	–30.63%	–29.00%	–27.66%	–26.88%	–26.20%	–25.61%
Forfeiture (10%)	–53.06%	–50.16%	–47.68%	–46.09%	–44.76%	–43.61%	–42.67%	–42.13%	–41.65%	–41.24%
Forfeiture (15%)	–61.88%	–59.74%	–57.94%	–56.80%	–55.85%	–55.04%	–54.37%	–53.99%	–53.66%	–53.37%
Forfeiture (20%)	–69.02%	–67.43%	–66.12%	–65.29%	–64.61%	–64.03%	–63.56%	–63.29%	–63.05%	–62.85%
Forfeiture (25%)	–74.80%	–73.62%	–72.65%	–72.05%	–71.56%	–71.15%	–70.81%	–70.62%	–70.45%	–70.30%
Forfeiture (30%)	–79.49%	–78.60%	–77.89%	–77.45%	–77.10%	–76.80%	–76.56%	–76.42%	–76.30%	–76.19%
Forfeiture (35%)	–83.30%	–82.63%	–82.10%	–81.78%	–81.52%	–81.30%	–81.13%	–81.03%	–80.94%	–80.87%
Forfeiture (40%)	–86.40%	–85.89%	–85.50%	–85.26%	–85.07%	–84.91%	–84.78%	–84.71%	–84.65%	–84.59%

MATURITY OF 10 YEARS AND VESTING OF 4 YEARS ON A $60 STOCK PRICE

Stock Price and Strike Price of $60, Maturity of 10 Years, Risk-Free Rate of 3.5%, 35% Volatility, 0% Dividends, Vesting of 4 Years, Employee Suboptimal Exercise Behavior from 1.2 to 3.0, and Forfeiture Rate from 0% to 40%.
Generalized Black-Scholes: $31.29

Customized Binomial Lattice	Suboptimal (1.2)	Suboptimal (1.4)	Suboptimal (1.6)	Suboptimal (1.8)	Suboptimal (2.0)	Suboptimal (2.2)	Suboptimal (2.4)	Suboptimal (2.6)	Suboptimal (2.8)	Suboptimal (3.0)
Forfeiture (0%)	$22.35	$24.05	$25.55	$26.53	$27.37	$28.10	$28.70	$29.05	$29.35	$29.62
Forfeiture (5%)	$18.11	$19.34	$20.42	$21.12	$21.70	$22.21	$22.63	$22.88	$23.09	$23.28
Forfeiture (10%)	$14.69	$15.59	$16.37	$16.87	$17.28	$17.64	$17.94	$18.11	$18.26	$18.39
Forfeiture (15%)	$11.93	$12.60	$13.16	$13.52	$13.81	$14.07	$14.28	$14.39	$14.50	$14.59
Forfeiture (20%)	$9.69	$10.19	$10.60	$10.86	$11.07	$11.25	$11.40	$11.49	$11.56	$11.62
Forfeiture (25%)	$7.88	$8.26	$8.56	$8.74	$8.90	$9.03	$9.13	$9.19	$9.25	$9.29
Forfeiture (30%)	$6.42	$6.69	$6.92	$7.05	$7.17	$7.26	$7.34	$7.38	$7.42	$7.45
Forfeiture (35%)	$5.23	$5.43	$5.60	$5.70	$5.78	$5.85	$5.90	$5.94	$5.96	$5.99
Forfeiture (40%)	$4.26	$4.41	$4.54	$4.61	$4.67	$4.72	$4.76	$4.78	$4.80	$4.82

Percentage Difference between Binomial and Black-Scholes Model	Suboptimal (1.2)	Suboptimal (1.4)	Suboptimal (1.6)	Suboptimal (1.8)	Suboptimal (2.0)	Suboptimal (2.2)	Suboptimal (2.4)	Suboptimal (2.6)	Suboptimal (2.8)	Suboptimal (3.0)
Forfeiture (0%)	–28.56%	–23.13%	–18.35%	–15.20%	–12.53%	–10.20%	–8.27%	–7.16%	–6.18%	–5.32%
Forfeiture (5%)	–42.13%	–38.17%	–34.74%	–32.51%	–30.63%	–29.00%	–27.66%	–26.88%	–26.20%	–25.61%
Forfeiture (10%)	–53.06%	–50.16%	–47.68%	–46.09%	–44.76%	–43.61%	–42.67%	–42.13%	–41.65%	–41.24%
Forfeiture (15%)	–61.88%	–59.74%	–57.94%	–56.80%	–55.85%	–55.04%	–54.37%	–53.99%	–53.66%	–53.37%
Forfeiture (20%)	–69.02%	–67.43%	–66.12%	–65.29%	–64.61%	–64.03%	–63.56%	–63.29%	–63.05%	–62.85%
Forfeiture (25%)	–74.80%	–73.62%	–72.65%	–72.05%	–71.56%	–71.15%	–70.81%	–70.62%	–70.45%	–70.30%
Forfeiture (30%)	–79.49%	–78.60%	–77.89%	–77.45%	–77.10%	–76.80%	–76.56%	–76.42%	–76.30%	–76.19%
Forfeiture (35%)	–83.30%	–82.63%	–82.10%	–81.78%	–81.52%	–81.30%	–81.13%	–81.03%	–80.94%	–80.87%
Forfeiture (40%)	–86.40%	–85.89%	–85.50%	–85.26%	–85.07%	–84.91%	–84.78%	–84.71%	–84.65%	–84.59%

MATURITY OF 10 YEARS AND VESTING OF 4 YEARS ON AN $80 STOCK PRICE

Stock Price and Strike Price of $80, Maturity of 10 Years, Risk-Free Rate of 3.5%, 35% Volatility, 0% Dividends, Vesting of 4 Years, Employee Suboptimal Exercise Behavior from 1.2 to 3.0, and Forfeiture Rate from 0% to 40%.
Generalized Black-Scholes: $41.72

Customized Binomial Lattice	Suboptimal (1.2)	Suboptimal (1.4)	Suboptimal (1.6)	Suboptimal (1.8)	Suboptimal (2.0)	Suboptimal (2.2)	Suboptimal (2.4)	Suboptimal (2.6)	Suboptimal (2.8)	Suboptimal (3.0)
Forfeiture (0%)	$29.80	$32.07	$34.06	$35.37	$36.49	$37.46	$38.27	$38.73	$39.14	$39.50
Forfeiture (5%)	$24.14	$25.79	$27.22	$28.15	$28.94	$29.62	$30.18	$30.50	$30.79	$31.03
Forfeiture (10%)	$19.58	$20.79	$21.83	$22.49	$23.05	$23.52	$23.92	$24.14	$24.34	$24.51
Forfeiture (15%)	$15.90	$16.80	$17.54	$18.02	$18.42	$18.76	$19.03	$19.19	$19.33	$19.45
Forfeiture (20%)	$12.92	$13.59	$14.13	$14.48	$14.76	$15.00	$15.20	$15.31	$15.41	$15.50
Forfeiture (25%)	$10.51	$11.01	$11.41	$11.66	$11.86	$12.04	$12.18	$12.26	$12.33	$12.39
Forfeiture (30%)	$8.56	$8.93	$9.22	$9.41	$9.55	$9.68	$9.78	$9.84	$9.89	$9.93
Forfeiture (35%)	$6.97	$7.25	$7.47	$7.60	$7.71	$7.80	$7.87	$7.91	$7.95	$7.98
Forfeiture (40%)	$5.68	$5.89	$6.05	$6.15	$6.23	$6.30	$6.35	$6.38	$6.40	$6.43

Percentage Difference between Binomial and Black-Scholes Model	Suboptimal (1.2)	Suboptimal (1.4)	Suboptimal (1.6)	Suboptimal (1.8)	Suboptimal (2.0)	Suboptimal (2.2)	Suboptimal (2.4)	Suboptimal (2.6)	Suboptimal (2.8)	Suboptimal (3.0)
Forfeiture (0%)	−28.56%	−23.13%	−18.35%	−15.20%	−12.53%	−10.20%	−8.27%	−7.16%	−6.18%	−5.32%
Forfeiture (5%)	−42.13%	−38.17%	−34.74%	−32.51%	−30.63%	−29.00%	−27.66%	−26.88%	−26.20%	−25.61%
Forfeiture (10%)	−53.06%	−50.16%	−47.68%	−46.09%	−44.76%	−43.61%	−42.67%	−42.13%	−41.65%	−41.24%
Forfeiture (15%)	−61.88%	−59.74%	−57.94%	−56.80%	−55.85%	−55.04%	−54.37%	−53.99%	−53.66%	−53.37%
Forfeiture (20%)	−69.02%	−67.43%	−66.12%	−65.29%	−64.61%	−64.03%	−63.56%	−63.29%	−63.05%	−62.85%
Forfeiture (25%)	−74.80%	−73.62%	−72.65%	−72.05%	−71.56%	−71.15%	−70.81%	−70.62%	−70.45%	−70.30%
Forfeiture (30%)	−79.49%	−78.60%	−77.89%	−77.45%	−77.10%	−76.80%	−76.56%	−76.42%	−76.30%	−76.19%
Forfeiture (35%)	−83.30%	−82.63%	−82.10%	−81.78%	−81.52%	−81.30%	−81.13%	−81.03%	−80.94%	−80.87%
Forfeiture (40%)	−86.40%	−85.89%	−85.50%	−85.26%	−85.07%	−84.91%	−84.78%	−84.71%	−84.65%	−84.59%

MATURITY OF 10 YEARS AND VESTING OF 5 YEARS ON A $20 STOCK PRICE

Stock Price and Strike Price of $20, Maturity of 10 Years, Risk-Free Rate of 3.5%, 35% Volatility, 0% Dividends, Vesting of 5 Years, Employee Suboptimal Exercise Behavior from 1.2 to 3.0, and Forfeiture Rate from 0% to 40%.
Generalized Black-Scholes: $10.43

Customized Binomial Lattice	Suboptimal (1.2)	Suboptimal (1.4)	Suboptimal (1.6)	Suboptimal (1.8)	Suboptimal (2.0)	Suboptimal (2.2)	Suboptimal (2.4)	Suboptimal (2.6)	Suboptimal (2.8)	Suboptimal (3.0)
Forfeiture (0%)	$8.11	$8.57	$8.95	$9.21	$9.42	$9.60	$9.75	$9.83	$9.91	$9.98
Forfeiture (5%)	$6.27	$6.59	$6.86	$7.03	$7.18	$7.30	$7.40	$7.46	$7.51	$7.56
Forfeiture (10%)	$4.85	$5.08	$5.27	$5.38	$5.48	$5.57	$5.64	$5.68	$5.71	$5.74
Forfeiture (15%)	$3.76	$3.92	$4.05	$4.13	$4.20	$4.26	$4.30	$4.33	$4.36	$4.38
Forfeiture (20%)	$2.91	$3.02	$3.12	$3.17	$3.22	$3.26	$3.29	$3.31	$3.33	$3.34
Forfeiture (25%)	$2.25	$2.34	$2.40	$2.44	$2.47	$2.50	$2.52	$2.54	$2.55	$2.56
Forfeiture (30%)	$1.75	$1.81	$1.85	$1.88	$1.90	$1.92	$1.94	$1.95	$1.96	$1.96
Forfeiture (35%)	$1.36	$1.40	$1.43	$1.45	$1.47	$1.48	$1.49	$1.50	$1.50	$1.51
Forfeiture (40%)	$1.05	$1.08	$1.10	$1.12	$1.13	$1.14	$1.15	$1.15	$1.16	$1.16

Percentage Difference between Binomial and Black-Scholes Model	Suboptimal (1.2)	Suboptimal (1.4)	Suboptimal (1.6)	Suboptimal (1.8)	Suboptimal (2.0)	Suboptimal (2.2)	Suboptimal (2.4)	Suboptimal (2.6)	Suboptimal (2.8)	Suboptimal (3.0)
Forfeiture (0%)	−22.19%	−17.86%	−14.14%	−11.74%	−9.72%	−7.98%	−6.54%	−5.71%	−4.97%	−4.33%
Forfeiture (5%)	−39.85%	−36.80%	−34.22%	−32.57%	−31.19%	−30.01%	−29.03%	−28.47%	−27.97%	−27.53%
Forfeiture (10%)	−53.47%	−51.31%	−49.51%	−48.37%	−47.43%	−46.62%	−45.95%	−45.57%	−45.23%	−44.93%
Forfeiture (15%)	−63.98%	−62.45%	−61.19%	−60.40%	−59.75%	−59.19%	−58.73%	−58.47%	−58.24%	−58.03%
Forfeiture (20%)	−72.10%	−71.01%	−70.13%	−69.58%	−69.13%	−68.74%	−68.43%	−68.25%	−68.09%	−67.94%
Forfeiture (25%)	−78.38%	−77.60%	−76.98%	−76.59%	−76.28%	−76.01%	−75.80%	−75.67%	−75.56%	−75.46%
Forfeiture (30%)	−83.24%	−82.68%	−82.24%	−81.97%	−81.75%	−81.57%	−81.42%	−81.33%	−81.25%	−81.19%
Forfeiture (35%)	−87.00%	−86.60%	−86.29%	−86.10%	−85.95%	−85.82%	−85.71%	−85.65%	−85.60%	−85.55%
Forfeiture (40%)	−89.92%	−89.63%	−89.41%	−89.27%	−89.17%	−89.07%	−89.00%	−88.96%	−88.92%	−88.89%

MATURITY OF 10 YEARS AND VESTING OF 5 YEARS ON A $40 STOCK PRICE

Stock Price and Strike Price of $40, Maturity of 10 Years, Risk-Free Rate of 3.5%, 35% Volatility, 0% Dividends, Vesting of 5 Years, Employee Suboptimal Exercise Behavior from 1.2 to 3.0, and Forfeiture Rate from 0% to 40%.
Generalized Black-Scholes: $20.86

Customized Binomial Lattice	Suboptimal (1.2)	Suboptimal (1.4)	Suboptimal (1.6)	Suboptimal (1.8)	Suboptimal (2.0)	Suboptimal (2.2)	Suboptimal (2.4)	Suboptimal (2.6)	Suboptimal (2.8)	Suboptimal (3.0)
Forfeiture (0%)	$16.23	$17.13	$17.91	$18.41	$18.83	$19.19	$19.49	$19.67	$19.82	$19.96
Forfeiture (5%)	$12.55	$13.18	$13.72	$14.06	$14.35	$14.60	$14.80	$14.92	$15.02	$15.12
Forfeiture (10%)	$9.71	$10.16	$10.53	$10.77	$10.97	$11.13	$11.27	$11.35	$11.42	$11.49
Forfeiture (15%)	$7.51	$7.83	$8.09	$8.26	$8.40	$8.51	$8.61	$8.66	$8.71	$8.75
Forfeiture (20%)	$5.82	$6.05	$6.23	$6.35	$6.44	$6.52	$6.59	$6.62	$6.66	$6.69
Forfeiture (25%)	$4.51	$4.67	$4.80	$4.88	$4.95	$5.00	$5.05	$5.07	$5.10	$5.12
Forfeiture (30%)	$3.50	$3.61	$3.70	$3.76	$3.81	$3.84	$3.88	$3.89	$3.91	$3.92
Forfeiture (35%)	$2.71	$2.79	$2.86	$2.90	$2.93	$2.96	$2.98	$2.99	$3.00	$3.01
Forfeiture (40%)	$2.10	$2.16	$2.21	$2.24	$2.26	$2.28	$2.29	$2.30	$2.31	$2.32

Percentage Difference between Binomial and Black-Scholes Model	Suboptimal (1.2)	Suboptimal (1.4)	Suboptimal (1.6)	Suboptimal (1.8)	Suboptimal (2.0)	Suboptimal (2.2)	Suboptimal (2.4)	Suboptimal (2.6)	Suboptimal (2.8)	Suboptimal (3.0)
Forfeiture (0%)	−22.19%	−17.86%	−14.14%	−11.74%	−9.72%	−7.98%	−6.54%	−5.71%	−4.97%	−4.33%
Forfeiture (5%)	−39.85%	−36.80%	−34.22%	−32.57%	−31.19%	−30.01%	−29.03%	−28.47%	−27.97%	−27.53%
Forfeiture (10%)	−53.47%	−51.31%	−49.51%	−48.37%	−47.43%	−46.62%	−45.95%	−45.57%	−45.23%	−44.93%
Forfeiture (15%)	−63.98%	−62.45%	−61.19%	−60.40%	−59.75%	−59.19%	−58.73%	−58.47%	−58.24%	−58.03%
Forfeiture (20%)	−72.10%	−71.01%	−70.13%	−69.58%	−69.13%	−68.74%	−68.43%	−68.25%	−68.09%	−67.94%
Forfeiture (25%)	−78.38%	−77.60%	−76.98%	−76.59%	−76.28%	−76.01%	−75.80%	−75.67%	−75.56%	−75.46%
Forfeiture (30%)	−83.24%	−82.68%	−82.24%	−81.97%	−81.75%	−81.57%	−81.42%	−81.33%	−81.25%	−81.19%
Forfeiture (35%)	−87.00%	−86.60%	−86.29%	−86.10%	−85.95%	−85.82%	−85.71%	−85.65%	−85.60%	−85.55%
Forfeiture (40%)	−89.92%	−89.63%	−89.41%	−89.27%	−89.17%	−89.07%	−89.00%	−88.96%	−88.92%	−88.89%

MATURITY OF 10 YEARS AND VESTING OF 5 YEARS ON A $60 STOCK PRICE

Stock Price and Strike Price of $60, Maturity of 10 Years, Risk-Free Rate of 3.5%, 35% Volatility, 0% Dividends, Vesting of 5 Years, Employee Suboptimal Exercise Behavior from 1.2 to 3.0, and Forfeiture Rate from 0% to 40%.
Generalized Black-Scholes: $31.29

Customized Binomial Lattice	Suboptimal (1.2)	Suboptimal (1.4)	Suboptimal (1.6)	Suboptimal (1.8)	Suboptimal (2.0)	Suboptimal (2.2)	Suboptimal (2.4)	Suboptimal (2.6)	Suboptimal (2.8)	Suboptimal (3.0)
Forfeiture (0%)	$24.34	$25.70	$26.86	$27.62	$28.25	$28.79	$29.24	$29.50	$29.73	$29.93
Forfeiture (5%)	$18.82	$19.77	$20.58	$21.10	$21.53	$21.90	$22.20	$22.38	$22.54	$22.68
Forfeiture (10%)	$14.56	$15.23	$15.80	$16.15	$16.45	$16.70	$16.91	$17.03	$17.14	$17.23
Forfeiture (15%)	$11.27	$11.75	$12.14	$12.39	$12.59	$12.77	$12.91	$12.99	$13.07	$13.13
Forfeiture (20%)	$8.73	$9.07	$9.35	$9.52	$9.66	$9.78	$9.88	$9.94	$9.99	$10.03
Forfeiture (25%)	$6.76	$7.01	$7.20	$7.32	$7.42	$7.50	$7.57	$7.61	$7.65	$7.68
Forfeiture (30%)	$5.24	$5.42	$5.56	$5.64	$5.71	$5.77	$5.81	$5.84	$5.87	$5.89
Forfeiture (35%)	$4.07	$4.19	$4.29	$4.35	$4.40	$4.44	$4.47	$4.49	$4.51	$4.52
Forfeiture (40%)	$3.15	$3.24	$3.31	$3.36	$3.39	$3.42	$3.44	$3.45	$3.47	$3.48

Percentage Difference between Binomial and Black-Scholes Model	Suboptimal (1.2)	Suboptimal (1.4)	Suboptimal (1.6)	Suboptimal (1.8)	Suboptimal (2.0)	Suboptimal (2.2)	Suboptimal (2.4)	Suboptimal (2.6)	Suboptimal (2.8)	Suboptimal (3.0)
Forfeiture (0%)	–22.19%	–17.86%	–14.14%	–11.74%	–9.72%	–7.98%	–6.54%	–5.71%	–4.97%	–4.33%
Forfeiture (5%)	–39.85%	–36.80%	–34.22%	–32.57%	–31.19%	–30.01%	–29.03%	–28.47%	–27.97%	–27.53%
Forfeiture (10%)	–53.47%	–51.31%	–49.51%	–48.37%	–47.43%	–46.62%	–45.95%	–45.57%	–45.23%	–44.93%
Forfeiture (15%)	–63.98%	–62.45%	–61.19%	–60.40%	–59.75%	–59.19%	–58.73%	–58.47%	–58.24%	–58.03%
Forfeiture (20%)	–72.10%	–71.01%	–70.13%	–69.58%	–69.13%	–68.74%	–68.43%	–68.25%	–68.09%	–67.94%
Forfeiture (25%)	–78.38%	–77.60%	–76.98%	–76.59%	–76.28%	–76.01%	–75.80%	–75.67%	–75.56%	–75.46%
Forfeiture (30%)	–83.24%	–82.68%	–82.24%	–81.97%	–81.75%	–81.57%	–81.42%	–81.33%	–81.25%	–81.19%
Forfeiture (35%)	–87.00%	–86.60%	–86.29%	–86.10%	–85.95%	–85.82%	–85.71%	–85.65%	–85.60%	–85.55%
Forfeiture (40%)	–89.92%	–89.63%	–89.41%	–89.27%	–89.17%	–89.07%	–89.00%	–88.96%	–88.92%	–88.89%

MATURITY OF 10 YEARS AND VESTING OF 5 YEARS ON AN $80 STOCK PRICE

Stock Price and Strike Price of $80, Maturity of 10 Years, Risk-Free Rate of 3.5%, 35% Volatility, 0% Dividends, Vesting of 5 Years, Employee Suboptimal Exercise Behavior from 1.2 to 3.0, and Forfeiture Rate from 0% to 40%.
Generalized Black-Scholes: $41.72

Customized Binomial Lattice	Suboptimal (1.2)	Suboptimal (1.4)	Suboptimal (1.6)	Suboptimal (1.8)	Suboptimal (2.0)	Suboptimal (2.2)	Suboptimal (2.4)	Suboptimal (2.6)	Suboptimal (2.8)	Suboptimal (3.0)
Forfeiture (0%)	$32.46	$34.27	$35.82	$36.82	$37.66	$38.39	$38.99	$39.33	$39.64	$39.91
Forfeiture (5%)	$25.09	$26.36	$27.44	$28.13	$28.70	$29.20	$29.61	$29.84	$30.05	$30.23
Forfeiture (10%)	$19.41	$20.31	$21.06	$21.54	$21.93	$22.27	$22.55	$22.71	$22.85	$22.97
Forfeiture (15%)	$15.03	$15.67	$16.19	$16.52	$16.79	$17.02	$17.21	$17.32	$17.42	$17.51
Forfeiture (20%)	$11.64	$12.09	$12.46	$12.69	$12.88	$13.04	$13.17	$13.25	$13.31	$13.37
Forfeiture (25%)	$9.02	$9.34	$9.60	$9.76	$9.89	$10.01	$10.10	$10.15	$10.20	$10.24
Forfeiture (30%)	$6.99	$7.22	$7.41	$7.52	$7.61	$7.69	$7.75	$7.79	$7.82	$7.85
Forfeiture (35%)	$5.42	$5.59	$5.72	$5.80	$5.86	$5.92	$5.96	$5.99	$6.01	$6.03
Forfeiture (40%)	$4.20	$4.33	$4.42	$4.47	$4.52	$4.56	$4.59	$4.61	$4.62	$4.64

Percentage Difference between Binomial and Black-Scholes Model	Suboptimal (1.2)	Suboptimal (1.4)	Suboptimal (1.6)	Suboptimal (1.8)	Suboptimal (2.0)	Suboptimal (2.2)	Suboptimal (2.4)	Suboptimal (2.6)	Suboptimal (2.8)	Suboptimal (3.0)
Forfeiture (0%)	−22.19%	−17.86%	−14.14%	−11.74%	−9.72%	−7.98%	−6.54%	−5.71%	−4.97%	−4.33%
Forfeiture (5%)	−39.85%	−36.80%	−34.22%	−32.57%	−31.19%	−30.01%	−29.03%	−28.47%	−27.97%	−27.53%
Forfeiture (10%)	−53.47%	−51.31%	−49.51%	−48.37%	−47.43%	−46.62%	−45.95%	−45.57%	−45.23%	−44.93%
Forfeiture (15%)	−63.98%	−62.45%	−61.19%	−60.40%	−59.75%	−59.19%	−58.73%	−58.47%	−58.24%	−58.03%
Forfeiture (20%)	−72.10%	−71.01%	−70.13%	−69.58%	−69.13%	−68.74%	−68.43%	−68.25%	−68.09%	−67.94%
Forfeiture (25%)	−78.38%	−77.60%	−76.98%	−76.59%	−76.28%	−76.01%	−75.80%	−75.67%	−75.56%	−75.46%
Forfeiture (30%)	−83.24%	−82.68%	−82.24%	−81.97%	−81.75%	−81.57%	−81.42%	−81.33%	−81.25%	−81.19%
Forfeiture (35%)	−87.00%	−86.60%	−86.29%	−86.10%	−85.95%	−85.82%	−85.71%	−85.65%	−85.60%	−85.55%
Forfeiture (40%)	−89.92%	−89.63%	−89.41%	−89.27%	−89.17%	−89.07%	−89.00%	−88.96%	−88.92%	−88.89%

MATURITY OF 10 YEARS AND VESTING OF 7 YEARS ON A $20 STOCK PRICE

Stock Price and Strike Price of $20, Maturity of 10 Years, Risk-Free Rate of 3.5%, 35% Volatility, 0% Dividends, Vesting of 7 Years, Employee Suboptimal Exercise Behavior from 1.2 to 3.0, and Forfeiture Rate from 0% to 40%.
Generalized Black-Scholes: $10.43

Customized Binomial Lattice	Suboptimal (1.2)	Suboptimal (1.4)	Suboptimal (1.6)	Suboptimal (1.8)	Suboptimal (2.0)	Suboptimal (2.2)	Suboptimal (2.4)	Suboptimal (2.6)	Suboptimal (2.8)	Suboptimal (3.0)
Forfeiture (0%)	$9.24	$9.50	$9.71	$9.83	$9.93	$10.01	$10.08	$10.12	$10.16	$10.19
Forfeiture (5%)	$6.49	$6.66	$6.80	$6.88	$6.94	$7.00	$7.04	$7.07	$7.09	$7.11
Forfeiture (10%)	$4.56	$4.67	$4.76	$4.81	$4.86	$4.89	$4.92	$4.94	$4.95	$4.96
Forfeiture (15%)	$3.21	$3.28	$3.34	$3.37	$3.40	$3.42	$3.44	$3.45	$3.46	$3.47
Forfeiture (20%)	$2.25	$2.30	$2.34	$2.36	$2.38	$2.39	$2.41	$2.41	$2.42	$2.42
Forfeiture (25%)	$1.58	$1.62	$1.64	$1.65	$1.67	$1.68	$1.68	$1.69	$1.69	$1.70
Forfeiture (30%)	$1.11	$1.13	$1.15	$1.16	$1.17	$1.17	$1.18	$1.18	$1.18	$1.19
Forfeiture (35%)	$0.78	$0.80	$0.81	$0.81	$0.82	$0.82	$0.82	$0.83	$0.83	$0.83
Forfeiture (40%)	$0.55	$0.56	$0.57	$0.57	$0.57	$0.58	$0.58	$0.58	$0.58	$0.58

Percentage Difference between Binomial and Black-Scholes Model	Suboptimal (1.2)	Suboptimal (1.4)	Suboptimal (1.6)	Suboptimal (1.8)	Suboptimal (2.0)	Suboptimal (2.2)	Suboptimal (2.4)	Suboptimal (2.6)	Suboptimal (2.8)	Suboptimal (3.0)
Forfeiture (0%)	−11.41%	−8.91%	−6.94%	−5.74%	−4.79%	−3.99%	−3.34%	−2.96%	−2.63%	−2.33%
Forfeiture (5%)	−37.76%	−36.11%	−34.83%	−34.05%	−33.43%	−32.91%	−32.49%	−32.25%	−32.03%	−31.83%
Forfeiture (10%)	−56.26%	−55.18%	−54.34%	−53.84%	−53.44%	−53.10%	−52.83%	−52.67%	−52.53%	−52.40%
Forfeiture (15%)	−69.27%	−68.55%	−68.01%	−67.68%	−67.42%	−67.20%	−67.02%	−66.92%	−66.82%	−66.74%
Forfeiture (20%)	−78.41%	−77.93%	−77.57%	−77.36%	−77.19%	−77.05%	−76.93%	−76.86%	−76.80%	−76.75%
Forfeiture (25%)	−84.83%	−84.51%	−84.28%	−84.14%	−84.03%	−83.93%	−83.86%	−83.82%	−83.78%	−83.74%
Forfeiture (30%)	−89.34%	−89.13%	−88.98%	−88.88%	−88.81%	−88.75%	−88.70%	−88.67%	−88.65%	−88.63%
Forfeiture (35%)	−92.51%	−92.37%	−92.27%	−92.21%	−92.16%	−92.12%	−92.09%	−92.07%	−92.06%	−92.04%
Forfeiture (40%)	−94.74%	−94.65%	−94.58%	−94.54%	−94.51%	−94.48%	−94.46%	−94.45%	−94.44%	−94.43%

MATURITY OF 10 YEARS AND VESTING OF 7 YEARS ON A $40 STOCK PRICE

Stock Price and Strike Price of $40, Maturity of 10 Years, Risk-Free Rate of 3.5%, 35% Volatility, 0% Dividends, Vesting of 7 Years, Employee Suboptimal Exercise Behavior from 1.2 to 3.0, and Forfeiture Rate from 0% to 40%.
Generalized Black-Scholes: $20.86

Customized Binomial Lattice	Suboptimal (1.2)	Suboptimal (1.4)	Suboptimal (1.6)	Suboptimal (1.8)	Suboptimal (2.0)	Suboptimal (2.2)	Suboptimal (2.4)	Suboptimal (2.6)	Suboptimal (2.8)	Suboptimal (3.0)
Forfeiture (0%)	$18.48	$19.00	$19.41	$19.66	$19.86	$20.03	$20.16	$20.24	$20.31	$20.37
Forfeiture (5%)	$12.98	$13.33	$13.59	$13.76	$13.88	$13.99	$14.08	$14.13	$14.18	$14.22
Forfeiture (10%)	$9.12	$9.35	$9.52	$9.63	$9.71	$9.78	$9.84	$9.87	$9.90	$9.93
Forfeiture (15%)	$6.41	$6.56	$6.67	$6.74	$6.80	$6.84	$6.88	$6.90	$6.92	$6.94
Forfeiture (20%)	$4.50	$4.60	$4.68	$4.72	$4.76	$4.79	$4.81	$4.83	$4.84	$4.85
Forfeiture (25%)	$3.16	$3.23	$3.28	$3.31	$3.33	$3.35	$3.37	$3.38	$3.38	$3.39
Forfeiture (30%)	$2.22	$2.27	$2.30	$2.32	$2.33	$2.35	$2.36	$2.36	$2.37	$2.37
Forfeiture (35%)	$1.56	$1.59	$1.61	$1.62	$1.63	$1.64	$1.65	$1.65	$1.66	$1.66
Forfeiture (40%)	$1.10	$1.12	$1.13	$1.14	$1.15	$1.15	$1.16	$1.16	$1.16	$1.16

Percentage Difference between Binomial and Black-Scholes Model	Suboptimal (1.2)	Suboptimal (1.4)	Suboptimal (1.6)	Suboptimal (1.8)	Suboptimal (2.0)	Suboptimal (2.2)	Suboptimal (2.4)	Suboptimal (2.6)	Suboptimal (2.8)	Suboptimal (3.0)
Forfeiture (0%)	–11.41%	–8.91%	–6.94%	–5.74%	–4.79%	–3.99%	–3.34%	–2.96%	–2.63%	–2.33%
Forfeiture (5%)	–37.76%	–36.11%	–34.83%	–34.05%	–33.43%	–32.91%	–32.49%	–32.25%	–32.03%	–31.83%
Forfeiture (10%)	–56.26%	–55.18%	–54.34%	–53.84%	–53.44%	–53.10%	–52.83%	–52.67%	–52.53%	–52.40%
Forfeiture (15%)	–69.27%	–68.55%	–68.01%	–67.68%	–67.42%	–67.20%	–67.02%	–66.92%	–66.82%	–66.74%
Forfeiture (20%)	–78.41%	–77.93%	–77.57%	–77.36%	–77.19%	–77.05%	–76.93%	–76.86%	–76.80%	–76.75%
Forfeiture (25%)	–84.83%	–84.51%	–84.28%	–84.14%	–84.03%	–83.93%	–83.86%	–83.82%	–83.78%	–83.74%
Forfeiture (30%)	–89.34%	–89.13%	–88.98%	–88.88%	–88.81%	–88.75%	–88.70%	–88.67%	–88.65%	–88.63%
Forfeiture (35%)	–92.51%	–92.37%	–92.27%	–92.21%	–92.16%	–92.12%	–92.09%	–92.07%	–92.06%	–92.04%
Forfeiture (40%)	–94.74%	–94.65%	–94.58%	–94.54%	–94.51%	–94.48%	–94.46%	–94.45%	–94.44%	–94.43%

MATURITY OF 10 YEARS AND VESTING OF 7 YEARS ON A $60 STOCK PRICE

Stock Price and Strike Price of $60, Maturity of 10 Years, Risk-Free Rate of 3.5%, 35% Volatility, 0% Dividends, Vesting of 7 Years, Employee Suboptimal Exercise Behavior from 1.2 to 3.0, and Forfeiture Rate from 0% to 40%.
Generalized Black-Scholes: $31.29

Customized Binomial Lattice	Suboptimal (1.2)	Suboptimal (1.4)	Suboptimal (1.6)	Suboptimal (1.8)	Suboptimal (2.0)	Suboptimal (2.2)	Suboptimal (2.4)	Suboptimal (2.6)	Suboptimal (2.8)	Suboptimal (3.0)
Forfeiture (0%)	$27.72	$28.50	$29.12	$29.49	$29.79	$30.04	$30.24	$30.36	$30.47	$30.56
Forfeiture (5%)	$19.47	$19.99	$20.39	$20.63	$20.83	$20.99	$21.12	$21.20	$21.27	$21.33
Forfeiture (10%)	$13.68	$14.02	$14.29	$14.44	$14.57	$14.67	$14.76	$14.81	$14.85	$14.89
Forfeiture (15%)	$9.62	$9.84	$10.01	$10.11	$10.19	$10.26	$10.32	$10.35	$10.38	$10.41
Forfeiture (20%)	$6.76	$6.90	$7.02	$7.08	$7.14	$7.18	$7.22	$7.24	$7.26	$7.27
Forfeiture (25%)	$4.75	$4.85	$4.92	$4.96	$5.00	$5.03	$5.05	$5.06	$5.08	$5.09
Forfeiture (30%)	$3.34	$3.40	$3.45	$3.48	$3.50	$3.52	$3.53	$3.54	$3.55	$3.56
Forfeiture (35%)	$2.34	$2.39	$2.42	$2.44	$2.45	$2.46	$2.47	$2.48	$2.49	$2.49
Forfeiture (40%)	$1.65	$1.68	$1.70	$1.71	$1.72	$1.73	$1.73	$1.74	$1.74	$1.74

Percentage Difference between Binomial and Black-Scholes Model	Suboptimal (1.2)	Suboptimal (1.4)	Suboptimal (1.6)	Suboptimal (1.8)	Suboptimal (2.0)	Suboptimal (2.2)	Suboptimal (2.4)	Suboptimal (2.6)	Suboptimal (2.8)	Suboptimal (3.0)
Forfeiture (0%)	−11.41%	−8.91%	−6.94%	−5.74%	−4.79%	−3.99%	−3.34%	−2.96%	−2.63%	−2.33%
Forfeiture (5%)	−37.76%	−36.11%	−34.83%	−34.05%	−33.43%	−32.91%	−32.49%	−32.25%	−32.03%	−31.83%
Forfeiture (10%)	−56.26%	−55.18%	−54.34%	−53.84%	−53.44%	−53.10%	−52.83%	−52.67%	−52.53%	−52.40%
Forfeiture (15%)	−69.27%	−68.55%	−68.01%	−67.68%	−67.42%	−67.20%	−67.02%	−66.92%	−66.82%	−66.74%
Forfeiture (20%)	−78.41%	−77.93%	−77.57%	−77.36%	−77.19%	−77.05%	−76.93%	−76.86%	−76.80%	−76.75%
Forfeiture (25%)	−84.83%	−84.51%	−84.28%	−84.14%	−84.03%	−83.93%	−83.86%	−83.82%	−83.78%	−83.74%
Forfeiture (30%)	−89.34%	−89.13%	−88.98%	−88.88%	−88.81%	−88.75%	−88.70%	−88.67%	−88.65%	−88.63%
Forfeiture (35%)	−92.51%	−92.37%	−92.27%	−92.21%	−92.16%	−92.12%	−92.09%	−92.07%	−92.06%	−92.04%
Forfeiture (40%)	−94.74%	−94.65%	−94.58%	−94.54%	−94.51%	−94.48%	−94.46%	−94.45%	−94.44%	−94.43%

MATURITY OF 10 YEARS AND VESTING OF 7 YEARS ON AN $80 STOCK PRICE

Stock Price and Strike Price of $80, Maturity of 10 Years, Risk-Free Rate of 3.5%, 35% Volatility, 0% Dividends, Vesting of 7 Years, Employee Suboptimal Exercise Behavior from 1.2 to 3.0, and Forfeiture Rate from 0% to 40%.
Generalized Black-Scholes: $41.72

Customized Binomial Lattice	Suboptimal (1.2)	Suboptimal (1.4)	Suboptimal (1.6)	Suboptimal (1.8)	Suboptimal (2.0)	Suboptimal (2.2)	Suboptimal (2.4)	Suboptimal (2.6)	Suboptimal (2.8)	Suboptimal (3.0)
Forfeiture (0%)	$36.96	$38.00	$38.82	$39.32	$39.72	$40.05	$40.32	$40.48	$40.62	$40.75
Forfeiture (5%)	$25.97	$26.65	$27.19	$27.51	$27.77	$27.99	$28.16	$28.26	$28.36	$28.44
Forfeiture (10%)	$18.25	$18.70	$19.05	$19.26	$19.42	$19.57	$19.68	$19.75	$19.80	$19.86
Forfeiture (15%)	$12.82	$13.12	$13.35	$13.48	$13.59	$13.68	$13.76	$13.80	$13.84	$13.87
Forfeiture (20%)	$9.01	$9.21	$9.36	$9.44	$9.52	$9.58	$9.62	$9.65	$9.68	$9.70
Forfeiture (25%)	$6.33	$6.46	$6.56	$6.62	$6.66	$6.70	$6.73	$6.75	$6.77	$6.78
Forfeiture (30%)	$4.45	$4.53	$4.60	$4.64	$4.67	$4.69	$4.71	$4.72	$4.74	$4.75
Forfeiture (35%)	$3.13	$3.18	$3.22	$3.25	$3.27	$3.29	$3.30	$3.31	$3.31	$3.32
Forfeiture (40%)	$2.20	$2.23	$2.26	$2.28	$2.29	$2.30	$2.31	$2.32	$2.32	$2.32

Percentage Difference between Binomial and Black-Scholes Model	Suboptimal (1.2)	Suboptimal (1.4)	Suboptimal (1.6)	Suboptimal (1.8)	Suboptimal (2.0)	Suboptimal (2.2)	Suboptimal (2.4)	Suboptimal (2.6)	Suboptimal (2.8)	Suboptimal (3.0)
Forfeiture (0%)	–11.41%	–8.91%	–6.94%	–5.74%	–4.79%	–3.99%	–3.34%	–2.96%	–2.63%	–2.33%
Forfeiture (5%)	–37.76%	–36.11%	–34.83%	–34.05%	–33.43%	–32.91%	–32.49%	–32.25%	–32.03%	–31.83%
Forfeiture (10%)	–56.26%	–55.18%	–54.34%	–53.84%	–53.44%	–53.10%	–52.83%	–52.67%	–52.53%	–52.40%
Forfeiture (15%)	–69.27%	–68.55%	–68.01%	–67.68%	–67.42%	–67.20%	–67.02%	–66.92%	–66.82%	–66.74%
Forfeiture (20%)	–78.41%	–77.93%	–77.57%	–77.36%	–77.19%	–77.05%	–76.93%	–76.86%	–76.80%	–76.75%
Forfeiture (25%)	–84.83%	–84.51%	–84.28%	–84.14%	–84.03%	–83.93%	–83.86%	–83.82%	–83.78%	–83.74%
Forfeiture (30%)	–89.34%	–89.13%	–88.98%	–88.88%	–88.81%	–88.75%	–88.70%	–88.67%	–88.65%	–88.63%
Forfeiture (35%)	–92.51%	–92.37%	–92.27%	–92.21%	–92.16%	–92.12%	–92.09%	–92.07%	–92.06%	–92.04%
Forfeiture (40%)	–94.74%	–94.65%	–94.58%	–94.54%	–94.51%	–94.48%	–94.46%	–94.45%	–94.44%	–94.43%

SEVENTY PERCENT VOLATILITY AND 10-YEAR MATURITY ESOs WITH VARYING STOCK PRICE, SUBOPTIMAL BEHAVIOR, VESTING PERIOD, AND FORFEITURE RATES

This section provides ESO valuation results on an underlying stock with 70 percent volatility and a 10-year maturity. The analysis is divided into 1-month, 1-year, 3-year, 4-year, 5-year, and 7-year vesting periods, and accounts for stock prices at grant date of $20, $40, $60, and $80.

MATURITY OF 10 YEARS AND VESTING OF 1 MONTH ON A $20 STOCK PRICE

Stock Price and Strike Price of $20, Maturity of 10 Years, Risk-Free Rate of 3.5%, 70% Volatility, 0% Dividends, Vesting of 1 Month, Employee Suboptimal Exercise Behavior from 1.2 to 3.0, and Forfeiture Rate from 0% to 40%.
Generalized Black-Scholes: $15.53

Customized Binomial Lattice	Suboptimal (1.2)	Suboptimal (1.4)	Suboptimal (1.6)	Suboptimal (1.8)	Suboptimal (2.0)	Suboptimal (2.2)	Suboptimal (2.4)	Suboptimal (2.6)	Suboptimal (2.8)	Suboptimal (3.0)
Forfeiture (0%)	$4.03	$5.85	$7.54	$9.00	$9.64	$10.77	$11.26	$11.70	$12.10	$12.47
Forfeiture (5%)	$3.92	$5.61	$7.13	$8.41	$8.97	$9.91	$10.32	$10.68	$11.01	$11.30
Forfeiture (10%)	$3.83	$5.40	$6.79	$7.92	$8.40	$9.21	$9.55	$9.85	$10.12	$10.36
Forfeiture (15%)	$3.74	$5.22	$6.49	$7.51	$7.93	$8.63	$8.91	$9.17	$9.39	$9.58
Forfeiture (20%)	$3.67	$5.06	$6.23	$7.15	$7.52	$8.13	$8.38	$8.59	$8.78	$8.94
Forfeiture (25%)	$3.60	$4.91	$6.01	$6.84	$7.17	$7.70	$7.92	$8.10	$8.26	$8.39
Forfeiture (30%)	$3.53	$4.79	$5.80	$6.56	$6.86	$7.33	$7.52	$7.68	$7.81	$7.93
Forfeiture (35%)	$3.47	$4.67	$5.62	$6.32	$6.59	$7.01	$7.17	$7.31	$7.42	$7.52
Forfeiture (40%)	$3.42	$4.56	$5.45	$6.10	$6.34	$6.72	$6.86	$6.98	$7.08	$7.17

Percentage Difference between Binomial and Black-Scholes Model	Suboptimal (1.2)	Suboptimal (1.4)	Suboptimal (1.6)	Suboptimal (1.8)	Suboptimal (2.0)	Suboptimal (2.2)	Suboptimal (2.4)	Suboptimal (2.6)	Suboptimal (2.8)	Suboptimal (3.0)
Forfeiture (0%)	–74.02%	–62.33%	–51.44%	–42.02%	–37.89%	–30.65%	–27.51%	–24.64%	–22.05%	–19.69%
Forfeiture (5%)	–74.73%	–63.89%	–54.07%	–45.81%	–42.25%	–36.15%	–33.55%	–31.21%	–29.11%	–27.23%
Forfeiture (10%)	–75.35%	–65.23%	–56.28%	–48.96%	–45.87%	–40.67%	–38.49%	–36.55%	–34.83%	–33.30%
Forfeiture (15%)	–75.90%	–66.39%	–58.19%	–51.64%	–48.93%	–44.44%	–42.59%	–40.97%	–39.54%	–38.28%
Forfeiture (20%)	–76.39%	–67.42%	–59.85%	–53.95%	–51.54%	–47.64%	–46.05%	–44.67%	–43.47%	–42.43%
Forfeiture (25%)	–76.84%	–68.34%	–61.32%	–55.96%	–53.81%	–50.38%	–49.01%	–47.83%	–46.81%	–45.94%
Forfeiture (30%)	–77.26%	–69.18%	–62.63%	–57.73%	–55.80%	–52.76%	–51.57%	–50.55%	–49.68%	–48.94%
Forfeiture (35%)	–77.64%	–69.94%	–63.80%	–59.31%	–57.57%	–54.86%	–53.81%	–52.93%	–52.18%	–51.55%
Forfeiture (40%)	–78.00%	–70.64%	–64.88%	–60.73%	–59.15%	–56.72%	–55.80%	–55.02%	–54.37%	–53.83%

MATURITY OF 10 YEARS AND VESTING OF 1 MONTH ON A $40 STOCK PRICE

Stock Price and Strike Price of $40, Maturity of 10 Years, Risk-Free Rate of 3.5%, 70% Volatility, 0% Dividends, Vesting of 1 Month, Employee Suboptimal Exercise Behavior from 1.2 to 3.0, and Forfeiture Rate from 0% to 40%.
Generalized Black-Scholes: $31.05

Customized Binomial Lattice	Suboptimal (1.2)	Suboptimal (1.4)	Suboptimal (1.6)	Suboptimal (1.8)	Suboptimal (2.0)	Suboptimal (2.2)	Suboptimal (2.4)	Suboptimal (2.6)	Suboptimal (2.8)	Suboptimal (3.0)
Forfeiture (0%)	$8.07	$11.70	$15.08	$18.00	$19.29	$21.53	$22.51	$23.40	$24.20	$24.94
Forfeiture (5%)	$7.85	$11.21	$14.26	$16.83	$17.93	$19.82	$20.63	$21.36	$22.01	$22.60
Forfeiture (10%)	$7.66	$10.80	$13.57	$15.85	$16.81	$18.42	$19.10	$19.70	$20.24	$20.71
Forfeiture (15%)	$7.48	$10.44	$12.98	$15.02	$15.86	$17.25	$17.83	$18.33	$18.77	$19.16
Forfeiture (20%)	$7.33	$10.12	$12.47	$14.30	$15.05	$16.26	$16.75	$17.18	$17.55	$17.88
Forfeiture (25%)	$7.19	$9.83	$12.01	$13.68	$14.34	$15.41	$15.83	$16.20	$16.51	$16.79
Forfeiture (30%)	$7.06	$9.57	$11.60	$13.13	$13.72	$14.67	$15.04	$15.35	$15.62	$15.85
Forfeiture (35%)	$6.94	$9.33	$11.24	$12.63	$13.18	$14.02	$14.34	$14.62	$14.85	$15.05
Forfeiture (40%)	$6.83	$9.12	$10.91	$12.19	$12.68	$13.44	$13.73	$13.97	$14.17	$14.34

Percentage Difference between Binomial and Black-Scholes Model	Suboptimal (1.2)	Suboptimal (1.4)	Suboptimal (1.6)	Suboptimal (1.8)	Suboptimal (2.0)	Suboptimal (2.2)	Suboptimal (2.4)	Suboptimal (2.6)	Suboptimal (2.8)	Suboptimal (3.0)
Forfeiture (0%)	−74.02%	−62.33%	−51.44%	−42.02%	−37.89%	−30.65%	−27.51%	−24.64%	−22.05%	−19.69%
Forfeiture (5%)	−74.73%	−63.89%	−54.07%	−45.81%	−42.25%	−36.15%	−33.55%	−31.21%	−29.11%	−27.23%
Forfeiture (10%)	−75.35%	−65.23%	−56.28%	−48.96%	−45.87%	−40.67%	−38.49%	−36.55%	−34.83%	−33.30%
Forfeiture (15%)	−75.90%	−66.39%	−58.19%	−51.64%	−48.93%	−44.44%	−42.59%	−40.97%	−39.54%	−38.28%
Forfeiture (20%)	−76.39%	−67.42%	−59.85%	−53.95%	−51.54%	−47.64%	−46.05%	−44.67%	−43.47%	−42.43%
Forfeiture (25%)	−76.84%	−68.34%	−61.32%	−55.96%	−53.81%	−50.38%	−49.01%	−47.83%	−46.81%	−45.94%
Forfeiture (30%)	−77.26%	−69.18%	−62.63%	−57.73%	−55.80%	−52.76%	−51.57%	−50.55%	−49.68%	−48.94%
Forfeiture (35%)	−77.64%	−69.94%	−63.80%	−59.31%	−57.57%	−54.86%	−53.81%	−52.93%	−52.18%	−51.55%
Forfeiture (40%)	−78.00%	−70.64%	−64.88%	−60.73%	−59.15%	−56.72%	−55.80%	−55.02%	−54.37%	−53.83%

MATURITY OF 10 YEARS AND VESTING OF 1 MONTH ON A $60 STOCK PRICE

Stock Price and Strike Price of $60, Maturity of 10 Years, Risk-Free Rate of 3.5%, 70% Volatility, 0% Dividends, Vesting of 1 Month, Employee Suboptimal Exercise Behavior from 1.2 to 3.0, and Forfeiture Rate from 0% to 40%.
Generalized Black-Scholes: $46.58

Customized Binomial Lattice	Suboptimal (1.2)	Suboptimal (1.4)	Suboptimal (1.6)	Suboptimal (1.8)	Suboptimal (2.0)	Suboptimal (2.2)	Suboptimal (2.4)	Suboptimal (2.6)	Suboptimal (2.8)	Suboptimal (3.0)
Forfeiture (0%)	$12.10	$17.54	$22.62	$27.00	$28.93	$32.30	$33.77	$35.10	$36.31	$37.40
Forfeiture (5%)	$11.77	$16.82	$21.39	$25.24	$26.90	$29.74	$30.95	$32.04	$33.02	$33.90
Forfeiture (10%)	$11.48	$16.20	$20.36	$23.77	$25.21	$27.63	$28.65	$29.55	$30.35	$31.07
Forfeiture (15%)	$11.23	$15.65	$19.47	$22.52	$23.79	$25.88	$26.74	$27.50	$28.16	$28.75
Forfeiture (20%)	$11.00	$15.17	$18.70	$21.45	$22.57	$24.39	$25.13	$25.77	$26.33	$26.81
Forfeiture (25%)	$10.79	$14.74	$18.02	$20.51	$21.51	$23.11	$23.75	$24.30	$24.77	$25.18
Forfeiture (30%)	$10.59	$14.36	$17.41	$19.69	$20.59	$22.00	$22.56	$23.03	$23.44	$23.78
Forfeiture (35%)	$10.41	$14.00	$16.86	$18.95	$19.76	$21.02	$21.51	$21.92	$22.27	$22.57
Forfeiture (40%)	$10.25	$13.68	$16.36	$18.29	$19.03	$20.16	$20.59	$20.95	$21.25	$21.51

Percentage Difference between Binomial and Black-Scholes Model	Suboptimal (1.2)	Suboptimal (1.4)	Suboptimal (1.6)	Suboptimal (1.8)	Suboptimal (2.0)	Suboptimal (2.2)	Suboptimal (2.4)	Suboptimal (2.6)	Suboptimal (2.8)	Suboptimal (3.0)
Forfeiture (0%)	–74.02%	–62.33%	–51.44%	–42.02%	–37.89%	–30.65%	–27.51%	–24.64%	–22.05%	–19.69%
Forfeiture (5%)	–74.73%	–63.89%	–54.07%	–45.81%	–42.25%	–36.15%	–33.55%	–31.21%	–29.11%	–27.23%
Forfeiture (10%)	–75.35%	–65.23%	–56.28%	–48.96%	–45.87%	–40.67%	–38.49%	–36.55%	–34.83%	–33.30%
Forfeiture (15%)	–75.90%	–66.39%	–58.19%	–51.64%	–48.93%	–44.44%	–42.59%	–40.97%	–39.54%	–38.28%
Forfeiture (20%)	–76.39%	–67.42%	–59.85%	–53.95%	–51.54%	–47.64%	–46.05%	–44.67%	–43.47%	–42.43%
Forfeiture (25%)	–76.84%	–68.34%	–61.32%	–55.96%	–53.81%	–50.38%	–49.01%	–47.83%	–46.81%	–45.94%
Forfeiture (30%)	–77.26%	–69.18%	–62.63%	–57.73%	–55.80%	–52.76%	–51.57%	–50.55%	–49.68%	–48.94%
Forfeiture (35%)	–77.64%	–69.94%	–63.80%	–59.31%	–57.57%	–54.86%	–53.81%	–52.93%	–52.18%	–51.55%
Forfeiture (40%)	–78.00%	–70.64%	–64.88%	–60.73%	–59.15%	–56.72%	–55.80%	–55.02%	–54.37%	–53.83%

MATURITY OF 10 YEARS AND VESTING OF 1 MONTH ON AN $80 STOCK PRICE

Stock Price and Strike Price of $80, Maturity of 10 Years, Risk-Free Rate of 3.5%, 70% Volatility, 0% Dividends, Vesting of 1 Month, Employee Suboptimal Exercise Behavior from 1.2 to 3.0, and Forfeiture Rate from 0% to 40%.
Generalized Black-Scholes: $62.10

Customized Binomial Lattice	Suboptimal (1.2)	Suboptimal (1.4)	Suboptimal (1.6)	Suboptimal (1.8)	Suboptimal (2.0)	Suboptimal (2.2)	Suboptimal (2.4)	Suboptimal (2.6)	Suboptimal (2.8)	Suboptimal (3.0)
Forfeiture (0%)	$16.13	$23.39	$30.16	$36.00	$38.57	$43.07	$45.02	$46.80	$48.41	$49.87
Forfeiture (5%)	$15.69	$22.42	$28.53	$33.66	$35.86	$39.65	$41.27	$42.72	$44.02	$45.19
Forfeiture (10%)	$15.31	$21.59	$27.15	$31.69	$33.61	$36.84	$38.20	$39.40	$40.47	$41.42
Forfeiture (15%)	$14.97	$20.87	$25.96	$30.03	$31.72	$34.50	$35.65	$36.66	$37.55	$38.33
Forfeiture (20%)	$14.66	$20.23	$24.93	$28.60	$30.09	$32.52	$33.50	$34.36	$35.10	$35.75
Forfeiture (25%)	$14.38	$19.66	$24.02	$27.35	$28.68	$30.82	$31.67	$32.40	$33.03	$33.57
Forfeiture (30%)	$14.12	$19.14	$23.21	$26.25	$27.45	$29.33	$30.08	$30.71	$31.25	$31.71
Forfeiture (35%)	$13.89	$18.67	$22.48	$25.27	$26.35	$28.03	$28.68	$29.23	$29.70	$30.09
Forfeiture (40%)	$13.66	$18.24	$21.81	$24.39	$25.37	$26.88	$27.45	$27.93	$28.34	$28.68

Percentage Difference between Binomial and Black-Scholes Model	Suboptimal (1.2)	Suboptimal (1.4)	Suboptimal (1.6)	Suboptimal (1.8)	Suboptimal (2.0)	Suboptimal (2.2)	Suboptimal (2.4)	Suboptimal (2.6)	Suboptimal (2.8)	Suboptimal (3.0)
Forfeiture (0%)	–74.02%	–62.33%	–51.44%	–42.02%	–37.89%	–30.65%	–27.51%	–24.64%	–22.05%	–19.69%
Forfeiture (5%)	–74.73%	–63.89%	–54.07%	–45.81%	–42.25%	–36.15%	–33.55%	–31.21%	–29.11%	–27.23%
Forfeiture (10%)	–75.35%	–65.23%	–56.28%	–48.96%	–45.87%	–40.67%	–38.49%	–36.55%	–34.83%	–33.30%
Forfeiture (15%)	–75.90%	–66.39%	–58.19%	–51.64%	–48.93%	–44.44%	–42.59%	–40.97%	–39.54%	–38.28%
Forfeiture (20%)	–76.39%	–67.42%	–59.85%	–53.95%	–51.54%	–47.64%	–46.05%	–44.67%	–43.47%	–42.43%
Forfeiture (25%)	–76.84%	–68.34%	–61.32%	–55.96%	–53.81%	–50.38%	–49.01%	–47.83%	–46.81%	–45.94%
Forfeiture (30%)	–77.26%	–69.18%	–62.63%	–57.73%	–55.80%	–52.76%	–51.57%	–50.55%	–49.68%	–48.94%
Forfeiture (35%)	–77.64%	–69.94%	–63.80%	–59.31%	–57.57%	–54.86%	–53.81%	–52.93%	–52.18%	–51.55%
Forfeiture (40%)	–78.00%	–70.64%	–64.88%	–60.73%	–59.15%	–56.72%	–55.80%	–55.02%	–54.37%	–53.83%

MATURITY OF 10 YEARS AND VESTING OF 1 YEAR ON A $20 STOCK PRICE

Stock Price and Strike Price of $20, Maturity of 10 Years, Risk-Free Rate of 3.5%, 70% Volatility, 0% Dividends, Vesting of 1 Year, Employee Suboptimal Exercise Behavior from 1.2 to 3.0, and Forfeiture Rate from 0% to 40%.
Generalized Black-Scholes: $15.53

Customized Binomial Lattice	Suboptimal (1.2)	Suboptimal (1.4)	Suboptimal (1.6)	Suboptimal (1.8)	Suboptimal (2.0)	Suboptimal (2.2)	Suboptimal (2.4)	Suboptimal (2.6)	Suboptimal (2.8)	Suboptimal (3.0)
Forfeiture (0%)	$7.18	$8.15	$9.11	$10.03	$10.45	$11.27	$11.65	$12.00	$12.34	$12.64
Forfeiture (5%)	$6.74	$7.58	$8.40	$9.16	$9.51	$10.18	$10.49	$10.76	$11.03	$11.27
Forfeiture (10%)	$6.33	$7.07	$7.77	$8.42	$8.71	$9.26	$9.51	$9.73	$9.95	$10.14
Forfeiture (15%)	$5.97	$6.62	$7.22	$7.77	$8.02	$8.47	$8.68	$8.86	$9.04	$9.19
Forfeiture (20%)	$5.63	$6.20	$6.73	$7.20	$7.41	$7.79	$7.97	$8.12	$8.26	$8.38
Forfeiture (25%)	$5.31	$5.82	$6.29	$6.70	$6.87	$7.20	$7.34	$7.47	$7.59	$7.69
Forfeiture (30%)	$5.02	$5.48	$5.89	$6.24	$6.39	$6.67	$6.79	$6.90	$7.00	$7.08
Forfeiture (35%)	$4.74	$5.16	$5.52	$5.83	$5.96	$6.20	$6.31	$6.39	$6.48	$6.55
Forfeiture (40%)	$4.49	$4.86	$5.18	$5.46	$5.57	$5.78	$5.87	$5.94	$6.01	$6.07

Percentage Difference between Binomial and Black-Scholes Model	Suboptimal (1.2)	Suboptimal (1.4)	Suboptimal (1.6)	Suboptimal (1.8)	Suboptimal (2.0)	Suboptimal (2.2)	Suboptimal (2.4)	Suboptimal (2.6)	Suboptimal (2.8)	Suboptimal (3.0)
Forfeiture (0%)	–53.77%	–47.48%	–41.31%	–35.42%	–32.68%	–27.42%	–24.95%	–22.70%	–20.53%	–18.56%
Forfeiture (5%)	–56.61%	–51.17%	–45.92%	–40.99%	–38.75%	–34.46%	–32.46%	–30.68%	–28.95%	–27.41%
Forfeiture (10%)	–59.20%	–54.44%	–49.93%	–45.78%	–43.91%	–40.38%	–38.75%	–37.31%	–35.92%	–34.70%
Forfeiture (15%)	–61.57%	–57.38%	–53.48%	–49.94%	–48.37%	–45.43%	–44.09%	–42.91%	–41.79%	–40.80%
Forfeiture (20%)	–63.76%	–60.05%	–56.65%	–53.60%	–52.27%	–49.80%	–48.69%	–47.72%	–46.80%	–46.00%
Forfeiture (25%)	–65.79%	–62.49%	–59.50%	–56.87%	–55.73%	–53.64%	–52.70%	–51.90%	–51.13%	–50.48%
Forfeiture (30%)	–67.68%	–64.73%	–62.09%	–59.80%	–58.82%	–57.03%	–56.24%	–55.56%	–54.93%	–54.38%
Forfeiture (35%)	–69.45%	–66.79%	–64.45%	–62.44%	–61.60%	–60.06%	–59.39%	–58.82%	–58.28%	–57.83%
Forfeiture (40%)	–71.10%	–68.70%	–66.62%	–64.86%	–64.12%	–62.79%	–62.21%	–61.73%	–61.28%	–60.90%

MATURITY OF 10 YEARS AND VESTING OF 1 YEAR ON A $40 STOCK PRICE

Stock Price and Strike Price of $40, Maturity of 10 Years, Risk-Free Rate of 3.5%, 70% Volatility, 0% Dividends, Vesting of 1 Year, Employee Suboptimal Exercise Behavior from 1.2 to 3.0, and Forfeiture Rate from 0% to 40%.
Generalized Black-Scholes: $31.05

Customized Binomial Lattice	Suboptimal (1.2)	Suboptimal (1.4)	Suboptimal (1.6)	Suboptimal (1.8)	Suboptimal (2.0)	Suboptimal (2.2)	Suboptimal (2.4)	Suboptimal (2.6)	Suboptimal (2.8)	Suboptimal (3.0)
Forfeiture (0%)	$14.35	$16.31	$18.22	$20.05	$20.90	$22.54	$23.30	$24.00	$24.68	$25.29
Forfeiture (5%)	$13.47	$15.16	$16.79	$18.32	$19.02	$20.35	$20.97	$21.53	$22.06	$22.54
Forfeiture (10%)	$12.67	$14.15	$15.55	$16.84	$17.42	$18.51	$19.02	$19.47	$19.90	$20.28
Forfeiture (15%)	$11.93	$13.23	$14.44	$15.54	$16.03	$16.95	$17.36	$17.73	$18.08	$18.38
Forfeiture (20%)	$11.25	$12.40	$13.46	$14.41	$14.82	$15.59	$15.93	$16.23	$16.52	$16.77
Forfeiture (25%)	$10.62	$11.65	$12.58	$13.39	$13.75	$14.40	$14.69	$14.94	$15.17	$15.38
Forfeiture (30%)	$10.03	$10.95	$11.77	$12.48	$12.79	$13.34	$13.59	$13.80	$14.00	$14.16
Forfeiture (35%)	$9.49	$10.31	$11.04	$11.66	$11.92	$12.40	$12.61	$12.79	$12.95	$13.09
Forfeiture (40%)	$8.97	$9.72	$10.36	$10.91	$11.14	$11.55	$11.73	$11.88	$12.02	$12.14

Percentage Difference between Binomial and Black-Scholes Model	Suboptimal (1.2)	Suboptimal (1.4)	Suboptimal (1.6)	Suboptimal (1.8)	Suboptimal (2.0)	Suboptimal (2.2)	Suboptimal (2.4)	Suboptimal (2.6)	Suboptimal (2.8)	Suboptimal (3.0)
Forfeiture (0%)	−53.77%	−47.48%	−41.31%	−35.42%	−32.68%	−27.42%	−24.95%	−22.70%	−20.53%	−18.56%
Forfeiture (5%)	−56.61%	−51.17%	−45.92%	−40.99%	−38.75%	−34.46%	−32.46%	−30.68%	−28.95%	−27.41%
Forfeiture (10%)	−59.20%	−54.44%	−49.93%	−45.78%	−43.91%	−40.38%	−38.75%	−37.31%	−35.92%	−34.70%
Forfeiture (15%)	−61.57%	−57.38%	−53.48%	−49.94%	−48.37%	−45.43%	−44.09%	−42.91%	−41.79%	−40.80%
Forfeiture (20%)	−63.76%	−60.05%	−56.65%	−53.60%	−52.27%	−49.80%	−48.69%	−47.72%	−46.80%	−46.00%
Forfeiture (25%)	−65.79%	−62.49%	−59.50%	−56.87%	−55.73%	−53.64%	−52.70%	−51.90%	−51.13%	−50.48%
Forfeiture (30%)	−67.68%	−64.73%	−62.09%	−59.80%	−58.82%	−57.03%	−56.24%	−55.56%	−54.93%	−54.38%
Forfeiture (35%)	−69.45%	−66.79%	−64.45%	−62.44%	−61.60%	−60.06%	−59.39%	−58.82%	−58.28%	−57.83%
Forfeiture (40%)	−71.10%	−68.70%	−66.62%	−64.86%	−64.12%	−62.79%	−62.21%	−61.73%	−61.28%	−60.90%

MATURITY OF 10 YEARS AND VESTING OF 1 YEAR ON A $60 STOCK PRICE

Stock Price and Strike Price of $60, Maturity of 10 Years, Risk-Free Rate of 3.5%, 70% Volatility, 0% Dividends, Vesting of 1 Year, Employee Suboptimal Exercise Behavior from 1.2 to 3.0, and Forfeiture Rate from 0% to 40%.
Generalized Black-Scholes: $46.58

Customized Binomial Lattice	Suboptimal (1.2)	Suboptimal (1.4)	Suboptimal (1.6)	Suboptimal (1.8)	Suboptimal (2.0)	Suboptimal (2.2)	Suboptimal (2.4)	Suboptimal (2.6)	Suboptimal (2.8)	Suboptimal (3.0)
Forfeiture (0%)	$21.53	$24.46	$27.33	$30.08	$31.35	$33.80	$34.96	$36.00	$37.01	$37.93
Forfeiture (5%)	$20.21	$22.74	$25.19	$27.48	$28.53	$30.53	$31.46	$32.29	$33.09	$33.81
Forfeiture (10%)	$19.00	$21.22	$23.32	$25.26	$26.13	$27.77	$28.53	$29.20	$29.84	$30.42
Forfeiture (15%)	$17.90	$19.85	$21.67	$23.32	$24.05	$25.42	$26.04	$26.59	$27.11	$27.57
Forfeiture (20%)	$16.88	$18.61	$20.19	$21.61	$22.23	$23.38	$23.90	$24.35	$24.78	$25.15
Forfeiture (25%)	$15.93	$17.47	$18.86	$20.09	$20.62	$21.59	$22.03	$22.41	$22.76	$23.07
Forfeiture (30%)	$15.05	$16.43	$17.66	$18.73	$19.18	$20.01	$20.38	$20.70	$20.99	$21.25
Forfeiture (35%)	$14.23	$15.47	$16.56	$17.49	$17.89	$18.60	$18.92	$19.18	$19.43	$19.64
Forfeiture (40%)	$13.46	$14.58	$15.55	$16.37	$16.71	$17.33	$17.60	$17.82	$18.04	$18.21

Percentage Difference between Binomial and Black-Scholes Model	Suboptimal (1.2)	Suboptimal (1.4)	Suboptimal (1.6)	Suboptimal (1.8)	Suboptimal (2.0)	Suboptimal (2.2)	Suboptimal (2.4)	Suboptimal (2.6)	Suboptimal (2.8)	Suboptimal (3.0)
Forfeiture (0%)	−53.77%	−47.48%	−41.31%	−35.42%	−32.68%	−27.42%	−24.95%	−22.70%	−20.53%	−18.56%
Forfeiture (5%)	−56.61%	−51.17%	−45.92%	−40.99%	−38.75%	−34.46%	−32.46%	−30.68%	−28.95%	−27.41%
Forfeiture (10%)	−59.20%	−54.44%	−49.93%	−45.78%	−43.91%	−40.38%	−38.75%	−37.31%	−35.92%	−34.70%
Forfeiture (15%)	−61.57%	−57.38%	−53.48%	−49.94%	−48.37%	−45.43%	−44.09%	−42.91%	−41.79%	−40.80%
Forfeiture (20%)	−63.76%	−60.05%	−56.65%	−53.60%	−52.27%	−49.80%	−48.69%	−47.72%	−46.80%	−46.00%
Forfeiture (25%)	−65.79%	−62.49%	−59.50%	−56.87%	−55.73%	−53.64%	−52.70%	−51.90%	−51.13%	−50.48%
Forfeiture (30%)	−67.68%	−64.73%	−62.09%	−59.80%	−58.82%	−57.03%	−56.24%	−55.56%	−54.93%	−54.38%
Forfeiture (35%)	−69.45%	−66.79%	−64.45%	−62.44%	−61.60%	−60.06%	−59.39%	−58.82%	−58.28%	−57.83%
Forfeiture (40%)	−71.10%	−68.70%	−66.62%	−64.86%	−64.12%	−62.79%	−62.21%	−61.73%	−61.28%	−60.90%

MATURITY OF 10 YEARS AND VESTING OF 1 YEAR ON AN $80 STOCK PRICE

Stock Price and Strike Price of $80, Maturity of 10 Years, Risk-Free Rate of 3.5%, 70% Volatility, 0% Dividends, Vesting of 1 Year, Employee Suboptimal Exercise Behavior from 1.2 to 3.0, and Forfeiture Rate from 0% to 40%.
Generalized Black-Scholes: $62.10

Customized Binomial Lattice	Suboptimal (1.2)	Suboptimal (1.4)	Suboptimal (1.6)	Suboptimal (1.8)	Suboptimal (2.0)	Suboptimal (2.2)	Suboptimal (2.4)	Suboptimal (2.6)	Suboptimal (2.8)	Suboptimal (3.0)
Forfeiture (0%)	$28.71	$32.61	$36.45	$40.11	$41.80	$45.07	$46.61	$48.00	$49.35	$50.57
Forfeiture (5%)	$26.94	$30.33	$33.59	$36.64	$38.04	$40.70	$41.94	$43.05	$44.12	$45.08
Forfeiture (10%)	$25.34	$28.29	$31.09	$33.67	$34.84	$37.03	$38.04	$38.93	$39.79	$40.55
Forfeiture (15%)	$23.86	$26.47	$28.89	$31.09	$32.06	$33.89	$34.72	$35.45	$36.15	$36.76
Forfeiture (20%)	$22.50	$24.81	$26.92	$28.81	$29.64	$31.17	$31.87	$32.47	$33.04	$33.54
Forfeiture (25%)	$21.24	$23.30	$25.15	$26.79	$27.49	$28.79	$29.37	$29.87	$30.35	$30.75
Forfeiture (30%)	$20.07	$21.91	$23.54	$24.97	$25.58	$26.69	$27.18	$27.60	$27.99	$28.33
Forfeiture (35%)	$18.97	$20.62	$22.08	$23.32	$23.85	$24.80	$25.22	$25.57	$25.91	$26.19
Forfeiture (40%)	$17.95	$19.43	$20.73	$21.83	$22.28	$23.11	$23.47	$23.77	$24.05	$24.28

Percentage Difference between Binomial and Black-Scholes Model	Suboptimal (1.2)	Suboptimal (1.4)	Suboptimal (1.6)	Suboptimal (1.8)	Suboptimal (2.0)	Suboptimal (2.2)	Suboptimal (2.4)	Suboptimal (2.6)	Suboptimal (2.8)	Suboptimal (3.0)
Forfeiture (0%)	−53.77%	−47.48%	−41.31%	−35.42%	−32.68%	−27.42%	−24.95%	−22.70%	−20.53%	−18.56%
Forfeiture (5%)	−56.61%	−51.17%	−45.92%	−40.99%	−38.75%	−34.46%	−32.46%	−30.68%	−28.95%	−27.41%
Forfeiture (10%)	−59.20%	−54.44%	−49.93%	−45.78%	−43.91%	−40.38%	−38.75%	−37.31%	−35.92%	−34.70%
Forfeiture (15%)	−61.57%	−57.38%	−53.48%	−49.94%	−48.37%	−45.43%	−44.09%	−42.91%	−41.79%	−40.80%
Forfeiture (20%)	−63.76%	−60.05%	−56.65%	−53.60%	−52.27%	−49.80%	−48.69%	−47.72%	−46.80%	−46.00%
Forfeiture (25%)	−65.79%	−62.49%	−59.50%	−56.87%	−55.73%	−53.64%	−52.70%	−51.90%	−51.13%	−50.48%
Forfeiture (30%)	−67.68%	−64.73%	−62.09%	−59.80%	−58.82%	−57.03%	−56.24%	−55.56%	−54.93%	−54.38%
Forfeiture (35%)	−69.45%	−66.79%	−64.45%	−62.44%	−61.60%	−60.06%	−59.39%	−58.82%	−58.28%	−57.83%
Forfeiture (40%)	−71.10%	−68.70%	−66.62%	−64.86%	−64.12%	−62.79%	−62.21%	−61.73%	−61.28%	−60.90%

MATURITY OF 10 YEARS AND VESTING OF 3 YEARS ON A $20 STOCK PRICE

Stock Price and Strike Price of $20, Maturity of 10 Years, Risk-Free Rate of 3.5%, 70% Volatility, 0% Dividends, Vesting of 3 Years, Employee Suboptimal Exercise Behavior from 1.2 to 3.0, and Forfeiture Rate from 0% to 40%.
Generalized Black-Scholes: $15.53

Customized Binomial Lattice	Suboptimal (1.2)	Suboptimal (1.4)	Suboptimal (1.6)	Suboptimal (1.8)	Suboptimal (2.0)	Suboptimal (2.2)	Suboptimal (2.4)	Suboptimal (2.6)	Suboptimal (2.8)	Suboptimal (3.0)
Forfeiture (0%)	$10.59	$11.17	$11.71	$12.22	$12.45	$12.89	$13.10	$13.29	$13.48	$13.65
Forfeiture (5%)	$9.06	$9.51	$9.93	$10.31	$10.49	$10.82	$10.98	$11.12	$11.26	$11.38
Forfeiture (10%)	$7.75	$8.11	$8.43	$8.73	$8.86	$9.11	$9.23	$9.33	$9.44	$9.53
Forfeiture (15%)	$6.64	$6.92	$7.18	$7.40	$7.50	$7.70	$7.79	$7.86	$7.94	$8.01
Forfeiture (20%)	$5.69	$5.91	$6.11	$6.29	$6.37	$6.52	$6.58	$6.64	$6.70	$6.75
Forfeiture (25%)	$4.88	$5.06	$5.22	$5.36	$5.42	$5.53	$5.58	$5.62	$5.67	$5.71
Forfeiture (30%)	$4.18	$4.33	$4.45	$4.56	$4.61	$4.70	$4.74	$4.77	$4.81	$4.83
Forfeiture (35%)	$3.59	$3.71	$3.81	$3.89	$3.93	$4.00	$4.03	$4.05	$4.08	$4.10
Forfeiture (40%)	$3.08	$3.17	$3.25	$3.32	$3.35	$3.41	$3.43	$3.45	$3.47	$3.49

Percentage Difference between Binomial and Black-Scholes Model	Suboptimal (1.2)	Suboptimal (1.4)	Suboptimal (1.6)	Suboptimal (1.8)	Suboptimal (2.0)	Suboptimal (2.2)	Suboptimal (2.4)	Suboptimal (2.6)	Suboptimal (2.8)	Suboptimal (3.0)
Forfeiture (0%)	–31.76%	–28.07%	–24.57%	–21.31%	–19.83%	–16.96%	–15.59%	–14.37%	–13.15%	–12.07%
Forfeiture (5%)	–41.65%	–38.76%	–36.06%	–33.58%	–32.46%	–30.31%	–29.29%	–28.39%	–27.50%	–26.70%
Forfeiture (10%)	–50.06%	–47.78%	–45.69%	–43.78%	–42.93%	–41.31%	–40.55%	–39.88%	–39.21%	–38.63%
Forfeiture (15%)	–57.22%	–55.42%	–53.78%	–52.31%	–51.66%	–50.43%	–49.85%	–49.35%	–48.85%	–48.42%
Forfeiture (20%)	–63.34%	–61.91%	–60.62%	–59.47%	–58.97%	–58.03%	–57.59%	–57.21%	–56.84%	–56.51%
Forfeiture (25%)	–68.57%	–67.42%	–66.40%	–65.51%	–65.12%	–64.39%	–64.06%	–63.77%	–63.49%	–63.24%
Forfeiture (30%)	–73.05%	–72.12%	–71.31%	–70.61%	–70.31%	–69.74%	–69.48%	–69.26%	–69.05%	–68.86%
Forfeiture (35%)	–76.88%	–76.13%	–75.48%	–74.93%	–74.69%	–74.25%	–74.05%	–73.88%	–73.71%	–73.57%
Forfeiture (40%)	–80.16%	–79.55%	–79.03%	–78.59%	–78.41%	–78.06%	–77.91%	–77.78%	–77.65%	–77.54%

MATURITY OF 10 YEARS AND VESTING OF 3 YEARS ON A $40 STOCK PRICE

Stock Price and Strike Price of $40, Maturity of 10 Years, Risk-Free Rate of 3.5%, 70% Volatility, 0% Dividends, Vesting of 3 Years, Employee Suboptimal Exercise Behavior from 1.2 to 3.0, and Forfeiture Rate from 0% to 40%.
Generalized Black-Scholes: $31.05

Customized Binomial Lattice	Suboptimal (1.2)	Suboptimal (1.4)	Suboptimal (1.6)	Suboptimal (1.8)	Suboptimal (2.0)	Suboptimal (2.2)	Suboptimal (2.4)	Suboptimal (2.6)	Suboptimal (2.8)	Suboptimal (3.0)
Forfeiture (0%)	$21.19	$22.34	$23.42	$24.43	$24.89	$25.79	$26.21	$26.59	$26.97	$27.30
Forfeiture (5%)	$18.12	$19.02	$19.85	$20.62	$20.97	$21.64	$21.95	$22.23	$22.51	$22.76
Forfeiture (10%)	$15.51	$16.21	$16.86	$17.46	$17.72	$18.22	$18.46	$18.67	$18.88	$19.06
Forfeiture (15%)	$13.28	$13.84	$14.35	$14.81	$15.01	$15.39	$15.57	$15.73	$15.88	$16.02
Forfeiture (20%)	$11.38	$11.83	$12.23	$12.58	$12.74	$13.03	$13.17	$13.29	$13.40	$13.50
Forfeiture (25%)	$9.76	$10.12	$10.43	$10.71	$10.83	$11.06	$11.16	$11.25	$11.34	$11.41
Forfeiture (30%)	$8.37	$8.66	$8.91	$9.13	$9.22	$9.40	$9.48	$9.54	$9.61	$9.67
Forfeiture (35%)	$7.18	$7.41	$7.61	$7.79	$7.86	$8.00	$8.06	$8.11	$8.16	$8.21
Forfeiture (40%)	$6.16	$6.35	$6.51	$6.65	$6.71	$6.81	$6.86	$6.90	$6.94	$6.97

Percentage Difference between Binomial and Black-Scholes Model	Suboptimal (1.2)	Suboptimal (1.4)	Suboptimal (1.6)	Suboptimal (1.8)	Suboptimal (2.0)	Suboptimal (2.2)	Suboptimal (2.4)	Suboptimal (2.6)	Suboptimal (2.8)	Suboptimal (3.0)
Forfeiture (0%)	–31.76%	–28.07%	–24.57%	–21.31%	–19.83%	–16.96%	–15.59%	–14.37%	–13.15%	–12.07%
Forfeiture (5%)	–41.65%	–38.76%	–36.06%	–33.58%	–32.46%	–30.31%	–29.29%	–28.39%	–27.50%	–26.70%
Forfeiture (10%)	–50.06%	–47.78%	–45.69%	–43.78%	–42.93%	–41.31%	–40.55%	–39.88%	–39.21%	–38.63%
Forfeiture (15%)	–57.22%	–55.42%	–53.78%	–52.31%	–51.66%	–50.43%	–49.85%	–49.35%	–48.85%	–48.42%
Forfeiture (20%)	–63.34%	–61.91%	–60.62%	–59.47%	–58.97%	–58.03%	–57.59%	–57.21%	–56.84%	–56.51%
Forfeiture (25%)	–68.57%	–67.42%	–66.40%	–65.51%	–65.12%	–64.39%	–64.06%	–63.77%	–63.49%	–63.24%
Forfeiture (30%)	–73.05%	–72.12%	–71.31%	–70.61%	–70.31%	–69.74%	–69.48%	–69.26%	–69.05%	–68.86%
Forfeiture (35%)	–76.88%	–76.13%	–75.48%	–74.93%	–74.69%	–74.25%	–74.05%	–73.88%	–73.71%	–73.57%
Forfeiture (40%)	–80.16%	–79.55%	–79.03%	–78.59%	–78.41%	–78.06%	–77.91%	–77.78%	–77.65%	–77.54%

MATURITY OF 10 YEARS AND VESTING OF 3 YEARS ON A $60 STOCK PRICE

Stock Price and Strike Price of $60, Maturity of 10 Years, Risk-Free Rate of 3.5%, 70% Volatility, 0% Dividends, Vesting of 3 Years, Employee Suboptimal Exercise Behavior from 1.2 to 3.0, and Forfeiture Rate from 0% to 40%.
Generalized Black-Scholes: $46.58

Customized Binomial Lattice	Suboptimal (1.2)	Suboptimal (1.4)	Suboptimal (1.6)	Suboptimal (1.8)	Suboptimal (2.0)	Suboptimal (2.2)	Suboptimal (2.4)	Suboptimal (2.6)	Suboptimal (2.8)	Suboptimal (3.0)
Forfeiture (0%)	$31.78	$33.50	$35.13	$36.65	$37.34	$38.68	$39.31	$39.88	$40.45	$40.96
Forfeiture (5%)	$27.18	$28.52	$29.78	$30.94	$31.46	$32.46	$32.93	$33.35	$33.77	$34.14
Forfeiture (10%)	$23.26	$24.32	$25.30	$26.18	$26.58	$27.34	$27.69	$28.00	$28.31	$28.58
Forfeiture (15%)	$19.92	$20.76	$21.53	$22.21	$22.51	$23.09	$23.36	$23.59	$23.82	$24.02
Forfeiture (20%)	$17.07	$17.74	$18.34	$18.88	$19.11	$19.55	$19.75	$19.93	$20.10	$20.25
Forfeiture (25%)	$14.64	$15.17	$15.65	$16.07	$16.25	$16.58	$16.74	$16.87	$17.01	$17.12
Forfeiture (30%)	$12.55	$12.98	$13.36	$13.69	$13.83	$14.09	$14.21	$14.32	$14.42	$14.50
Forfeiture (35%)	$10.77	$11.12	$11.42	$11.68	$11.79	$11.99	$12.09	$12.16	$12.24	$12.31
Forfeiture (40%)	$9.24	$9.52	$9.76	$9.97	$10.06	$10.22	$10.29	$10.35	$10.41	$10.46

Percentage Difference between Binomial and Black-Scholes Model	Suboptimal (1.2)	Suboptimal (1.4)	Suboptimal (1.6)	Suboptimal (1.8)	Suboptimal (2.0)	Suboptimal (2.2)	Suboptimal (2.4)	Suboptimal (2.6)	Suboptimal (2.8)	Suboptimal (3.0)
Forfeiture (0%)	−31.76%	−28.07%	−24.57%	−21.31%	−19.83%	−16.96%	−15.59%	−14.37%	−13.15%	−12.07%
Forfeiture (5%)	−41.65%	−38.76%	−36.06%	−33.58%	−32.46%	−30.31%	−29.29%	−28.39%	−27.50%	−26.70%
Forfeiture (10%)	−50.06%	−47.78%	−45.69%	−43.78%	−42.93%	−41.31%	−40.55%	−39.88%	−39.21%	−38.63%
Forfeiture (15%)	−57.22%	−55.42%	−53.78%	−52.31%	−51.66%	−50.43%	−49.85%	−49.35%	−48.85%	−48.42%
Forfeiture (20%)	−63.34%	−61.91%	−60.62%	−59.47%	−58.97%	−58.03%	−57.59%	−57.21%	−56.84%	−56.51%
Forfeiture (25%)	−68.57%	−67.42%	−66.40%	−65.51%	−65.12%	−64.39%	−64.06%	−63.77%	−63.49%	−63.24%
Forfeiture (30%)	−73.05%	−72.12%	−71.31%	−70.61%	−70.31%	−69.74%	−69.48%	−69.26%	−69.05%	−68.86%
Forfeiture (35%)	−76.88%	−76.13%	−75.48%	−74.93%	−74.69%	−74.25%	−74.05%	−73.88%	−73.71%	−73.57%
Forfeiture (40%)	−80.16%	−79.55%	−79.03%	−78.59%	−78.41%	−78.06%	−77.91%	−77.78%	−77.65%	−77.54%

MATURITY OF 10 YEARS AND VESTING OF 3 YEARS ON AN $80 STOCK PRICE

Stock Price and Strike Price of $80, Maturity of 10 Years, Risk-Free Rate of 3.5%, 70% Volatility, 0% Dividends, Vesting of 3 Years, Employee Suboptimal Exercise Behavior from 1.2 to 3.0, and Forfeiture Rate from 0% to 40%.
Generalized Black-Scholes: $46.58

Customized Binomial Lattice	Suboptimal (1.2)	Suboptimal (1.4)	Suboptimal (1.6)	Suboptimal (1.8)	Suboptimal (2.0)	Suboptimal (2.2)	Suboptimal (2.4)	Suboptimal (2.6)	Suboptimal (2.8)	Suboptimal (3.0)
Forfeiture (0%)	$31.78	$33.50	$35.13	$36.65	$37.34	$38.68	$39.31	$39.88	$40.45	$40.96
Forfeiture (5%)	$27.18	$28.52	$29.78	$30.94	$31.46	$32.46	$32.93	$33.35	$33.77	$34.14
Forfeiture (10%)	$23.26	$24.32	$25.30	$26.18	$26.58	$27.34	$27.69	$28.00	$28.31	$28.58
Forfeiture (15%)	$19.92	$20.76	$21.53	$22.21	$22.51	$23.09	$23.36	$23.59	$23.82	$24.02
Forfeiture (20%)	$17.07	$17.74	$18.34	$18.88	$19.11	$19.55	$19.75	$19.93	$20.10	$20.25
Forfeiture (25%)	$14.64	$15.17	$15.65	$16.07	$16.25	$16.58	$16.74	$16.87	$17.01	$17.12
Forfeiture (30%)	$12.55	$12.98	$13.36	$13.69	$13.83	$14.09	$14.21	$14.32	$14.42	$14.50
Forfeiture (35%)	$10.77	$11.12	$11.42	$11.68	$11.79	$11.99	$12.09	$12.16	$12.24	$12.31
Forfeiture (40%)	$9.24	$9.52	$9.76	$9.97	$10.06	$10.22	$10.29	$10.35	$10.41	$10.46

Percentage Difference between Binomial and Black-Scholes Model	Suboptimal (1.2)	Suboptimal (1.4)	Suboptimal (1.6)	Suboptimal (1.8)	Suboptimal (2.0)	Suboptimal (2.2)	Suboptimal (2.4)	Suboptimal (2.6)	Suboptimal (2.8)	Suboptimal (3.0)
Forfeiture (0%)	−31.76%	−28.07%	−24.57%	−21.31%	−19.83%	−16.96%	−15.59%	−14.37%	−13.15%	−12.07%
Forfeiture (5%)	−41.65%	−38.76%	−36.06%	−33.58%	−32.46%	−30.31%	−29.29%	−28.39%	−27.50%	−26.70%
Forfeiture (10%)	−50.06%	−47.78%	−45.69%	−43.78%	−42.93%	−41.31%	−40.55%	−39.88%	−39.21%	−38.63%
Forfeiture (15%)	−57.22%	−55.42%	−53.78%	−52.31%	−51.66%	−50.43%	−49.85%	−49.35%	−48.85%	−48.42%
Forfeiture (20%)	−63.34%	−61.91%	−60.62%	−59.47%	−58.97%	−58.03%	−57.59%	−57.21%	−56.84%	−56.51%
Forfeiture (25%)	−68.57%	−67.42%	−66.40%	−65.51%	−65.12%	−64.39%	−64.06%	−63.77%	−63.49%	−63.24%
Forfeiture (30%)	−73.05%	−72.12%	−71.31%	−70.61%	−70.31%	−69.74%	−69.48%	−69.26%	−69.05%	−68.86%
Forfeiture (35%)	−76.88%	−76.13%	−75.48%	−74.93%	−74.69%	−74.25%	−74.05%	−73.88%	−73.71%	−73.57%
Forfeiture (40%)	−80.16%	−79.55%	−79.03%	−78.59%	−78.41%	−78.06%	−77.91%	−77.78%	−77.65%	−77.54%

MATURITY OF 10 YEARS AND VESTING OF 4 YEARS ON A $20 STOCK PRICE

Stock Price and Strike Price of $20, Maturity of 10 Years, Risk-Free Rate of 3.5%, 70% Volatility, 0% Dividends, Vesting of 4 Years, Employee Suboptimal Exercise Behavior from 1.2 to 3.0, and Forfeiture Rate from 0% to 40%.
Generalized Black-Scholes: $15.53

Customized Binomial Lattice	Suboptimal (1.2)	Suboptimal (1.4)	Suboptimal (1.6)	Suboptimal (1.8)	Suboptimal (2.0)	Suboptimal (2.2)	Suboptimal (2.4)	Suboptimal (2.6)	Suboptimal (2.8)	Suboptimal (3.0)
Forfeiture (0%)	$11.74	$12.20	$12.63	$13.02	$13.20	$13.54	$13.70	$13.84	$13.98	$14.11
Forfeiture (5%)	$9.57	$9.91	$10.23	$10.51	$10.64	$10.89	$11.00	$11.11	$11.21	$11.30
Forfeiture (10%)	$7.80	$8.06	$8.29	$8.51	$8.60	$8.78	$8.86	$8.93	$9.01	$9.07
Forfeiture (15%)	$6.36	$6.56	$6.73	$6.89	$6.96	$7.09	$7.15	$7.20	$7.25	$7.30
Forfeiture (20%)	$5.19	$5.34	$5.47	$5.59	$5.64	$5.73	$5.78	$5.82	$5.86	$5.89
Forfeiture (25%)	$4.24	$4.35	$4.45	$4.54	$4.58	$4.65	$4.68	$4.71	$4.73	$4.76
Forfeiture (30%)	$3.46	$3.55	$3.62	$3.69	$3.71	$3.77	$3.79	$3.81	$3.83	$3.85
Forfeiture (35%)	$2.82	$2.89	$2.95	$3.00	$3.02	$3.06	$3.08	$3.09	$3.10	$3.12
Forfeiture (40%)	$2.31	$2.36	$2.40	$2.44	$2.45	$2.48	$2.50	$2.51	$2.52	$2.53

Percentage Difference between Binomial and Black-Scholes Model	Suboptimal (1.2)	Suboptimal (1.4)	Suboptimal (1.6)	Suboptimal (1.8)	Suboptimal (2.0)	Suboptimal (2.2)	Suboptimal (2.4)	Suboptimal (2.6)	Suboptimal (2.8)	Suboptimal (3.0)
Forfeiture (0%)	–24.39%	–21.43%	–18.68%	–16.14%	–15.00%	–12.80%	–11.76%	–10.84%	–9.92%	–9.11%
Forfeiture (5%)	–38.38%	–36.17%	–34.13%	–32.28%	–31.45%	–29.87%	–29.12%	–28.46%	–27.81%	–27.24%
Forfeiture (10%)	–49.75%	–48.09%	–46.58%	–45.21%	–44.61%	–43.46%	–42.92%	–42.45%	–41.99%	–41.58%
Forfeiture (15%)	–59.01%	–57.76%	–56.62%	–55.62%	–55.17%	–54.34%	–53.95%	–53.61%	–53.27%	–52.98%
Forfeiture (20%)	–66.56%	–65.60%	–64.75%	–64.00%	–63.67%	–63.06%	–62.78%	–62.53%	–62.29%	–62.08%
Forfeiture (25%)	–72.70%	–71.97%	–71.33%	–70.77%	–70.53%	–70.08%	–69.87%	–69.69%	–69.51%	–69.36%
Forfeiture (30%)	–77.72%	–77.16%	–76.67%	–76.25%	–76.07%	–75.74%	–75.58%	–75.45%	–75.32%	–75.21%
Forfeiture (35%)	–81.81%	–81.38%	–81.01%	–80.69%	–80.56%	–80.31%	–80.19%	–80.10%	–80.00%	–79.92%
Forfeiture (40%)	–85.14%	–84.81%	–84.53%	–84.29%	–84.19%	–84.00%	–83.92%	–83.85%	–83.78%	–83.72%

MATURITY OF 10 YEARS AND VESTING OF 4 YEARS ON A $40 STOCK PRICE

Stock Price and Strike Price of $40, Maturity of 10 Years, Risk-Free Rate of 3.5%, 70% Volatility, 0% Dividends, Vesting of 4 Years, Employee Suboptimal Exercise Behavior from 1.2 to 3.0, and Forfeiture Rate from 0% to 40%.
Generalized Black-Scholes: $31.05

Customized Binomial Lattice	Suboptimal (1.2)	Suboptimal (1.4)	Suboptimal (1.6)	Suboptimal (1.8)	Suboptimal (2.0)	Suboptimal (2.2)	Suboptimal (2.4)	Suboptimal (2.6)	Suboptimal (2.8)	Suboptimal (3.0)
Forfeiture (0%)	$23.48	$24.40	$25.25	$26.04	$26.39	$27.08	$27.40	$27.68	$27.97	$28.22
Forfeiture (5%)	$19.13	$19.82	$20.45	$21.03	$21.29	$21.78	$22.01	$22.21	$22.42	$22.59
Forfeiture (10%)	$15.60	$16.12	$16.59	$17.01	$17.20	$17.56	$17.72	$17.87	$18.01	$18.14
Forfeiture (15%)	$12.73	$13.12	$13.47	$13.78	$13.92	$14.18	$14.30	$14.41	$14.51	$14.60
Forfeiture (20%)	$10.38	$10.68	$10.95	$11.18	$11.28	$11.47	$11.56	$11.63	$11.71	$11.78
Forfeiture (25%)	$8.48	$8.70	$8.90	$9.08	$9.15	$9.29	$9.36	$9.41	$9.47	$9.51
Forfeiture (30%)	$6.92	$7.09	$7.24	$7.37	$7.43	$7.53	$7.58	$7.62	$7.66	$7.70
Forfeiture (35%)	$5.65	$5.78	$5.90	$6.00	$6.04	$6.12	$6.15	$6.18	$6.21	$6.23
Forfeiture (40%)	$4.61	$4.72	$4.80	$4.88	$4.91	$4.97	$4.99	$5.02	$5.04	$5.06

Percentage Difference between Binomial and Black-Scholes Model	Suboptimal (1.2)	Suboptimal (1.4)	Suboptimal (1.6)	Suboptimal (1.8)	Suboptimal (2.0)	Suboptimal (2.2)	Suboptimal (2.4)	Suboptimal (2.6)	Suboptimal (2.8)	Suboptimal (3.0)
Forfeiture (0%)	−24.39%	−21.43%	−18.68%	−16.14%	−15.00%	−12.80%	−11.76%	−10.84%	−9.92%	−9.11%
Forfeiture (5%)	−38.38%	−36.17%	−34.13%	−32.28%	−31.45%	−29.87%	−29.12%	−28.46%	−27.81%	−27.24%
Forfeiture (10%)	−49.75%	−48.09%	−46.58%	−45.21%	−44.61%	−43.46%	−42.92%	−42.45%	−41.99%	−41.58%
Forfeiture (15%)	−59.01%	−57.76%	−56.62%	−55.62%	−55.17%	−54.34%	−53.95%	−53.61%	−53.27%	−52.98%
Forfeiture (20%)	−66.56%	−65.60%	−64.75%	−64.00%	−63.67%	−63.06%	−62.78%	−62.53%	−62.29%	−62.08%
Forfeiture (25%)	−72.70%	−71.97%	−71.33%	−70.77%	−70.53%	−70.08%	−69.87%	−69.69%	−69.51%	−69.36%
Forfeiture (30%)	−77.72%	−77.16%	−76.67%	−76.25%	−76.07%	−75.74%	−75.58%	−75.45%	−75.32%	−75.21%
Forfeiture (35%)	−81.81%	−81.38%	−81.01%	−80.69%	−80.56%	−80.31%	−80.19%	−80.10%	−80.00%	−79.92%
Forfeiture (40%)	−85.14%	−84.81%	−84.53%	−84.29%	−84.19%	−84.00%	−83.92%	−83.85%	−83.78%	−83.72%

MATURITY OF 10 YEARS AND VESTING OF 4 YEARS ON A $60 STOCK PRICE

Stock Price and Strike Price of $60, Maturity of 10 Years, Risk-Free Rate of 3.5%, 70% Volatility, 0% Dividends, Vesting of 4 Years, Employee Suboptimal Exercise Behavior from 1.2 to 3.0, and Forfeiture Rate from 0% to 40%.
Generalized Black-Scholes: $46.58

Customized Binomial Lattice	Suboptimal (1.2)	Suboptimal (1.4)	Suboptimal (1.6)	Suboptimal (1.8)	Suboptimal (2.0)	Suboptimal (2.2)	Suboptimal (2.4)	Suboptimal (2.6)	Suboptimal (2.8)	Suboptimal (3.0)
Forfeiture (0%)	$35.22	$36.59	$37.88	$39.06	$39.59	$40.61	$41.10	$41.53	$41.95	$42.33
Forfeiture (5%)	$28.70	$29.73	$30.68	$31.54	$31.93	$32.67	$33.01	$33.32	$33.62	$33.89
Forfeiture (10%)	$23.40	$24.18	$24.88	$25.52	$25.80	$26.33	$26.58	$26.80	$27.02	$27.21
Forfeiture (15%)	$19.09	$19.68	$20.20	$20.67	$20.88	$21.27	$21.45	$21.61	$21.76	$21.90
Forfeiture (20%)	$15.58	$16.02	$16.42	$16.77	$16.92	$17.20	$17.34	$17.45	$17.57	$17.66
Forfeiture (25%)	$12.71	$13.05	$13.35	$13.61	$13.73	$13.94	$14.03	$14.12	$14.20	$14.27
Forfeiture (30%)	$10.38	$10.64	$10.87	$11.06	$11.14	$11.30	$11.37	$11.43	$11.49	$11.55
Forfeiture (35%)	$8.47	$8.67	$8.85	$8.99	$9.06	$9.17	$9.23	$9.27	$9.31	$9.35
Forfeiture (40%)	$6.92	$7.07	$7.21	$7.32	$7.36	$7.45	$7.49	$7.52	$7.56	$7.58

Percentage Difference between Binomial and Black-Scholes Model	Suboptimal (1.2)	Suboptimal (1.4)	Suboptimal (1.6)	Suboptimal (1.8)	Suboptimal (2.0)	Suboptimal (2.2)	Suboptimal (2.4)	Suboptimal (2.6)	Suboptimal (2.8)	Suboptimal (3.0)
Forfeiture (0%)	−24.39%	−21.43%	−18.68%	−16.14%	−15.00%	−12.80%	−11.76%	−10.84%	−9.92%	−9.11%
Forfeiture (5%)	−38.38%	−36.17%	−34.13%	−32.28%	−31.45%	−29.87%	−29.12%	−28.46%	−27.81%	−27.24%
Forfeiture (10%)	−49.75%	−48.09%	−46.58%	−45.21%	−44.61%	−43.46%	−42.92%	−42.45%	−41.99%	−41.58%
Forfeiture (15%)	−59.01%	−57.76%	−56.62%	−55.62%	−55.17%	−54.34%	−53.95%	−53.61%	−53.27%	−52.98%
Forfeiture (20%)	−66.56%	−65.60%	−64.75%	−64.00%	−63.67%	−63.06%	−62.78%	−62.53%	−62.29%	−62.08%
Forfeiture (25%)	−72.70%	−71.97%	−71.33%	−70.77%	−70.53%	−70.08%	−69.87%	−69.69%	−69.51%	−69.36%
Forfeiture (30%)	−77.72%	−77.16%	−76.67%	−76.25%	−76.07%	−75.74%	−75.58%	−75.45%	−75.32%	−75.21%
Forfeiture (35%)	−81.81%	−81.38%	−81.01%	−80.69%	−80.56%	−80.31%	−80.19%	−80.10%	−80.00%	−79.92%
Forfeiture (40%)	−85.14%	−84.81%	−84.53%	−84.29%	−84.19%	−84.00%	−83.92%	−83.85%	−83.78%	−83.72%

MATURITY OF 10 YEARS AND VESTING OF 4 YEARS ON AN $80 STOCK PRICE

Stock Price and Strike Price of $80, Maturity of 10 Years, Risk-Free Rate of 3.5%, 70% Volatility, 0% Dividends, Vesting of 4 Years, Employee Suboptimal Exercise Behavior from 1.2 to 3.0, and Forfeiture Rate from 0% to 40%.
Generalized Black-Scholes: $62.10

Customized Binomial Lattice	Suboptimal (1.2)	Suboptimal (1.4)	Suboptimal (1.6)	Suboptimal (1.8)	Suboptimal (2.0)	Suboptimal (2.2)	Suboptimal (2.4)	Suboptimal (2.6)	Suboptimal (2.8)	Suboptimal (3.0)
Forfeiture (0%)	$46.95	$48.79	$50.50	$52.08	$52.79	$54.15	$54.80	$55.37	$55.94	$56.44
Forfeiture (5%)	$38.27	$39.64	$40.91	$42.06	$42.57	$43.55	$44.02	$44.42	$44.83	$45.19
Forfeiture (10%)	$31.20	$32.24	$33.18	$34.02	$34.40	$35.11	$35.45	$35.74	$36.03	$36.28
Forfeiture (15%)	$25.45	$26.23	$26.94	$27.56	$27.84	$28.36	$28.60	$28.81	$29.02	$29.20
Forfeiture (20%)	$20.77	$21.36	$21.89	$22.36	$22.56	$22.94	$23.12	$23.27	$23.42	$23.55
Forfeiture (25%)	$16.95	$17.40	$17.80	$18.15	$18.30	$18.58	$18.71	$18.82	$18.93	$19.03
Forfeiture (30%)	$13.84	$14.19	$14.49	$14.75	$14.86	$15.07	$15.16	$15.24	$15.33	$15.39
Forfeiture (35%)	$11.30	$11.57	$11.80	$11.99	$12.08	$12.23	$12.30	$12.36	$12.42	$12.47
Forfeiture (40%)	$9.23	$9.43	$9.61	$9.76	$9.82	$9.93	$9.99	$10.03	$10.07	$10.11

Percentage Difference between Binomial and Black-Scholes Model	Suboptimal (1.2)	Suboptimal (1.4)	Suboptimal (1.6)	Suboptimal (1.8)	Suboptimal (2.0)	Suboptimal (2.2)	Suboptimal (2.4)	Suboptimal (2.6)	Suboptimal (2.8)	Suboptimal (3.0)
Forfeiture (0%)	−24.39%	−21.43%	−18.68%	−16.14%	−15.00%	−12.80%	−11.76%	−10.84%	−9.92%	−9.11%
Forfeiture (5%)	−38.38%	−36.17%	−34.13%	−32.28%	−31.45%	−29.87%	−29.12%	−28.46%	−27.81%	−27.24%
Forfeiture (10%)	−49.75%	−48.09%	−46.58%	−45.21%	−44.61%	−43.46%	−42.92%	−42.45%	−41.99%	−41.58%
Forfeiture (15%)	−59.01%	−57.76%	−56.62%	−55.62%	−55.17%	−54.34%	−53.95%	−53.61%	−53.27%	−52.98%
Forfeiture (20%)	−66.56%	−65.60%	−64.75%	−64.00%	−63.67%	−63.06%	−62.78%	−62.53%	−62.29%	−62.08%
Forfeiture (25%)	−72.70%	−71.97%	−71.33%	−70.77%	−70.53%	−70.08%	−69.87%	−69.69%	−69.51%	−69.36%
Forfeiture (30%)	−77.72%	−77.16%	−76.67%	−76.25%	−76.07%	−75.74%	−75.58%	−75.45%	−75.32%	−75.21%
Forfeiture (35%)	−81.81%	−81.38%	−81.01%	−80.69%	−80.56%	−80.31%	−80.19%	−80.10%	−80.00%	−79.92%
Forfeiture (40%)	−85.14%	−84.81%	−84.53%	−84.29%	−84.19%	−84.00%	−83.92%	−83.85%	−83.78%	−83.72%

MATURITY OF 10 YEARS AND VESTING OF 5 YEARS ON A $20 STOCK PRICE

Stock Price and Strike Price of $20, Maturity of 10 Years, Risk-Free Rate of 3.5%, 70% Volatility, 0% Dividends, Vesting of 5 Years, Employee Suboptimal Exercise Behavior from 1.2 to 3.0, and Forfeiture Rate from 0% to 40%.
Generalized Black-Scholes: $15.53

Customized Binomial Lattice	Suboptimal (1.2)	Suboptimal (1.4)	Suboptimal (1.6)	Suboptimal (1.8)	Suboptimal (2.0)	Suboptimal (2.2)	Suboptimal (2.4)	Suboptimal (2.6)	Suboptimal (2.8)	Suboptimal (3.0)
Forfeiture (0%)	$12.68	$13.05	$13.38	$13.69	$13.82	$14.08	$14.20	$14.31	$14.41	$14.51
Forfeiture (5%)	$9.84	$10.11	$10.35	$10.56	$10.65	$10.83	$10.92	$10.99	$11.06	$11.13
Forfeiture (10%)	$7.64	$7.83	$8.00	$8.16	$8.22	$8.35	$8.41	$8.46	$8.51	$8.55
Forfeiture (15%)	$5.94	$6.07	$6.20	$6.30	$6.35	$6.44	$6.48	$6.51	$6.55	$6.58
Forfeiture (20%)	$4.61	$4.71	$4.80	$4.88	$4.91	$4.97	$5.00	$5.02	$5.05	$5.07
Forfeiture (25%)	$3.58	$3.65	$3.72	$3.77	$3.80	$3.84	$3.86	$3.88	$3.89	$3.91
Forfeiture (30%)	$2.78	$2.84	$2.88	$2.92	$2.94	$2.97	$2.98	$3.00	$3.01	$3.02
Forfeiture (35%)	$2.16	$2.20	$2.23	$2.26	$2.27	$2.30	$2.31	$2.32	$2.32	$2.33
Forfeiture (40%)	$1.68	$1.71	$1.73	$1.75	$1.76	$1.78	$1.78	$1.79	$1.80	$1.80

Percentage Difference between Binomial and Black-Scholes Model	Suboptimal (1.2)	Suboptimal (1.4)	Suboptimal (1.6)	Suboptimal (1.8)	Suboptimal (2.0)	Suboptimal (2.2)	Suboptimal (2.4)	Suboptimal (2.6)	Suboptimal (2.8)	Suboptimal (3.0)
Forfeiture (0%)	−18.33%	−15.97%	−13.80%	−11.84%	−10.97%	−9.31%	−8.53%	−7.85%	−7.16%	−6.57%
Forfeiture (5%)	−36.60%	−34.90%	−33.36%	−31.98%	−31.37%	−30.22%	−29.68%	−29.21%	−28.74%	−28.33%
Forfeiture (10%)	−50.77%	−49.55%	−48.45%	−47.47%	−47.05%	−46.24%	−45.86%	−45.54%	−45.21%	−44.93%
Forfeiture (15%)	−61.76%	−60.88%	−60.09%	−59.40%	−59.10%	−58.53%	−58.27%	−58.05%	−57.82%	−57.63%
Forfeiture (20%)	−70.30%	−69.66%	−69.09%	−68.60%	−68.39%	−67.99%	−67.80%	−67.65%	−67.49%	−67.35%
Forfeiture (25%)	−76.93%	−76.46%	−76.05%	−75.70%	−75.55%	−75.27%	−75.14%	−75.03%	−74.92%	−74.82%
Forfeiture (30%)	−82.08%	−81.73%	−81.44%	−81.18%	−81.08%	−80.88%	−80.79%	−80.71%	−80.63%	−80.57%
Forfeiture (35%)	−86.07%	−85.82%	−85.61%	−85.43%	−85.35%	−85.21%	−85.14%	−85.09%	−85.03%	−84.99%
Forfeiture (40%)	−89.18%	−89.00%	−88.84%	−88.71%	−88.65%	−88.55%	−88.50%	−88.47%	−88.43%	−88.40%

MATURITY OF 10 YEARS AND VESTING OF 5 YEARS ON A $40 STOCK PRICE

Stock Price and Strike Price of $40, Maturity of 10 Years, Risk-Free Rate of 3.5%, 70% Volatility, 0% Dividends, Vesting of 5 Years, Employee Suboptimal Exercise Behavior from 1.2 to 3.0, and Forfeiture Rate from 0% to 40%.
Generalized Black-Scholes: $31.05

Customized Binomial Lattice	Suboptimal (1.2)	Suboptimal (1.4)	Suboptimal (1.6)	Suboptimal (1.8)	Suboptimal (2.0)	Suboptimal (2.2)	Suboptimal (2.4)	Suboptimal (2.6)	Suboptimal (2.8)	Suboptimal (3.0)
Forfeiture (0%)	$25.36	$26.09	$26.77	$27.37	$27.64	$28.16	$28.40	$28.61	$28.83	$29.01
Forfeiture (5%)	$19.69	$20.21	$20.69	$21.12	$21.31	$21.67	$21.84	$21.98	$22.13	$22.25
Forfeiture (10%)	$15.29	$15.67	$16.01	$16.31	$16.44	$16.69	$16.81	$16.91	$17.01	$17.10
Forfeiture (15%)	$11.87	$12.15	$12.39	$12.61	$12.70	$12.88	$12.96	$13.03	$13.10	$13.16
Forfeiture (20%)	$9.22	$9.42	$9.60	$9.75	$9.82	$9.94	$10.00	$10.05	$10.10	$10.14
Forfeiture (25%)	$7.16	$7.31	$7.44	$7.55	$7.59	$7.68	$7.72	$7.75	$7.79	$7.82
Forfeiture (30%)	$5.57	$5.67	$5.76	$5.84	$5.88	$5.94	$5.97	$5.99	$6.01	$6.03
Forfeiture (35%)	$4.32	$4.40	$4.47	$4.53	$4.55	$4.59	$4.61	$4.63	$4.65	$4.66
Forfeiture (40%)	$3.36	$3.42	$3.47	$3.51	$3.52	$3.56	$3.57	$3.58	$3.59	$3.60

Percentage Difference between Binomial and Black-Scholes Model	Suboptimal (1.2)	Suboptimal (1.4)	Suboptimal (1.6)	Suboptimal (1.8)	Suboptimal (2.0)	Suboptimal (2.2)	Suboptimal (2.4)	Suboptimal (2.6)	Suboptimal (2.8)	Suboptimal (3.0)
Forfeiture (0%)	−18.33%	−15.97%	−13.80%	−11.84%	−10.97%	−9.31%	−8.53%	−7.85%	−7.16%	−6.57%
Forfeiture (5%)	−36.60%	−34.90%	−33.36%	−31.98%	−31.37%	−30.22%	−29.68%	−29.21%	−28.74%	−28.33%
Forfeiture (10%)	−50.77%	−49.55%	−48.45%	−47.47%	−47.05%	−46.24%	−45.86%	−45.54%	−45.21%	−44.93%
Forfeiture (15%)	−61.76%	−60.88%	−60.09%	−59.40%	−59.10%	−58.53%	−58.27%	−58.05%	−57.82%	−57.63%
Forfeiture (20%)	−70.30%	−69.66%	−69.09%	−68.60%	−68.39%	−67.99%	−67.80%	−67.65%	−67.49%	−67.35%
Forfeiture (25%)	−76.93%	−76.46%	−76.05%	−75.70%	−75.55%	−75.27%	−75.14%	−75.03%	−74.92%	−74.82%
Forfeiture (30%)	−82.08%	−81.73%	−81.44%	−81.18%	−81.08%	−80.88%	−80.79%	−80.71%	−80.63%	−80.57%
Forfeiture (35%)	−86.07%	−85.82%	−85.61%	−85.43%	−85.35%	−85.21%	−85.14%	−85.09%	−85.03%	−84.99%
Forfeiture (40%)	−89.18%	−89.00%	−88.84%	−88.71%	−88.65%	−88.55%	−88.50%	−88.47%	−88.43%	−88.40%

MATURITY OF 10 YEARS AND VESTING OF 5 YEARS ON A $60 STOCK PRICE

Stock Price and Strike Price of $60, Maturity of 10 Years, Risk-Free Rate of 3.5%, 70% Volatility, 0% Dividends, Vesting of 5 Years, Employee Suboptimal Exercise Behavior from 1.2 to 3.0, and Forfeiture Rate from 0% to 40%.
Generalized Black-Scholes: $46.58

Customized Binomial Lattice	Suboptimal (1.2)	Suboptimal (1.4)	Suboptimal (1.6)	Suboptimal (1.8)	Suboptimal (2.0)	Suboptimal (2.2)	Suboptimal (2.4)	Suboptimal (2.6)	Suboptimal (2.8)	Suboptimal (3.0)
Forfeiture (0%)	$38.04	$39.14	$40.15	$41.06	$41.47	$42.24	$42.60	$42.92	$43.24	$43.52
Forfeiture (5%)	$29.53	$30.32	$31.04	$31.68	$31.96	$32.50	$32.75	$32.97	$33.19	$33.38
Forfeiture (10%)	$22.93	$23.50	$24.01	$24.47	$24.66	$25.04	$25.22	$25.37	$25.52	$25.65
Forfeiture (15%)	$17.81	$18.22	$18.59	$18.91	$19.05	$19.31	$19.44	$19.54	$19.65	$19.74
Forfeiture (20%)	$13.83	$14.13	$14.40	$14.63	$14.72	$14.91	$15.00	$15.07	$15.14	$15.20
Forfeiture (25%)	$10.75	$10.96	$11.15	$11.32	$11.39	$11.52	$11.58	$11.63	$11.68	$11.73
Forfeiture (30%)	$8.35	$8.51	$8.65	$8.76	$8.81	$8.91	$8.95	$8.99	$9.02	$9.05
Forfeiture (35%)	$6.49	$6.60	$6.70	$6.79	$6.82	$6.89	$6.92	$6.95	$6.97	$6.99
Forfeiture (40%)	$5.04	$5.13	$5.20	$5.26	$5.29	$5.33	$5.35	$5.37	$5.39	$5.40

Percentage Difference between Binomial and Black-Scholes Model	Suboptimal (1.2)	Suboptimal (1.4)	Suboptimal (1.6)	Suboptimal (1.8)	Suboptimal (2.0)	Suboptimal (2.2)	Suboptimal (2.4)	Suboptimal (2.6)	Suboptimal (2.8)	Suboptimal (3.0)
Forfeiture (0%)	–18.33%	–15.97%	–13.80%	–11.84%	–10.97%	–9.31%	–8.53%	–7.85%	–7.16%	–6.57%
Forfeiture (5%)	–36.60%	–34.90%	–33.36%	–31.98%	–31.37%	–30.22%	–29.68%	–29.21%	–28.74%	–28.33%
Forfeiture (10%)	–50.77%	–49.55%	–48.45%	–47.47%	–47.05%	–46.24%	–45.86%	–45.54%	–45.21%	–44.93%
Forfeiture (15%)	–61.76%	–60.88%	–60.09%	–59.40%	–59.10%	–58.53%	–58.27%	–58.05%	–57.82%	–57.63%
Forfeiture (20%)	–70.30%	–69.66%	–69.09%	–68.60%	–68.39%	–67.99%	–67.80%	–67.65%	–67.49%	–67.35%
Forfeiture (25%)	–76.93%	–76.46%	–76.05%	–75.70%	–75.55%	–75.27%	–75.14%	–75.03%	–74.92%	–74.82%
Forfeiture (30%)	–82.08%	–81.73%	–81.44%	–81.18%	–81.08%	–80.88%	–80.79%	–80.71%	–80.63%	–80.57%
Forfeiture (35%)	–86.07%	–85.82%	–85.61%	–85.43%	–85.35%	–85.21%	–85.14%	–85.09%	–85.03%	–84.99%
Forfeiture (40%)	–89.18%	–89.00%	–88.84%	–88.71%	–88.65%	–88.55%	–88.50%	–88.47%	–88.43%	–88.40%

MATURITY OF 10 YEARS AND VESTING OF 5 YEARS ON AN $80 STOCK PRICE

Stock Price and Strike Price of $80, Maturity of 10 Years, Risk-Free Rate of 3.5%, 70% Volatility, 0% Dividends, Vesting of 5 Years, Employee Suboptimal Exercise Behavior from 1.2 to 3.0, and Forfeiture Rate from 0% to 40%.
Generalized Black-Scholes: $62.10

Customized Binomial Lattice	Suboptimal (1.2)	Suboptimal (1.4)	Suboptimal (1.6)	Suboptimal (1.8)	Suboptimal (2.0)	Suboptimal (2.2)	Suboptimal (2.4)	Suboptimal (2.6)	Suboptimal (2.8)	Suboptimal (3.0)
Forfeiture (0%)	$50.72	$52.19	$53.53	$54.75	$55.29	$56.32	$56.81	$57.23	$57.65	$58.02
Forfeiture (5%)	$39.37	$40.43	$41.38	$42.24	$42.62	$43.34	$43.67	$43.96	$44.26	$44.51
Forfeiture (10%)	$30.57	$31.33	$32.01	$32.62	$32.89	$33.39	$33.62	$33.82	$34.02	$34.20
Forfeiture (15%)	$23.74	$24.29	$24.78	$25.21	$25.40	$25.75	$25.91	$26.05	$26.19	$26.31
Forfeiture (20%)	$18.44	$18.84	$19.19	$19.50	$19.63	$19.88	$19.99	$20.09	$20.19	$20.27
Forfeiture (25%)	$14.33	$14.62	$14.87	$15.09	$15.18	$15.36	$15.44	$15.51	$15.58	$15.64
Forfeiture (30%)	$11.13	$11.34	$11.53	$11.68	$11.75	$11.88	$11.93	$11.98	$12.03	$12.07
Forfeiture (35%)	$8.65	$8.80	$8.94	$9.05	$9.10	$9.19	$9.23	$9.26	$9.29	$9.32
Forfeiture (40%)	$6.72	$6.83	$6.93	$7.01	$7.05	$7.11	$7.14	$7.16	$7.19	$7.21

Percentage Difference between Binomial and Black-Scholes Model	Suboptimal (1.2)	Suboptimal (1.4)	Suboptimal (1.6)	Suboptimal (1.8)	Suboptimal (2.0)	Suboptimal (2.2)	Suboptimal (2.4)	Suboptimal (2.6)	Suboptimal (2.8)	Suboptimal (3.0)
Forfeiture (0%)	−18.33%	−15.97%	−13.80%	−11.84%	−10.97%	−9.31%	−8.53%	−7.85%	−7.16%	−6.57%
Forfeiture (5%)	−36.60%	−34.90%	−33.36%	−31.98%	−31.37%	−30.22%	−29.68%	−29.21%	−28.74%	−28.33%
Forfeiture (10%)	−50.77%	−49.55%	−48.45%	−47.47%	−47.05%	−46.24%	−45.86%	−45.54%	−45.21%	−44.93%
Forfeiture (15%)	−61.76%	−60.88%	−60.09%	−59.40%	−59.10%	−58.53%	−58.27%	−58.05%	−57.82%	−57.63%
Forfeiture (20%)	−70.30%	−69.66%	−69.09%	−68.60%	−68.39%	−67.99%	−67.80%	−67.65%	−67.49%	−67.35%
Forfeiture (25%)	−76.93%	−76.46%	−76.05%	−75.70%	−75.55%	−75.27%	−75.14%	−75.03%	−74.92%	−74.82%
Forfeiture (30%)	−82.08%	−81.73%	−81.44%	−81.18%	−81.08%	−80.88%	−80.79%	−80.71%	−80.63%	−80.57%
Forfeiture (35%)	−86.07%	−85.82%	−85.61%	−85.43%	−85.35%	−85.21%	−85.14%	−85.09%	−85.03%	−84.99%
Forfeiture (40%)	−89.18%	−89.00%	−88.84%	−88.71%	−88.65%	−88.55%	−88.50%	−88.47%	−88.43%	−88.40%

MATURITY OF 10 YEARS AND VESTING OF 7 YEARS ON A $20 STOCK PRICE

Stock Price and Strike Price of $20, Maturity of 10 Years, Risk-Free Rate of 3.5%, 70% Volatility, 0% Dividends, Vesting of 7 Years, Employee Suboptimal Exercise Behavior from 1.2 to 3.0, and Forfeiture Rate from 0% to 40%.
Generalized Black-Scholes: $15.53

Customized Binomial Lattice	Suboptimal (1.2)	Suboptimal (1.4)	Suboptimal (1.6)	Suboptimal (1.8)	Suboptimal (2.0)	Suboptimal (2.2)	Suboptimal (2.4)	Suboptimal (2.6)	Suboptimal (2.8)	Suboptimal (3.0)
Forfeiture (0%)	$14.14	$14.36	$14.55	$14.71	$14.78	$14.91	$14.97	$15.02	$15.07	$15.11
Forfeiture (5%)	$9.95	$10.09	$10.22	$10.33	$10.37	$10.46	$10.50	$10.53	$10.56	$10.59
Forfeiture (10%)	$7.00	$7.10	$7.18	$7.25	$7.28	$7.34	$7.36	$7.38	$7.40	$7.42
Forfeiture (15%)	$4.93	$4.99	$5.05	$5.09	$5.11	$5.15	$5.17	$5.18	$5.19	$5.20
Forfeiture (20%)	$3.47	$3.51	$3.55	$3.58	$3.59	$3.61	$3.62	$3.63	$3.64	$3.65
Forfeiture (25%)	$2.44	$2.47	$2.49	$2.51	$2.52	$2.54	$2.54	$2.55	$2.55	$2.56
Forfeiture (30%)	$1.72	$1.73	$1.75	$1.76	$1.77	$1.78	$1.78	$1.79	$1.79	$1.80
Forfeiture (35%)	$1.21	$1.22	$1.23	$1.24	$1.24	$1.25	$1.25	$1.25	$1.26	$1.26
Forfeiture (40%)	$0.85	$0.86	$0.86	$0.87	$0.87	$0.88	$0.88	$0.88	$0.88	$0.88

Percentage Difference between Binomial and Black-Scholes Model	Suboptimal (1.2)	Suboptimal (1.4)	Suboptimal (1.6)	Suboptimal (1.8)	Suboptimal (2.0)	Suboptimal (2.2)	Suboptimal (2.4)	Suboptimal (2.6)	Suboptimal (2.8)	Suboptimal (3.0)
Forfeiture (0%)	−8.94%	−7.54%	−6.31%	−5.25%	−4.80%	−3.97%	−3.58%	−3.26%	−2.94%	−2.68%
Forfeiture (5%)	−35.92%	−34.98%	−34.17%	−33.48%	−33.18%	−32.64%	−32.39%	−32.18%	−31.97%	−31.80%
Forfeiture (10%)	−54.90%	−54.28%	−53.75%	−53.29%	−53.10%	−52.74%	−52.58%	−52.44%	−52.31%	−52.20%
Forfeiture (15%)	−68.27%	−67.85%	−67.50%	−67.20%	−67.07%	−66.84%	−66.73%	−66.64%	−66.56%	−66.48%
Forfeiture (20%)	−77.68%	−77.40%	−77.16%	−76.96%	−76.88%	−76.73%	−76.66%	−76.60%	−76.54%	−76.50%
Forfeiture (25%)	−84.30%	−84.11%	−83.95%	−83.82%	−83.77%	−83.67%	−83.62%	−83.58%	−83.55%	−83.52%
Forfeiture (30%)	−88.95%	−88.83%	−88.72%	−88.64%	−88.60%	−88.54%	−88.51%	−88.48%	−88.46%	−88.44%
Forfeiture (35%)	−92.23%	−92.15%	−92.08%	−92.02%	−92.00%	−91.95%	−91.93%	−91.92%	−91.90%	−91.89%
Forfeiture (40%)	−94.54%	−94.48%	−94.43%	−94.40%	−94.38%	−94.35%	−94.34%	−94.33%	−94.32%	−94.31%

MATURITY OF 10 YEARS AND VESTING OF 7 YEARS ON A $40 STOCK PRICE

Stock Price and Strike Price of $40, Maturity of 10 Years, Risk-Free Rate of 3.5%, 70% Volatility, 0% Dividends, Vesting of 7 Years, Employee Suboptimal Exercise Behavior from 1.2 to 3.0, and Forfeiture Rate from 0% to 40%.
Generalized Black-Scholes: $31.05

Customized Binomial Lattice	Suboptimal (1.2)	Suboptimal (1.4)	Suboptimal (1.6)	Suboptimal (1.8)	Suboptimal (2.0)	Suboptimal (2.2)	Suboptimal (2.4)	Suboptimal (2.6)	Suboptimal (2.8)	Suboptimal (3.0)
Forfeiture (0%)	$28.28	$28.71	$29.09	$29.42	$29.56	$29.82	$29.94	$30.04	$30.14	$30.22
Forfeiture (5%)	$19.90	$20.19	$20.44	$20.66	$20.75	$20.92	$20.99	$21.06	$21.12	$21.18
Forfeiture (10%)	$14.00	$14.20	$14.36	$14.50	$14.56	$14.67	$14.73	$14.77	$14.81	$14.84
Forfeiture (15%)	$9.85	$9.98	$10.09	$10.19	$10.22	$10.30	$10.33	$10.36	$10.38	$10.41
Forfeiture (20%)	$6.93	$7.02	$7.09	$7.15	$7.18	$7.23	$7.25	$7.27	$7.28	$7.30
Forfeiture (25%)	$4.88	$4.93	$4.98	$5.02	$5.04	$5.07	$5.09	$5.10	$5.11	$5.12
Forfeiture (30%)	$3.43	$3.47	$3.50	$3.53	$3.54	$3.56	$3.57	$3.58	$3.58	$3.59
Forfeiture (35%)	$2.41	$2.44	$2.46	$2.48	$2.49	$2.50	$2.50	$2.51	$2.51	$2.52
Forfeiture (40%)	$1.70	$1.71	$1.73	$1.74	$1.75	$1.75	$1.76	$1.76	$1.76	$1.77

Percentage Difference between Binomial and Black-Scholes Model	Suboptimal (1.2)	Suboptimal (1.4)	Suboptimal (1.6)	Suboptimal (1.8)	Suboptimal (2.0)	Suboptimal (2.2)	Suboptimal (2.4)	Suboptimal (2.6)	Suboptimal (2.8)	Suboptimal (3.0)
Forfeiture (0%)	−8.94%	−7.54%	−6.31%	−5.25%	−4.80%	−3.97%	−3.58%	−3.26%	−2.94%	−2.68%
Forfeiture (5%)	−35.92%	−34.98%	−34.17%	−33.48%	−33.18%	−32.64%	−32.39%	−32.18%	−31.97%	−31.80%
Forfeiture (10%)	−54.90%	−54.28%	−53.75%	−53.29%	−53.10%	−52.74%	−52.58%	−52.44%	−52.31%	−52.20%
Forfeiture (15%)	−68.27%	−67.85%	−67.50%	−67.20%	−67.07%	−66.84%	−66.73%	−66.64%	−66.56%	−66.48%
Forfeiture (20%)	−77.68%	−77.40%	−77.16%	−76.96%	−76.88%	−76.73%	−76.66%	−76.60%	−76.54%	−76.50%
Forfeiture (25%)	−84.30%	−84.11%	−83.95%	−83.82%	−83.77%	−83.67%	−83.62%	−83.58%	−83.55%	−83.52%
Forfeiture (30%)	−88.95%	−88.83%	−88.72%	−88.64%	−88.60%	−88.54%	−88.51%	−88.48%	−88.46%	−88.44%
Forfeiture (35%)	−92.23%	−92.15%	−92.08%	−92.02%	−92.00%	−91.95%	−91.93%	−91.92%	−91.90%	−91.89%
Forfeiture (40%)	−94.54%	−94.48%	−94.43%	−94.40%	−94.38%	−94.35%	−94.34%	−94.33%	−94.32%	−94.31%

MATURITY OF 10 YEARS AND VESTING OF 7 YEARS ON A $60 STOCK PRICE

Stock Price and Strike Price of $60, Maturity of 10 Years, Risk–Free Rate of 3.5%, 70% Volatility, 0% Dividends, Vesting of 7 Years, Employee Suboptimal Exercise Behavior from 1.2 to 3.0, and Forfeiture Rate from 0% to 40%.
Generalized Black–Scholes: $46.58

Customized Binomial Lattice	Suboptimal (1.2)	Suboptimal (1.4)	Suboptimal (1.6)	Suboptimal (1.8)	Suboptimal (2.0)	Suboptimal (2.2)	Suboptimal (2.4)	Suboptimal (2.6)	Suboptimal (2.8)	Suboptimal (3.0)
Forfeiture (0%)	$42.41	$43.07	$43.64	$44.13	$44.34	$44.73	$44.91	$45.06	$45.21	$45.33
Forfeiture (5%)	$29.85	$30.28	$30.66	$30.98	$31.12	$31.38	$31.49	$31.59	$31.68	$31.76
Forfeiture (10%)	$21.00	$21.29	$21.54	$21.76	$21.85	$22.01	$22.09	$22.15	$22.21	$22.27
Forfeiture (15%)	$14.78	$14.97	$15.14	$15.28	$15.34	$15.45	$15.50	$15.54	$15.58	$15.61
Forfeiture (20%)	$10.40	$10.53	$10.64	$10.73	$10.77	$10.84	$10.87	$10.90	$10.93	$10.95
Forfeiture (25%)	$7.31	$7.40	$7.47	$7.54	$7.56	$7.61	$7.63	$7.65	$7.66	$7.68
Forfeiture (30%)	$5.15	$5.20	$5.25	$5.29	$5.31	$5.34	$5.35	$5.37	$5.38	$5.39
Forfeiture (35%)	$3.62	$3.66	$3.69	$3.72	$3.73	$3.75	$3.76	$3.76	$3.77	$3.78
Forfeiture (40%)	$2.54	$2.57	$2.59	$2.61	$2.62	$2.63	$2.64	$2.64	$2.65	$2.65

Percentage Difference between Binomial and Black-Scholes Model	Suboptimal (1.2)	Suboptimal (1.4)	Suboptimal (1.6)	Suboptimal (1.8)	Suboptimal (2.0)	Suboptimal (2.2)	Suboptimal (2.4)	Suboptimal (2.6)	Suboptimal (2.8)	Suboptimal (3.0)
Forfeiture (0%)	–8.94%	–7.54%	–6.31%	–5.25%	–4.80%	–3.97%	–3.58%	–3.26%	–2.94%	–2.68%
Forfeiture (5%)	–35.92%	–34.98%	–34.17%	–33.48%	–33.18%	–32.64%	–32.39%	–32.18%	–31.97%	–31.80%
Forfeiture (10%)	–54.90%	–54.28%	–53.75%	–53.29%	–53.10%	–52.74%	–52.58%	–52.44%	–52.31%	–52.20%
Forfeiture (15%)	–68.27%	–67.85%	–67.50%	–67.20%	–67.07%	–66.84%	–66.73%	–66.64%	–66.56%	–66.48%
Forfeiture (20%)	–77.68%	–77.40%	–77.16%	–76.96%	–76.88%	–76.73%	–76.66%	–76.60%	–76.54%	–76.50%
Forfeiture (25%)	–84.30%	–84.11%	–83.95%	–83.82%	–83.77%	–83.67%	–83.62%	–83.58%	–83.55%	–83.52%
Forfeiture (30%)	–88.95%	–88.83%	–88.72%	–88.64%	–88.60%	–88.54%	–88.51%	–88.48%	–88.46%	–88.44%
Forfeiture (35%)	–92.23%	–92.15%	–92.08%	–92.02%	–92.00%	–91.95%	–91.93%	–91.92%	–91.90%	–91.89%
Forfeiture (40%)	–94.54%	–94.48%	–94.43%	–94.40%	–94.38%	–94.35%	–94.34%	–94.33%	–94.32%	–94.31%

MATURITY OF 10 YEARS AND VESTING OF 7 YEARS ON AN $80 STOCK PRICE

Stock Price and Strike Price of $80, Maturity of 10 Years, Risk-Free Rate of 3.5%, 70% Volatility, 0% Dividends, Vesting of 7 Years, Employee Suboptimal Exercise Behavior from 1.2 to 3.0, and Forfeiture Rate from 0% to 40%.
Generalized Black-Scholes: $62.10

Customized Binomial Lattice	Suboptimal (1.2)	Suboptimal (1.4)	Suboptimal (1.6)	Suboptimal (1.8)	Suboptimal (2.0)	Suboptimal (2.2)	Suboptimal (2.4)	Suboptimal (2.6)	Suboptimal (2.8)	Suboptimal (3.0)
Forfeiture (0%)	$56.55	$57.42	$58.18	$58.84	$59.12	$59.64	$59.88	$60.07	$60.27	$60.44
Forfeiture (5%)	$39.80	$40.38	$40.88	$41.31	$41.49	$41.83	$41.99	$42.12	$42.25	$42.35
Forfeiture (10%)	$28.01	$28.39	$28.72	$29.01	$29.13	$29.35	$29.45	$29.53	$29.62	$29.69
Forfeiture (15%)	$19.71	$19.96	$20.18	$20.37	$20.45	$20.59	$20.66	$20.71	$20.77	$20.81
Forfeiture (20%)	$13.86	$14.04	$14.18	$14.31	$14.36	$14.45	$14.50	$14.53	$14.57	$14.60
Forfeiture (25%)	$9.75	$9.87	$9.97	$10.05	$10.08	$10.14	$10.17	$10.19	$10.22	$10.24
Forfeiture (30%)	$6.86	$6.94	$7.00	$7.06	$7.08	$7.12	$7.14	$7.15	$7.17	$7.18
Forfeiture (35%)	$4.83	$4.88	$4.92	$4.96	$4.97	$5.00	$5.01	$5.02	$5.03	$5.04
Forfeiture (40%)	$3.39	$3.43	$3.46	$3.48	$3.49	$3.51	$3.52	$3.52	$3.53	$3.53

Percentage Difference between Binomial and Black-Scholes Model	Suboptimal (1.2)	Suboptimal (1.4)	Suboptimal (1.6)	Suboptimal (1.8)	Suboptimal (2.0)	Suboptimal (2.2)	Suboptimal (2.4)	Suboptimal (2.6)	Suboptimal (2.8)	Suboptimal (3.0)
Forfeiture (0%)	–8.94%	–7.54%	–6.31%	–5.25%	–4.80%	–3.97%	–3.58%	–3.26%	–2.94%	–2.68%
Forfeiture (5%)	–35.92%	–34.98%	–34.17%	–33.48%	–33.18%	–32.64%	–32.39%	–32.18%	–31.97%	–31.80%
Forfeiture (10%)	–54.90%	–54.28%	–53.75%	–53.29%	–53.10%	–52.74%	–52.58%	–52.44%	–52.31%	–52.20%
Forfeiture (15%)	–68.27%	–67.85%	–67.50%	–67.20%	–67.07%	–66.84%	–66.73%	–66.64%	–66.56%	–66.48%
Forfeiture (20%)	–77.68%	–77.40%	–77.16%	–76.96%	–76.88%	–76.73%	–76.66%	–76.60%	–76.54%	–76.50%
Forfeiture (25%)	–84.30%	–84.11%	–83.95%	–83.82%	–83.77%	–83.67%	–83.62%	–83.58%	–83.55%	–83.52%
Forfeiture (30%)	–88.95%	–88.83%	–88.72%	–88.64%	–88.60%	–88.54%	–88.51%	–88.48%	–88.46%	–88.44%
Forfeiture (35%)	–92.23%	–92.15%	–92.08%	–92.02%	–92.00%	–91.95%	–91.93%	–91.92%	–91.90%	–91.89%
Forfeiture (40%)	–94.54%	–94.48%	–94.43%	–94.40%	–94.38%	–94.35%	–94.34%	–94.33%	–94.32%	–94.31%

Glossary

American closed-form approximation A family of partial-differential equation models used to approximate the American option value.

American option An option that can be executed at any time up to and including maturity.

at-the-money A call or put option where the stock price is exactly at the strike price.

backward induction A mathematical procedure used to calculate the binomial valuation lattice by weighting the future option values by a risk-neutral probability and discounting these values to the present.

binomial lattice A type of options valuation methodology using discrete simulation of the stock price where at every node the stock price can bifurcate into two directions.

Black-Scholes A type of options valuation closed-form model used primarily to value basic European call and put options without dividends. The Black-Scholes model is also known as the BSM.

blackout Certain periods when an option cannot be executed (usually weeks before and after an earnings announcement) by certain senior executives or personnel with fiduciary responsibilities.

bootstrapping A technique used to compute implied forward interest rates from spot interest rates.

Brownian Motion A type of stochastic process useful for forecasting stock prices, among other things. The process can be modeled by applying simulation.

BSM Acronym for the Black-Scholes model.

call option The contractual right but not the obligation, to purchase the underlying stock at some predetermined contractual strike price within a specified time.

closed-form models Types of models that can be solved using a predefined equation. For instance, $A + B = C$ is a closed-form model, where given any two of the three variables, the third can be determined.

Crystal Ball An Excel-based Monte Carlo simulation software.

dividend yield The total dividend payments computed as a percent of the stock price that is paid out over the course of a year.

employee stock options Call options issued to employees as an alternative means of compensation for their services.

ESO The acronym for employee stock options.

European option An option that can be executed only at maturity but not at any time before maturity.

fair-market value The price that a buyer could be reasonably expected to pay and a seller could be reasonably expected to accept, if an asset were for sale on the open market for a reasonable period of time, both buyer and seller being in possession of all pertinent facts, and neither being under any compulsion to act.

FAS 123 Financial Accounting Standard 123, which offers guidance on the accounting and valuation of employee stock options.

FASB The Financial Accounting Standards Board, responsible for determining accounting standards in the United States. Its rules and regulations are termed Financial Accounting Standards (FAS).

forward rate An interest rate that applies between two dates in the future.

forfeiture When an employee leaves or is terminated from a firm, he or she is forced to give up or forfeit the options granted. Forfeiture rates are established through turnover rates or proportion of option cancellations per year.

GARCH The family of econometric techniques termed the *G*eneralized *A*utoregressive *C*onditional *H*eteroskedasticity models. GARCH models are used primarily for modeling volatilities.

GBM Generalized Black-Scholes model.

Generalized Black-Scholes The Generalized Black-Scholes is similar to the Black-Scholes model but incorporates a dividend yield as one of its inputs.

grant date The date employee stock options are granted. This date is usually sometime in the future of the valuation date.

hypothesis test A statistical technique used to test a small data sample for particular characteristics of the population (e.g., types of distributions, confidence levels, error measurements, and so forth).

in-the-money Describes the condition of a call option when the stock price exceeds the strike price, or for a put option, when the strike price exceeds the stock price.

intrinsic valuation method The option valuation methodology that assumes volatility is zero and the option value is the stock price less the strike price. This means ESOs that are typically issued at-the-money will be worth nothing, and this approach is not allowed under the revised FAS 123.

lattice steps The number of steps to model in a binomial lattice, where the higher the number, the more precise the results. However, the results will converge after some optimal number of steps. In order to obtain the optimal number of steps, care must be taken to condition the lattice for convergence and timing of executions.

marketability discount A discount given to the fair-market value of an asset to reduce its value because the asset cannot be readily bought or sold in the open market.

maturity The date an option contract terminates.

Monte Carlo simulation An analytical technique of randomly drawing numbers from prespecified distributions, used to forecast or quantify uncertainties.

nonparametric simulation A type of simulation where no distributional assumptions are made of the input variables (e.g., a normal distribution with a mean of x and variance of y). Instead, the simulation uses historical data and selects them at random, letting the data tell the story, rather than imposing distributional parameters.

nonrecombining lattice A type of binomial lattice used to calculate an option with changing volatilities over time.

path-dependent simulation A type of Monte Carlo simulation technique used to forecast future stock prices, whose path in the future is dependent on the path taken in the past. An example path-dependent simulation is the Brownian Motion stochastic process.

put option A contractual right, but not the obligation, to sell the underlying stock at some predetermined contractual price within a specified time.

Real Options Analysis Toolkit A software for calculating financial options and real options (strategic options on real physical assets or projects) developed by the author.

recombining lattice A type of binomial lattice used to value most types of options. The recombining lattice is calculated faster than its nonrecombining counterpart.

risk-free rate The annualized rate of return on a riskless asset, typically defined as the interest rate of the U.S. Treasuries.

spot rate The interest rate applicable from the present to some time in the future.

stochastic process A mathematical equation that cannot be solved as a closed-form equation, as some of its variables are uncertain, constantly changing, or stochastic. One way to analyze a stochastic process is through the use of simulation.

stock price In ESO valuation, the stock price used is typically the forecast stock price at a future options grant date.

strike price The contractual price at which an option can be executed. A call option's strike price means the price at which the underlying stock can be bought. A put option's strike price means the price at which the underlying stock can be sold.

suboptimal exercise behavior multiple The ratio of the stock price to the strike price when an employee stock option was executed in the past.

trinomial lattice A type of options valuation methodology (a member of the lattice family, and related to the binomial lattice) using discrete simulation of the stock price where at every node the stock price branches into three directions. The results from a trinomial lattice are similar to a binomial lattice but a trinomial lattice converges faster and requires fewer steps to obtain the same value.

vesting The contractual period when an employee stock option cannot be executed.

volatility A statistical value calculated for describing the movements of stock prices. The higher the volatility, the higher the risk of the stock, and the higher the fluctuations of the stock price about its mean. In options analysis, this is usually calculated by taking the standard deviation of the natural logarithm of the stock returns in the past and annualizing it. Other approaches include using a GARCH model, market comparables, and implied volatilities from exchange-traded options and LEAPS.

Notes

CHAPTER 1 Implications of the New FAS 123 Requirements

1. *Wall Street Journal*, April 21, 2004.
2. Financial Accounting Standards Board web site: www.fasb.org.
3. This book is not intended to cover the subject of options management, tax or accounting implications, or other related FASB requirements or standards. Its goal is simply to expound on the issues of fair-market valuation.
4. Fischer Black and Myron Scholes, 1973. "The Pricing of Options and Corporate Liabilities," *Journal of Political Economy*, vol. 81 (May/June): 637.
5. The values used in these cases have been sufficiently changed to protect proprietary information of former clients. However, the results shown are still valid for interpretation.
6. The term *closed-form model* simply means there exists a mathematical representation of the model. For instance, $A = B + C$ is a closed-form model, where if one provides the values of B and C, the model yields an exact and unique result A.
7. In order to facilitate computation and test of robustness, Decisioneering, Inc.'s Crystal Ball Monte Carlo simulation software and my Real Options Analysis Toolkit and proprietary customized binomial valuation algorithms were used.
8. These are typical values found in my experience when working with Fortune 500 firms.
9. See Dr. Johnathan Mun's *Real Options Analysis* (New York: Wiley, 2003) for solved models of American options approximation approaches using the Real Options Analysis Toolkit software.
10. Crystal Ball professional software was used to calculate the option value in this case.

CHAPTER 2 The 2004 Proposed FAS 123 Requirements

1. This chapter is based on excerpts taken from the March 31, 2004 FAS 123 exposure draft.

CHAPTER 3 Impact on Valuation

1. For detailed examples of the risk-neutral and market-replicating portfolio approaches, see Dr. Johnathan Mun's *Real Options Analysis* (Wiley, 2003).

2. See Dr. Johnathan Mun's *Applied Risk Analysis: Moving Beyond Uncertainty*, (Wiley Finance, 2003) for details on the case study.
3. The GBM accounts for dividends on European options but the basic BSM does not.
4. American options are exercisable at any time up to and including the expiration date. European options are exercisable only at termination or maturity expiration date. Most employee stock options are a mixture of both—European option during the vesting period (the option cannot be exercised prior to vesting) and American option at and after the vesting period.
5. These could be cliff vesting (the options are all void if the employee leaves or is terminated before this cliff vesting period) or graded monthly/quarterly/annually vesting (a certain proportion of the options vest after a specified period of employment service to the firm).
6. This multiple is the ratio of the stock price when the option is exercised to the contractual strike price, and is tabulated based on historical information.
7. A *tornado chart* lists all the inputs that drive the model, starting from the input variable that has the most effect on the results. The chart is obtained by perturbing each input at some consistent range (e.g., ±10% from the base case) one at a time, and comparing their results to the base case.
8. Different input levels yield different tornado charts but in most cases, volatility is not the only dominant variable. Forfeiture, vesting, and suboptimal exercise behavior multiples all tend to either dominate over or be as dominant as volatility. The results illustrated in Figures 3.1 to 3.4 are highly specific and represent a special case, but were chosen to make a point that sometimes volatility may not always be the dominant input and that the other exotic inputs can also dominate the option value.
9. A *spider chart* looks like a spider with a central body and its many legs protruding. The positively sloped lines indicate a positive relationship (e.g., the higher the stock price, the higher the option value as seen in Figure 3.3), while a negatively sloped line indicates a negative relationship. Further, spider charts can be used to visualize linear and nonlinear relationships.
10. Assumptions used: stock and strike price of $25, 10-year maturity, 5 percent risk-free rate, 50 percent volatility, 0 percent dividends, suboptimal exercise behavior multiple range of 1–20, vesting period of 1–10 years, and tested with 100–5,000 binomial lattice steps.
11. Assumptions used: stock and strike price range of $5–$100, 10-year maturity, 5 percent risk-free rate, 50 percent volatility, 0 percent dividends, suboptimal exercise behavior multiple range of 1–20, vesting period of 4 years, and tested with 100–5,000 binomial lattice steps.
12. Assumptions used: stock and strike price of $25, 10-year maturity, 5 percent risk-free rate, 10 to 100 percent volatility range, 0 percent dividends, suboptimal exercise behavior multiple range of 1–20, vesting period of 1 year, and tested with 100–5,000 binomial lattice steps.
13. Assumptions used: stock and strike price of $25, 10-year maturity, 5 percent risk-free rate, 50 percent volatility, 0 percent dividends, suboptimal exercise

behavior multiple of 1.01, vesting period of 1–10 years, forfeiture range of 0 to 50 percent, and tested with 100–5,000 binomial lattice steps.

14. Stock price and strike price are set at $100, maturity of 5 years, 5 percent risk-free rate, 75 percent volatility, and 1,000 steps in the customized lattice. Other exotic variable inputs are listed in Table 3.10.
15. Stock price and strike price are set at $100, maturity of 5 years, 5 percent risk-free rate, 75 percent volatility, 1,000 steps in the customized lattice, 1.8 suboptimal exercise behavior multiple, 10 percent forfeiture rate, and 1-year vesting.
16. Stock and strike price of $100, 75 percent volatility, 5 percent risk-free rate, 10-year maturity, 0 percent dividends, 1-year vesting, 10 percent forfeiture rate, and 1,000 lattice steps.
17. Stock and strike price range of $30–$100, 45 percent volatility, 5 percent risk-free rate, 10-year maturity, dividend range of 0 to 10 percent, vesting of 1–4 years, 5 to 14 percent forfeiture rate, suboptimal exercise behavior multiple range of 1.8–3.0, and 1,000 lattice steps.

CHAPTER 4 Haircuts on Nonmarketability, Modified Black-Scholes with Expected Life, and Dilution

1. Assumptions used: stock and strike price of $100, 10-year maturity, 1-year vesting, 35 percent volatility, 0 percent dividends, 5 percent risk-free rate, suboptimal exercise behavior multiple range of 1.2–3.0, forfeiture range of 0 to 40 percent and 1,000-step customized lattice.
2. Cedric Jolidon finds the mean values of marketability discounts to be between 20 to 35 percent in his article, “The Application of the Marketability Discount in the Valuation of Swiss Companies” (Swiss Private Equity Corporate Finance Association). A typical marketability range of 10 to 40 percent was found in several discount court cases. In the *CPA Journal* (February 2001), M. Greene and D. Schnapp found that a typical range was somewhere between 30 and 35 percent. An article in the *Business Valuation Review* finds that 35 percent is the typical value (Jay Abrams, “Discount for Lack of Marketability”). In the *Fair Value* newsletter, Michael Paschall finds that 30 to 50 percent is the typical marketability discount used in the market.

CHAPTER 5 Applicability of Monte Carlo Simulation

1. Aswath Damodaran. *Investment Valuation.* New York: Wiley Finance, 1996.
2. Don M. Chance. *An Introduction to Derivatives,* 4th ed. Dryden Press, 1998.
3. This is due to the mathematical properties of American options, which require the knowledge of what the optimal stopping times and optimal execution barriers are. Using simulation to solve American-type options is very difficult and is beyond the scope of this book.
4. John C. Hull. *Options, Futures, and Other Derivatives*, 3rd ed. Englewood Cliffs, NJ: Prentice Hall, 1997.

5. See Dr. Johnathan Mun's *Real Options Analysis* (Wiley, 2002) for the technical details involved with solving binomial lattices.
6. A simulation running 100,000 trials under Latin Hypercube with a size of 1,000 at an initial seed of 1 was applied on 100 path-dependent time steps.
7. Crystal Ball software was used to simulate the input variables.
8. An autocorrelation and partial autocorrelation analysis was performed to determine the correlation coefficient.
9. Any level of precision and confidence can be chosen. Here, the 99.9 percent statistical confidence with a $0.01 error precision ($0.01 fluctuation around the average option value) is fairly restrictive. Of course the level of precision attained is contingent upon the inputs and inputs' distributional parameters being accurate.

CHAPTER 6 Expense Attribution Schedule

1. For details on how the valuation input parameters were obtained, see Chapter 10.
2. Due to the size of the worksheet, only parts of the calculations are shown in the figure.

CHAPTER 8 Binomial Lattices in Technical Detail

1. This is simply an illustration of the size and computational requirements for an exact binomial approximation where data from all the simulated trials are saved in order to perform other statistical analyses.
2. Please contact me at JohnathanMun@cs.com for more information regarding software applications and proprietary algorithms used.
3. See Chapter 9 for more technical details and Chapter 10 for an application of the appropriate number of steps to use in an analysis.
4. See my other book, *Real Options Analysis* (Wiley, 2002), for details on solving a lattice using market-replicating portfolios.
5. The simulated actual values are based on a geometric Brownian Motion with an annualized volatility of 20 percent calculated as the standard deviation of the natural logarithms of historical returns.
6. Chapter 5 illustrates the use of simulation to solve the options in three different ways: path-dependent simulation, BSM, and binomial lattices.
7. Please note that because the lattice is a discrete simulation, only certain discrete stock prices will be displayed. If you are trying to obtain a forecast of stock prices complete with their probabilities of being above or below a particular level, use Monte Carlo to simulate a continuous Brownian Motion stochastic process instead.
8. This multiple is the ratio of the stock price when the option is exercised to the contractual strike price, and is tabulated based on historical information.
9. Please contact me for additional details about the algorithms.

10. Based on the March 2004 whitepaper by Jeremy Bulow and John Shoven.
11. This has the same effect of multiplying the number of grants by (1 – Forfeiture) because total valuation is Price × Quantity × (1 – Forfeiture), so it does not matter whether the forfeiture adjustment is made on the option price or the quantity of option grants, as long as it is applied only once.

CHAPTER 9 The Model Inputs

1. Of the 6,553 stocks analyzed, 2,924 of them pay dividends, 2,140 of them yielding at or below 5 percent, 2,282 at or below 6 percent, 2,503 at or below 7 percent, and 2,830 at or below 10 percent.
2. An unexpected increase in dividend yield tends to increase the stock price and vice versa. See Dr. Johnathan Mun, "The Dividend Prize Puzzle: A Nonparametric Approach," *Journal of the Advances of Quantitative Accounting and Finance* (1998).
3. Carpenter, J. 1998. "The Exercise and Valuation of Executive Stock Options," *Journal of Financial Economics*, vol. 48, no. 2 (May).
4. S. Huddart, and M. Lang. 1996. "Employee Stock Option Exercises: An Empirical Analysis," *Journal of Accounting and Economics*, vol. 21, no. 1 (February).
5. Refer to Figure 3.8 for empirical details.

CHAPTER 10 A Sample Case Study

1. I developed this proprietary algorithm based on my analytical work with FASB in 2003 and 2004; my three books, *Real Options Analysis: Tools and Techniques* (Wiley, 2002), *Real Options Analysis Course* (Wiley, 2003), *Applied Risk Analysis: Moving Beyond Uncertainty* (Wiley, 2003); creation of my software, Real Options Analysis Toolkit (versions 1.0 and 2.0); academic research; and previous valuation consulting experience at KPMG Consulting.
2. A geometric Brownian Motion stochastic process with Monte Carlo simulation was used. See Chapter 7 for more details.
3. The spot rate curve used in the analysis was averaged around the past four weeks of the valuation date to obtain a better market consensus of the economic expectations.
4. The R-squared (R^2), or coefficient of determination, is an error measurement that looks at the percent variation of the dependent variable that can be explained by the variation in the independent variable for a regression analysis, and ranges from 0 to 1.0. The higher the R^2 value, the better the model fits and explains the data. In this case, an R^2 of 0.0105 means a bad fit and the model is not statistically significant and its results could not be relied on.
5. Examples of goodness-of-fit statistics include the t-statistic and the F-statistic. The former is used to test if *each* of the estimated slope and intercepts is statistically significant, that is, if it is statistically significantly different from zero (therefore making sure that the intercept and slope estimates are statistically valid). The latter applies the same concepts but simultaneously tests the entire

regression equation including the intercept and slopes. The calculated F-statistic of 1.8650 and a corresponding p-value of 0.1147 indicate collectively that the model is statistically insignificant and the results cannot be relied on.

6. See Chapter 9 for the technical details of obtaining periodic and annualizing volatilities.
7. Using an inverted Brownian Motion stochastic process, the 99.99 percent cut-off point was determined for the stock price within the specified time period given the volatility measure.
8. The higher the suboptimal exercise behavior multiple is set, the higher the option value—a conservative estimate of the multiple means that it is set higher so as not to undervalue the option.
9. A 1,000-step customized binomial lattice is generally used unless otherwise noted. Sometimes increments from 1,000 to 5,000 steps may be used to check for convergence. However, due to the nonrecombining nature of changing volatility options, a lower number of steps may have to be employed.
10. I developed this proprietary algorithm based on my analytical work with FASB in 2003 and 2004; my three books, *Real Options Analysis: Tools and Techniques* (Wiley, 2002), *Real Options Analysis Course* (Wiley, 2003), *Applied Risk Analysis: Moving Beyond Uncertainty* (Wiley, 2003); creation of my software, Real Options Analysis Toolkit (versions 1.0 and 2.0); academic research; and previous valuation consulting experience at KPMG Consulting.
11. A nonrecombining binomial lattice bifurcates (splits into two) every step it takes, so starting from one value, it branches out to two values on the first step (2^1), two becomes four in the second step (2^2), and four becomes eight in the third step (2^3) and so forth, until the 1,000th step (2^{1000} or over 10^{301} values to calculate). Even the world's fastest supercomputers will be unable to handle the computations within our lifetimes. Thus, software tricks and algorithms have to be employed.
12. The *Law of Large Numbers* stipulates that the central tendency (mean) of a distribution of averages is an unbiased estimator of the true population average. The results from 4,200 steps show a mean value that is comparable to the median of the distribution of averages, and hence, 4,200 steps is chosen as the input into the binomial lattice.
13. This is the extreme case where we assume 100 percent of the employee stock options will be executed once they become fully vested, to minimize the BSM results.
14. See Chapter 6 for details on the expense allocation procedure.

About the CD-ROM

INTRODUCTION

This appendix provides you with information on the contents of the CD-ROM that accompanies this book. For the latest and greatest information, please refer to the ReadMe file located at the root of the CD.

SYSTEM REQUIREMENTS

- IBM PC or compatible computer with Pentium II or higher processor.
- 128 MB RAM (256 MB RAM recommended).
- 10 MB hard-disk space.
- CD-ROM drive.
- SVGA monitor with 256 Color.
- Excel 2000, XP, or 2003.
- Windows 2000, NT 4.0 (SP 6a), XP, or higher.

Note: Many popular spreadsheet programs are capable of reading Microsoft Excel files. However, users should be aware that a slight amount of formatting might be lost when using a program other than Microsoft Excel.

USING THE CD WITH WINDOWS

To access the CD-ROM on your computer, follow these steps:

1. Insert the CD into your computer's CD-ROM drive.
2. The CD-ROM interface will appear. The interface provides a simple point-and-click way to explore the contents of the CD.

If the opening screen of the CD-ROM does not appear automatically, follow these steps to access the CD:

1. Click the Start button on the left end of the taskbar and then choose Run from the menu that pops up.
2. In the dialogue box that appears, type ***d*:\setup.exe**. (If your CD-ROM drive is not drive *d*, fill in the appropriate letter in place of *d*.) This brings up the CD interface described in the preceding set of steps.

WHAT'S ON THE CD

The following sections provide a summary of the software and other materials you'll find on the CD. Refer to Appendix 10A to get started using this demo.

Content

The enclosed CD-ROM contains a demo of the Employee Stock Option Valuation Toolkit version 1.1. This software solves valuation of employee stock options (ESOs) using closed-form models such as the Black-Scholes, as well as customized binomial lattices (thousands of lattice steps can be run in only a few seconds, compared to years if performed manually) in accordance with FAS 123 requirements. This functional demo version gives the user access to features such as the ESO Toolkit, which provides a graphical user interface of valuation models, and ESO Functions, which provides access to the valuation functions in Excel. It includes:

- *Sample Excel worksheets.* These show the manual computations of the ESOs, useful for auditing purposes.
- *User's manual.* This is complete with a step-by-step installation guide, glossary, and list of functions.

To run the setup program, do the following:

1. Insert the enclosed CD-ROM into the CD-ROM drive of your computer.
2. Open Windows Explorer and locate the folders on the CD-ROM drive.

3. Double click on the Setup.exe file to install the demo software. Read and follow the online instructions.
4. When prompted, enter the following user name: DEMO, and the following software key: 4D87-5FE2-DF38-D7B9.

To obtain a full version of the software or for additional information about the algorithms, please contact the author at JohnathanMun@cs.com.

Other Applications

The following applications are also included on the CD-ROM:

Adobe Reader
Adobe Reader is a freeware application for viewing files in the Adobe Portable Document format.

Excel Viewer
Excel Viewer is a freeware viewer that allows you to view, but not edit, most Microsoft Excel spreadsheets. Certain features of Microsoft Excel documents may not work as expected from within Excel Viewer.

Shareware programs are fully functional, trial versions of copyrighted programs. If you like particular programs, register with their authors for a nominal fee and receive licenses, enhanced versions, and technical support.

Freeware programs are copyrighted games, applications, and utilities that are free for personal use. Unlike shareware, these programs do not require a fee or provide technical support.

GNU software is governed by its own license, which is included inside the folder of the GNU product. See the GNU license for more details.

Trial, demo, or evaluation versions are usually limited either by time or by functionality (such as being unable to save projects). Some trial versions are very sensitive to system date changes. If you alter your computer's date, the programs will "time out" and no longer be functional.

CUSTOMER CARE

If you have trouble with the CD-ROM, please call the Wiley Product Technical Support phone number at (800) 762-2974. Outside the United States, call 1 (317) 572-3994. You can also contact Wiley Product Technical

Support at **www.wiley.com/techsupport**. John Wiley & Sons will provide technical support only for installation and other general quality control items. For technical support on the applications themselves, consult the program's vendor or author.

To place additional orders or to request information about other Wiley products, please call (877) 762-2974.

Index